Vampire Game

JUDAL

Vampire Game Vol. 12
Created by Judal

Translation - Ikoi Hiroe
English Adaptation - Jason Deitrich
Copy Editor - Suzanne Waldman
Retouch and Lettering - JUNEMOON Studios
Production Artist - Lucas Rivera
Cover Design - Gary Shum

Editor - Tim Beedle
Digital Imaging Manager - Chris Buford
Production Managers - Jennifer Miller and Mutsumi Miyazaki
Managing Editor - Jill Freshney
VP of Production - Ron Klamert
Publisher and E.I.C. - Mike Kiley
President and C.O.O. - John Parker
C.E.O. - Stuart Levy

A **TOKYOPOP** Manga

TOKYOPOP Inc.
5900 Wilshire Blvd. Suite 2000
Los Angeles, CA 90036

E-mail: info@TOKYOPOP.com
Come visit us online at www.TOKYOPOP.com

ISBN: 1-59532-442-9

First TOKYOPOP printing: August 2005
10 9 8 7 6 5 4 3 2
Printed in the USA

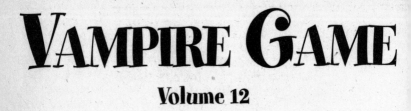

VAMPIRE GAME

Volume 12

by

JUDAL

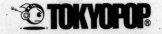

HAMBURG // LONDON // LOS ANGELES // TOKYO

VAMPIRE GAME

The Story Thus Far...

This is the tale of the Vampire King Duzell and his quest for revenge against the good King Phelios, a valiant warrior who slew the vampire a century ago. Now Duzell has returned, reincarnated as a feline foe to deliver woe to... well, that's the problem. Who is the reincarnation of King Phelios?

The princess Ishtar, heir to the Pheliostan throne, is required by law to wed a man from the royal family. However, she's set her heart on her protector, Sir Darres. But after Prince Yuujel announces that Darres is actually his half-brother, it would seem as if nothing could put off the sound of wedding bells...except for that very loud gasp of disbelief. You see, the only problem with Yuujel's announcement is that it's not true.

Lassen wants to be king of Pheliosta, and he's not about to let a little thing like romance get in his way. He's determined to prove that Darres is a fraud and marry Princess Ishtar himself. Or murder her. (They're practically the same thing with Lassen.) He's come up with a perfect little plan to do it, too. Sidia, the Holy Sword, has long been a symbol of justice and might in Pheliosta. Forged out of the souls of slain vampires, it can only be drawn by a direct descendent of St. Phelios, and for a former street urchin like Darres, that can present a bit of a problem. Of course, the poison Darres recently ingested is a problem as well. Along with the army of undead soldiers that showed up shortly after he drank it.

Duzell, on the other hand, has accompanied Ishtar to Mil Seii, where he's run into a soul from his past: Rishas, his former servant and lover. Rishas has been reincarnated into the body of a woman, and even more astonishing, has somehow managed to gain the affection of Lassen. Her heart still belongs to Duzell, though, which could be a problem, considering Duzell's growing affection for Ishtar...

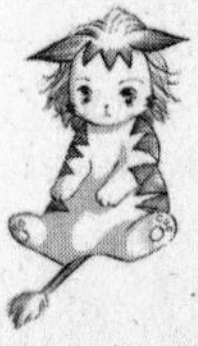

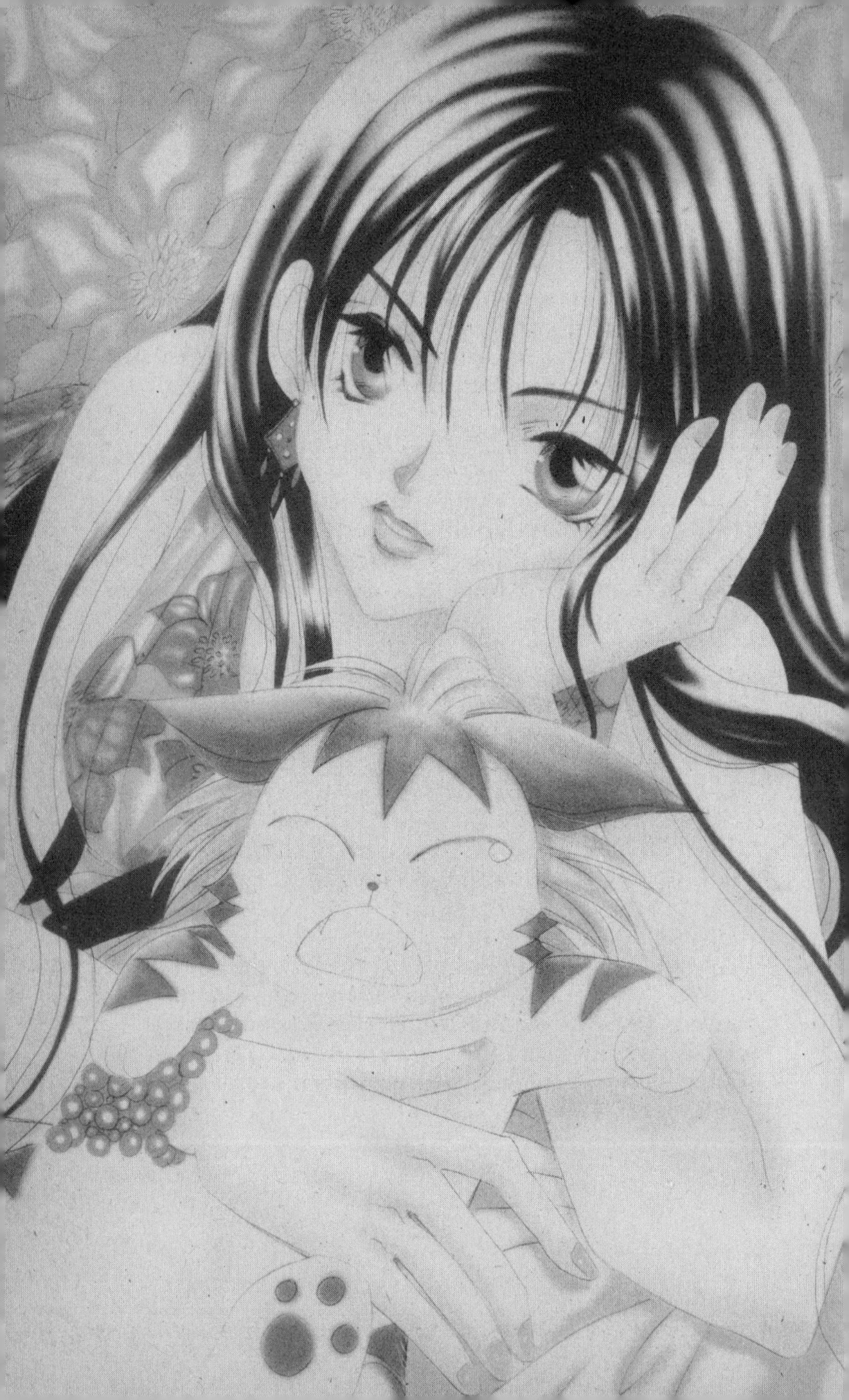

Table of Contents

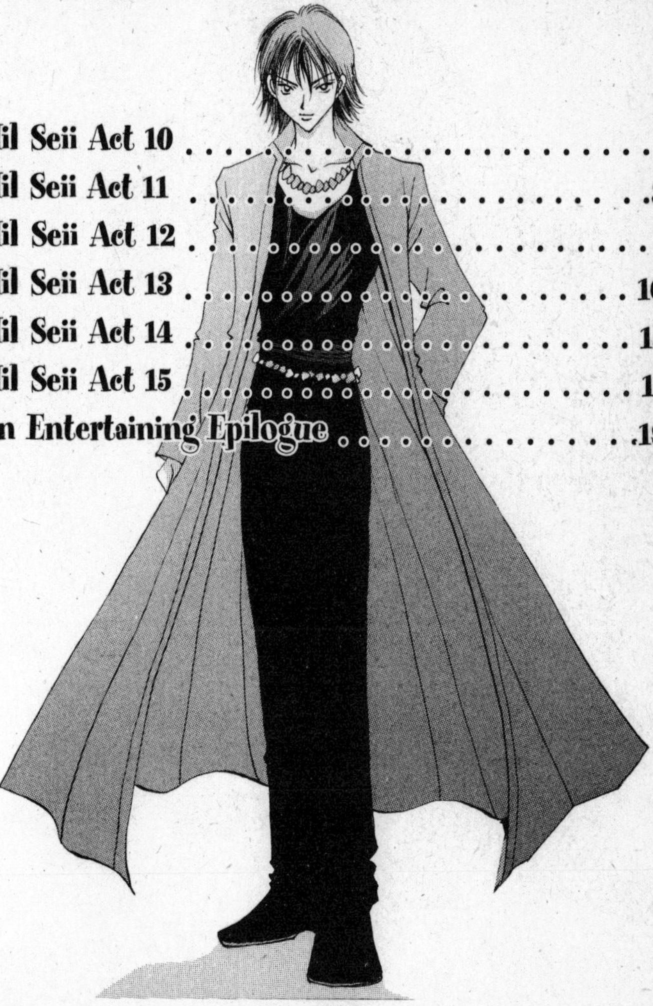

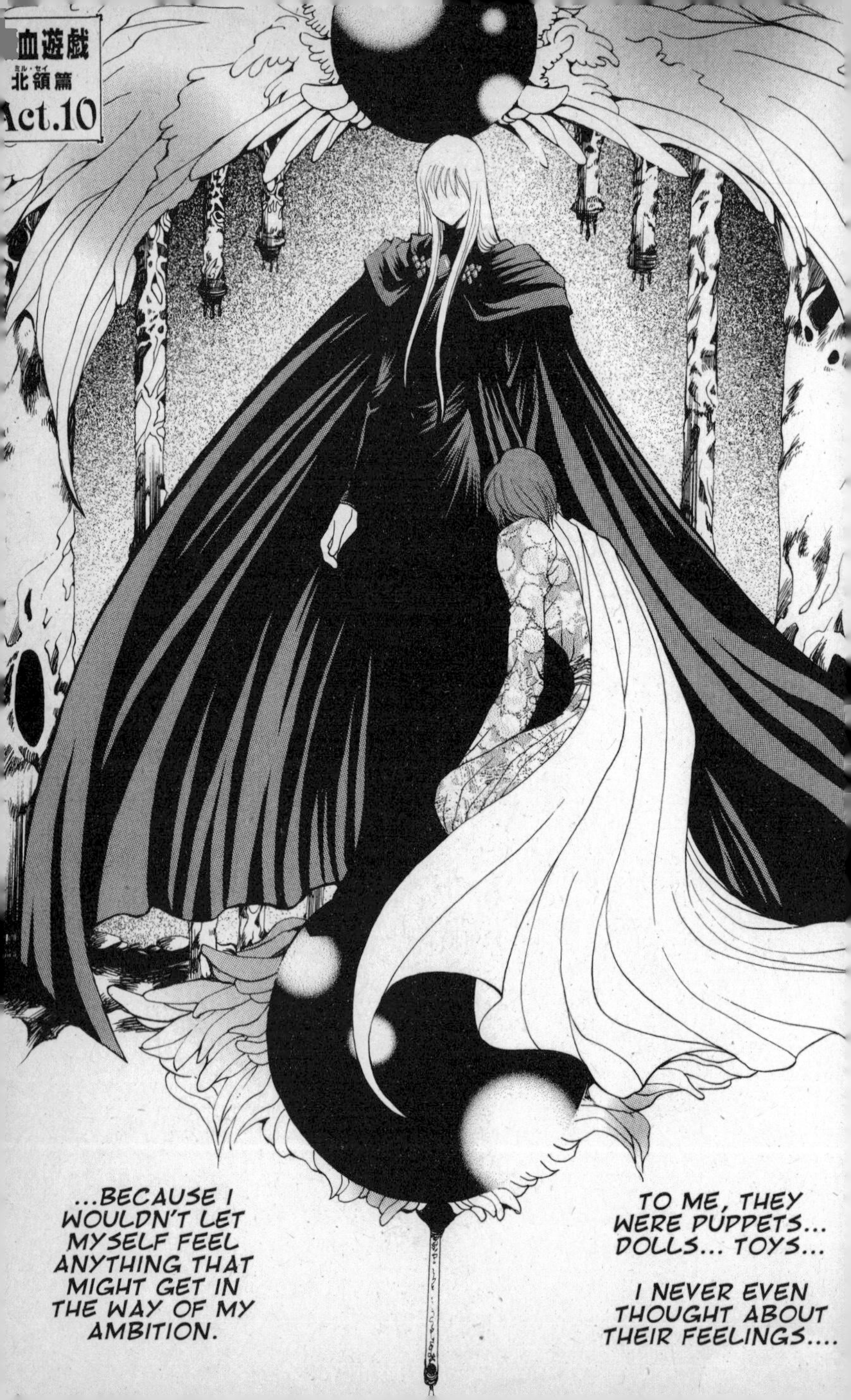
血遊戯
ミル・セイ
北領篇
Act.10
TO ME, THEY WERE PUPPETS... DOLLS... TOYS...
I NEVER EVEN THOUGHT ABOUT THEIR FEELINGS....
...BECAUSE I WOULDN'T LET MYSELF FEEL ANYTHING THAT MIGHT GET IN THE WAY OF MY AMBITION.

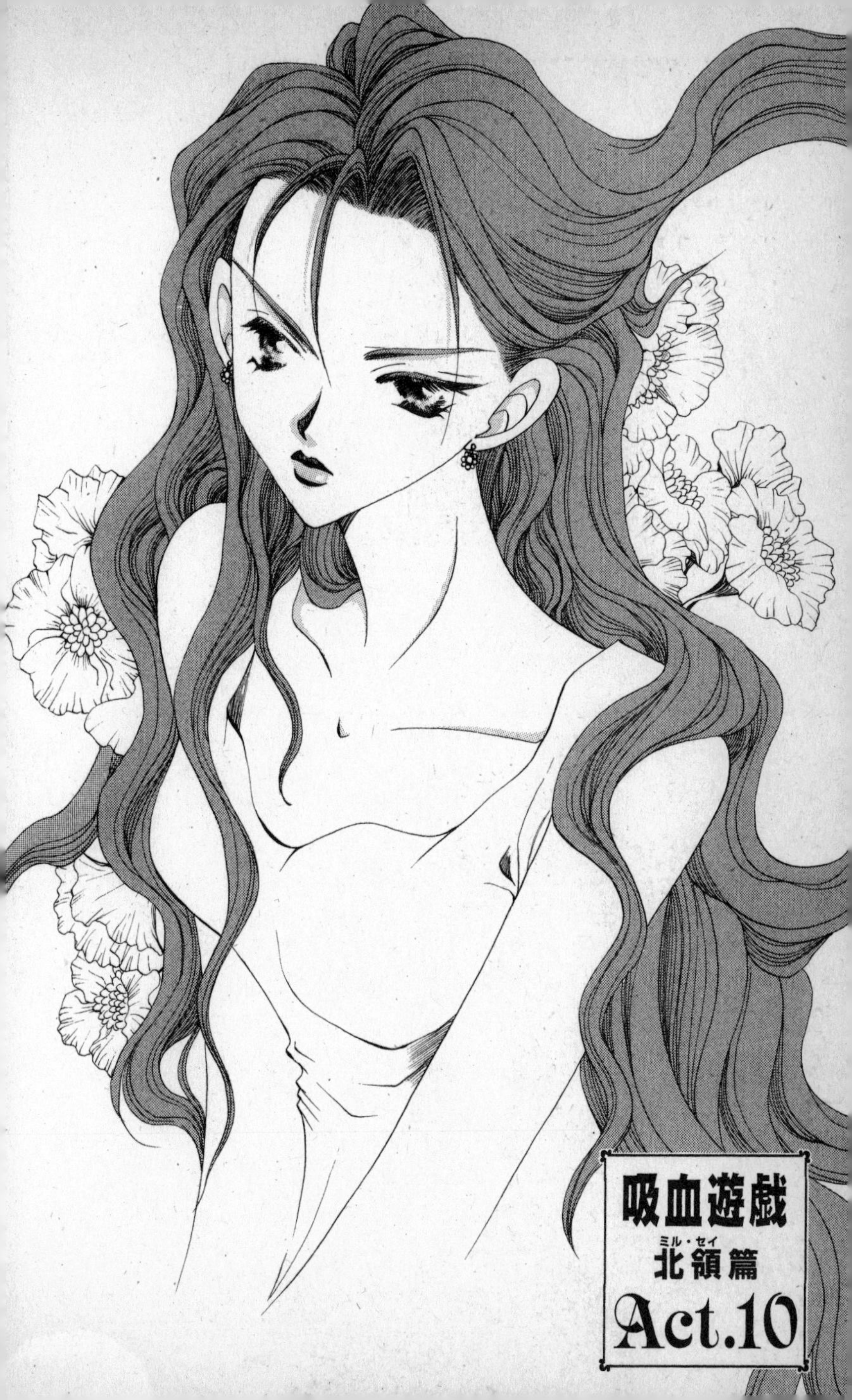
吸血遊戯
北領篇（ミル・セイ）
Act.10

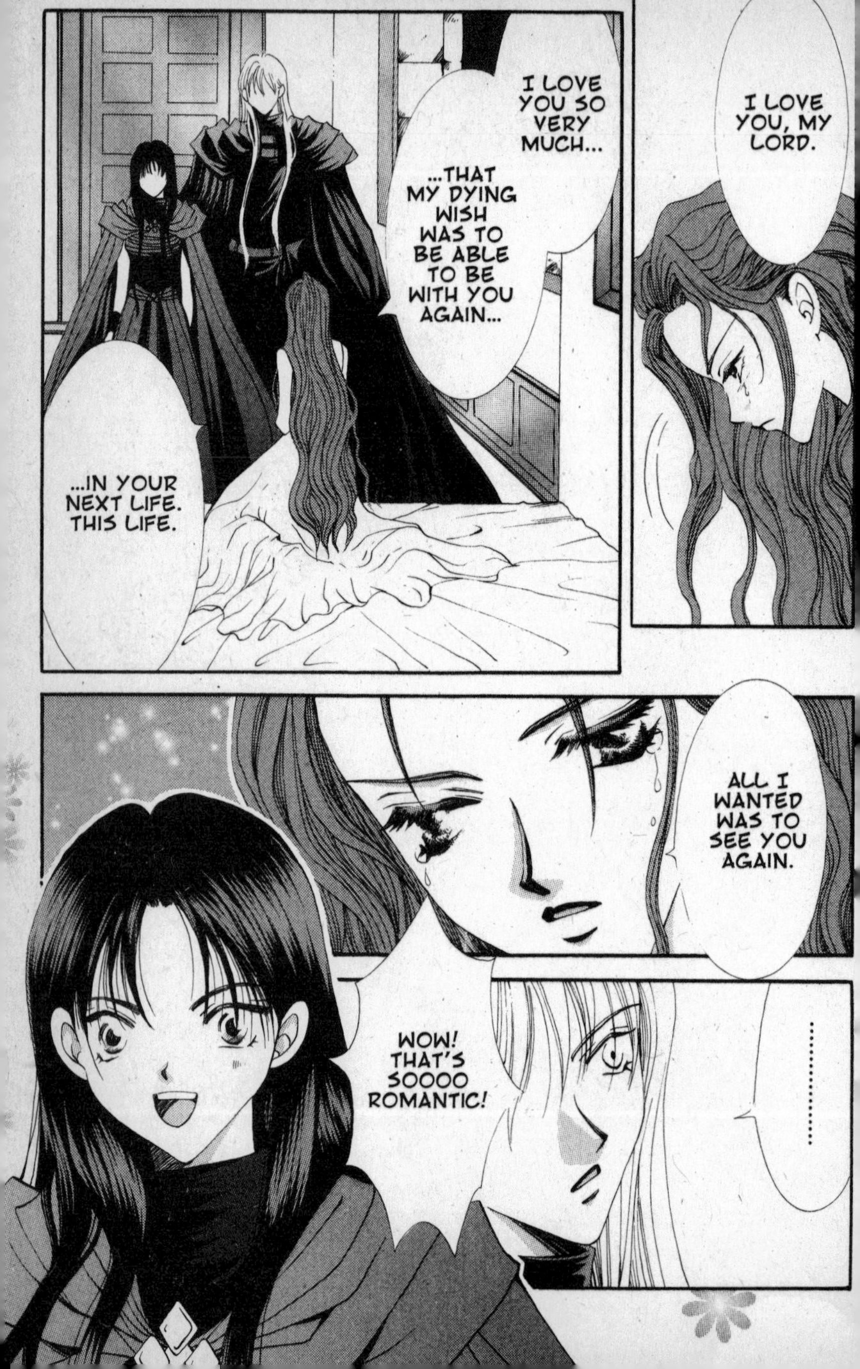
I LOVE YOU, MY LORD.
I LOVE YOU SO VERY MUCH...
...THAT MY DYING WISH WAS TO BE ABLE TO BE WITH YOU AGAIN...
...IN YOUR NEXT LIFE. THIS LIFE.
ALL I WANTED WAS TO SEE YOU AGAIN.
....
WOW! THAT'S SOOOO ROMANTIC!

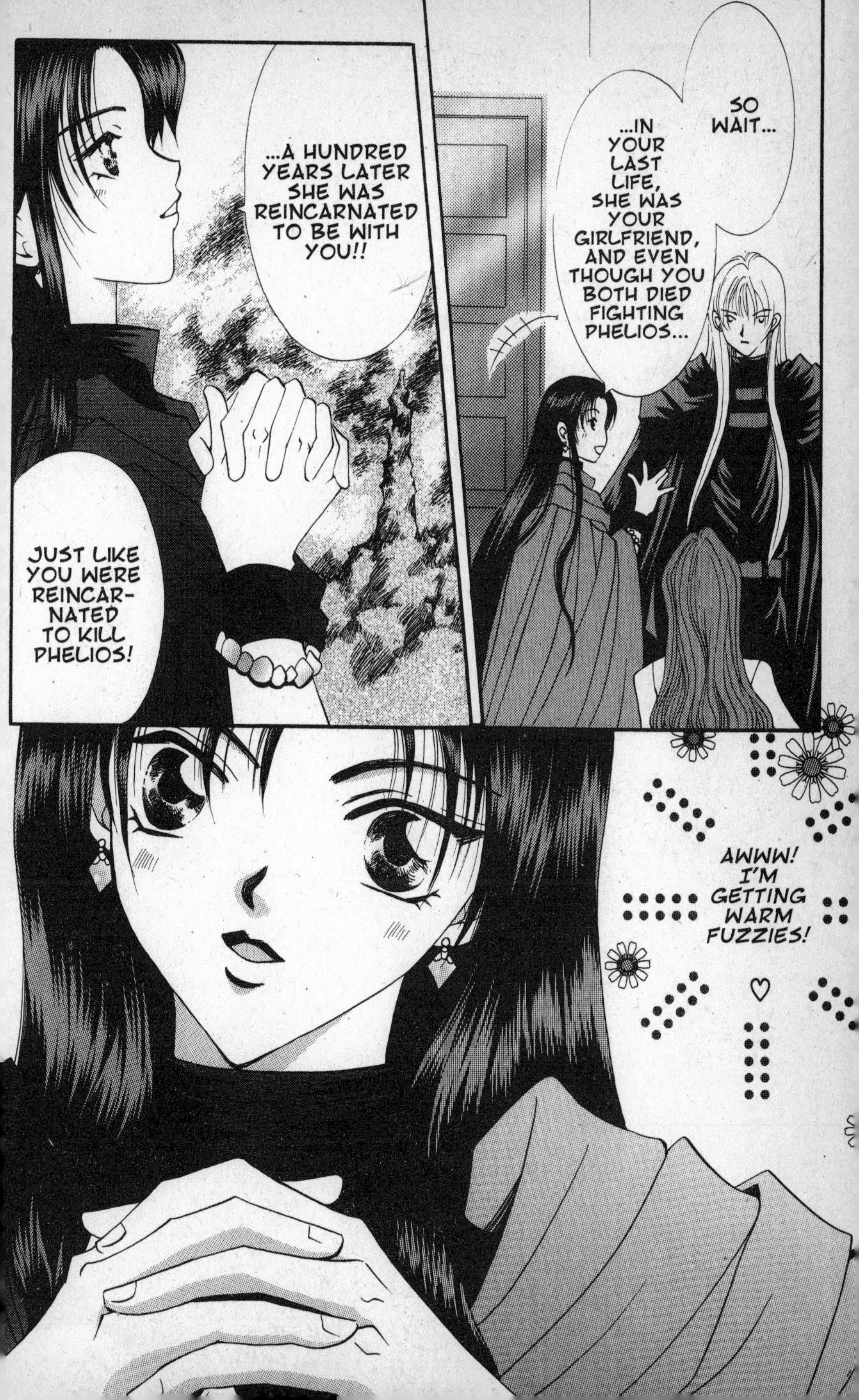
SO WAIT...
...IN YOUR LAST LIFE, SHE WAS YOUR GIRLFRIEND, AND EVEN THOUGH YOU BOTH DIED FIGHTING PHELIOS...
...A HUNDRED YEARS LATER SHE WAS REINCARNATED TO BE WITH YOU!!
JUST LIKE YOU WERE REINCAR-NATED TO KILL PHELIOS!
AWWW! I'M GETTING WARM FUZZIES!

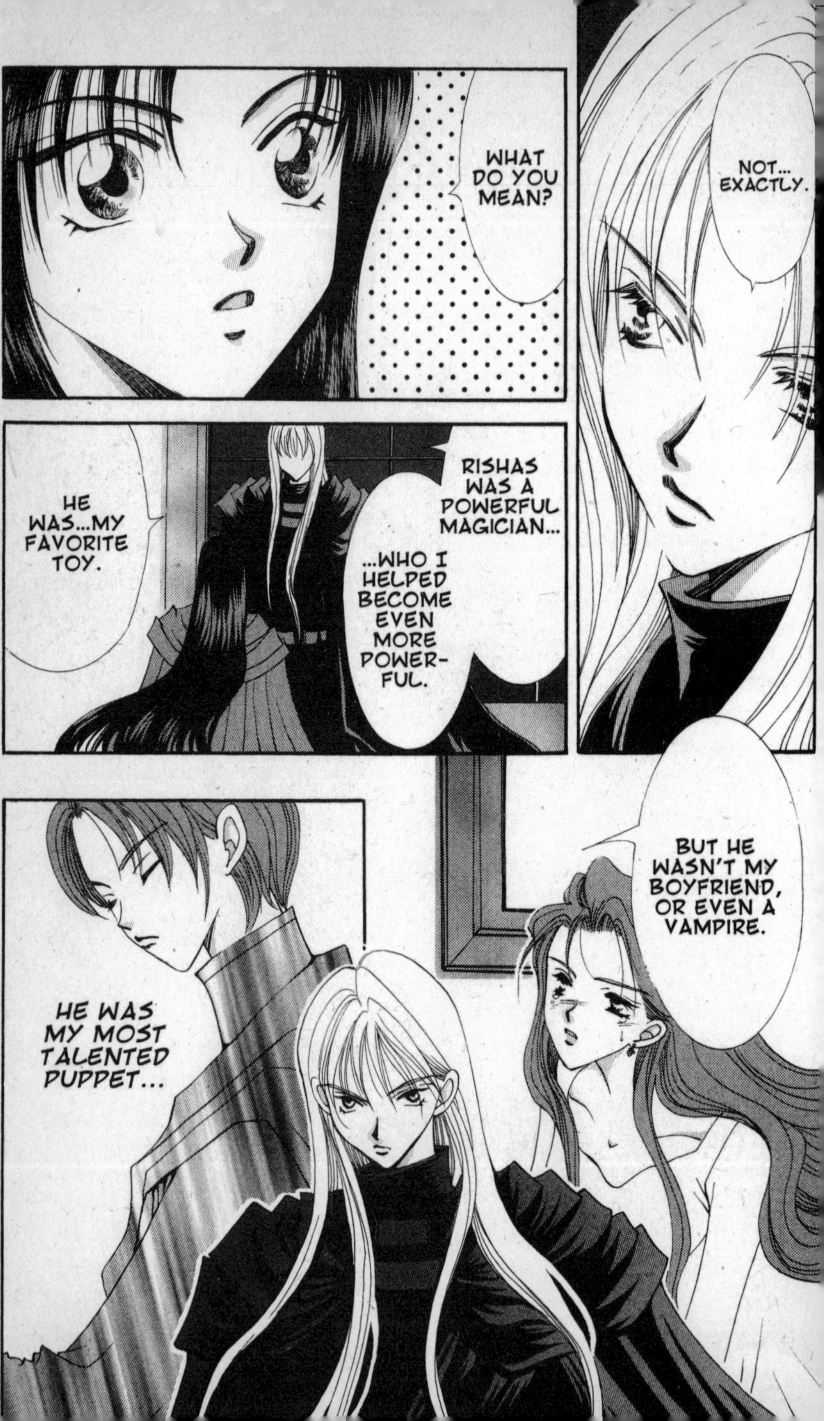
NOT... EXACTLY.
WHAT DO YOU MEAN?
RISHAS WAS A POWERFUL MAGICIAN...
...WHO I HELPED BECOME EVEN MORE POWER-FUL.
HE WAS...MY FAVORITE TOY.
BUT HE WASN'T MY BOYFRIEND, OR EVEN A VAMPIRE.
HE WAS MY MOST TALENTED PUPPET...

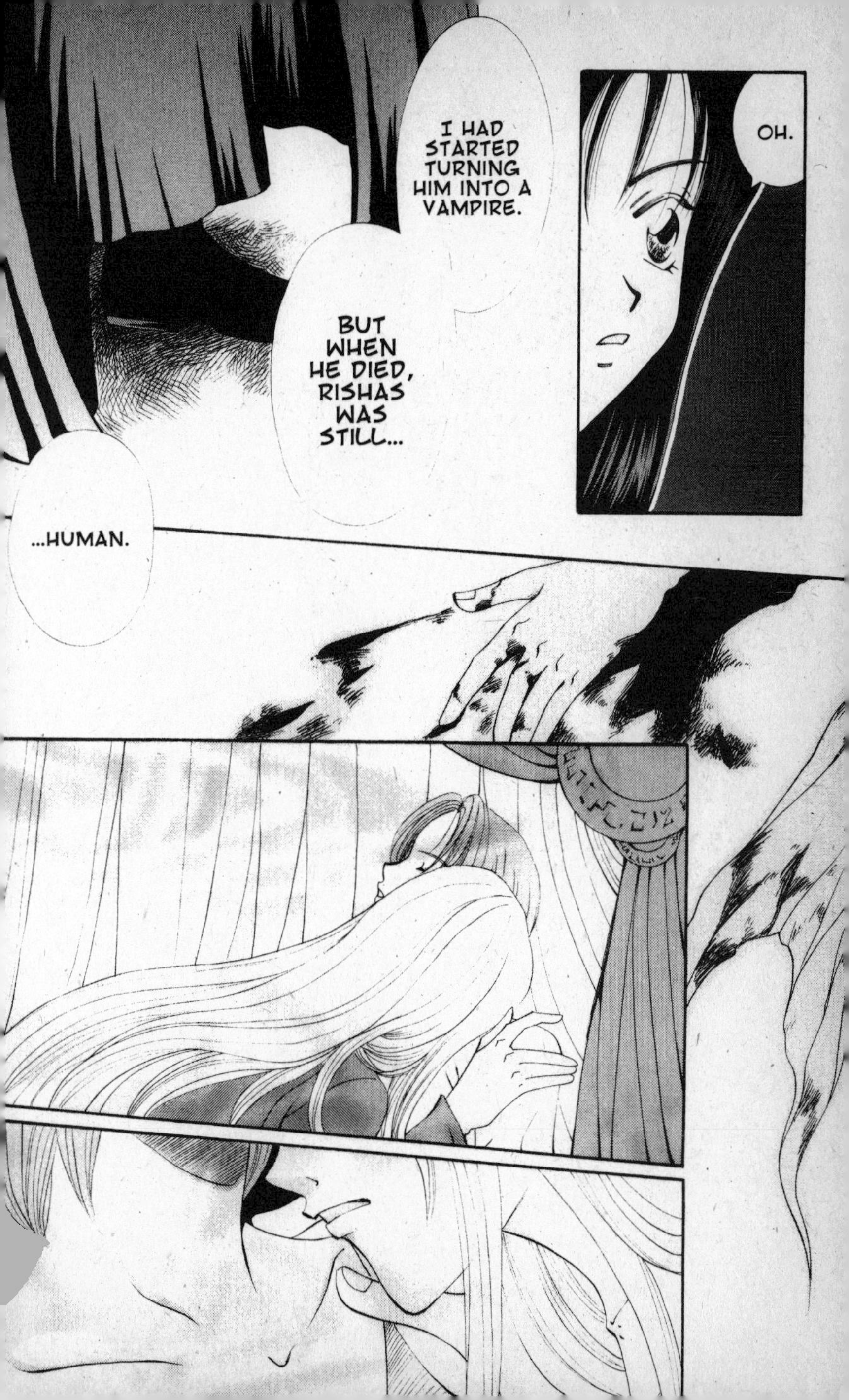
OH.
I HAD STARTED TURNING HIM INTO A VAMPIRE.
BUT WHEN HE DIED, RISHAS WAS STILL...
...HUMAN.

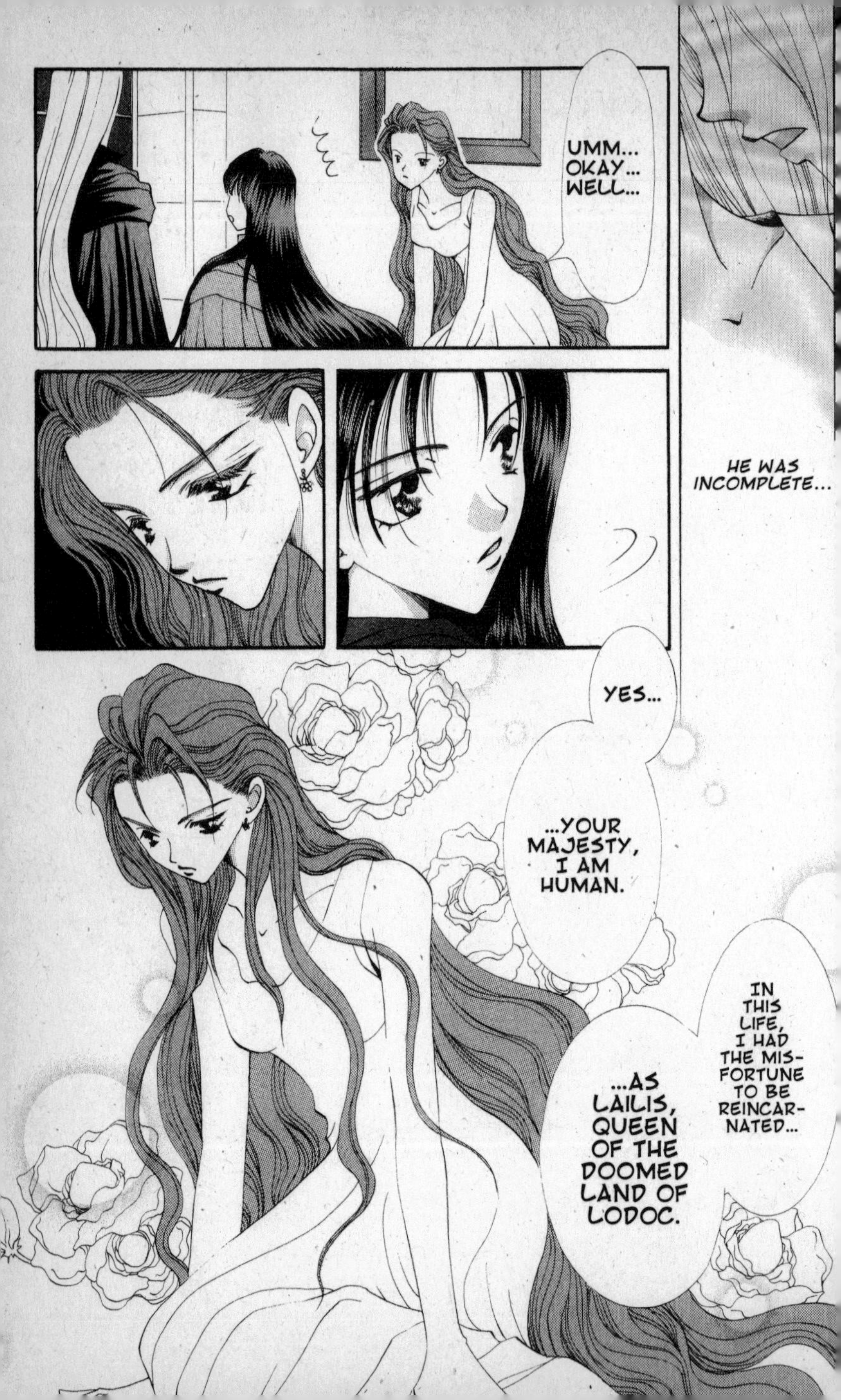
HE WAS INCOMPLETE...
UMM... OKAY... WELL...
YES...
...YOUR MAJESTY, I AM HUMAN.
IN THIS LIFE, I HAD THE MIS-FORTUNE TO BE REINCARNATED...
...AS LAILIS, QUEEN OF THE DOOMED LAND OF LODOC.

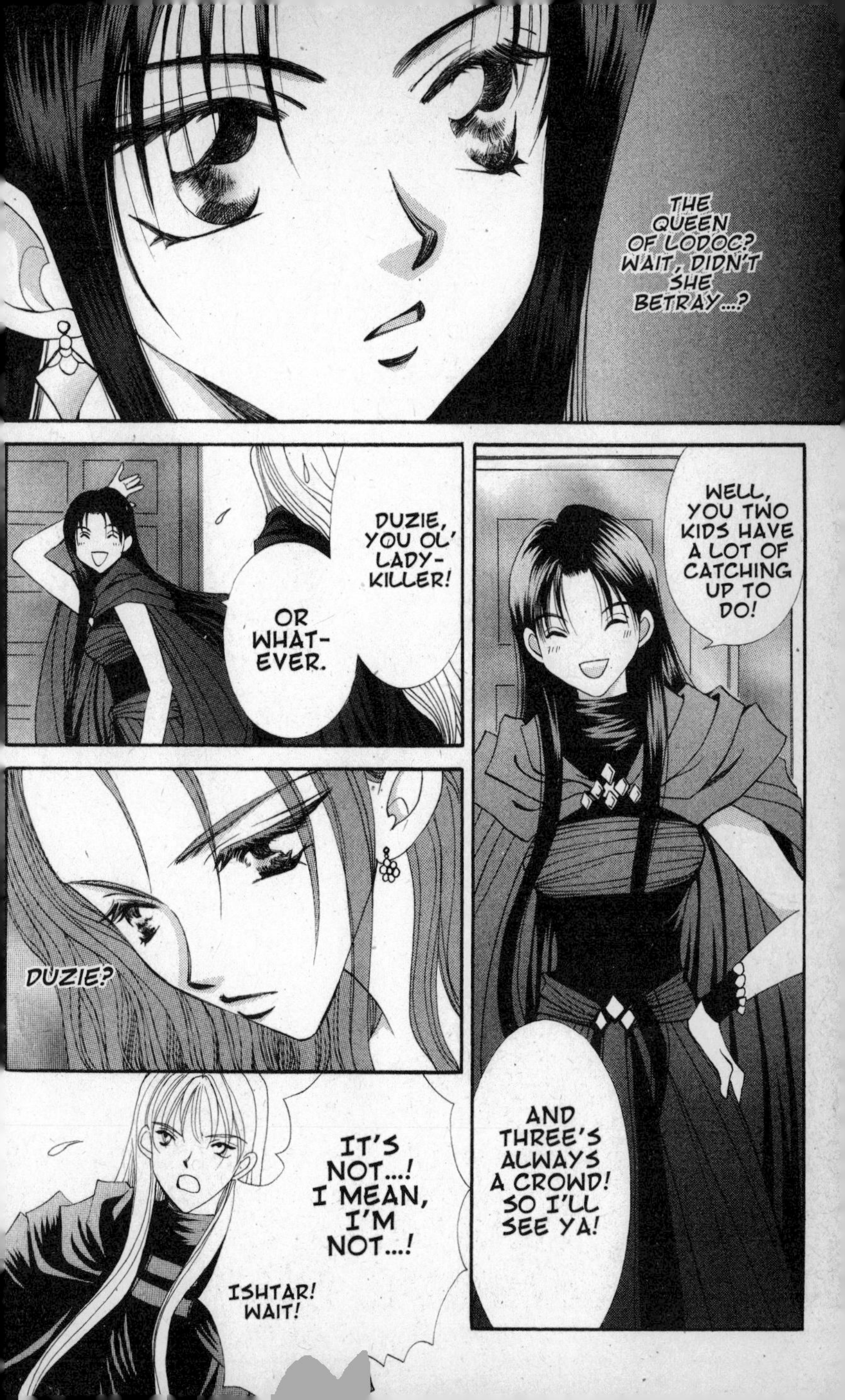

THE QUEEN OF LODOC? WAIT, DIDN'T SHE BETRAY...?
WELL, YOU TWO KIDS HAVE A LOT OF CATCHING UP TO DO!
AND THREE'S ALWAYS A CROWD! SO I'LL SEE YA!
DUZIE, YOU OL' LADY-KILLER!
OR WHAT-EVER.
DUZIE?
IT'S NOT...! I MEAN, I'M NOT...!
ISHTAR! WAIT!

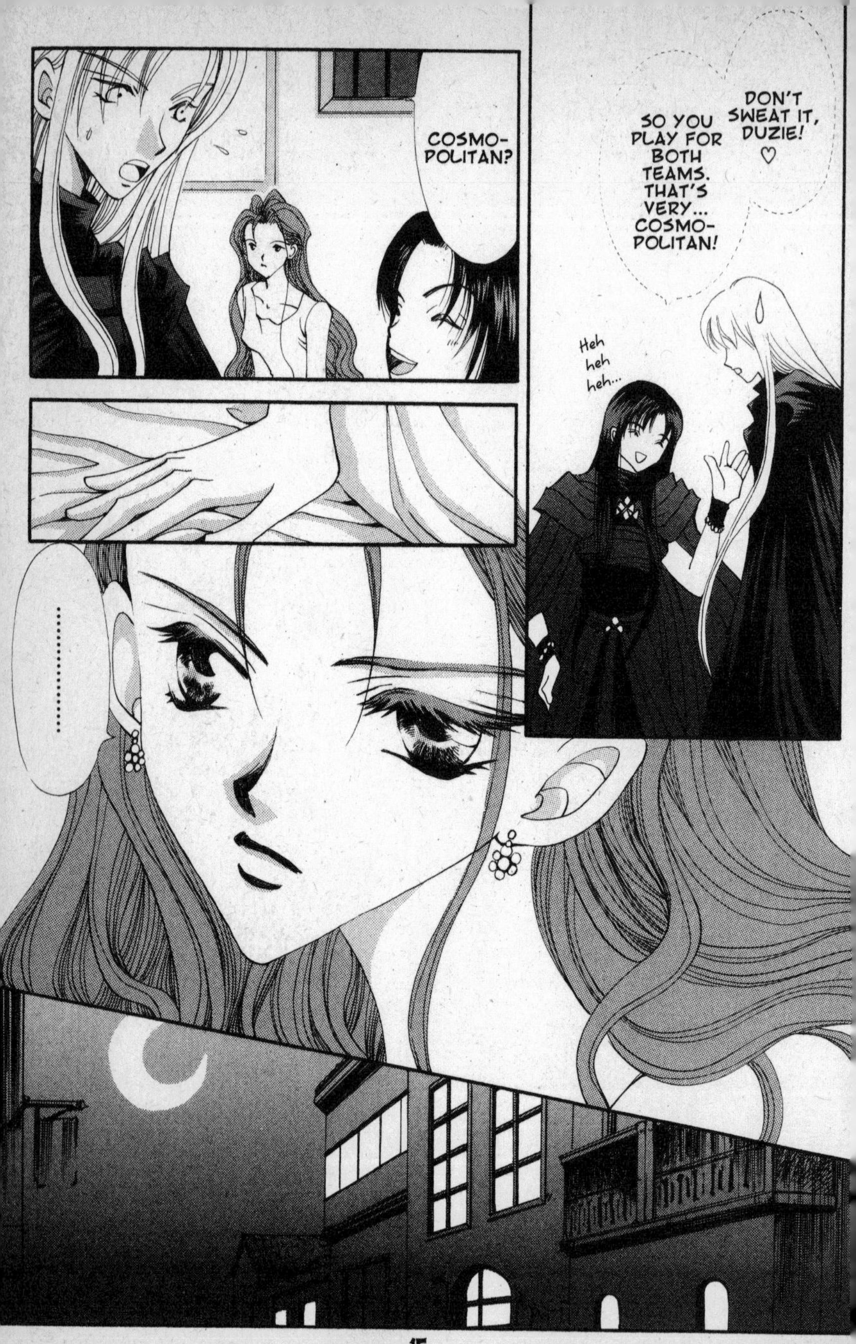
DON'T SWEAT IT, DUZIE! ♡
SO YOU PLAY FOR BOTH TEAMS. THAT'S VERY... COSMO-POLITAN!
Heh heh heh...
COSMO-POLITAN?
......

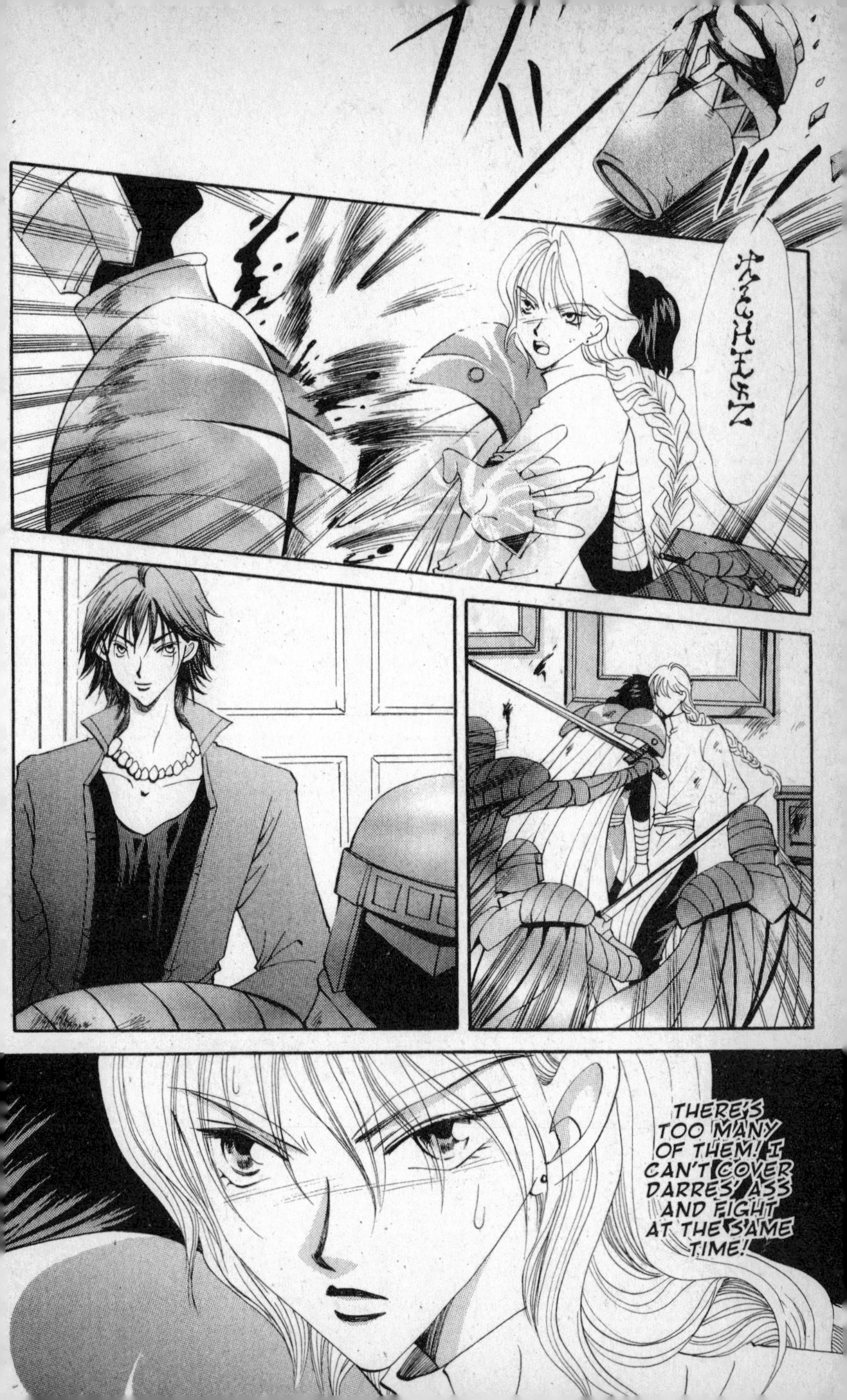
THERE'S TOO MANY OF THEM! I CAN'T COVER DARRES' ASS AND FIGHT AT THE SAME TIME!

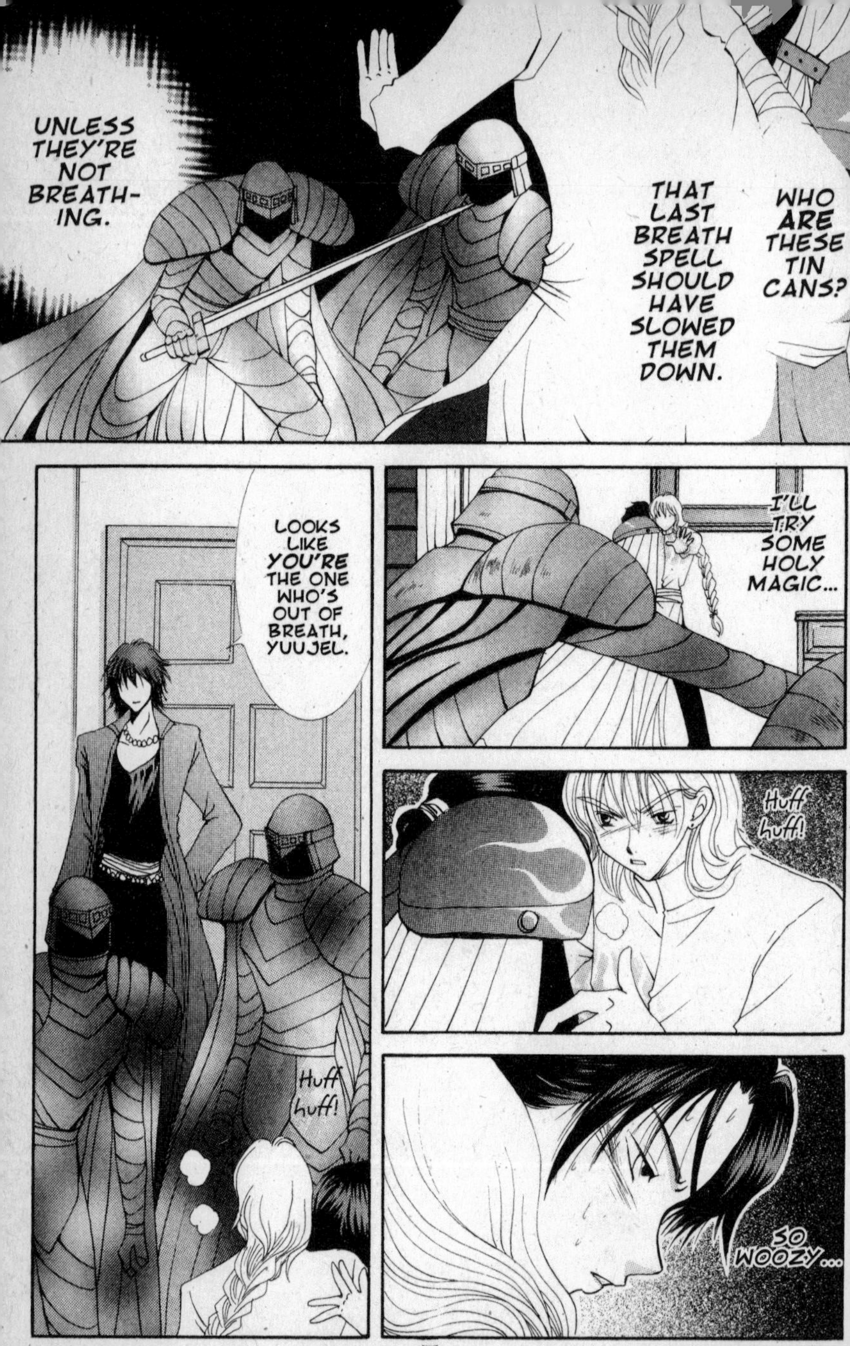
WHO ARE THESE TIN CANS?
THAT LAST BREATH SPELL SHOULD HAVE SLOWED THEM DOWN.
UNLESS THEY'RE NOT BREATHING.
I'LL TRY SOME HOLY MAGIC...
Huff huff!
SO WOOZY...
LOOKS LIKE *YOU'RE* THE ONE WHO'S OUT OF BREATH, YUUJEL.
Huff huff!

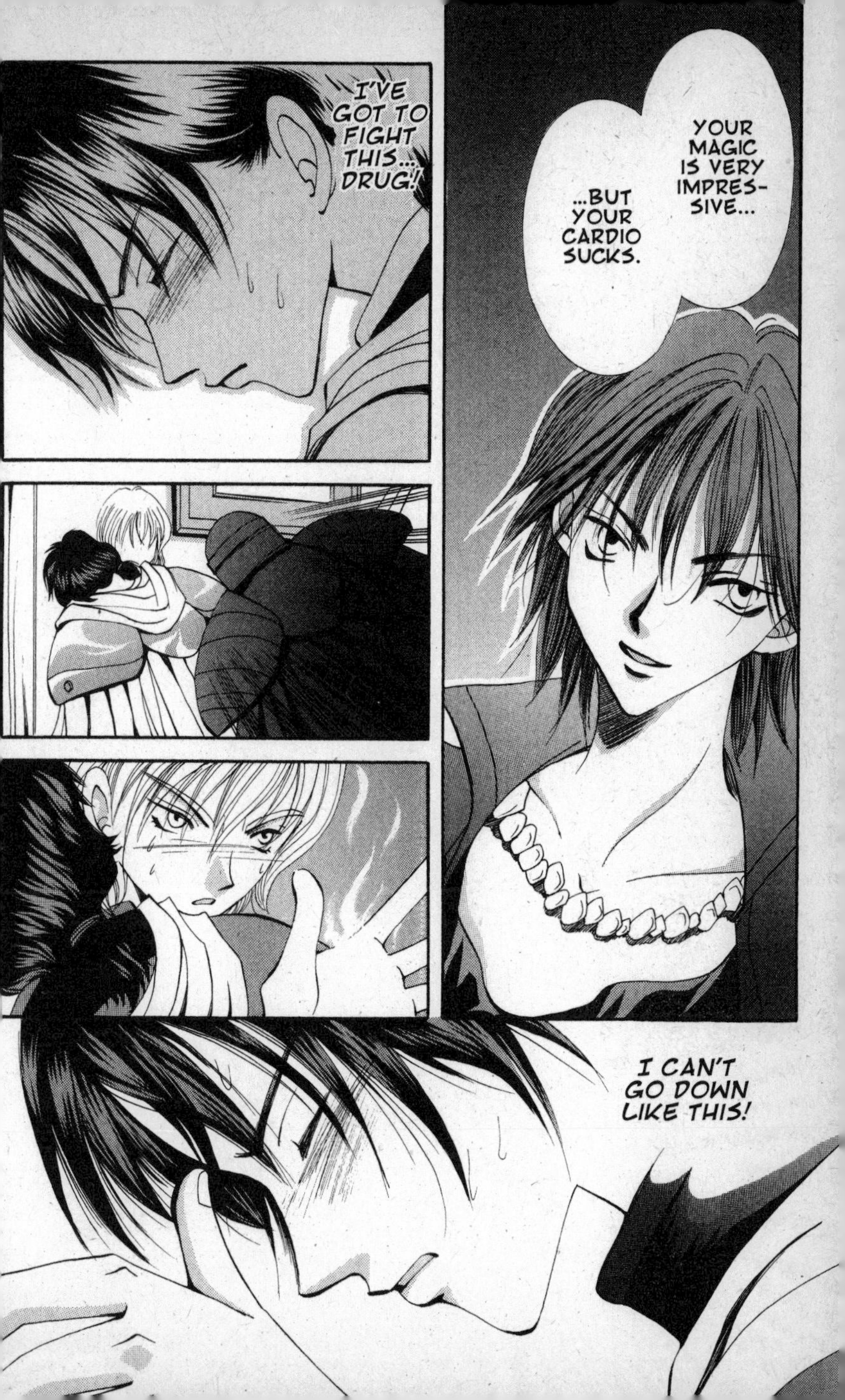
YOUR MAGIC IS VERY IMPRES-SIVE...
...BUT YOUR CARDIO SUCKS.
I'VE GOT TO FIGHT THIS... DRUG!
I CAN'T GO DOWN LIKE THIS!

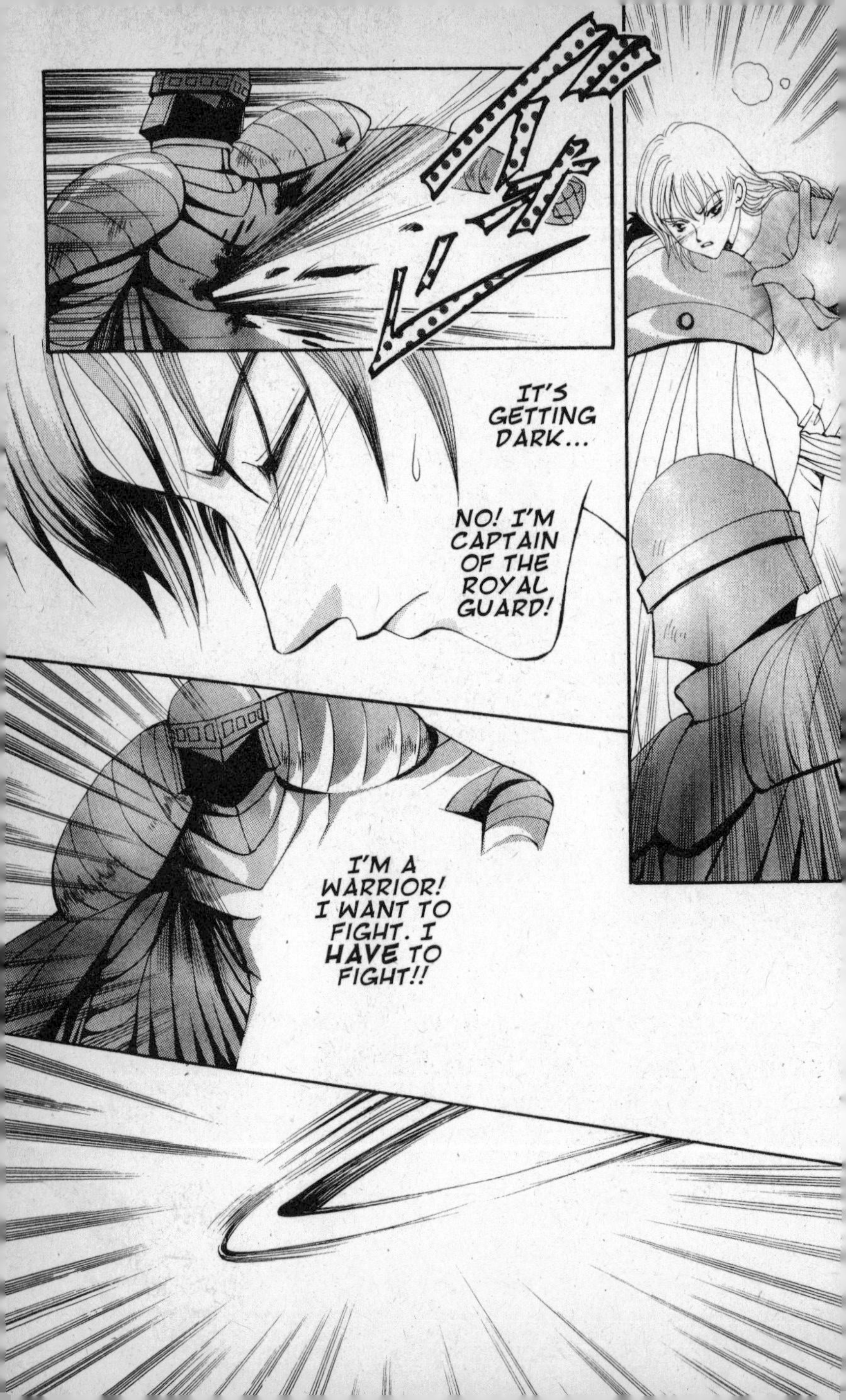
IT'S GETTING DARK...
NO! I'M CAPTAIN OF THE ROYAL GUARD!
I'M A WARRIOR! I WANT TO FIGHT. I **HAVE** TO FIGHT!!

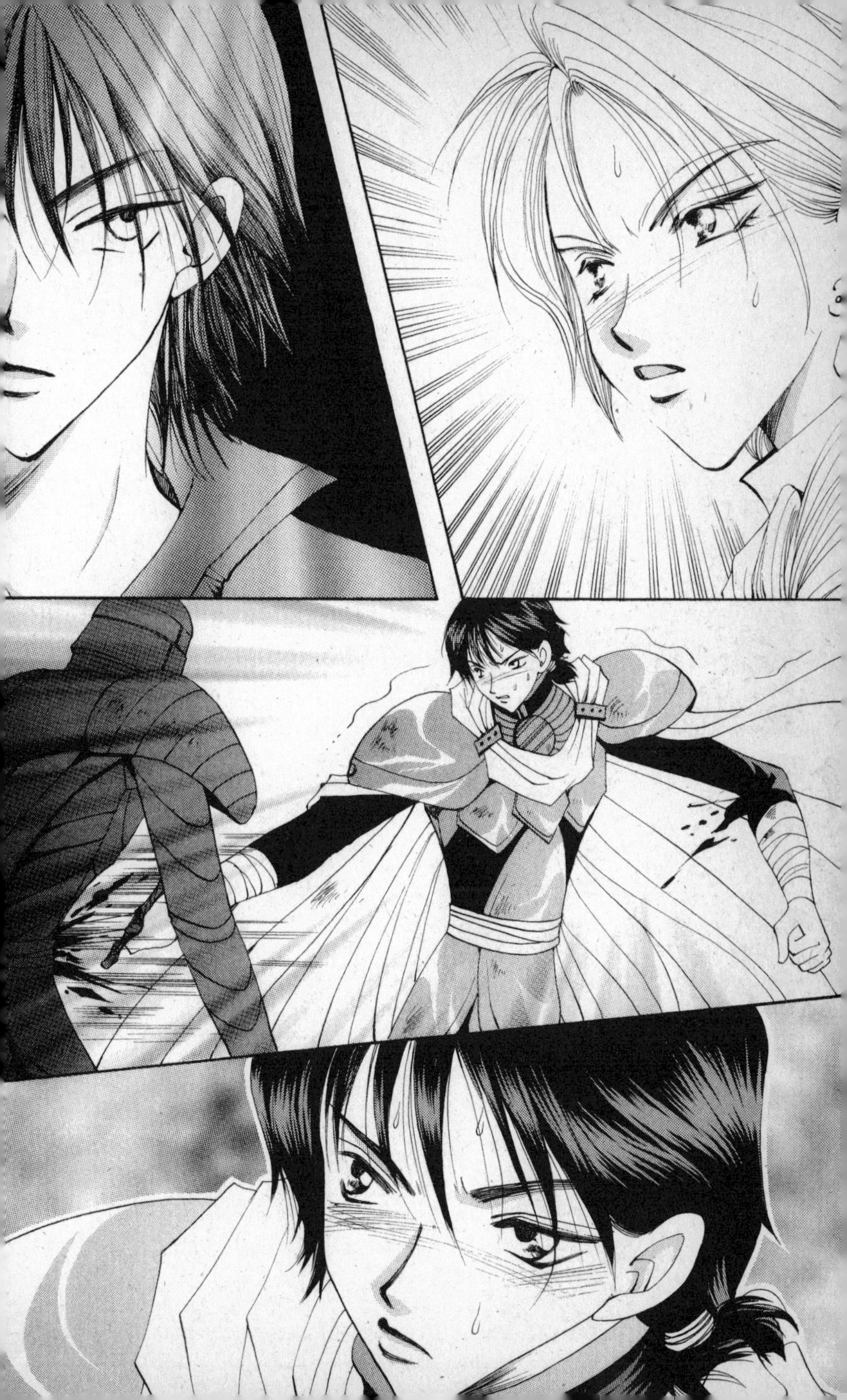

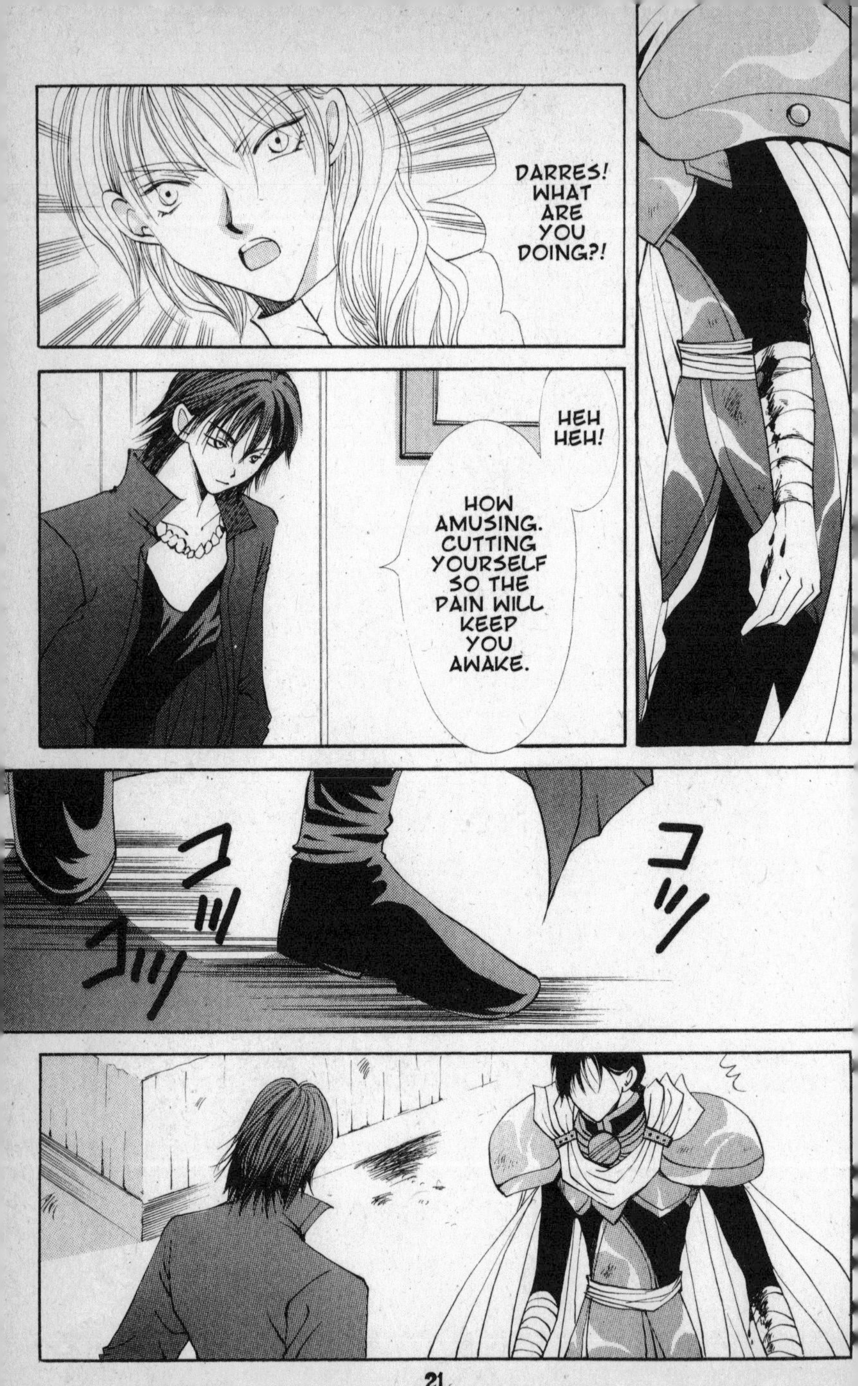
DARRES! WHAT ARE YOU DOING?!
HEH HEH!
HOW AMUSING. CUTTING YOURSELF SO THE PAIN WILL KEEP YOU AWAKE.
コッ
コッ
コッ

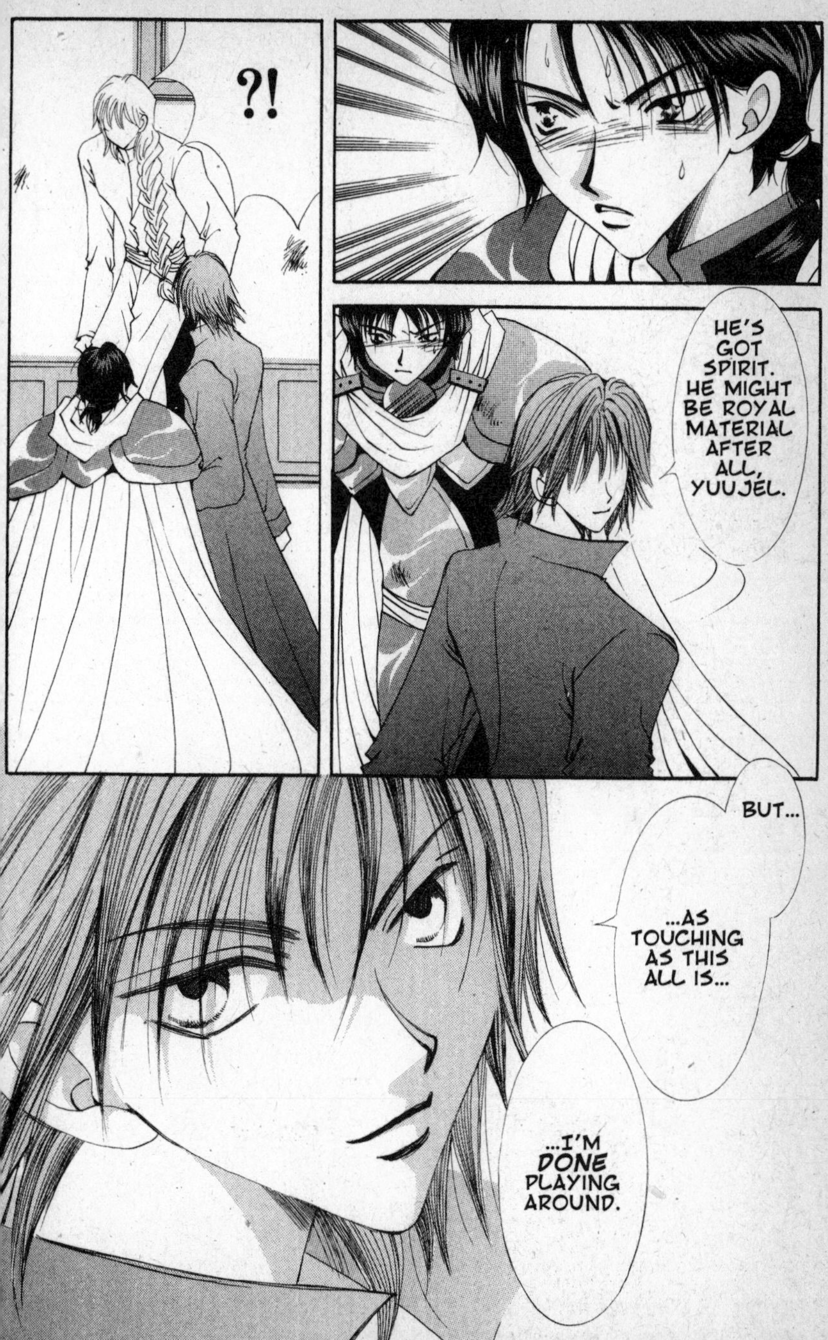
HE'S GOT SPIRIT. HE MIGHT BE ROYAL MATERIAL AFTER ALL, YUUJEL.
?!
BUT...
...AS TOUCHING AS THIS ALL IS...
...I'M DONE PLAYING AROUND.

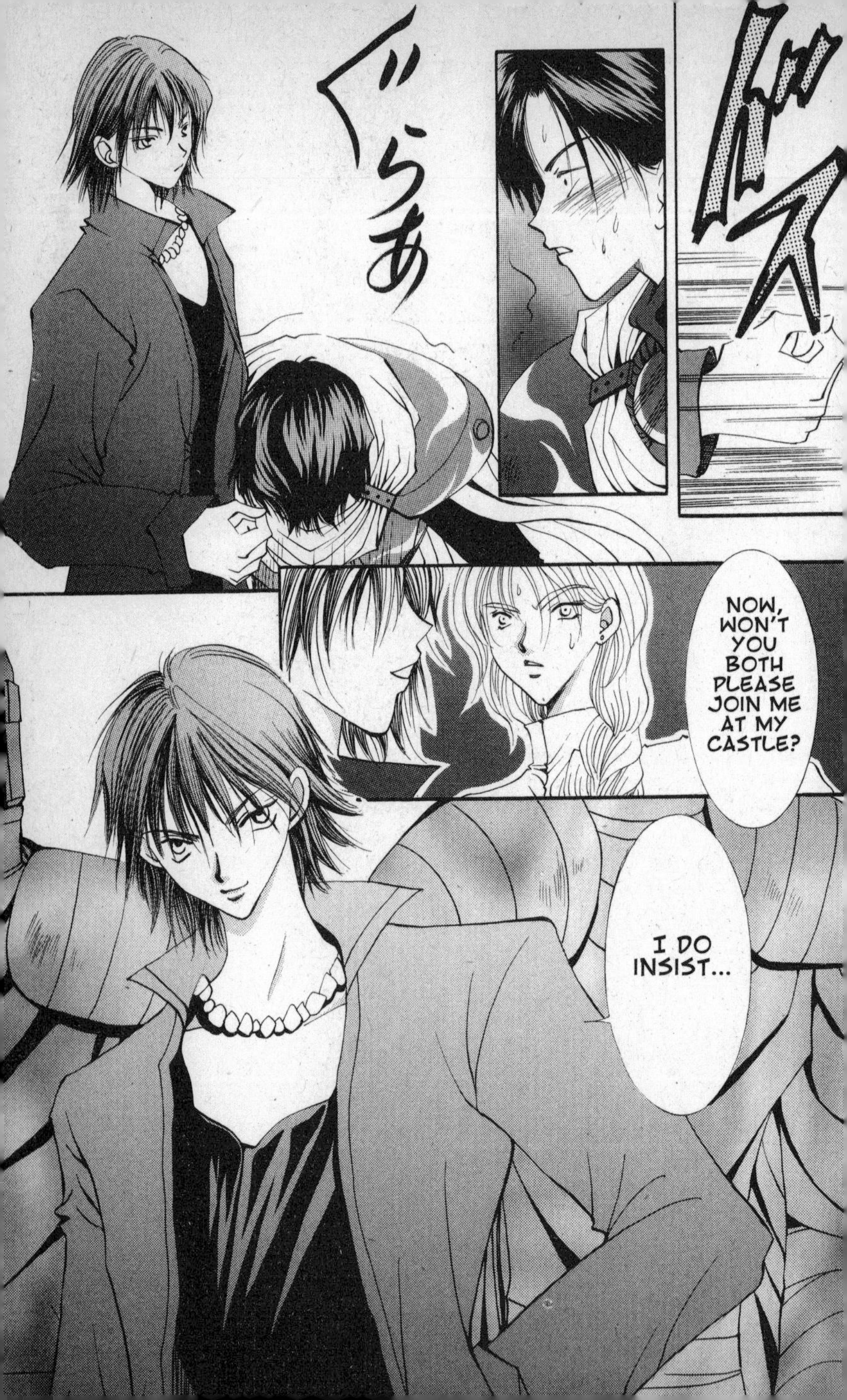
ドス
ぐらあ
NOW, WON'T YOU BOTH PLEASE JOIN ME AT MY CASTLE?
I DO INSIST...

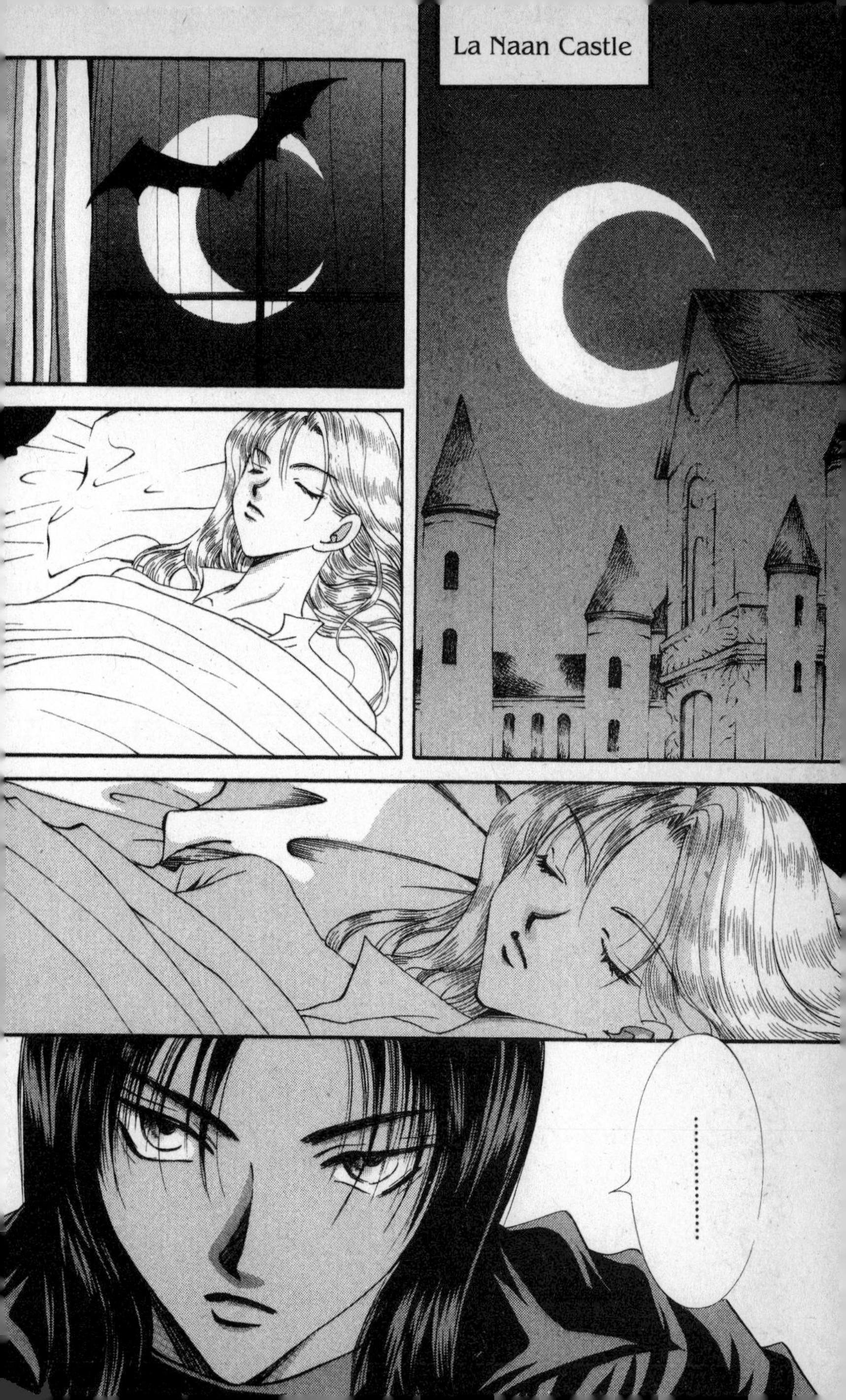
La Naan Castle
....

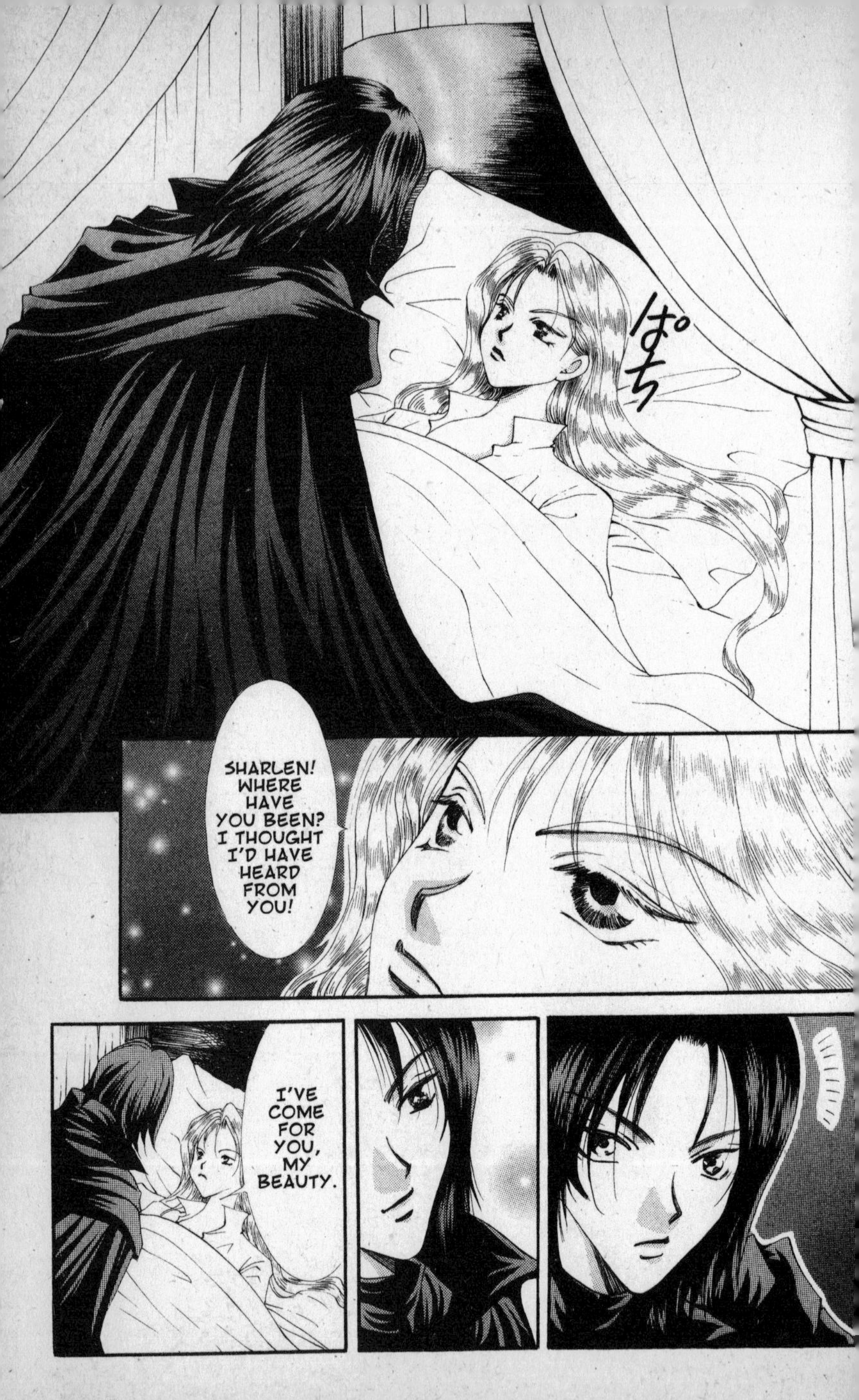
ぱち
SHARLEN! WHERE HAVE YOU BEEN? I THOUGHT I'D HAVE HEARD FROM YOU!
I'VE COME FOR YOU, MY BEAUTY.

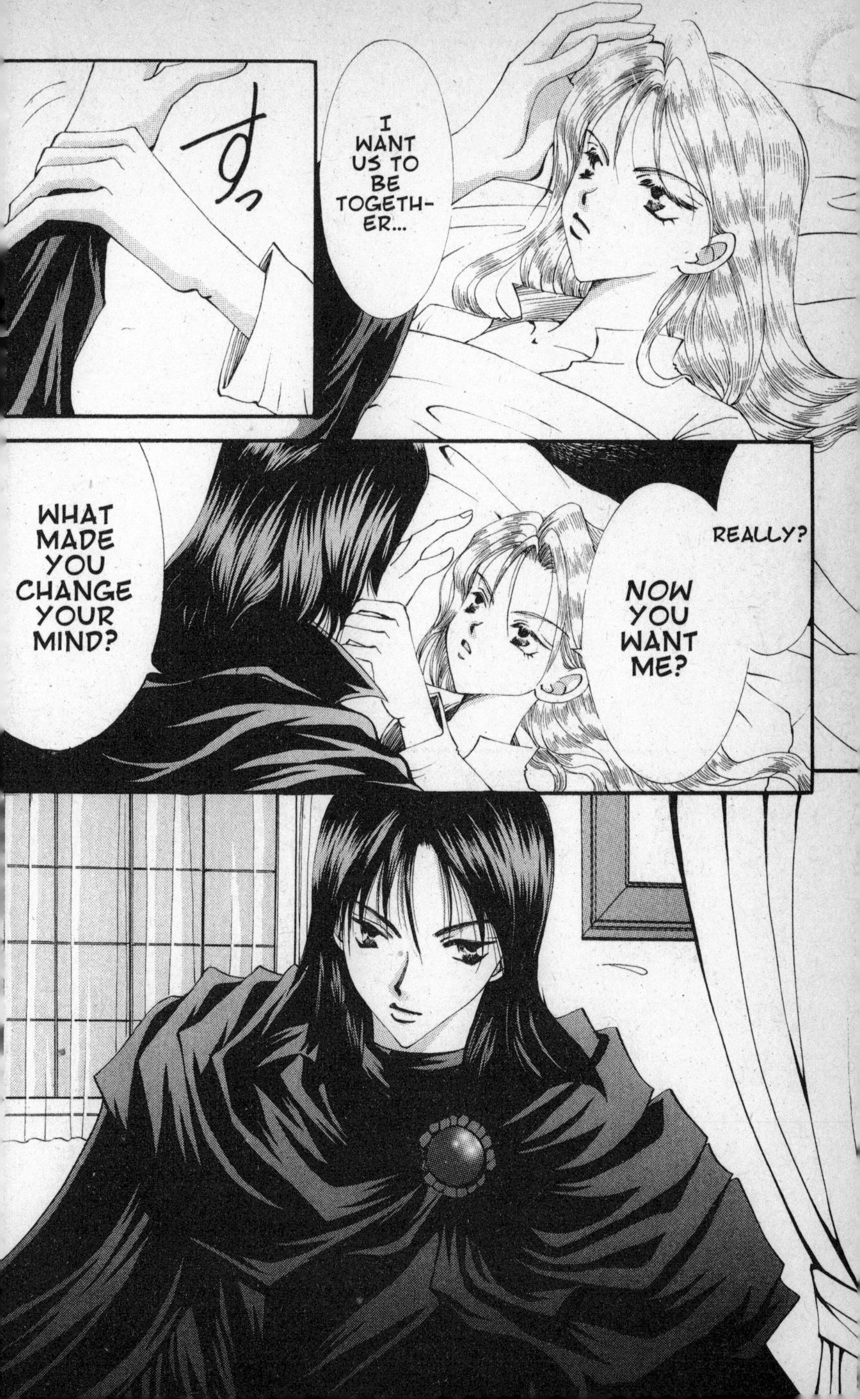
I WANT US TO BE TOGETH-ER...
すっ
REALLY?
NOW YOU WANT ME?
WHAT MADE YOU CHANGE YOUR MIND?

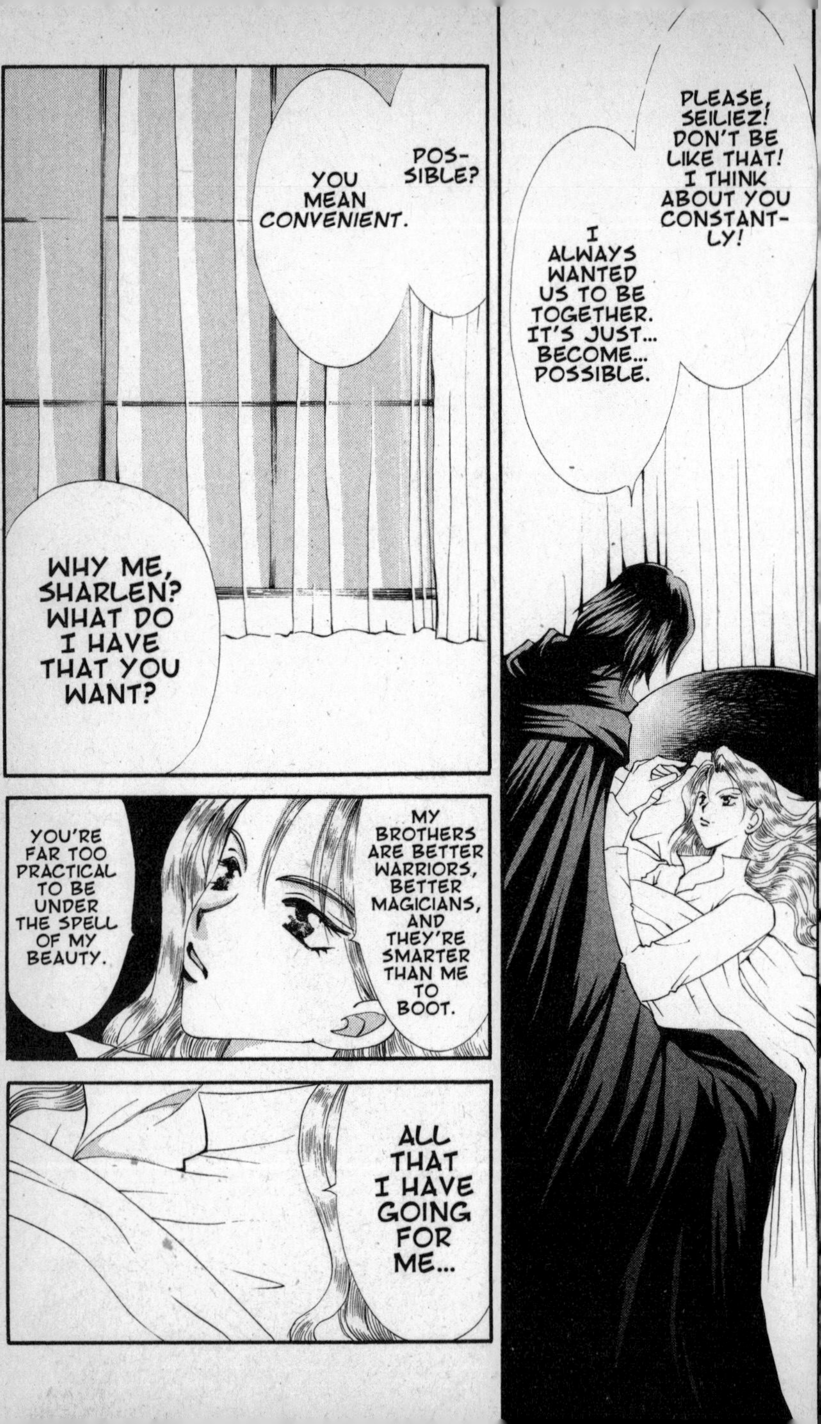
PLEASE, SEILIEZ! DON'T BE LIKE THAT! I THINK ABOUT YOU CONSTANT-LY!
I ALWAYS WANTED US TO BE TOGETHER. IT'S JUST... BECOME... POSSIBLE.
POS-SIBLE? YOU MEAN CONVENIENT.
WHY ME, SHARLEN? WHAT DO I HAVE THAT YOU WANT?
MY BROTHERS ARE BETTER WARRIORS, BETTER MAGICIANS, AND THEY'RE SMARTER THAN ME TO BOOT.
YOU'RE FAR TOO PRACTICAL TO BE UNDER THE SPELL OF MY BEAUTY.
ALL THAT I HAVE GOING FOR ME...

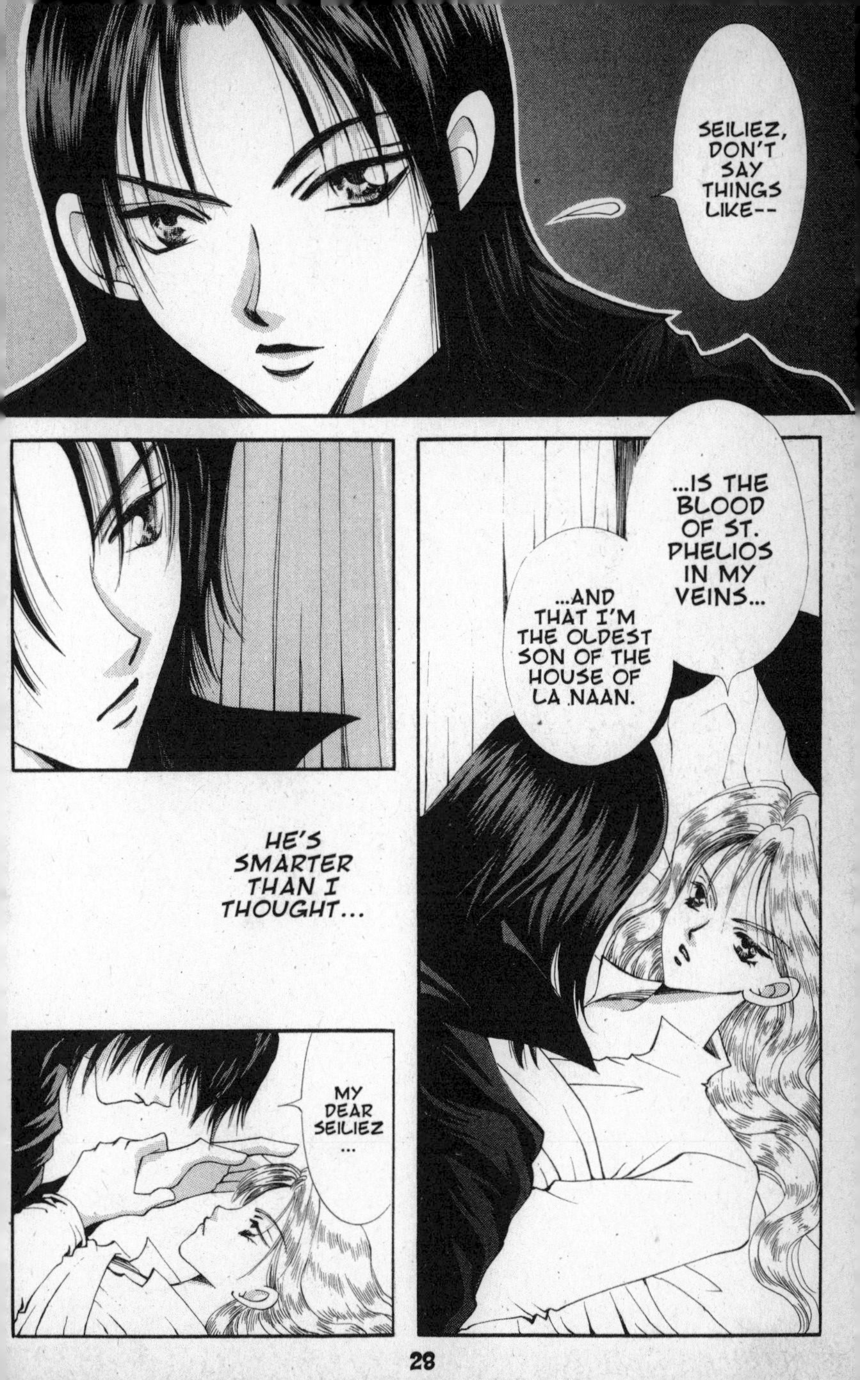
SEILIEZ, DON'T SAY THINGS LIKE--
...IS THE BLOOD OF ST. PHELIOS IN MY VEINS...
...AND THAT I'M THE OLDEST SON OF THE HOUSE OF LA NAAN.
HE'S SMARTER THAN I THOUGHT...
MY DEAR SEILIEZ ...

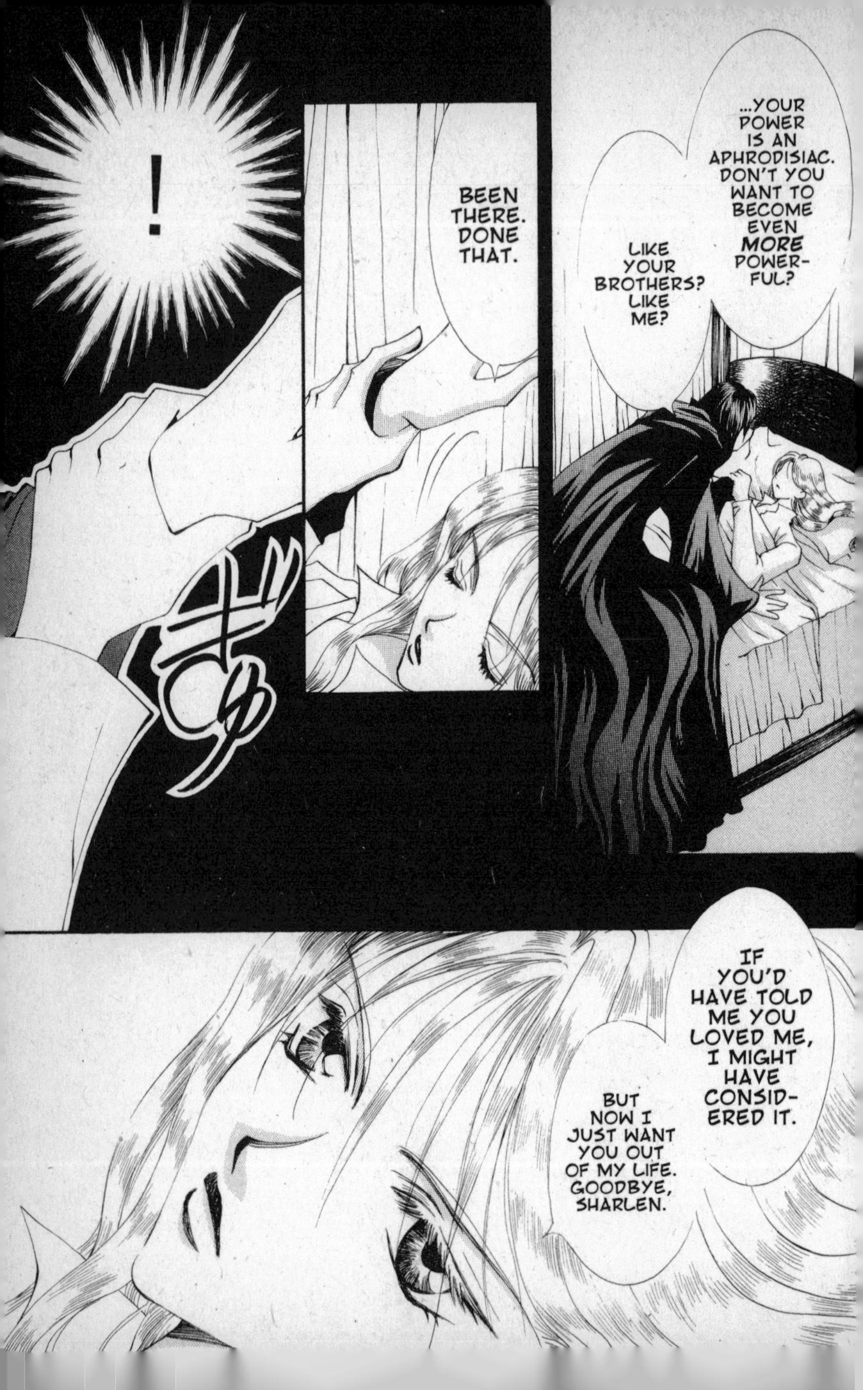
...YOUR POWER IS AN APHRODISIAC. DON'T YOU WANT TO BECOME EVEN MORE POWERFUL?
LIKE YOUR BROTHERS? LIKE ME?
BEEN THERE. DONE THAT.
!
IF YOU'D HAVE TOLD ME YOU LOVED ME, I MIGHT HAVE CONSIDERED IT.
BUT NOW I JUST WANT YOU OUT OF MY LIFE. GOODBYE, SHARLEN.

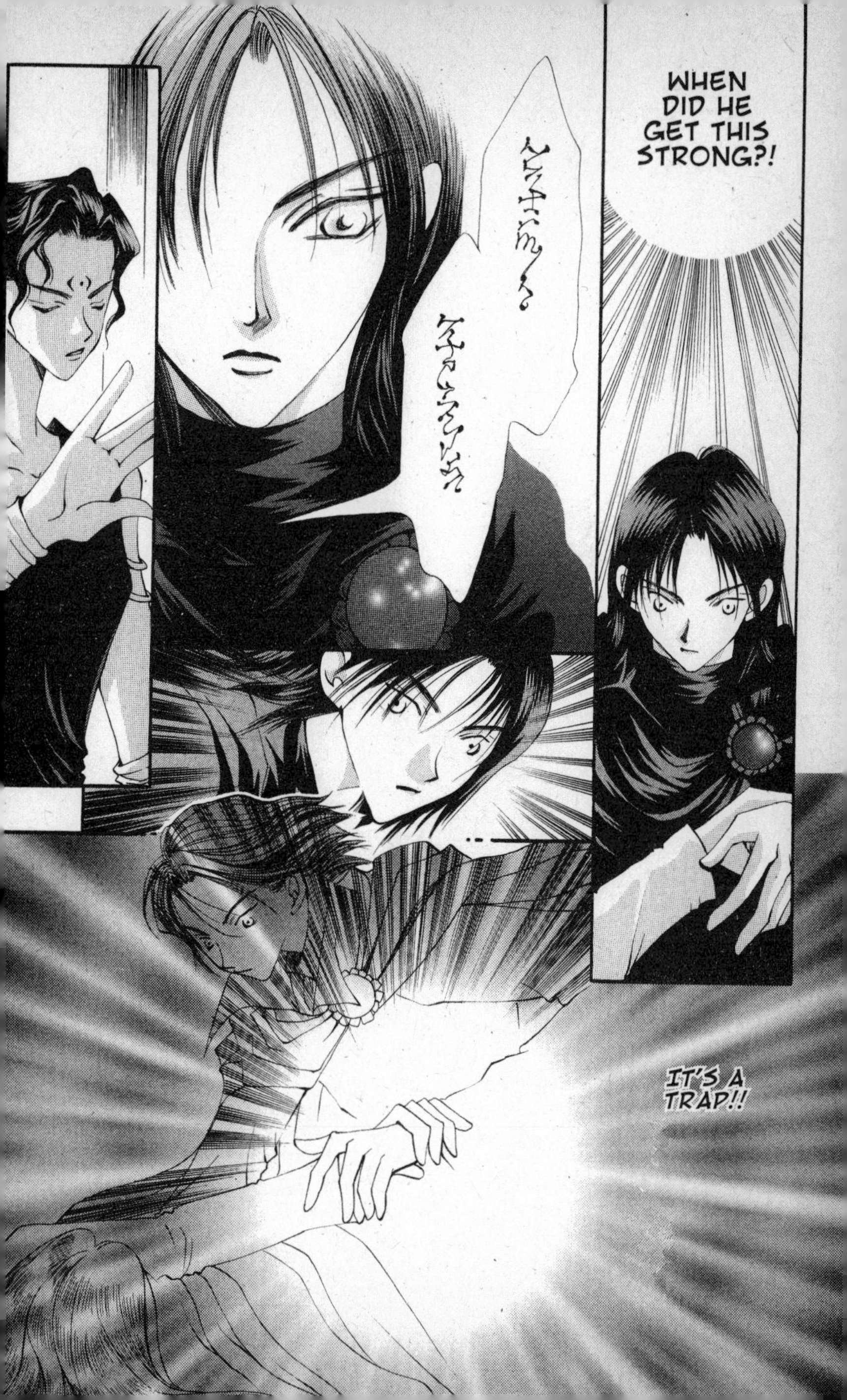
WHEN DID HE GET THIS STRONG?!
IT'S A TRAP!!

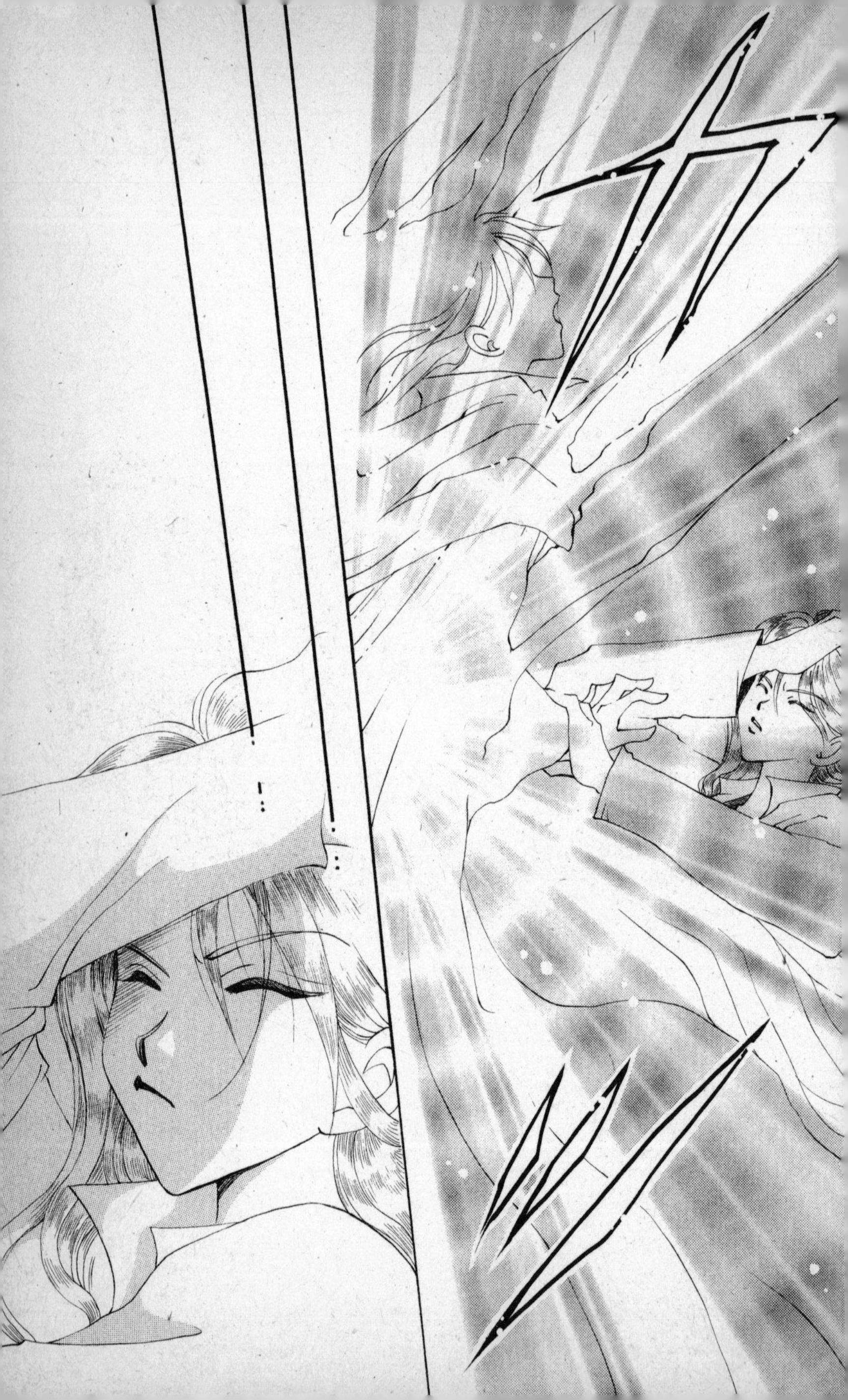

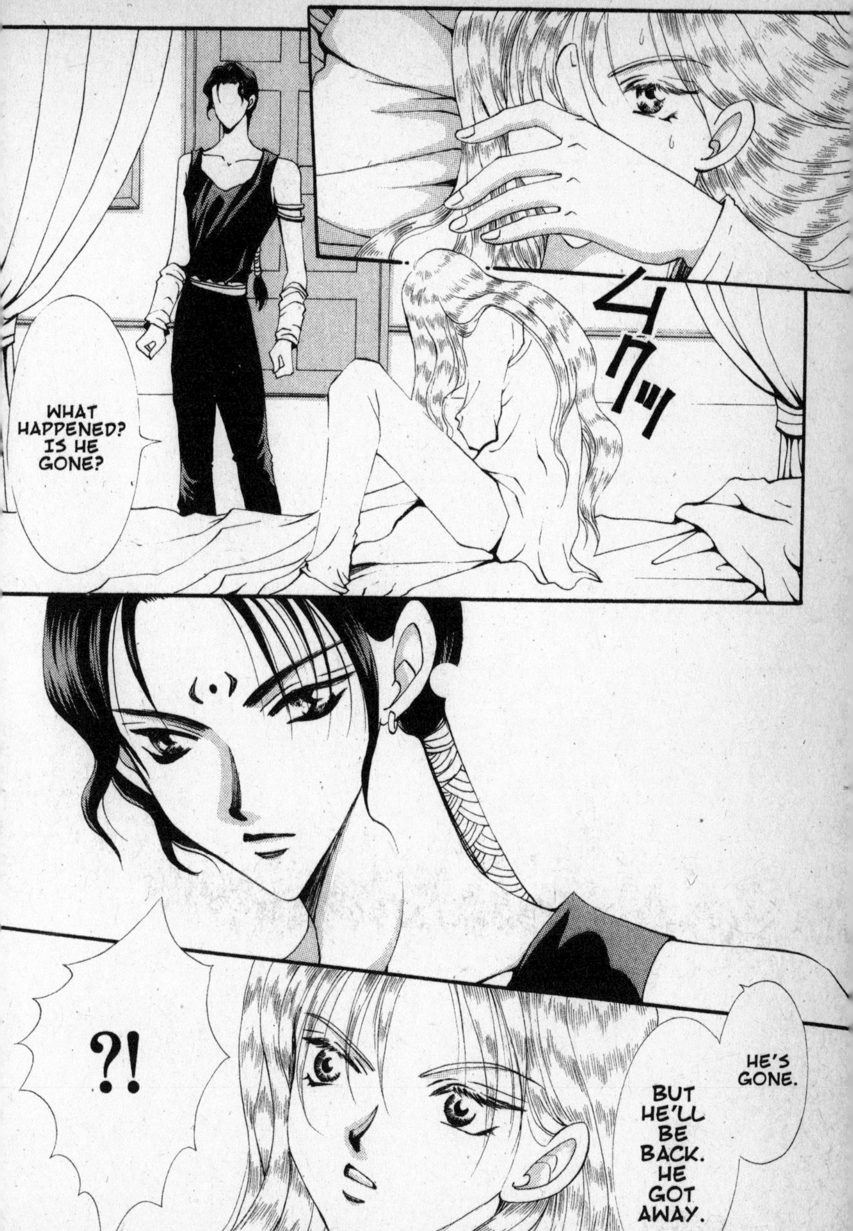
ムクッ
WHAT HAPPENED? IS HE GONE?
HE'S GONE.
BUT HE'LL BE BACK. HE GOT AWAY.
?!

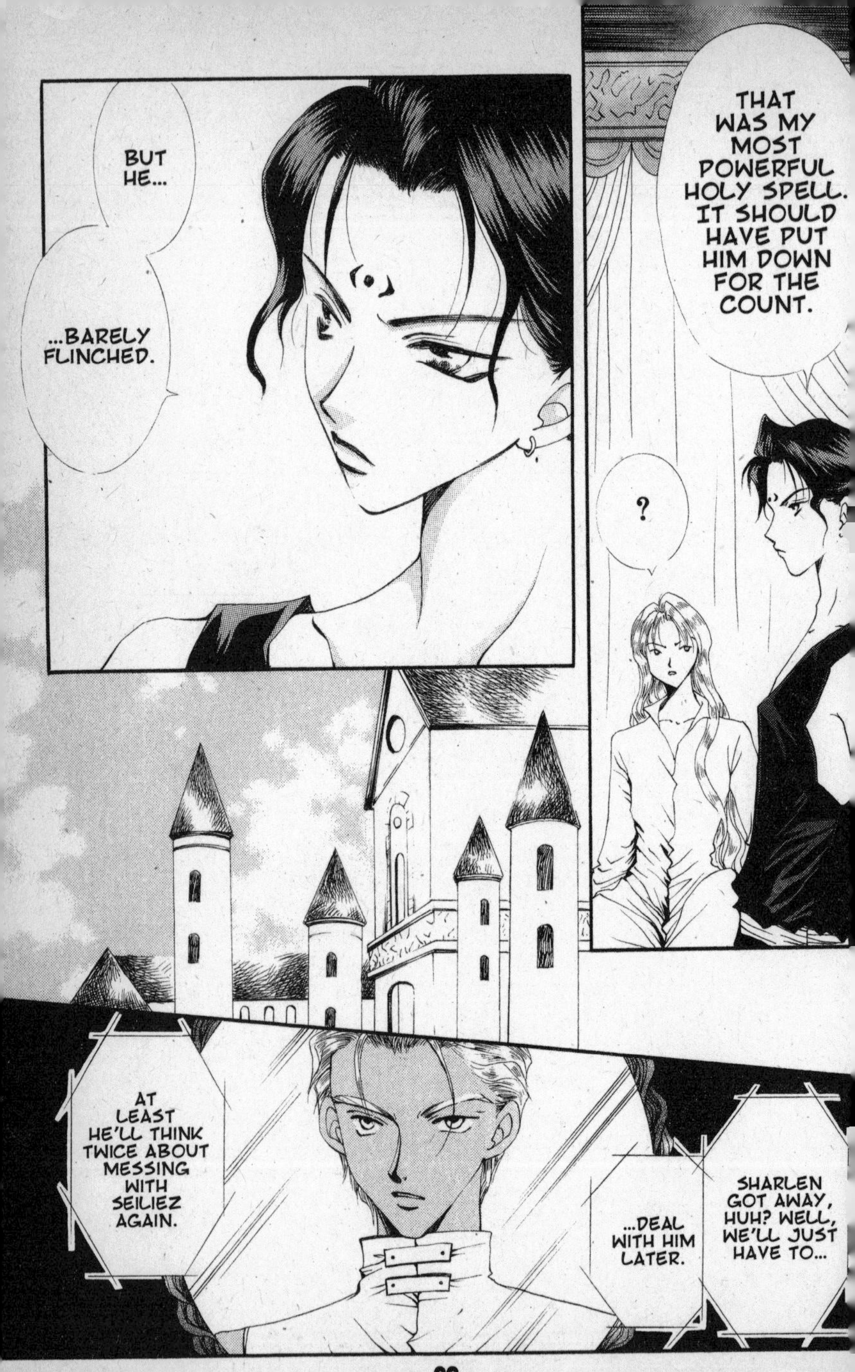
THAT WAS MY MOST POWERFUL HOLY SPELL. IT SHOULD HAVE PUT HIM DOWN FOR THE COUNT.
?
BUT HE...
...BARELY FLINCHED.
SHARLEN GOT AWAY, HUH? WELL, WE'LL JUST HAVE TO...
...DEAL WITH HIM LATER.
AT LEAST HE'LL THINK TWICE ABOUT MESSING WITH SEILIEZ AGAIN.

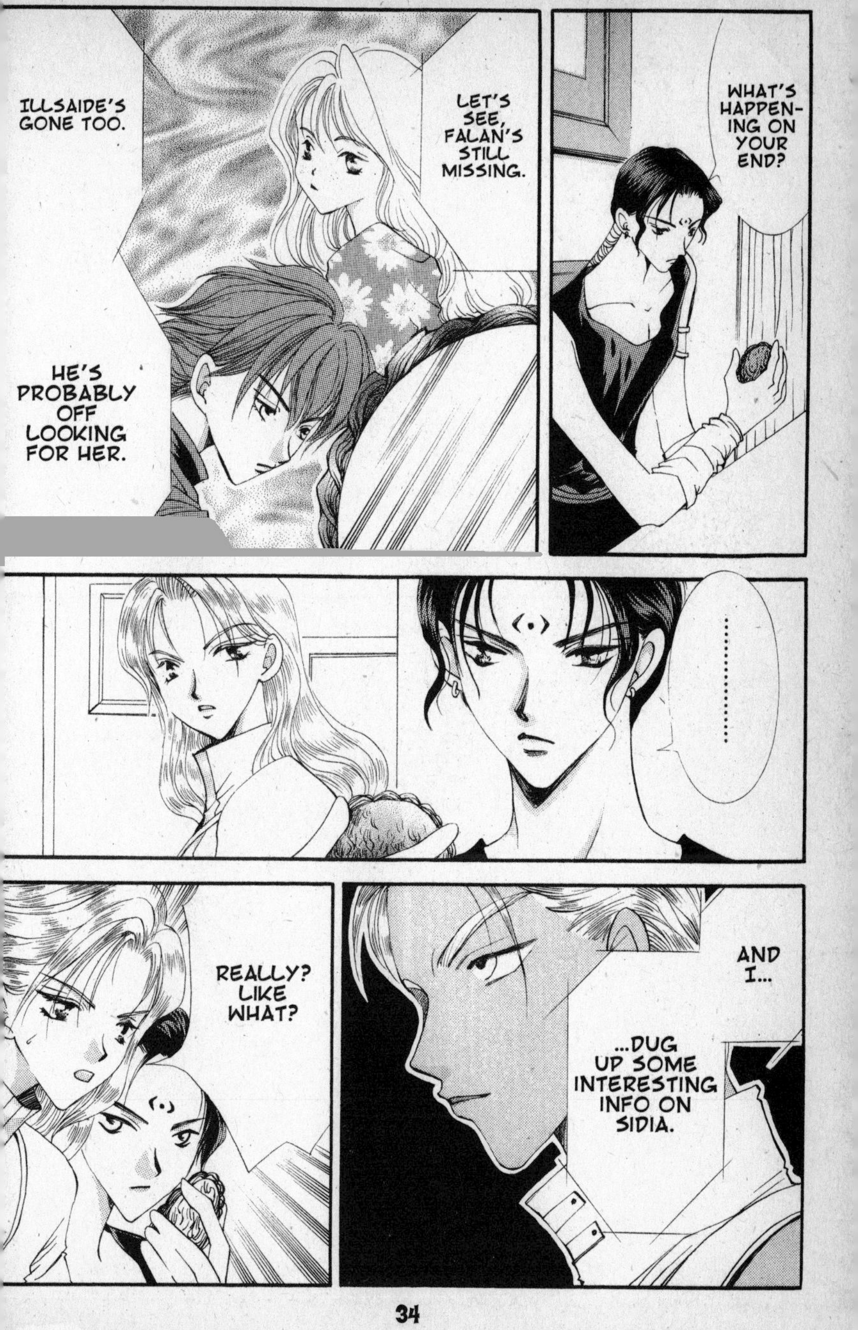
WHAT'S HAPPENING ON YOUR END?
LET'S SEE, FALAN'S STILL MISSING.
ILLSAIDE'S GONE TOO.
HE'S PROBABLY OFF LOOKING FOR HER.
......
AND I...
...DUG UP SOME INTERESTING INFO ON SIDIA.
REALLY? LIKE WHAT?

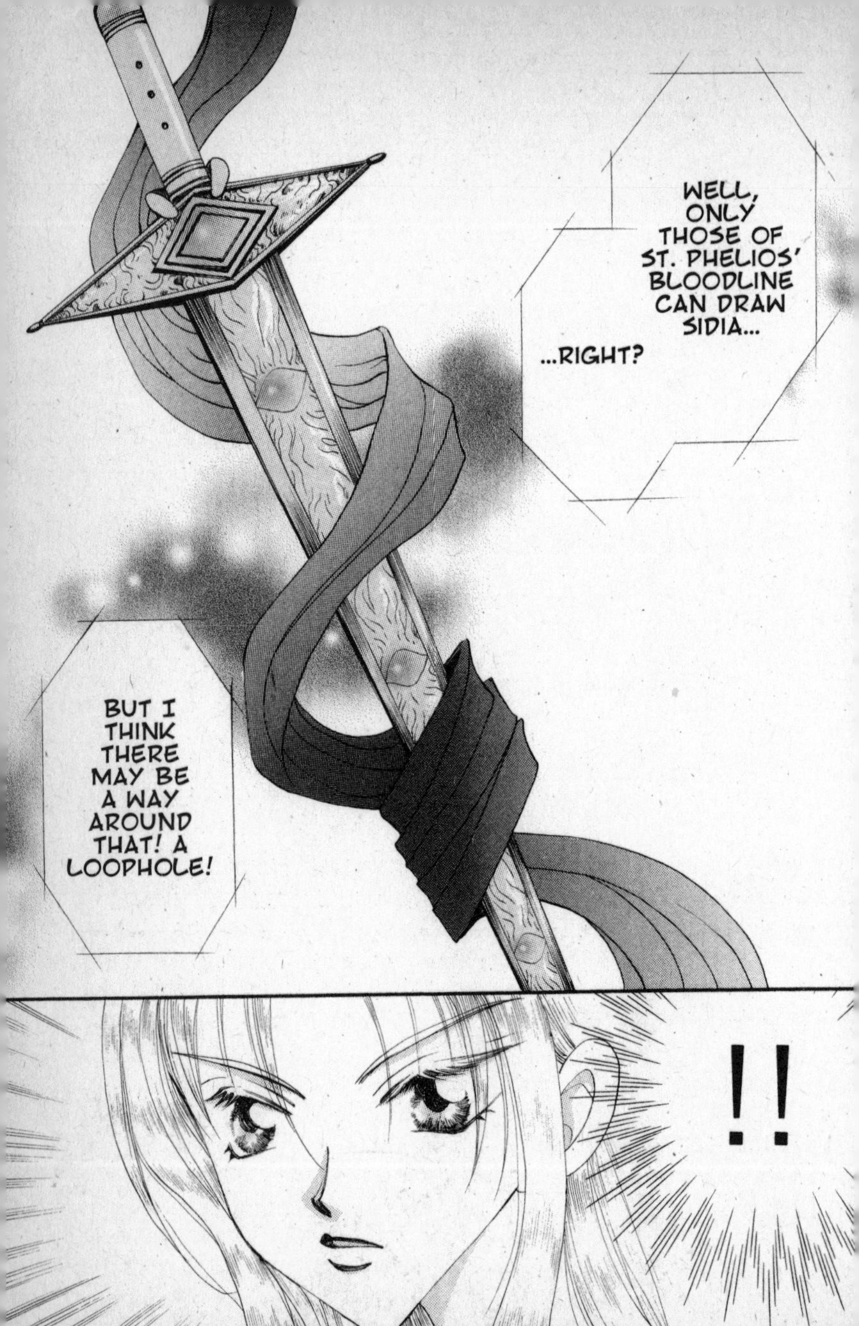
WELL, ONLY THOSE OF ST. PHELIOS' BLOODLINE CAN DRAW SIDIA...
...RIGHT?
BUT I THINK THERE MAY BE A WAY AROUND THAT! A LOOPHOLE!
!!

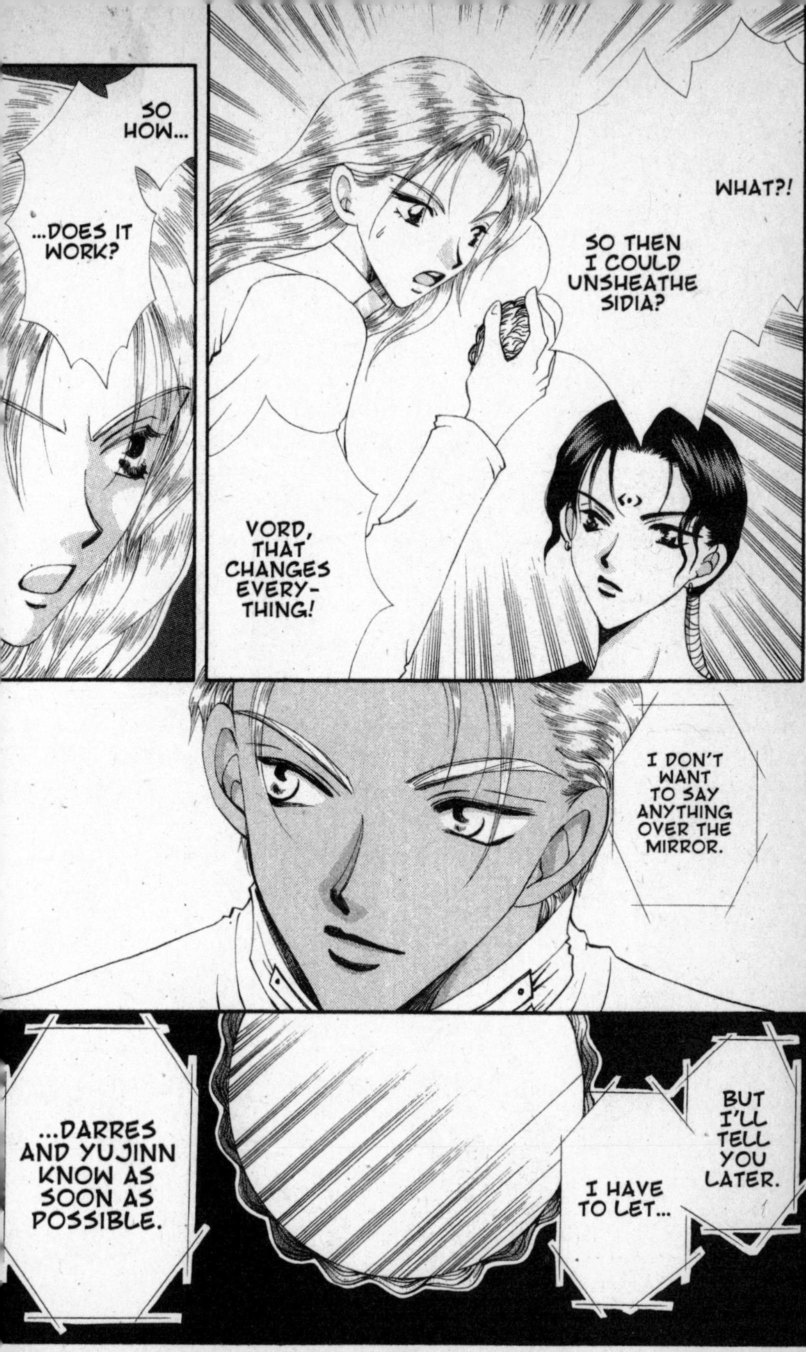
WHAT?!
SO THEN I COULD UNSHEATHE SIDIA?
VORD, THAT CHANGES EVERY-THING!
SO HOW...
...DOES IT WORK?
I DON'T WANT TO SAY ANYTHING OVER THE MIRROR.
BUT I'LL TELL YOU LATER.
I HAVE TO LET...
...DARRES AND YUJINN KNOW AS SOON AS POSSIBLE.

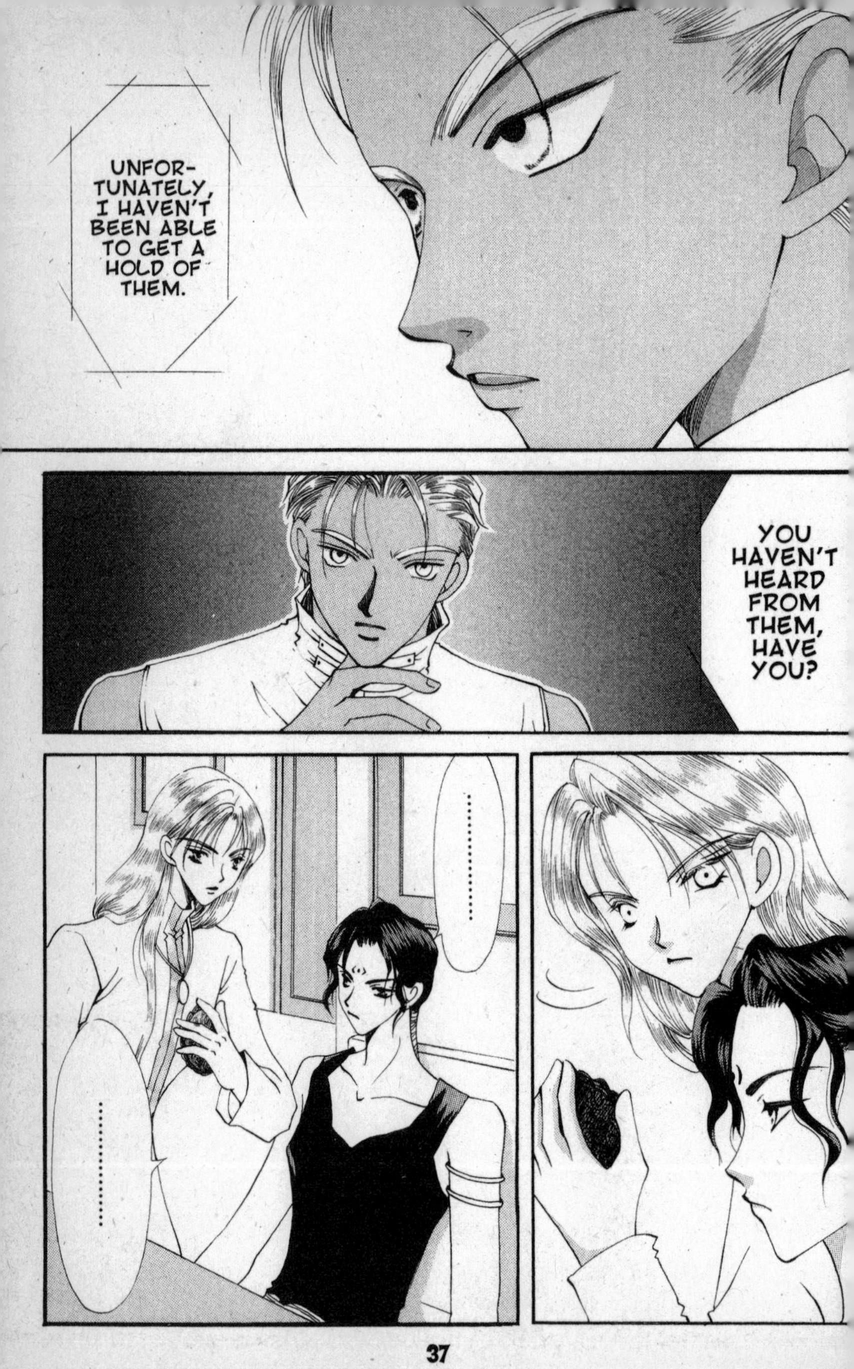
UNFOR-TUNATELY, I HAVEN'T BEEN ABLE TO GET A HOLD OF THEM.
YOU HAVEN'T HEARD FROM THEM, HAVE YOU?
......
......

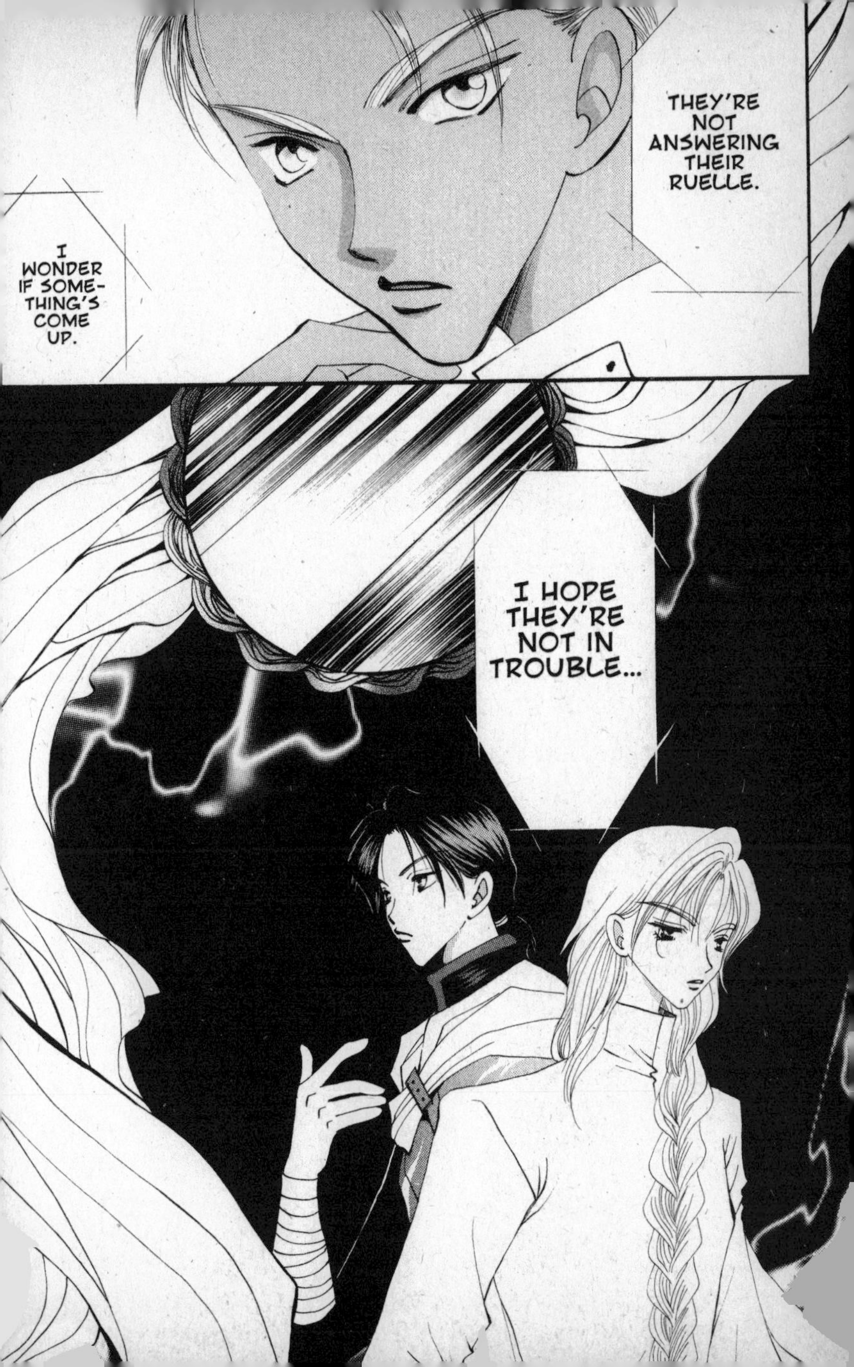
THEY'RE NOT ANSWERING THEIR RUELLE.
I WONDER IF SOME-THING'S COME UP.
I HOPE THEY'RE NOT IN TROUBLE...

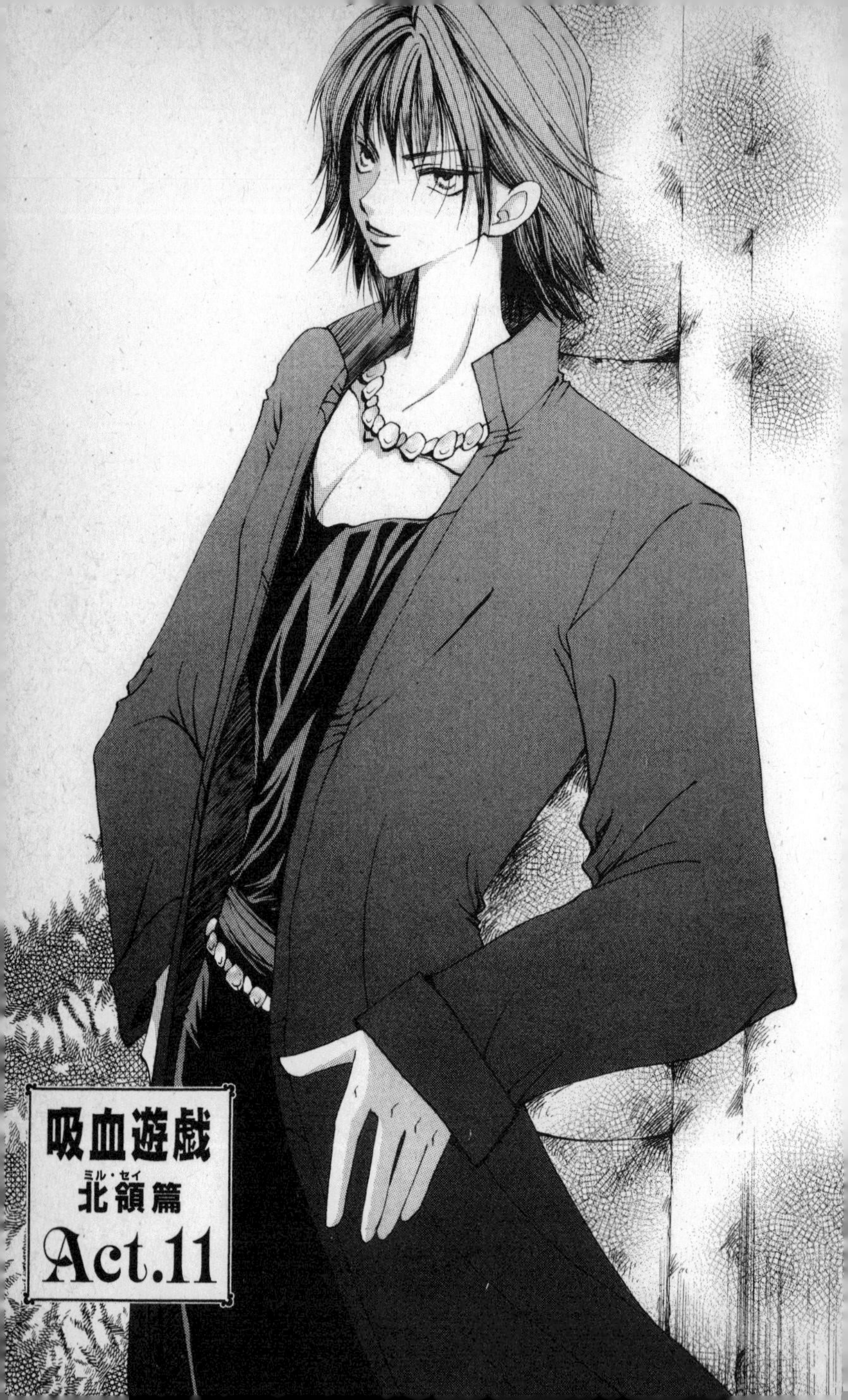
吸血遊戯
ミル・セイ
北領篇
Act.11

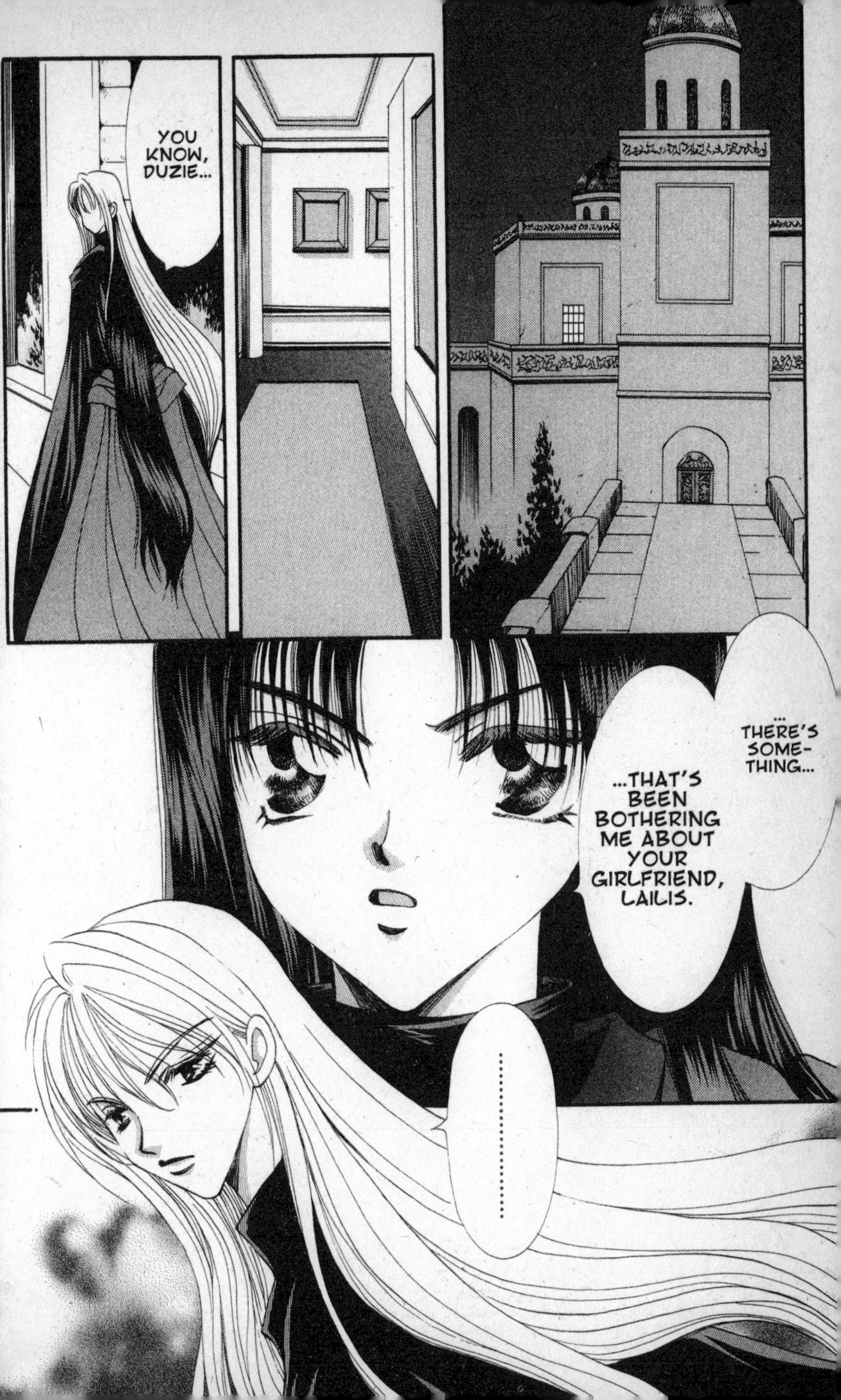
YOU KNOW, DUZIE...
... THERE'S SOME-THING...
...THAT'S BEEN BOTHERING ME ABOUT YOUR GIRLFRIEND, LAILIS.
....

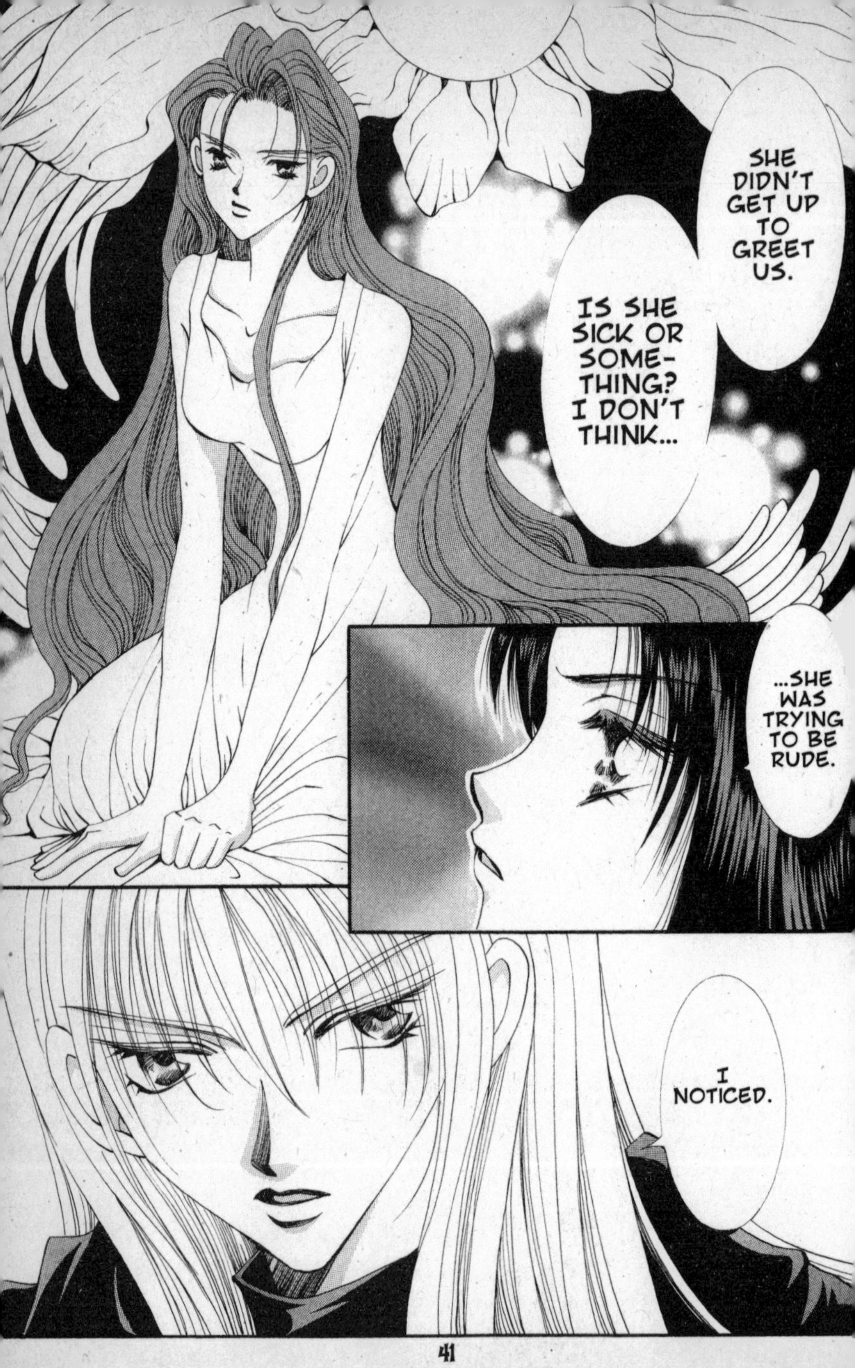
SHE DIDN'T GET UP TO GREET US.
IS SHE SICK OR SOME-THING? I DON'T THINK...
...SHE WAS TRYING TO BE RUDE.
I NOTICED.

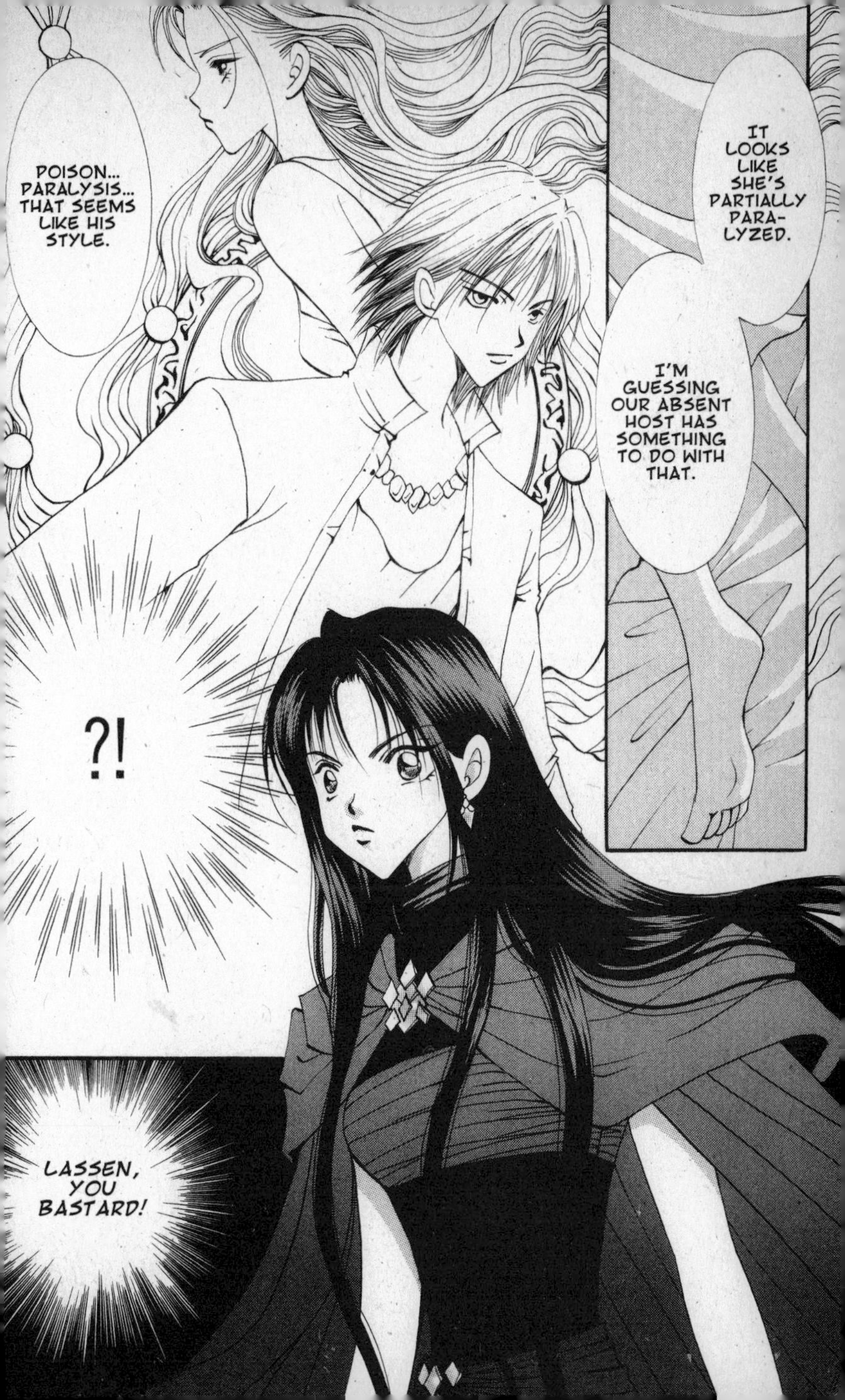
IT LOOKS LIKE SHE'S PARTIALLY PARA-LYZED.
I'M GUESSING OUR ABSENT HOST HAS SOMETHING TO DO WITH THAT.
POISON... PARALYSIS... THAT SEEMS LIKE HIS STYLE.
?!
LASSEN, YOU BASTARD!

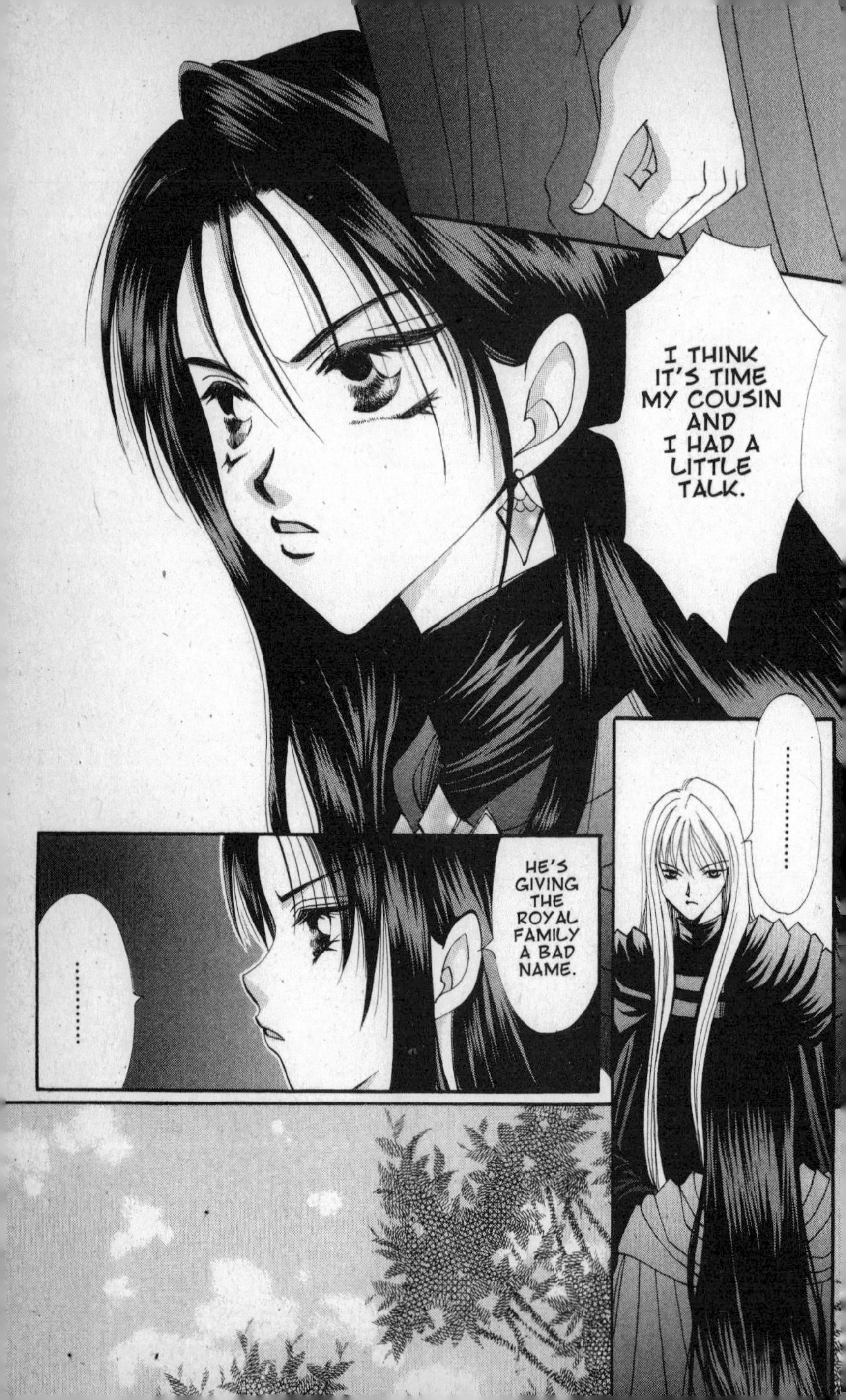
I THINK IT'S TIME MY COUSIN AND I HAD A LITTLE TALK.
......
HE'S GIVING THE ROYAL FAMILY A BAD NAME.
......

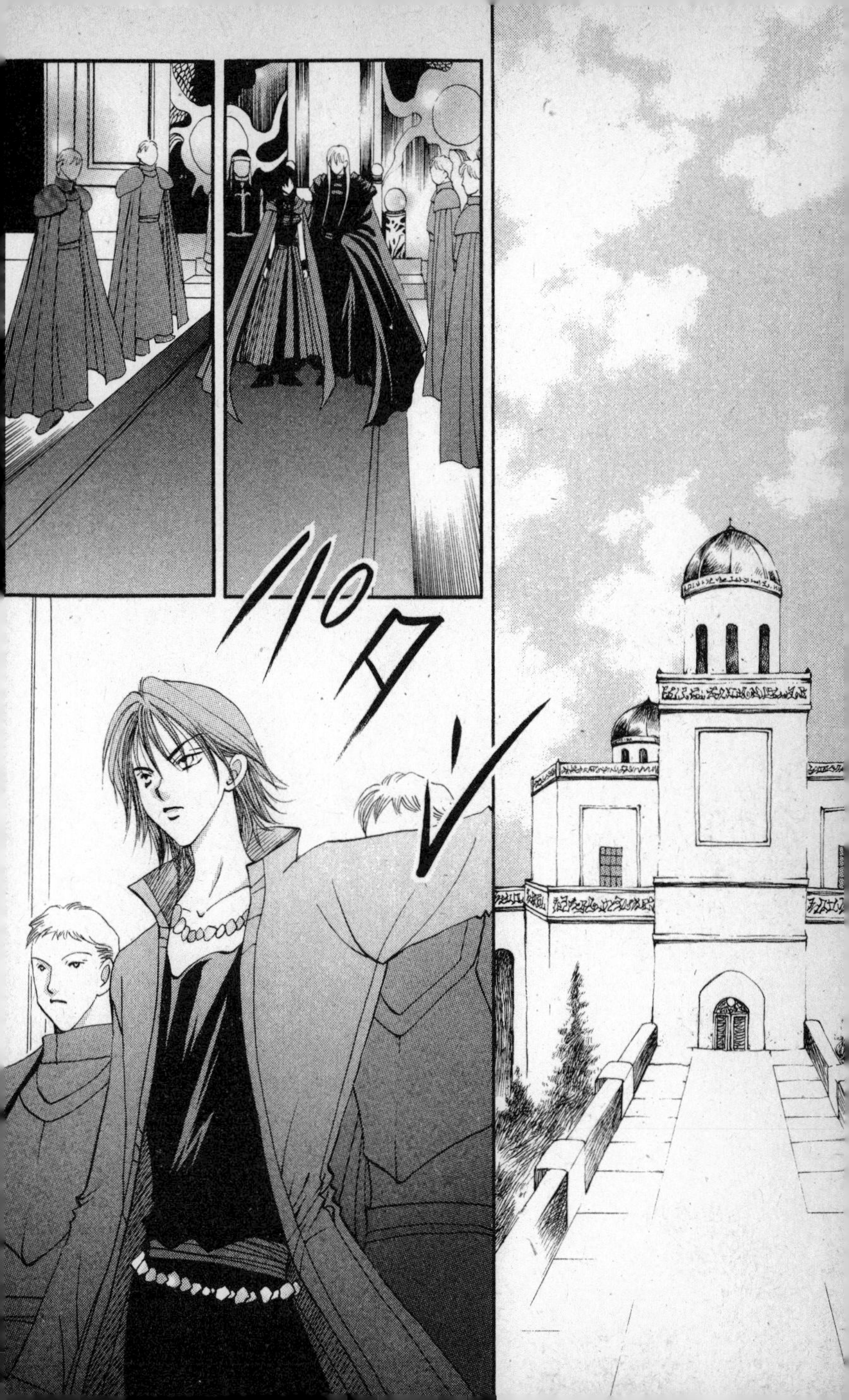
パタン

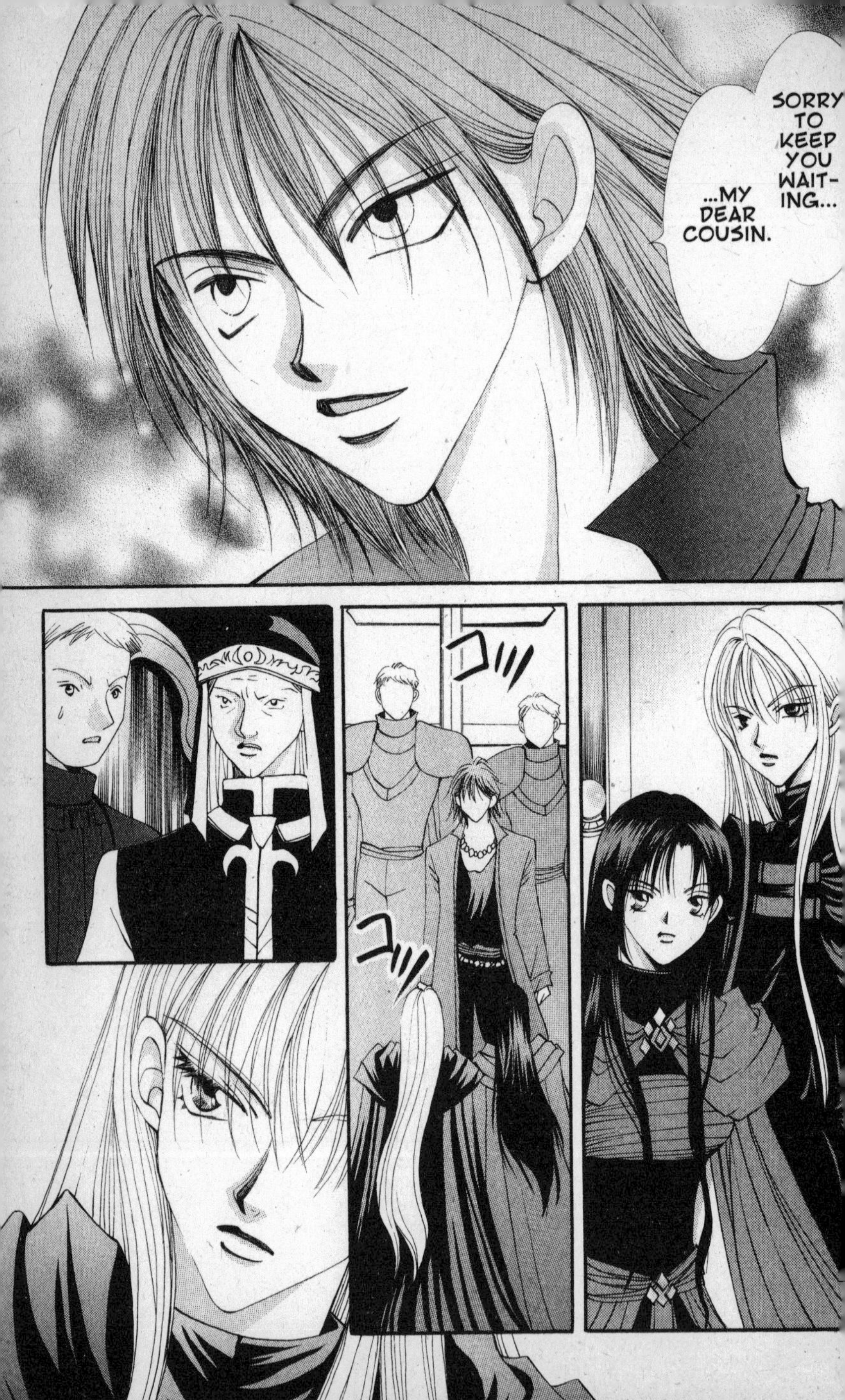
SORRY TO KEEP YOU WAITING...
...MY DEAR COUSIN.
コッ
コッ

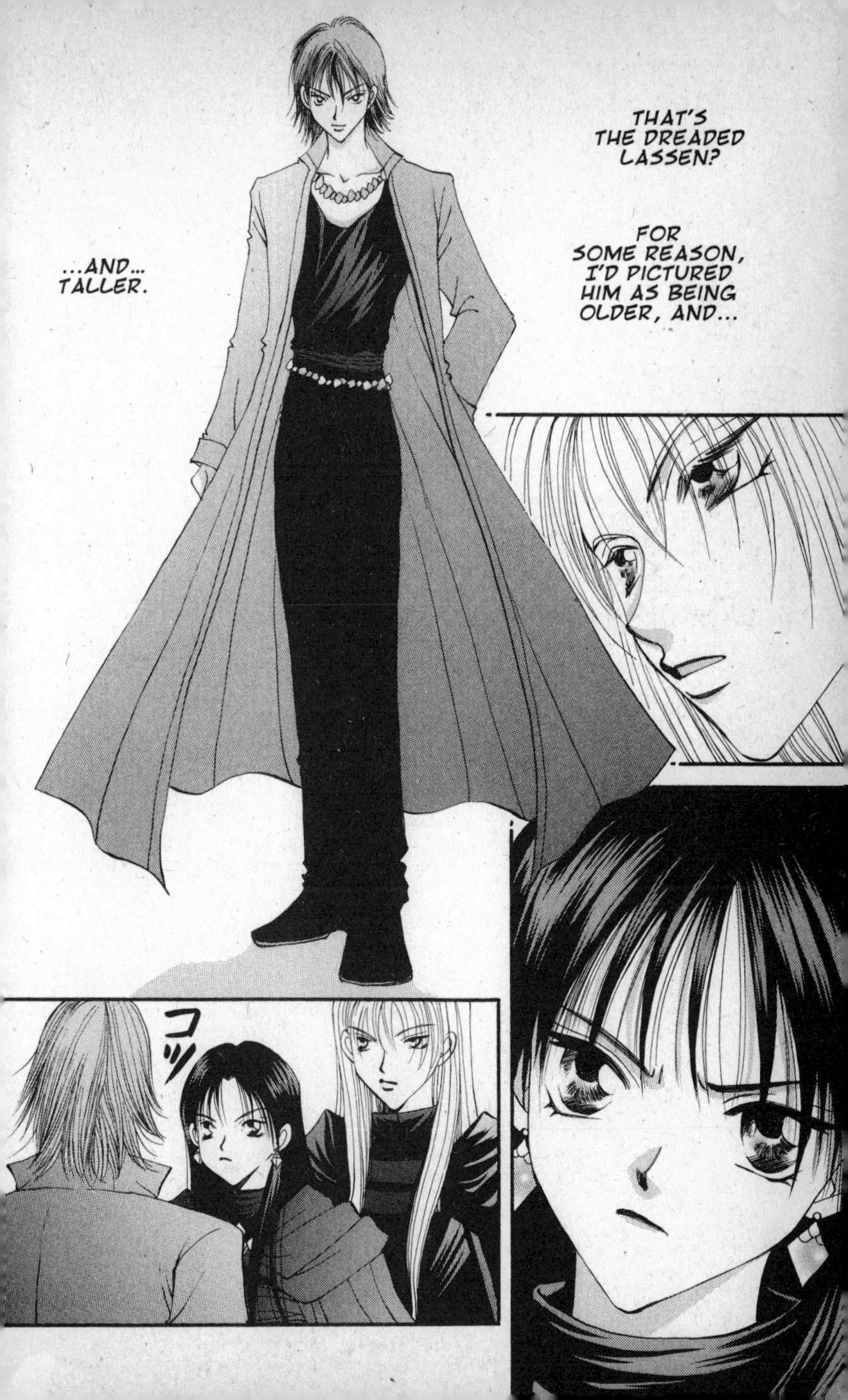
THAT'S THE DREADED LASSEN?
FOR SOME REASON, I'D PICTURED HIM AS BEING OLDER, AND...
...AND... TALLER.
コッ

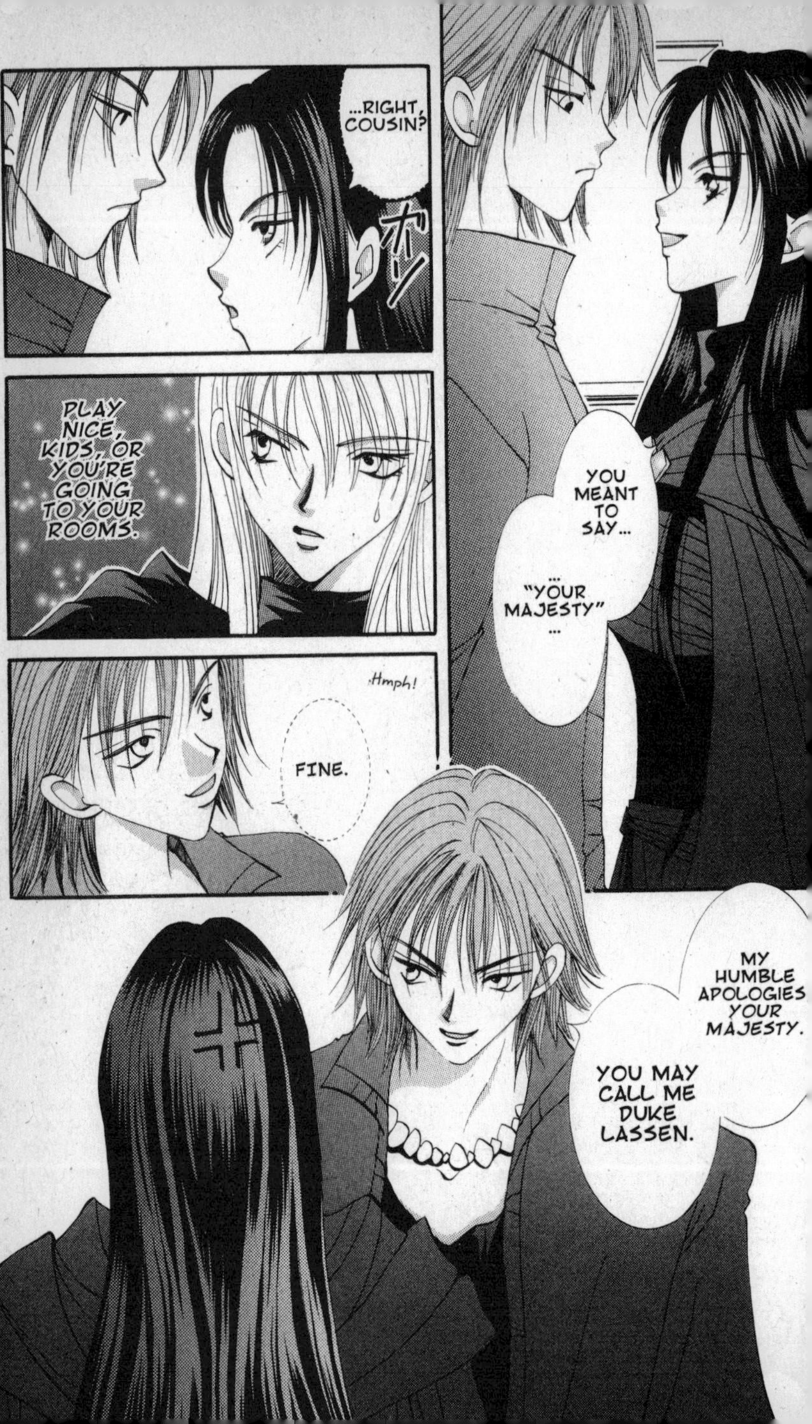
YOU MEANT TO SAY...
..."YOUR MAJESTY"...
...RIGHT, COUSIN?
PLAY NICE, KIDS, OR YOU'RE GOING TO YOUR ROOMS.
Hmph!
FINE.
MY HUMBLE APOLOGIES YOUR MAJESTY.
YOU MAY CALL ME DUKE LASSEN.

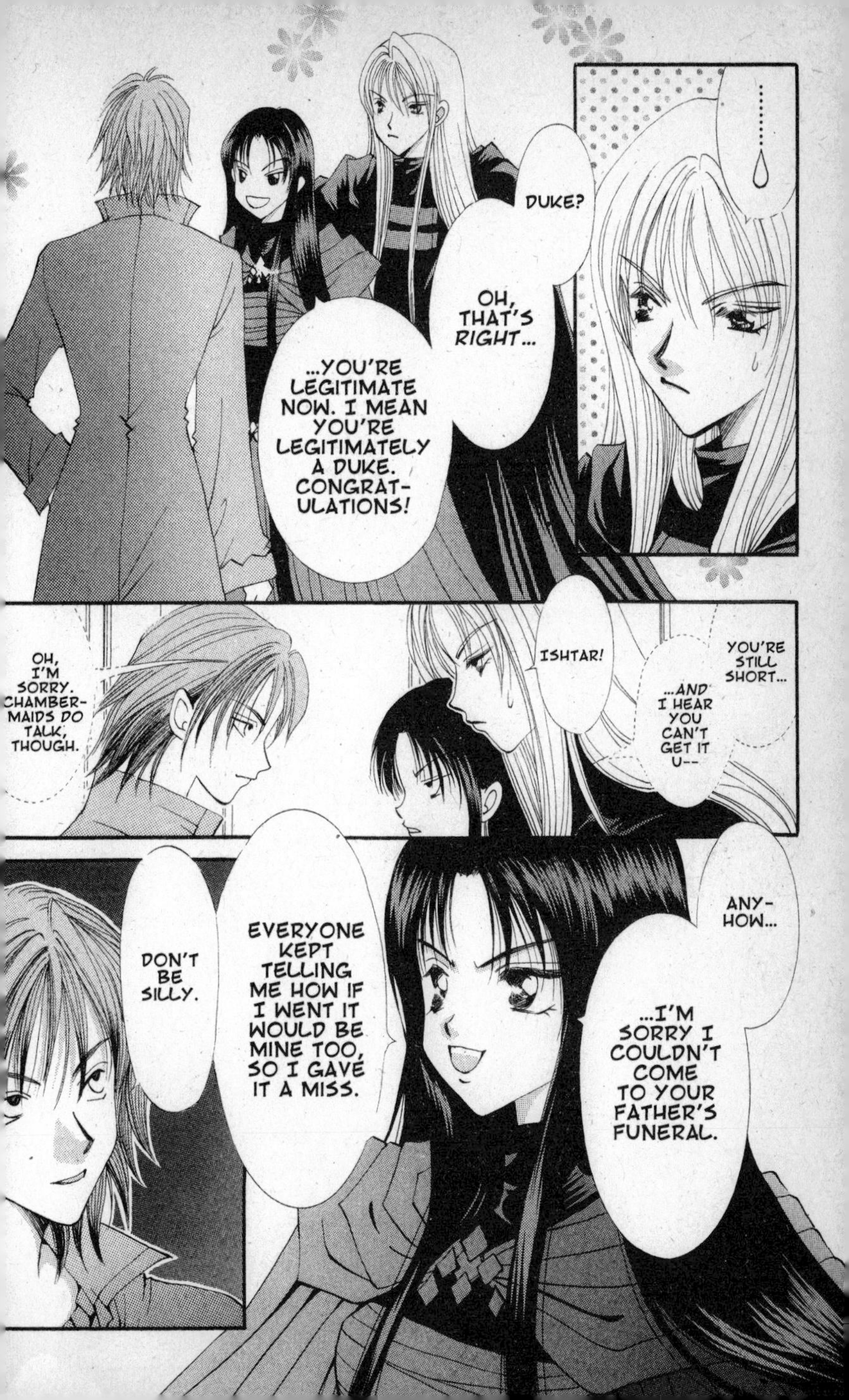
DUKE?
OH, THAT'S RIGHT...
...YOU'RE LEGITIMATE NOW. I MEAN YOU'RE LEGITIMATELY A DUKE. CONGRAT-ULATIONS!
YOU'RE STILL SHORT...
...AND I HEAR YOU CAN'T GET IT U--
ISHTAR!
OH, I'M SORRY. CHAMBER-MAIDS DO TALK, THOUGH.
ANY-HOW...
...I'M SORRY I COULDN'T COME TO YOUR FATHER'S FUNERAL.
EVERYONE KEPT TELLING ME HOW IF I WENT IT WOULD BE MINE TOO, SO I GAVE IT A MISS.
DON'T BE SILLY.

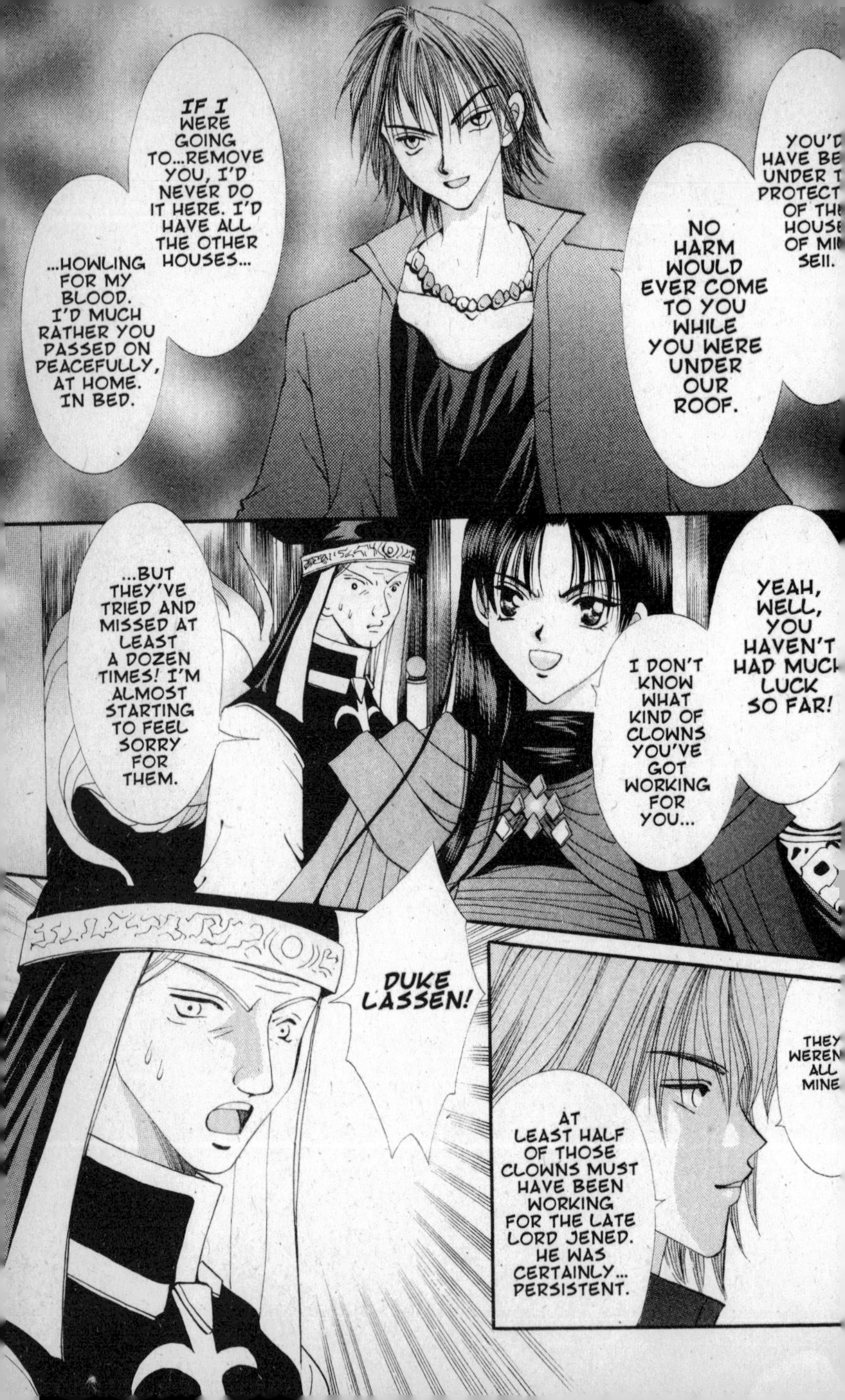
YOU'D HAVE BE UNDER T PROTECT OF THE HOUSE OF MI SEII.
NO HARM WOULD EVER COME TO YOU WHILE YOU WERE UNDER OUR ROOF.
IF I WERE GOING TO...REMOVE YOU, I'D NEVER DO IT HERE. I'D HAVE ALL THE OTHER HOUSES...
...HOWLING FOR MY BLOOD. I'D MUCH RATHER YOU PASSED ON PEACEFULLY, AT HOME. IN BED.
YEAH, WELL, YOU HAVEN'T HAD MUC LUCK SO FAR!
I DON'T KNOW WHAT KIND OF CLOWNS YOU'VE GOT WORKING FOR YOU...
...BUT THEY'VE TRIED AND MISSED AT LEAST A DOZEN TIMES! I'M ALMOST STARTING TO FEEL SORRY FOR THEM.
THEY WEREN ALL MINE
AT LEAST HALF OF THOSE CLOWNS MUST HAVE BEEN WORKING FOR THE LATE LORD JENED. HE WAS CERTAINLY... PERSISTENT.
DUKE LASSEN!

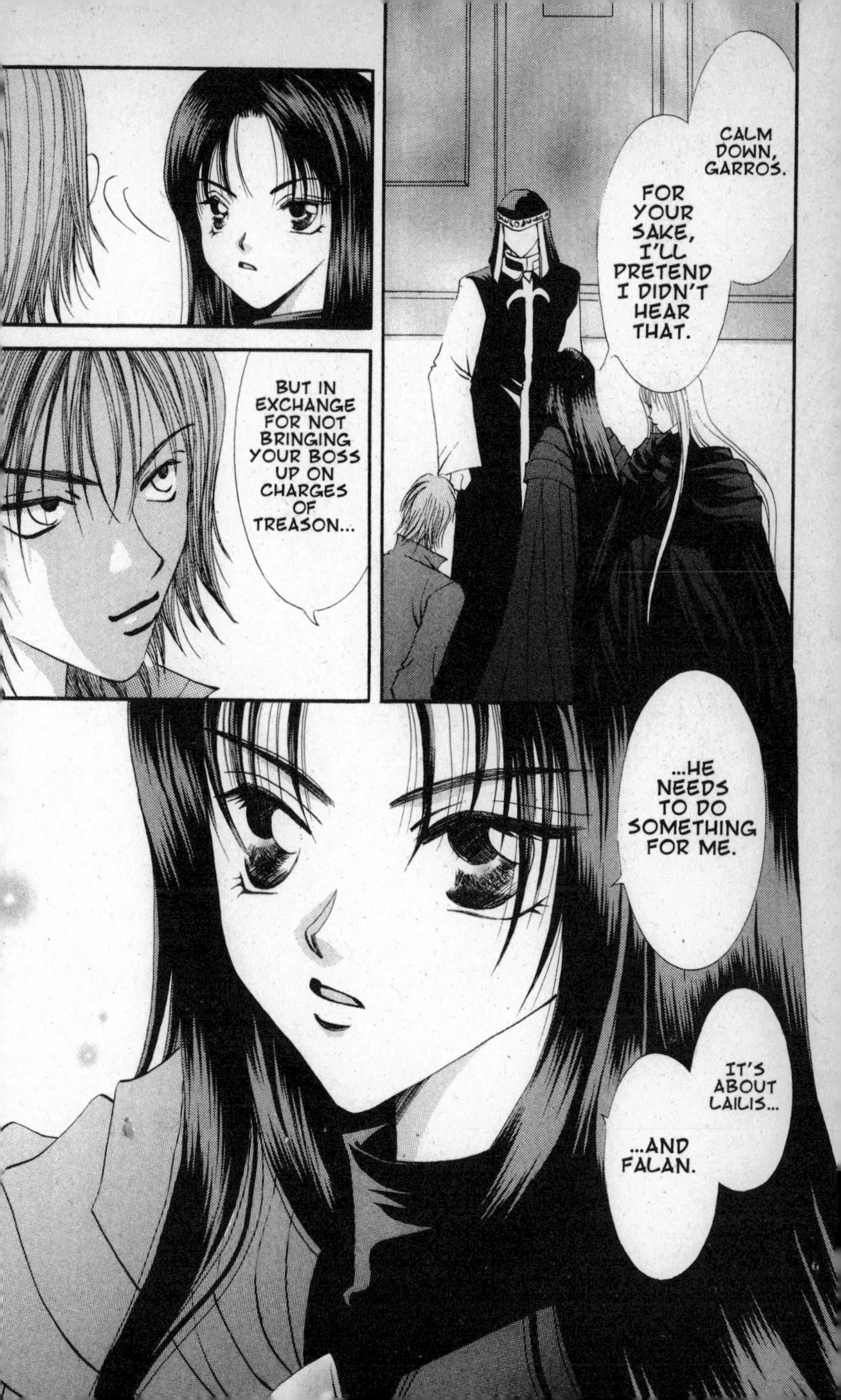
CALM DOWN, GARROS.
FOR YOUR SAKE, I'LL PRETEND I DIDN'T HEAR THAT.
BUT IN EXCHANGE FOR NOT BRINGING YOUR BOSS UP ON CHARGES OF TREASON...
...HE NEEDS TO DO SOMETHING FOR ME.
IT'S ABOUT LAILIS...
...AND FALAN.

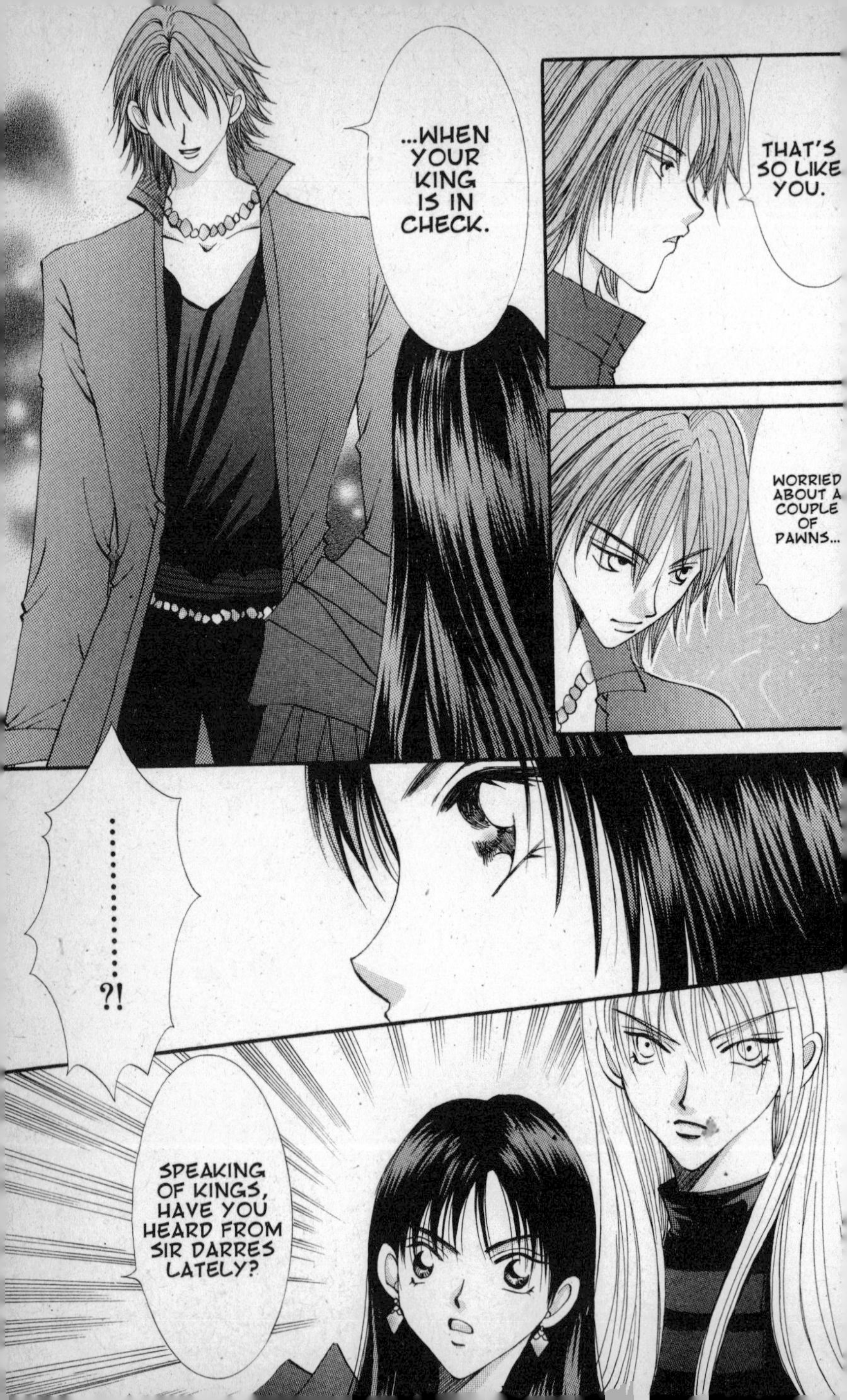
THAT'S SO LIKE YOU.
WORRIED ABOUT A COUPLE OF PAWNS...
...WHEN YOUR KING IS IN CHECK.
..........?!
SPEAKING OF KINGS, HAVE YOU HEARD FROM SIR DARRES LATELY?

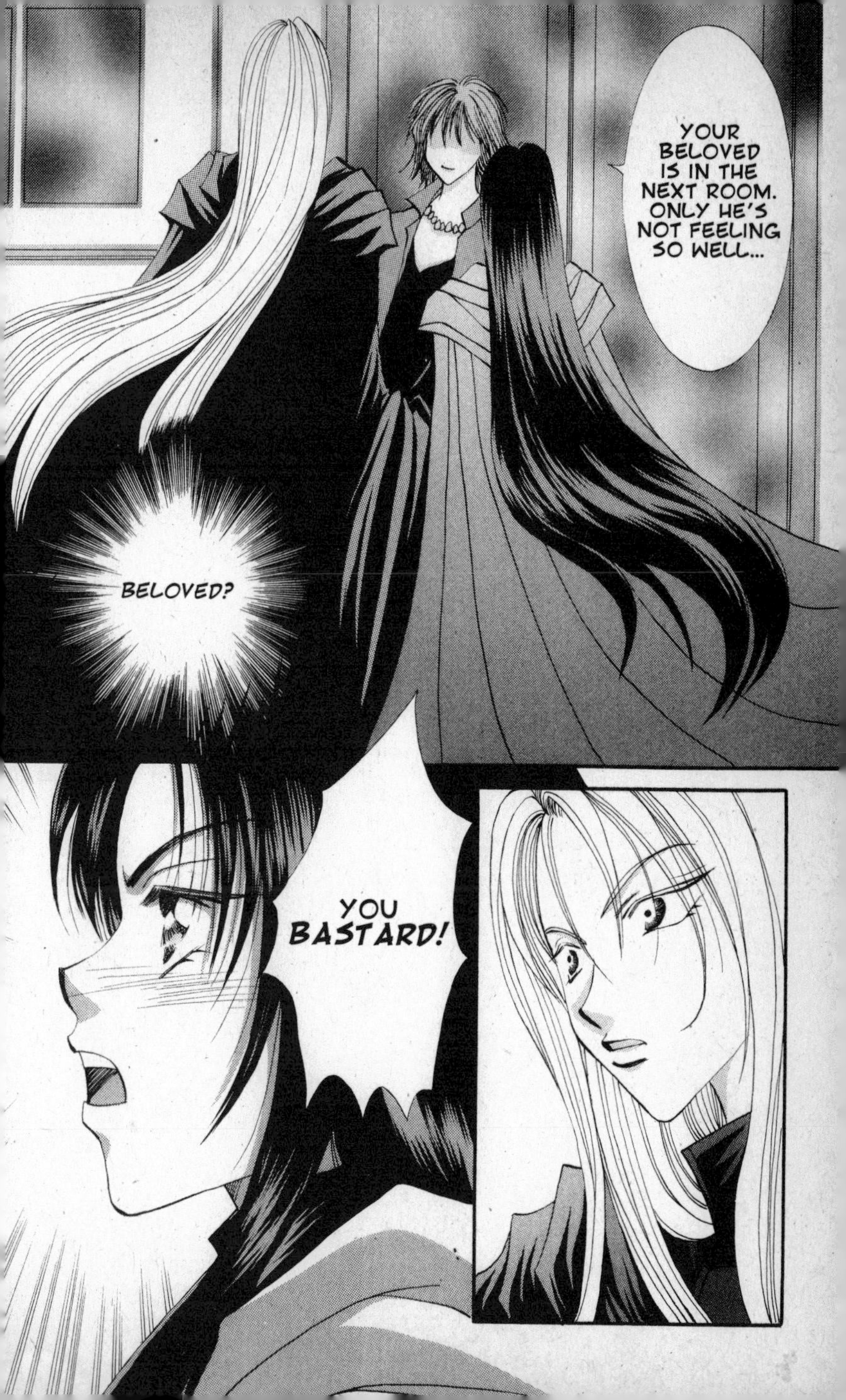
YOUR BELOVED IS IN THE NEXT ROOM. ONLY HE'S NOT FEELING SO WELL...
BELOVED?
YOU BASTARD!

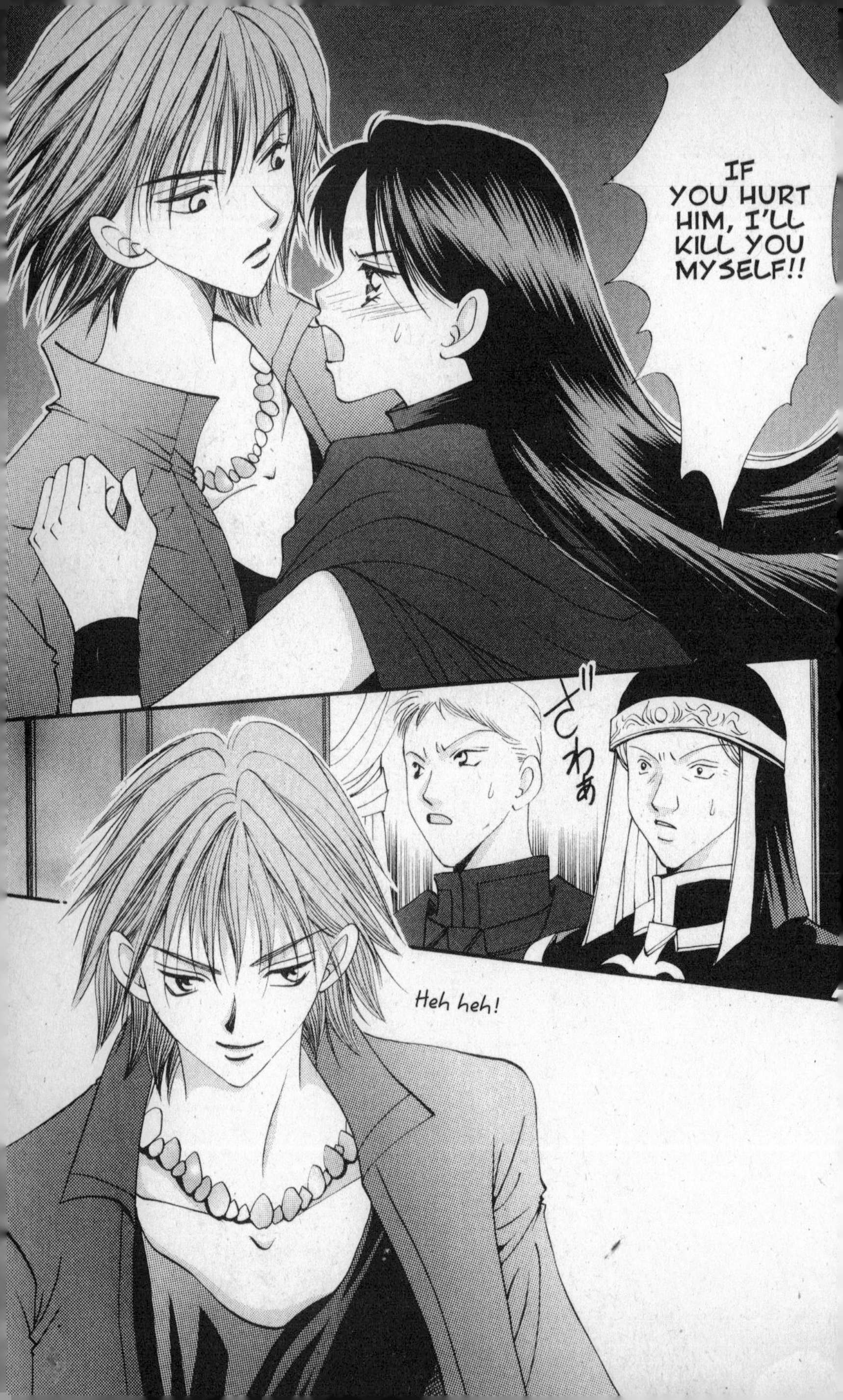
IF YOU HURT HIM, I'LL KILL YOU MYSELF!!
ざわぁ
Heh heh!

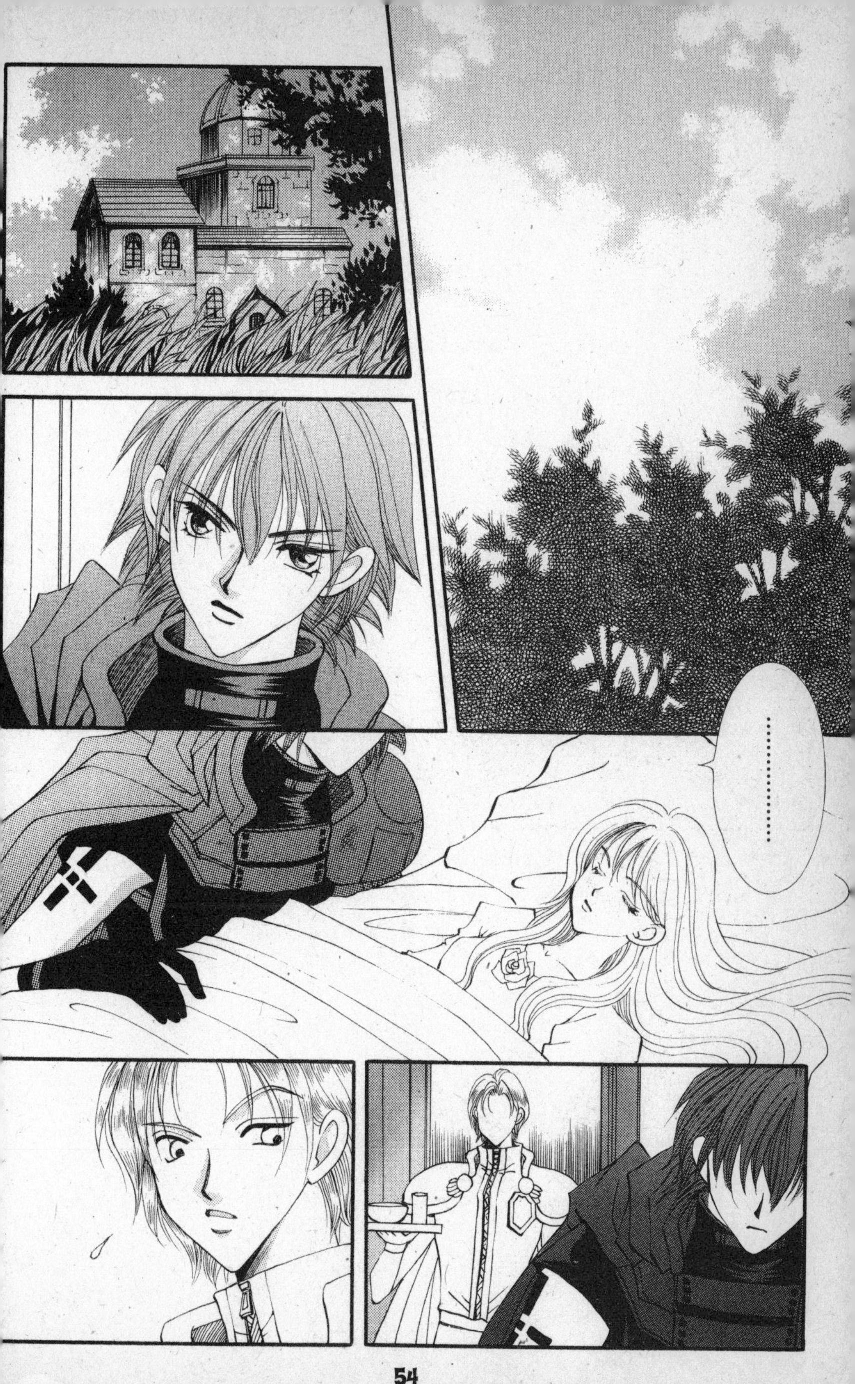
....

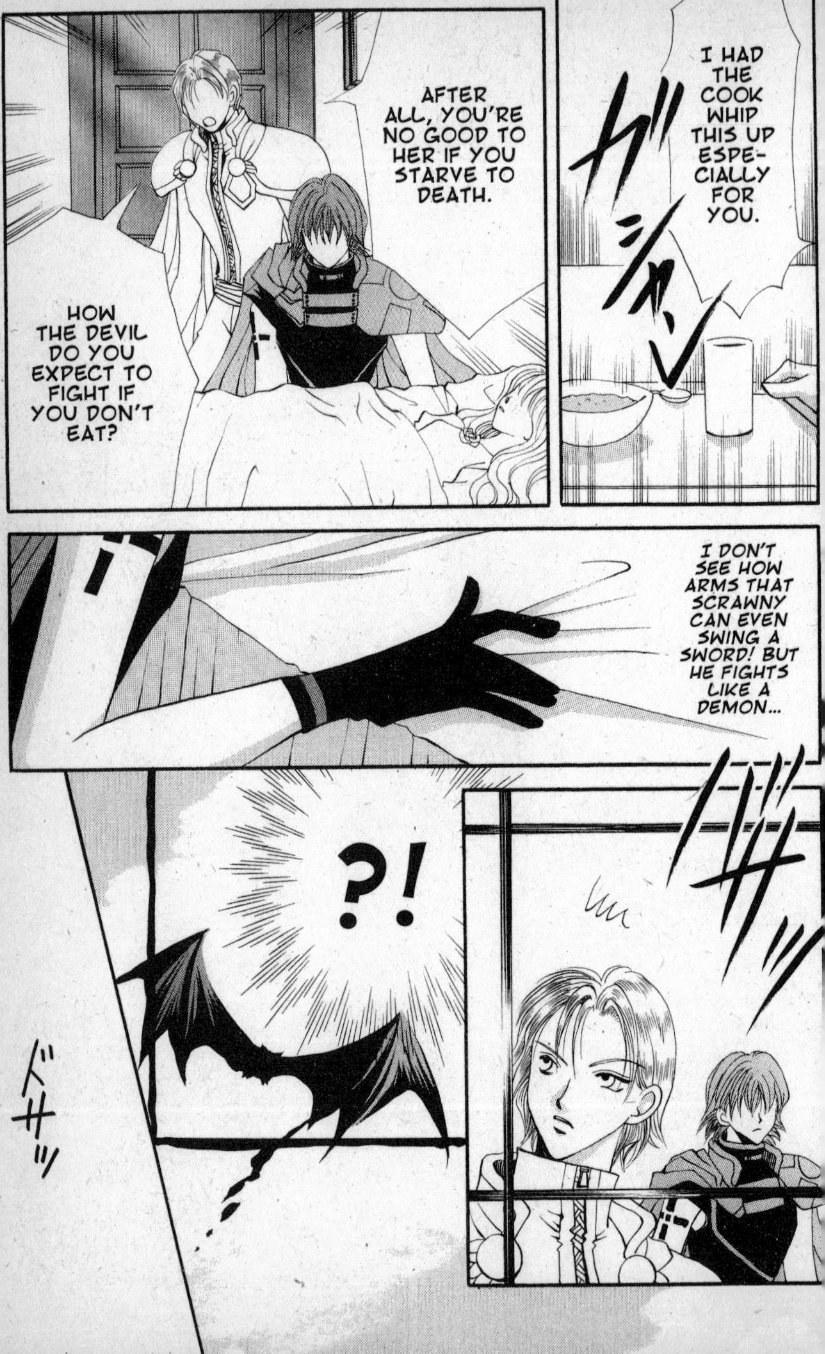
I HAD THE COOK WHIP THIS UP ESPE-CIALLY FOR YOU.
ガシャン
AFTER ALL, YOU'RE NO GOOD TO HER IF YOU STARVE TO DEATH.
HOW THE DEVIL DO YOU EXPECT TO FIGHT IF YOU DON'T EAT?
I DON'T SEE HOW ARMS THAT SCRAWNY CAN EVEN SWING A SWORD! BUT HE FIGHTS LIKE A DEMON...
バサッ
?!
ギクッ

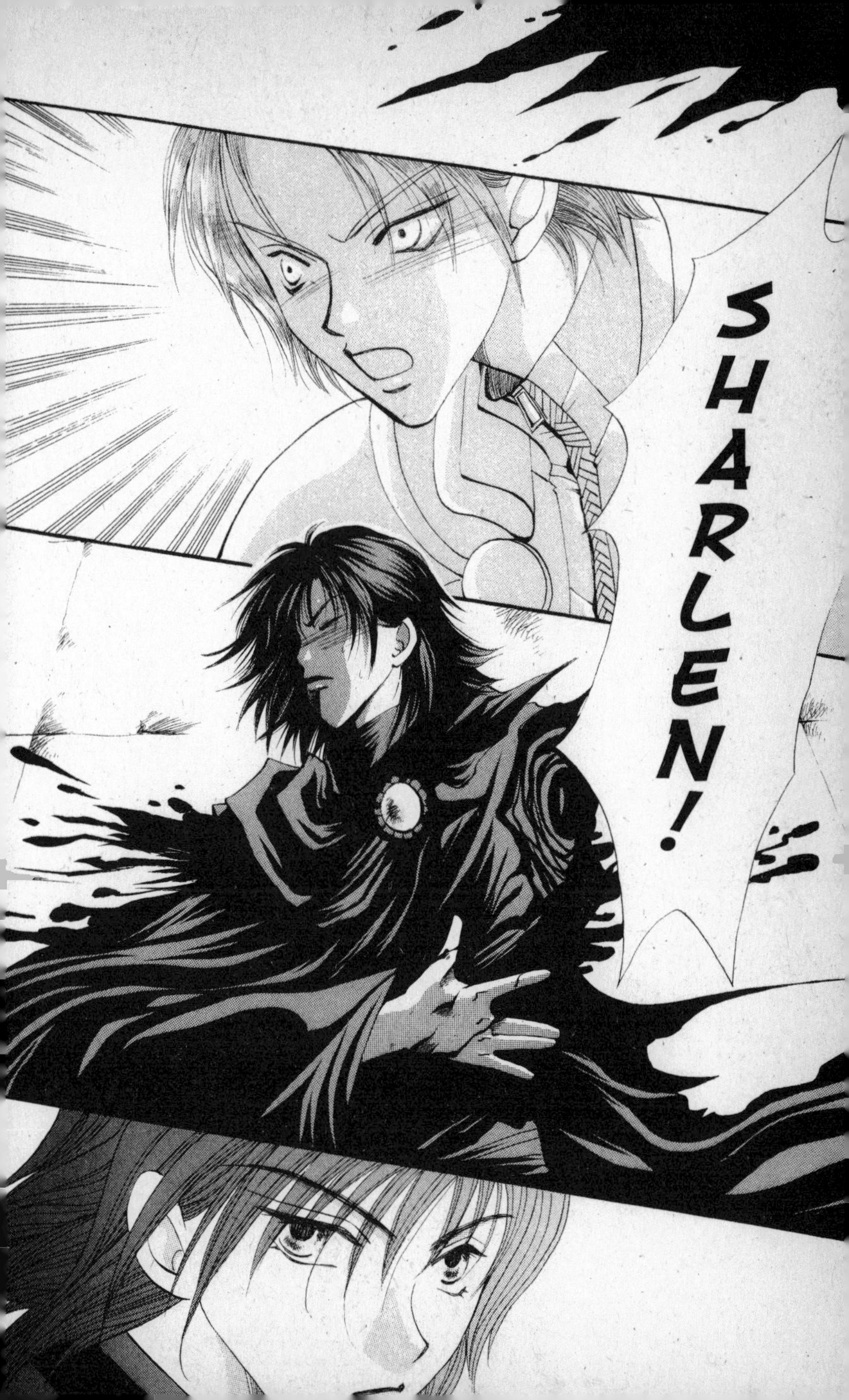
SHARLEN!

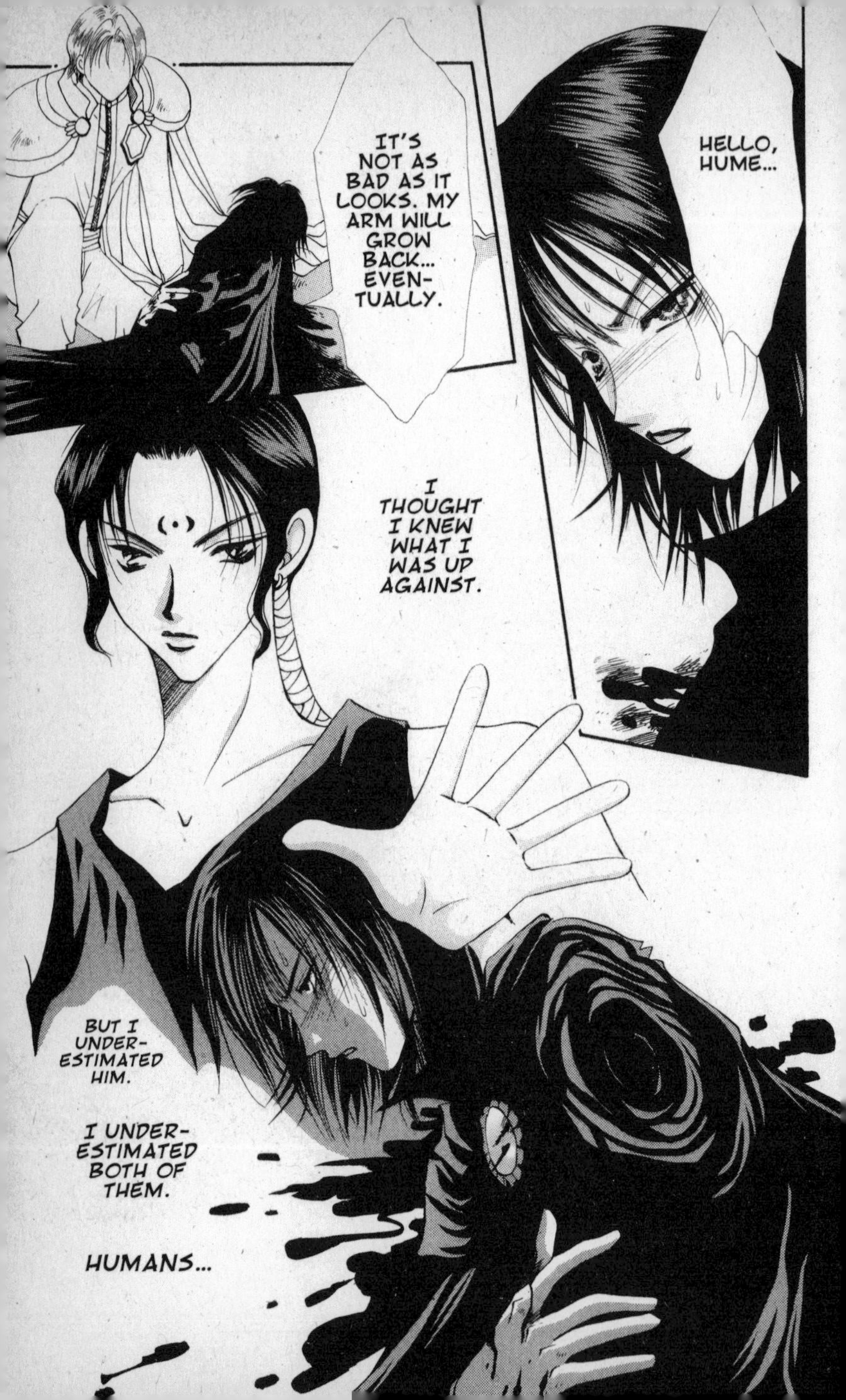
HELLO, HUME...
IT'S NOT AS BAD AS IT LOOKS. MY ARM WILL GROW BACK... EVEN-TUALLY.
I THOUGHT I KNEW WHAT I WAS UP AGAINST.
BUT I UNDER-ESTIMATED HIM.
I UNDER-ESTIMATED BOTH OF THEM.
HUMANS...

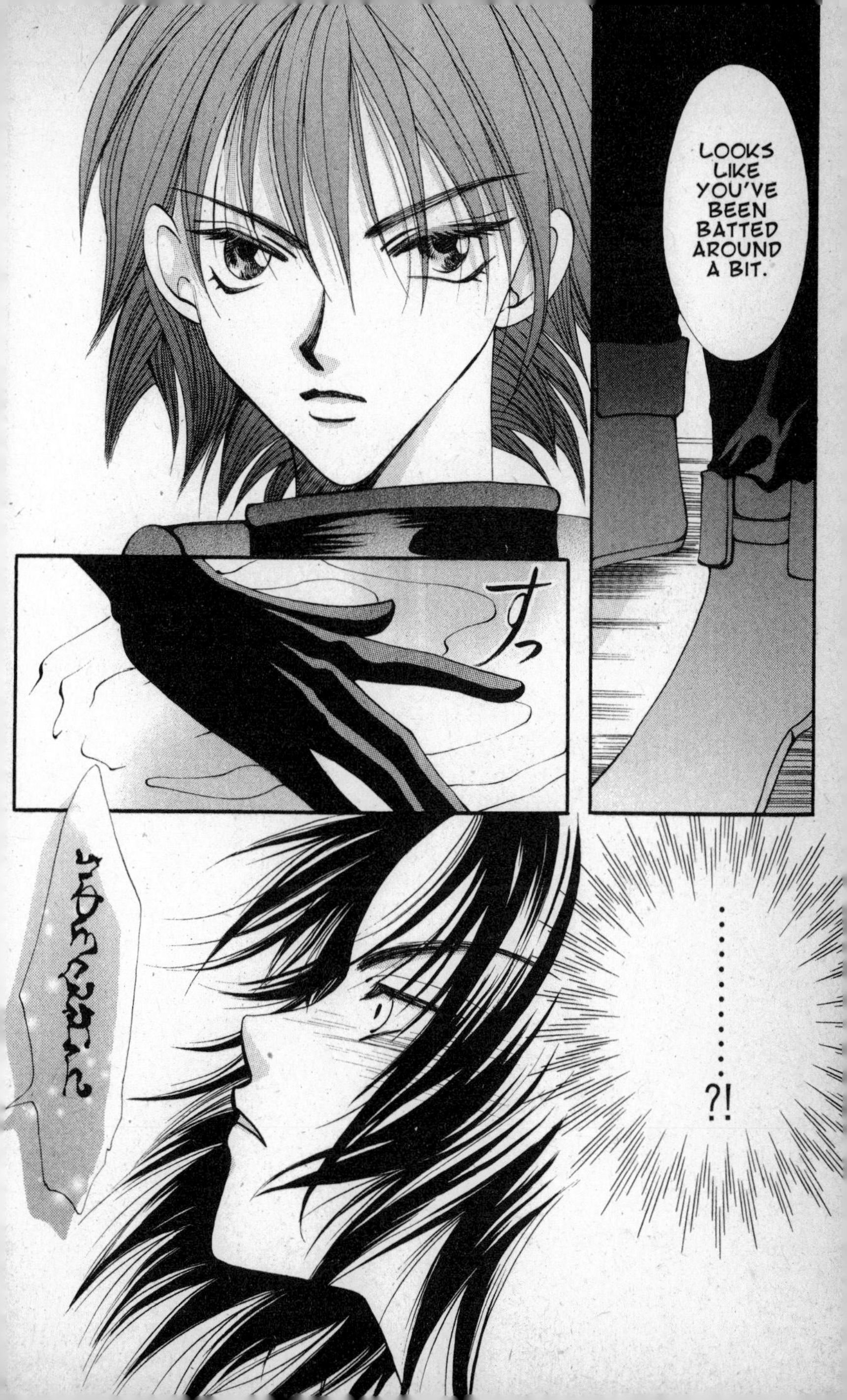
LOOKS LIKE YOU'VE BEEN BATTED AROUND A BIT.
すっ
......?!

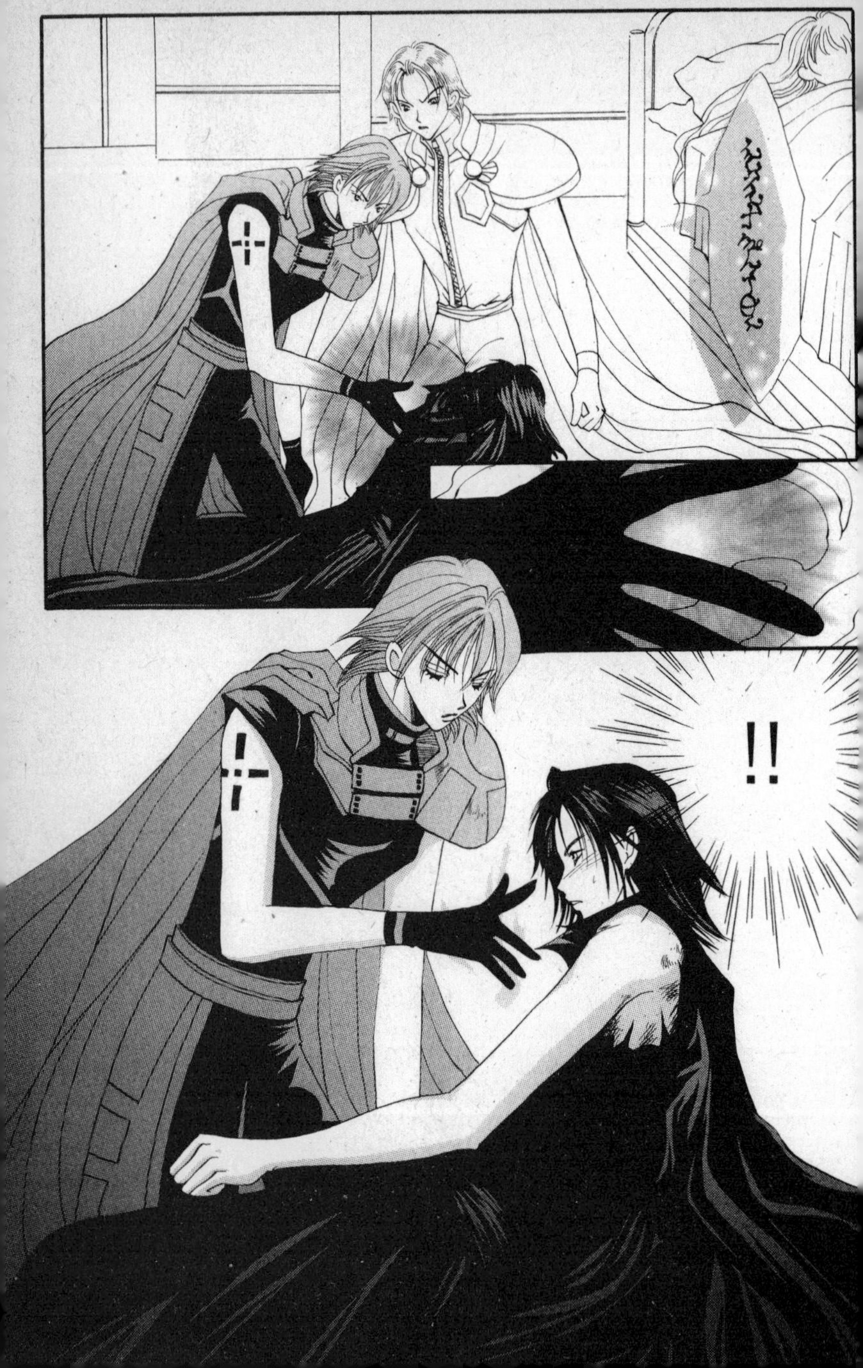
!!

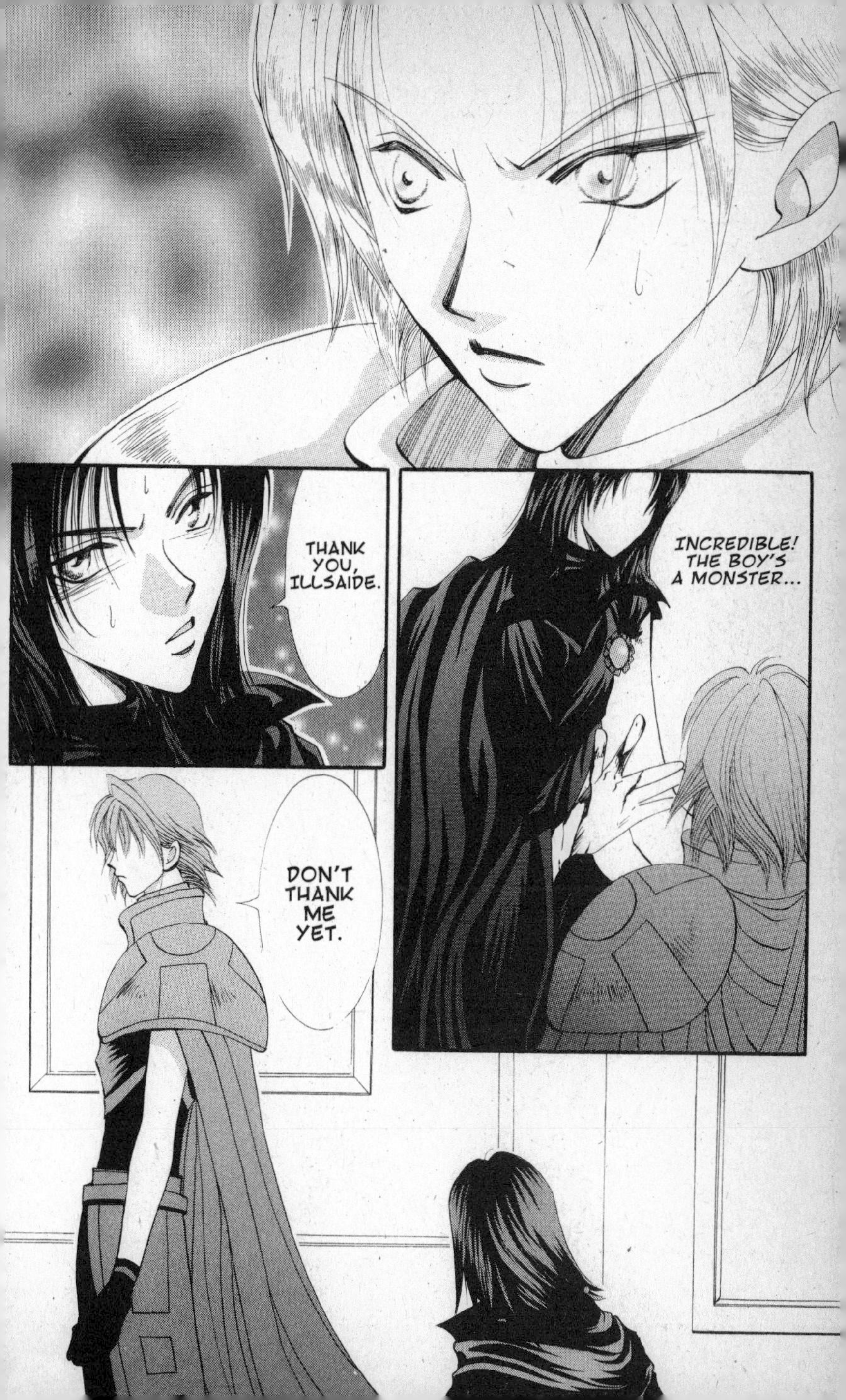
INCREDIBLE! THE BOY'S A MONSTER...
THANK YOU, ILLSAIDE.
DON'T THANK ME YET.

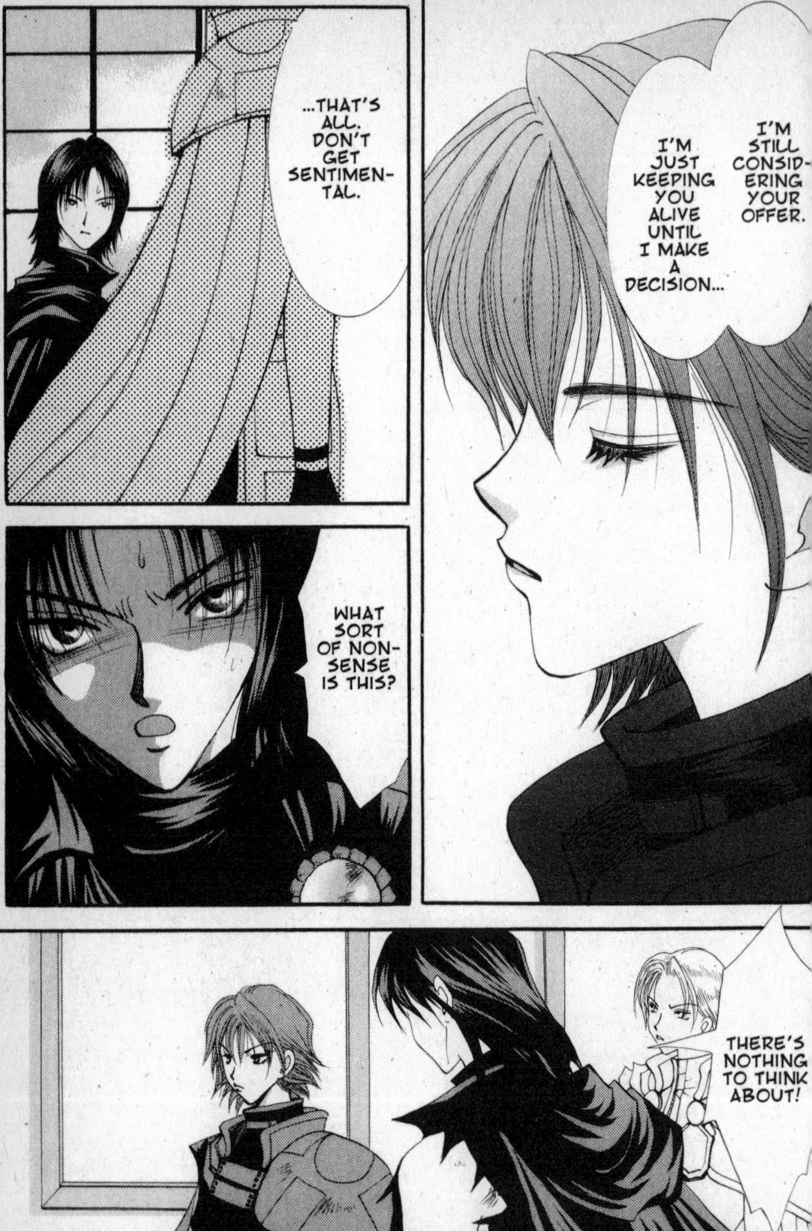
I'M STILL CONSIDERING YOUR OFFER.
I'M JUST KEEPING YOU ALIVE UNTIL I MAKE A DECISION...
...THAT'S ALL. DON'T GET SENTIMENTAL.
WHAT SORT OF NONSENSE IS THIS?
THERE'S NOTHING TO THINK ABOUT!

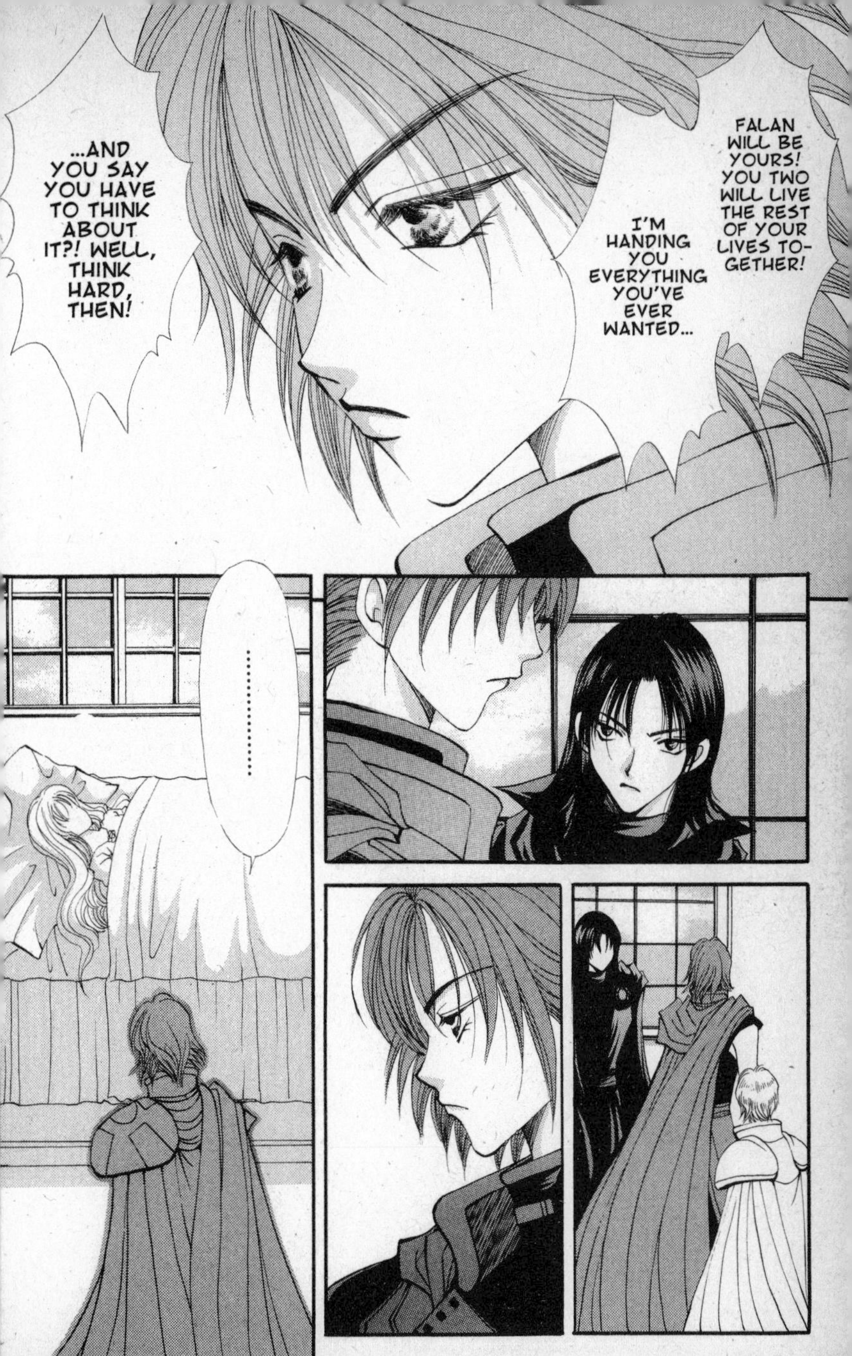
FALAN WILL BE YOURS! YOU TWO WILL LIVE THE REST OF YOUR LIVES TO-GETHER!
I'M HANDING YOU EVERYTHING YOU'VE EVER WANTED...
...AND YOU SAY YOU HAVE TO THINK ABOUT IT?! WELL, THINK HARD, THEN!
....

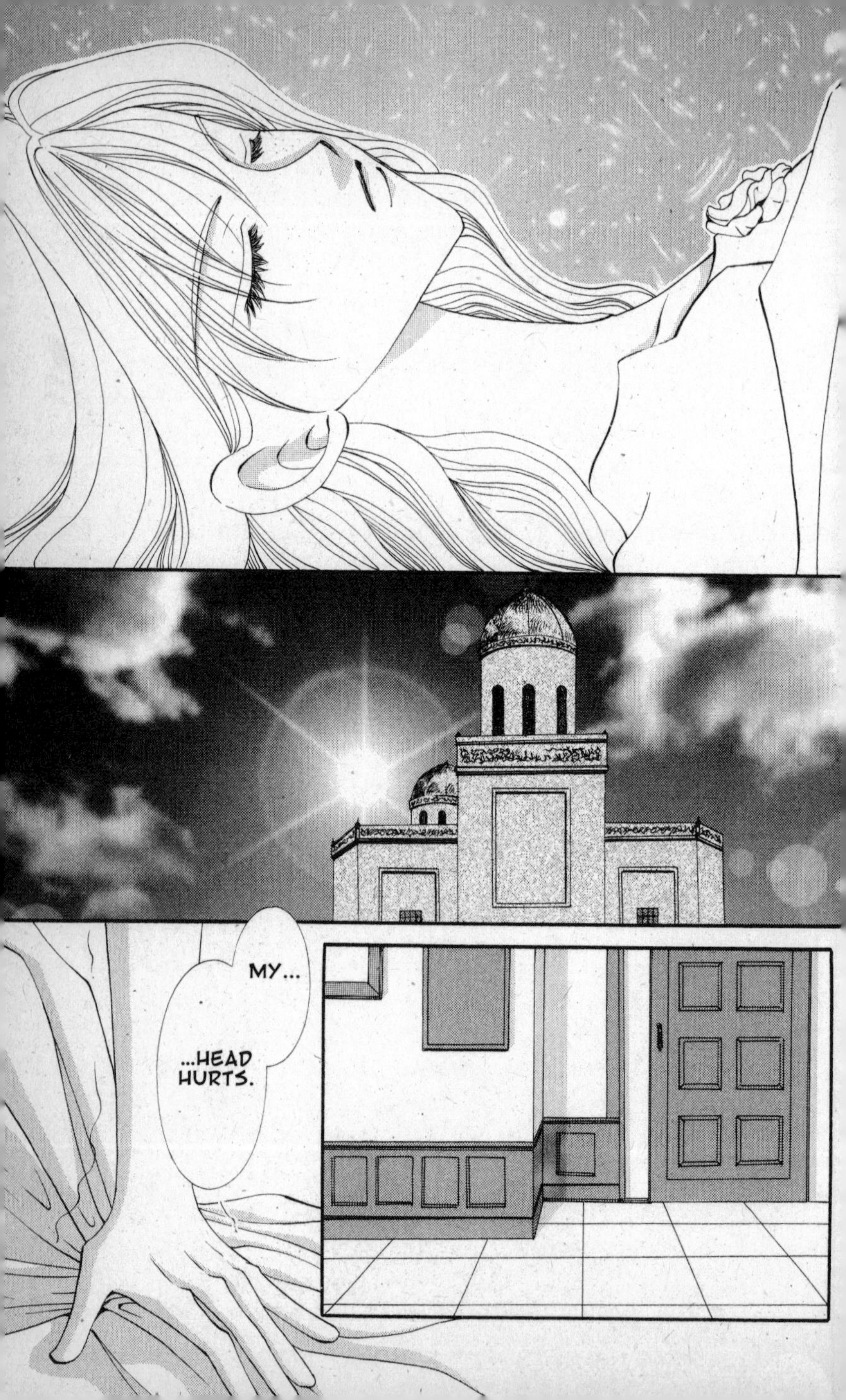
MY...
...HEAD HURTS.

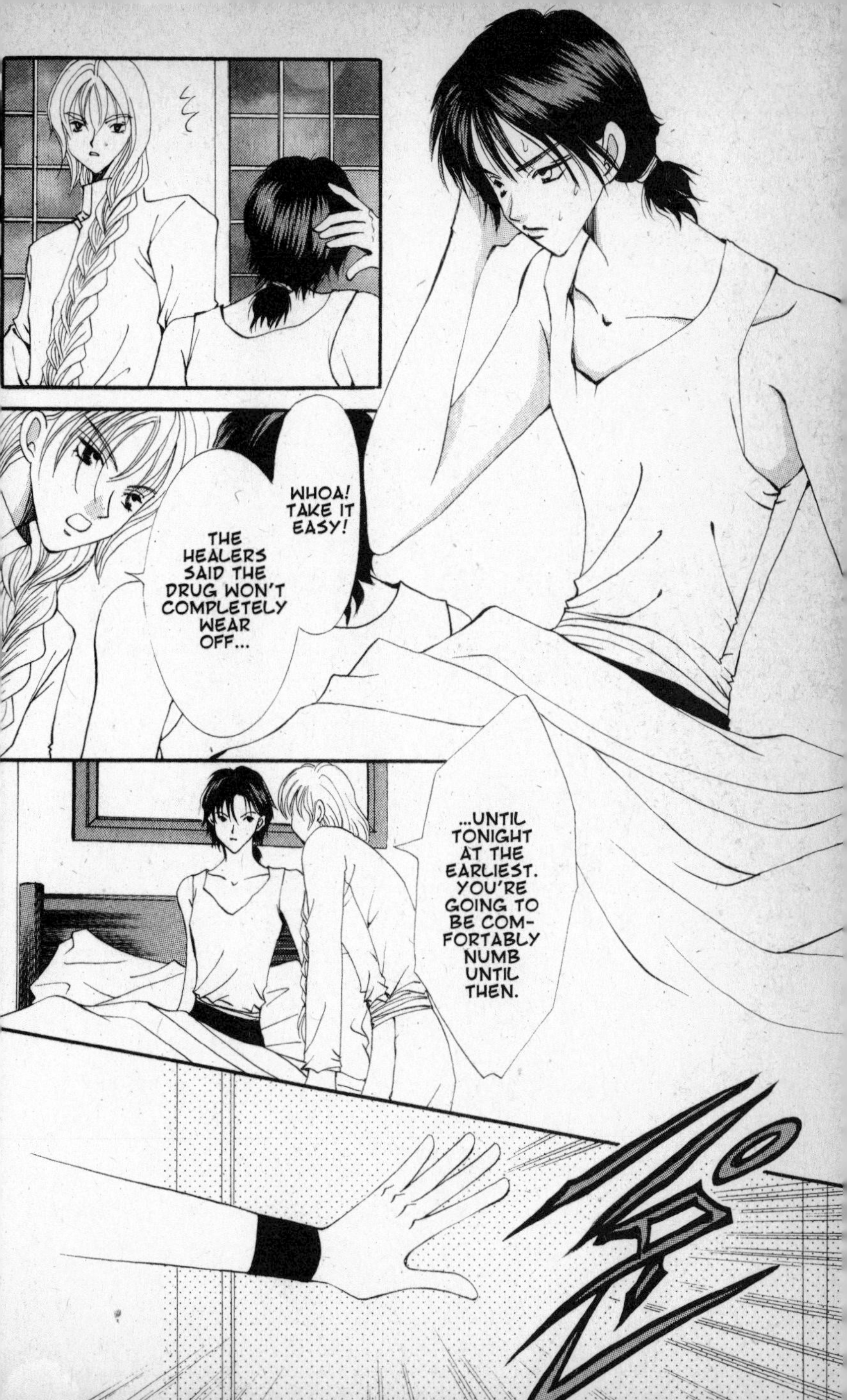
WHOA! TAKE IT EASY!
THE HEALERS SAID THE DRUG WON'T COMPLETELY WEAR OFF...
...UNTIL TONIGHT AT THE EARLIEST. YOU'RE GOING TO BE COM-FORTABLY NUMB UNTIL THEN.

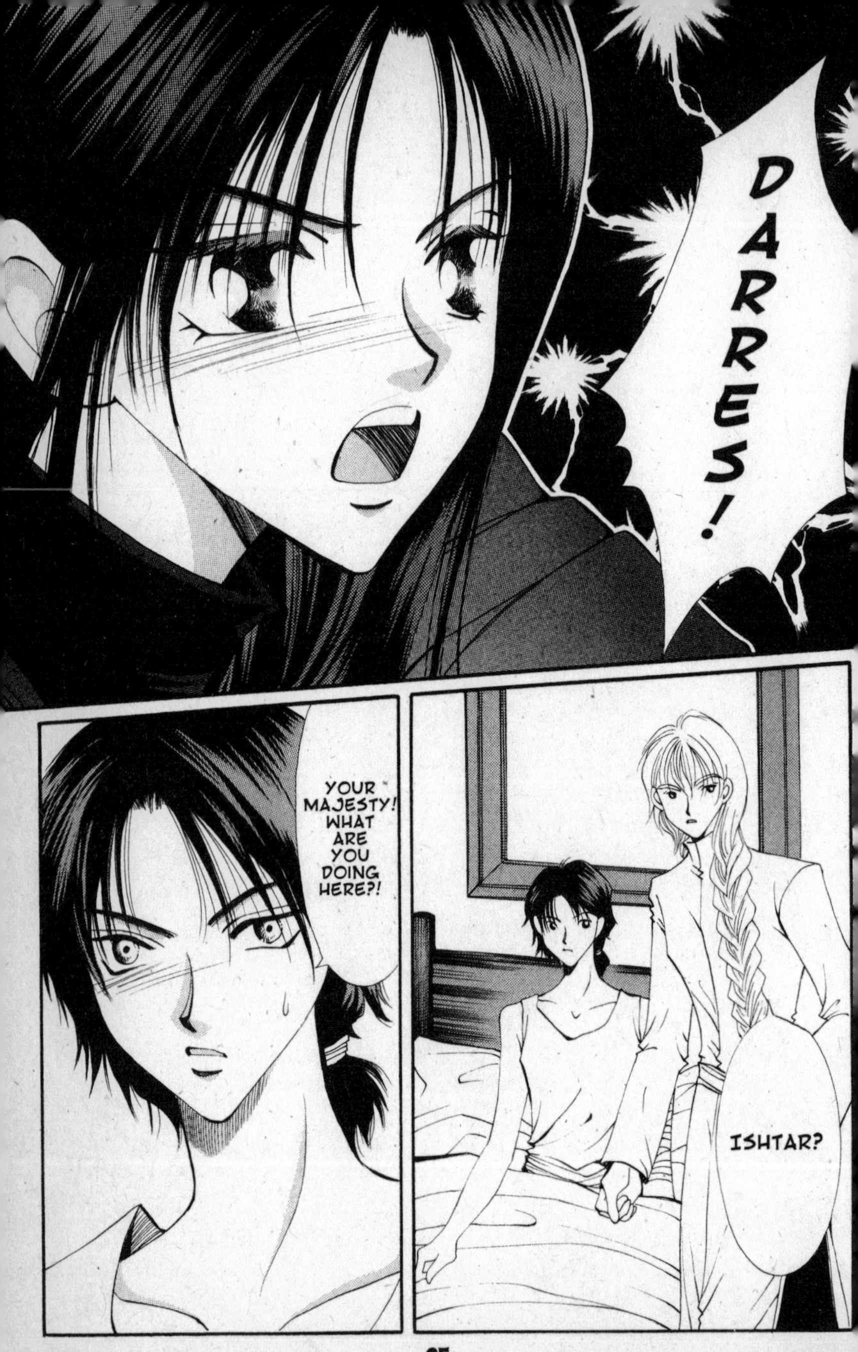
DARRES!
ISHTAR?
YOUR MAJESTY! WHAT ARE YOU DOING HERE?!

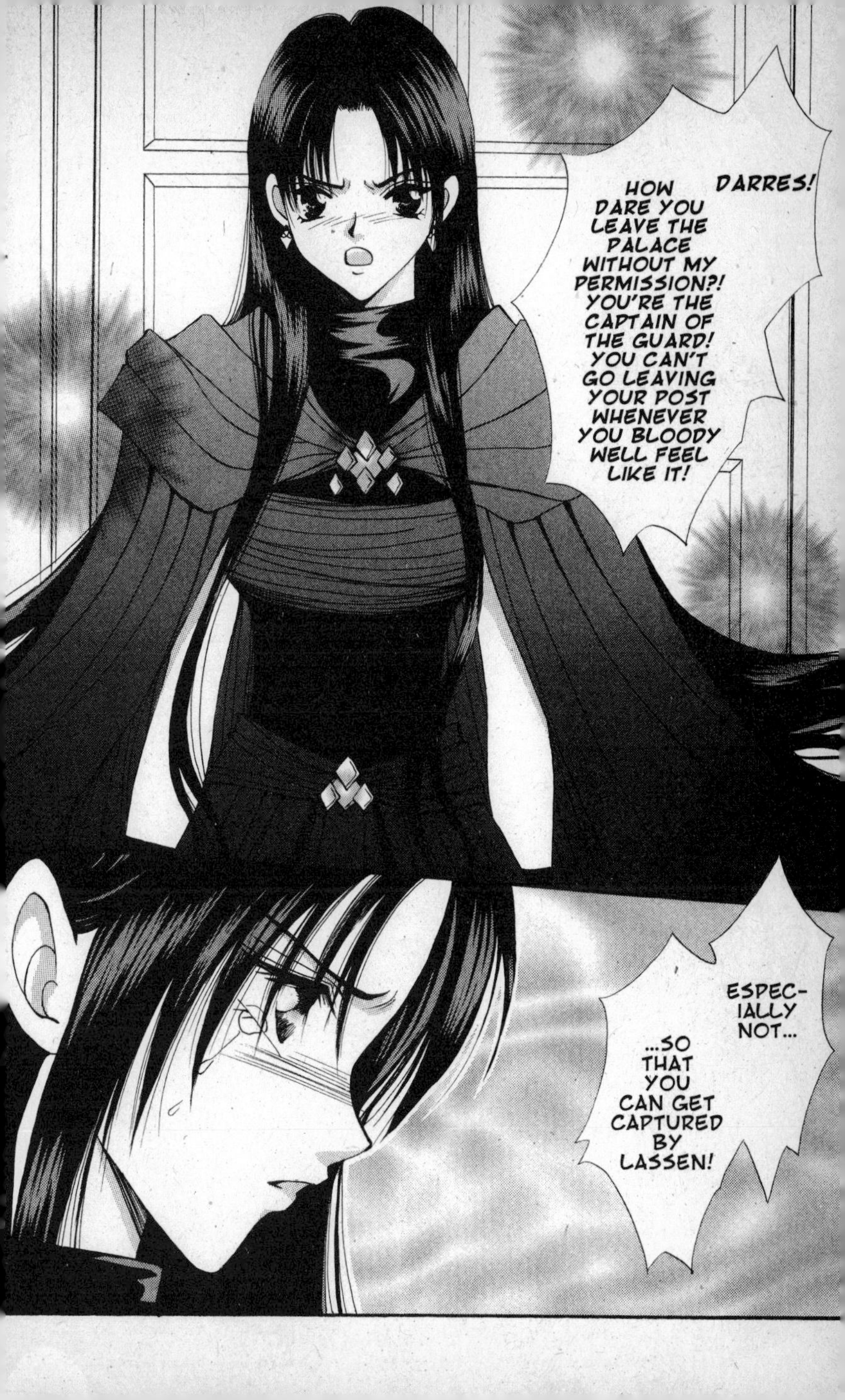
DARRES!
HOW DARE YOU LEAVE THE PALACE WITHOUT MY PERMISSION?! YOU'RE THE CAPTAIN OF THE GUARD! YOU CAN'T GO LEAVING YOUR POST WHENEVER YOU BLOODY WELL FEEL LIKE IT!
ESPEC-IALLY NOT...
...SO THAT YOU CAN GET CAPTURED BY LASSEN!

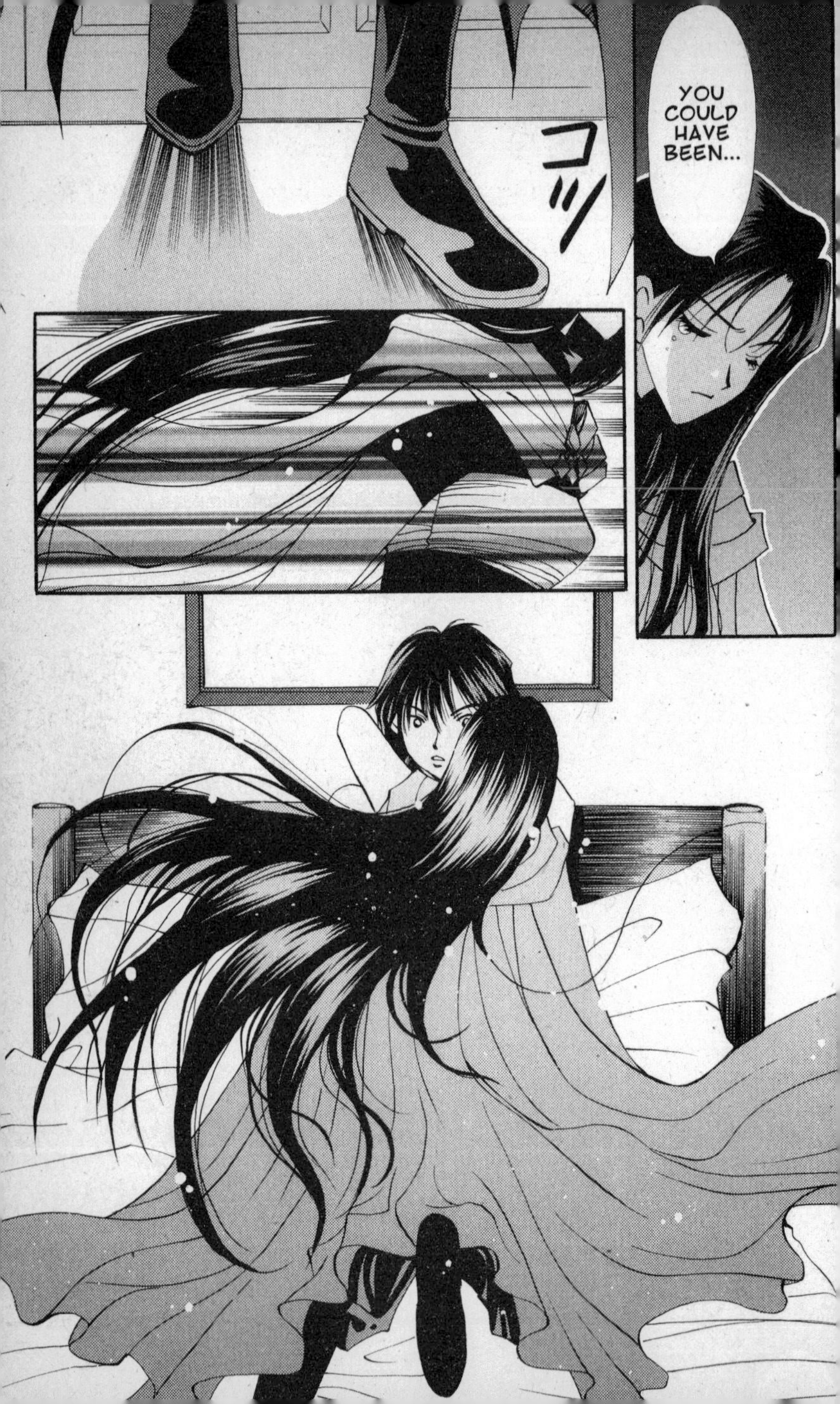

コッ
YOU COULD HAVE BEEN...

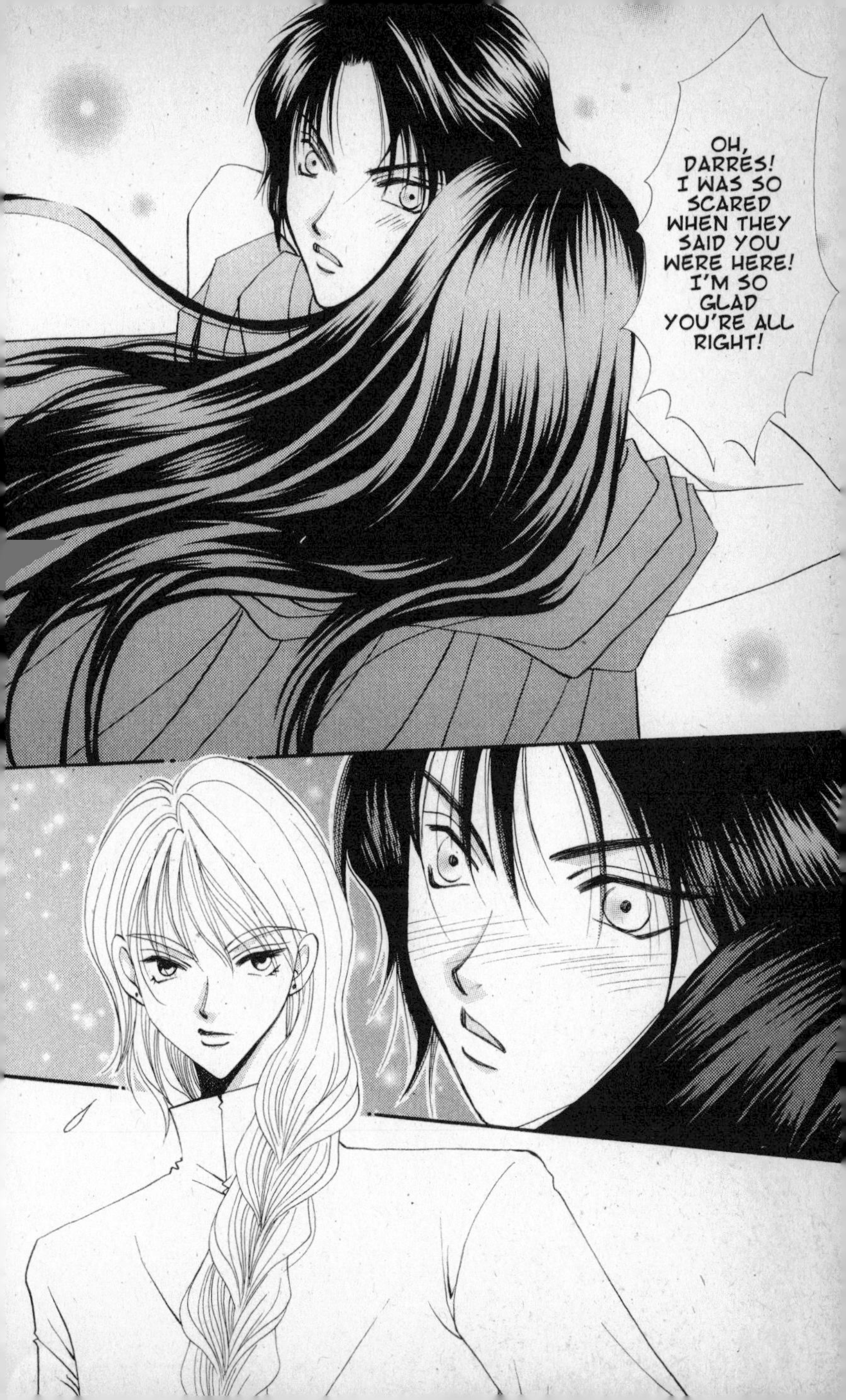
OH, DARRES! I WAS SO SCARED WHEN THEY SAID YOU WERE HERE! I'M SO GLAD YOU'RE ALL RIGHT!

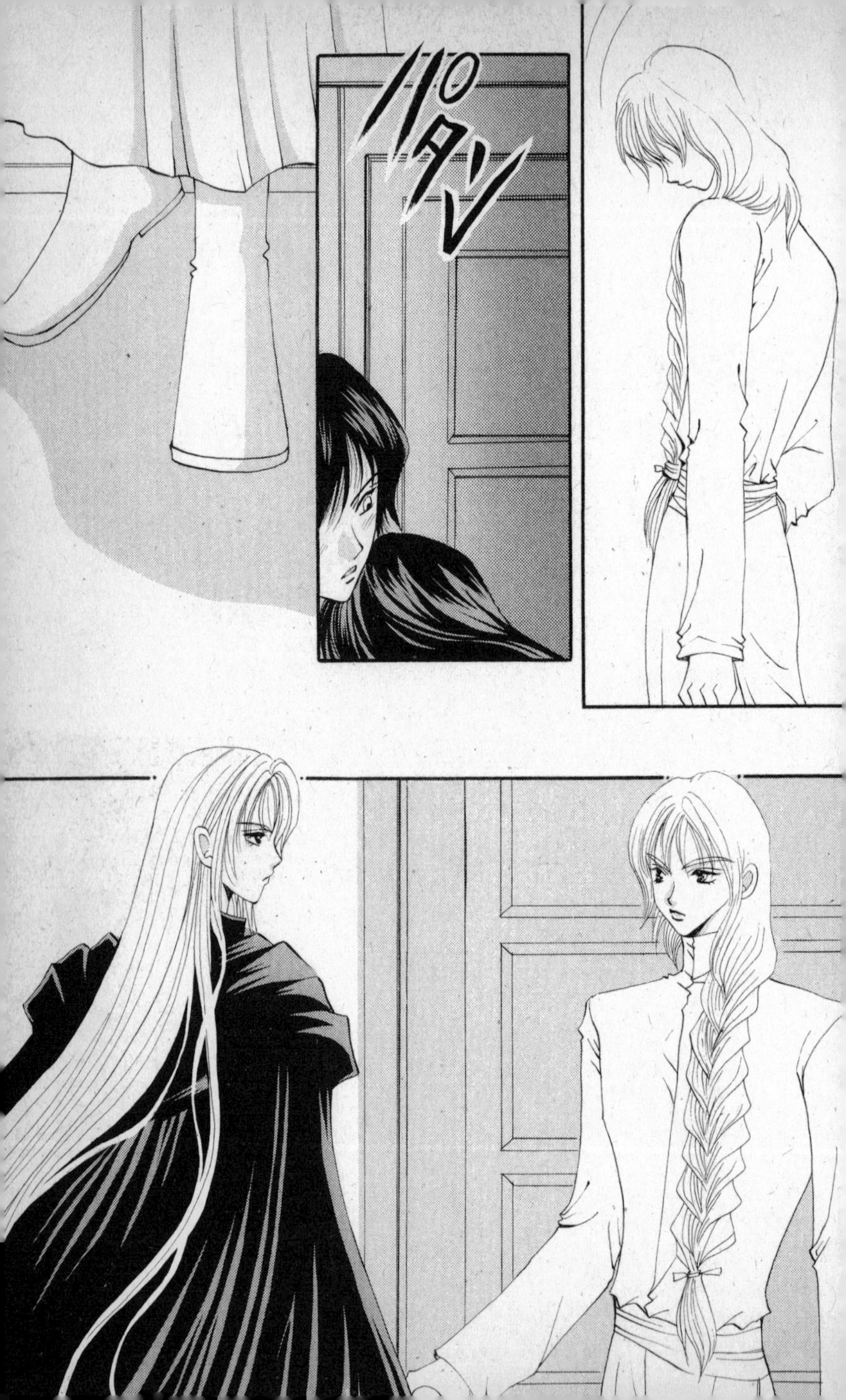
パタン

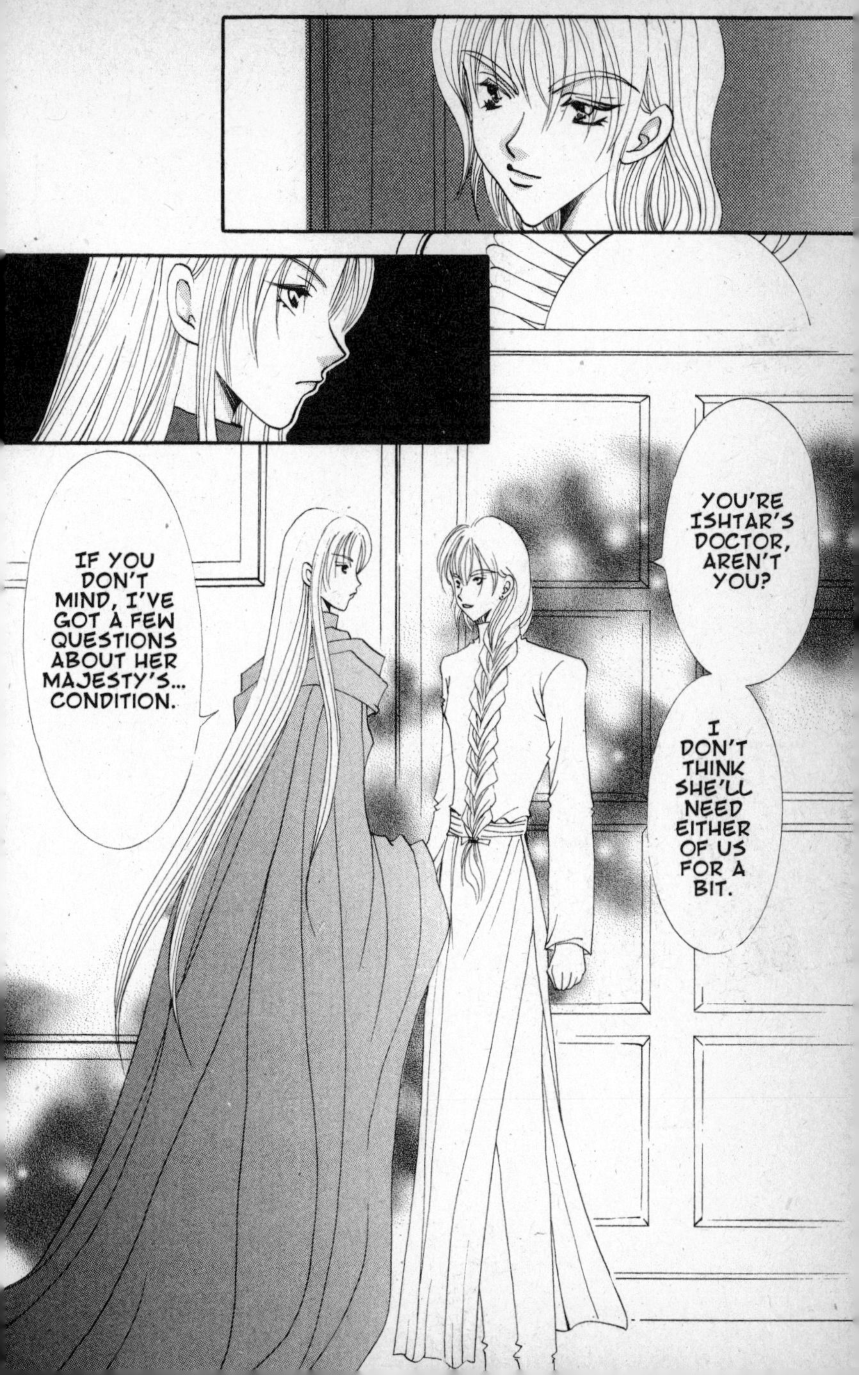
YOU'RE ISHTAR'S DOCTOR, AREN'T YOU?
I DON'T THINK SHE'LL NEED EITHER OF US FOR A BIT.
IF YOU DON'T MIND, I'VE GOT A FEW QUESTIONS ABOUT HER MAJESTY'S... CONDITION.

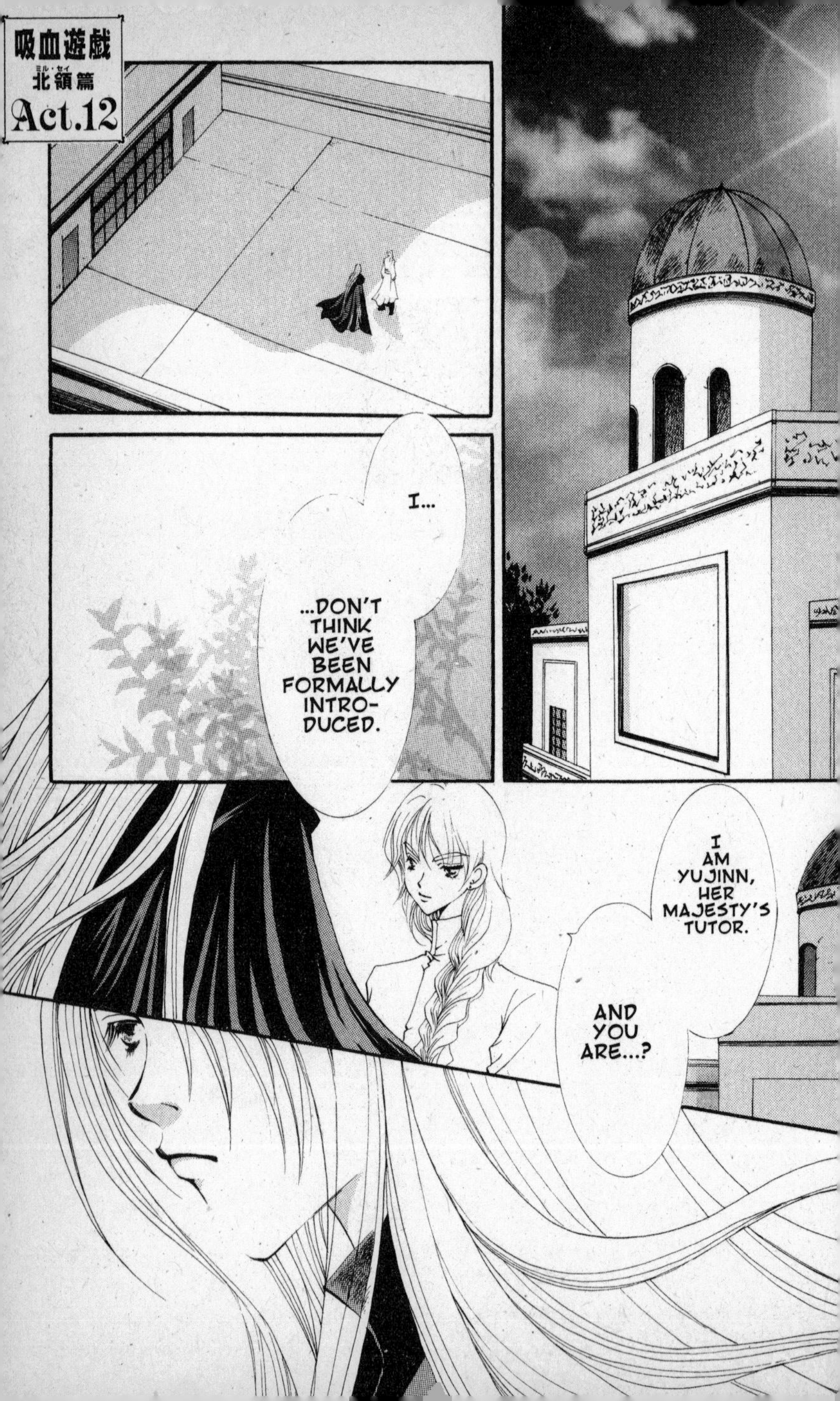
吸血遊戯
北領篇
Act.12
I...
...DON'T THINK WE'VE BEEN FORMALLY INTRO-DUCED.
I AM YUJINN, HER MAJESTY'S TUTOR.
AND YOU ARE...?

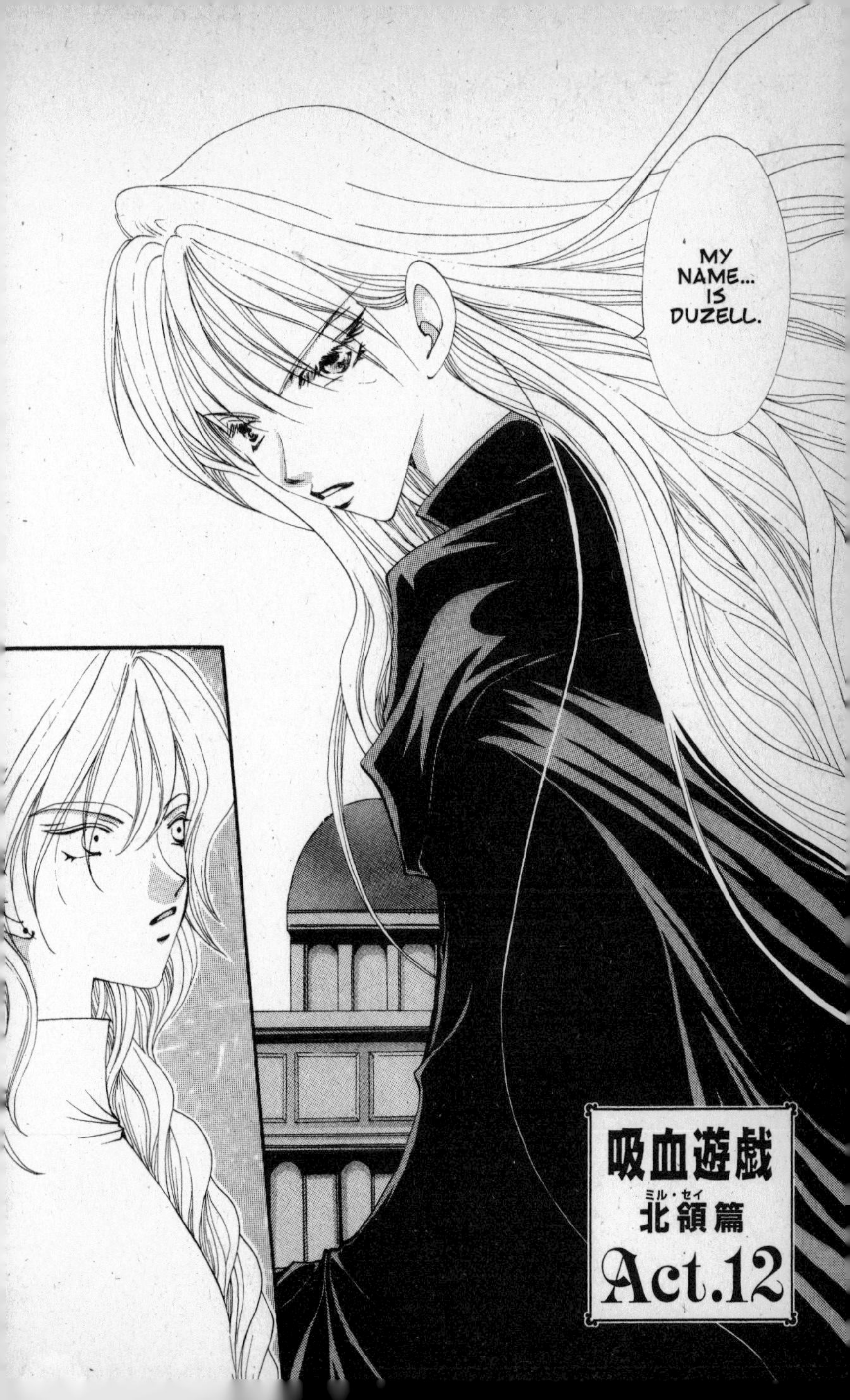
MY NAME... IS DUZELL.
吸血遊戯
ミル・セイ
北領篇
Act.12

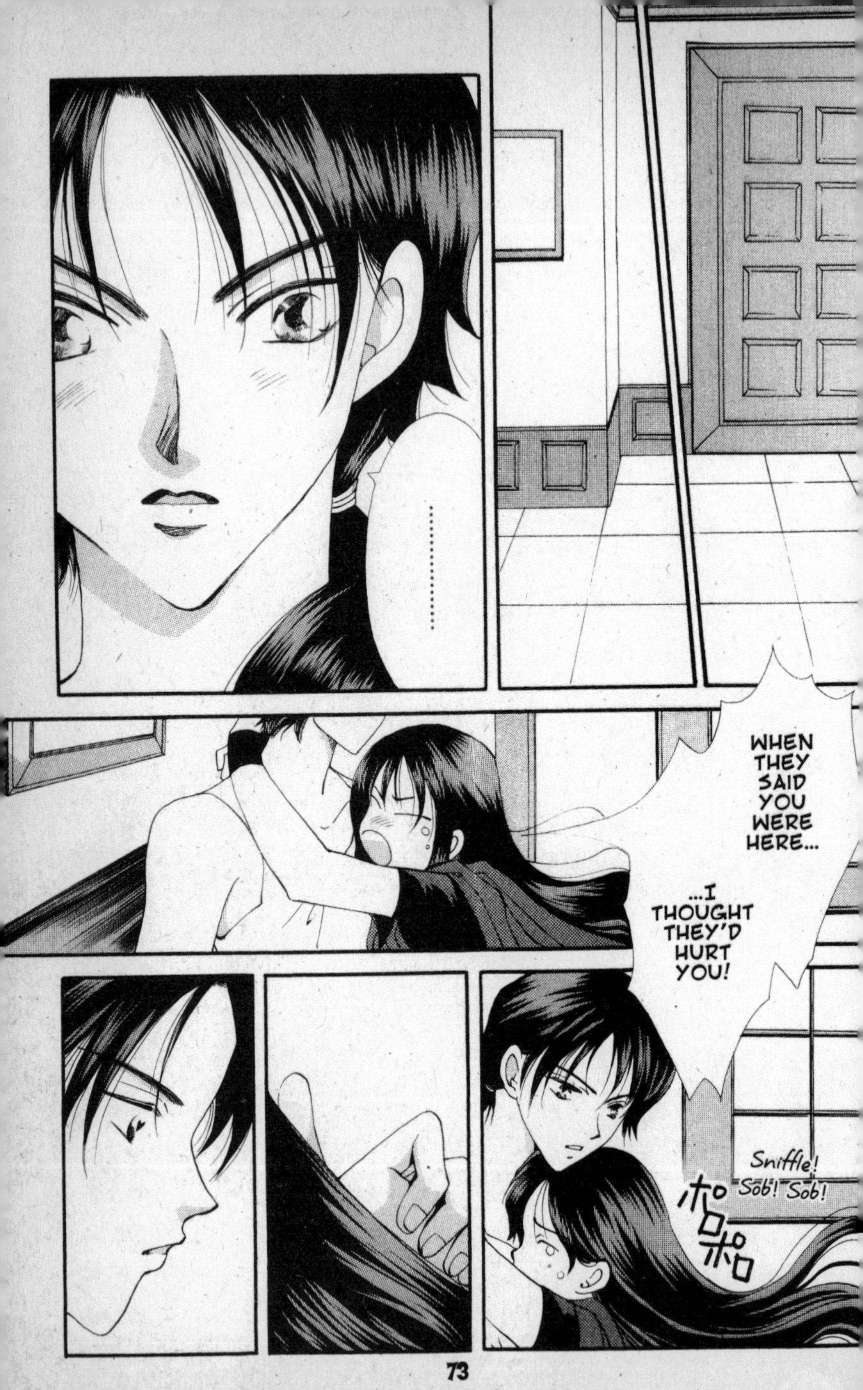

......
WHEN THEY SAID YOU WERE HERE...
...I THOUGHT THEY'D HURT YOU!
Sniffle! Sob! Sob!
ポロポロ

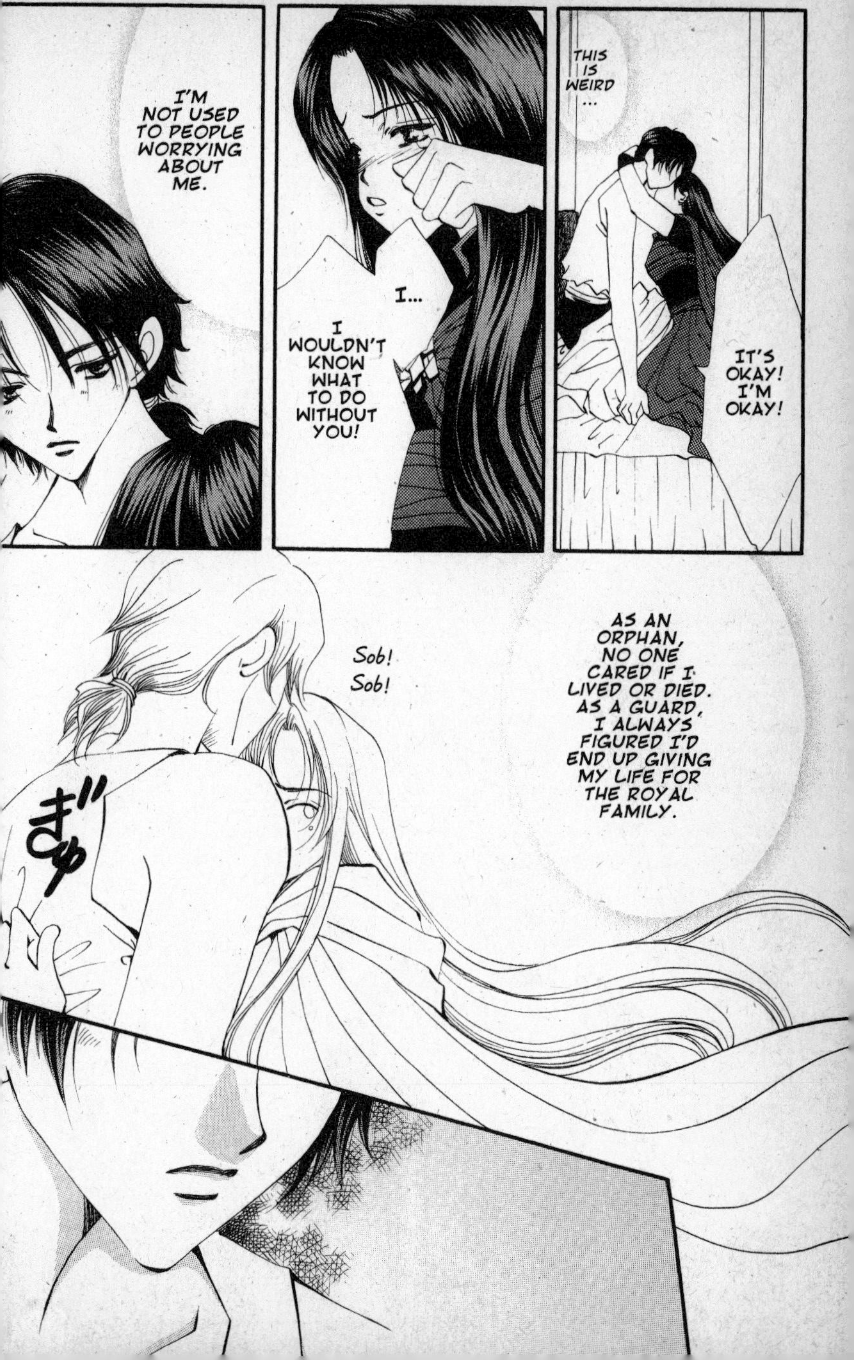
THIS IS WEIRD...
IT'S OKAY! I'M OKAY!
I...
I WOULDN'T KNOW WHAT TO DO WITHOUT YOU!
I'M NOT USED TO PEOPLE WORRYING ABOUT ME.
AS AN ORPHAN, NO ONE CARED IF I LIVED OR DIED. AS A GUARD, I ALWAYS FIGURED I'D END UP GIVING MY LIFE FOR THE ROYAL FAMILY.
Sob! Sob!
ぎゅ

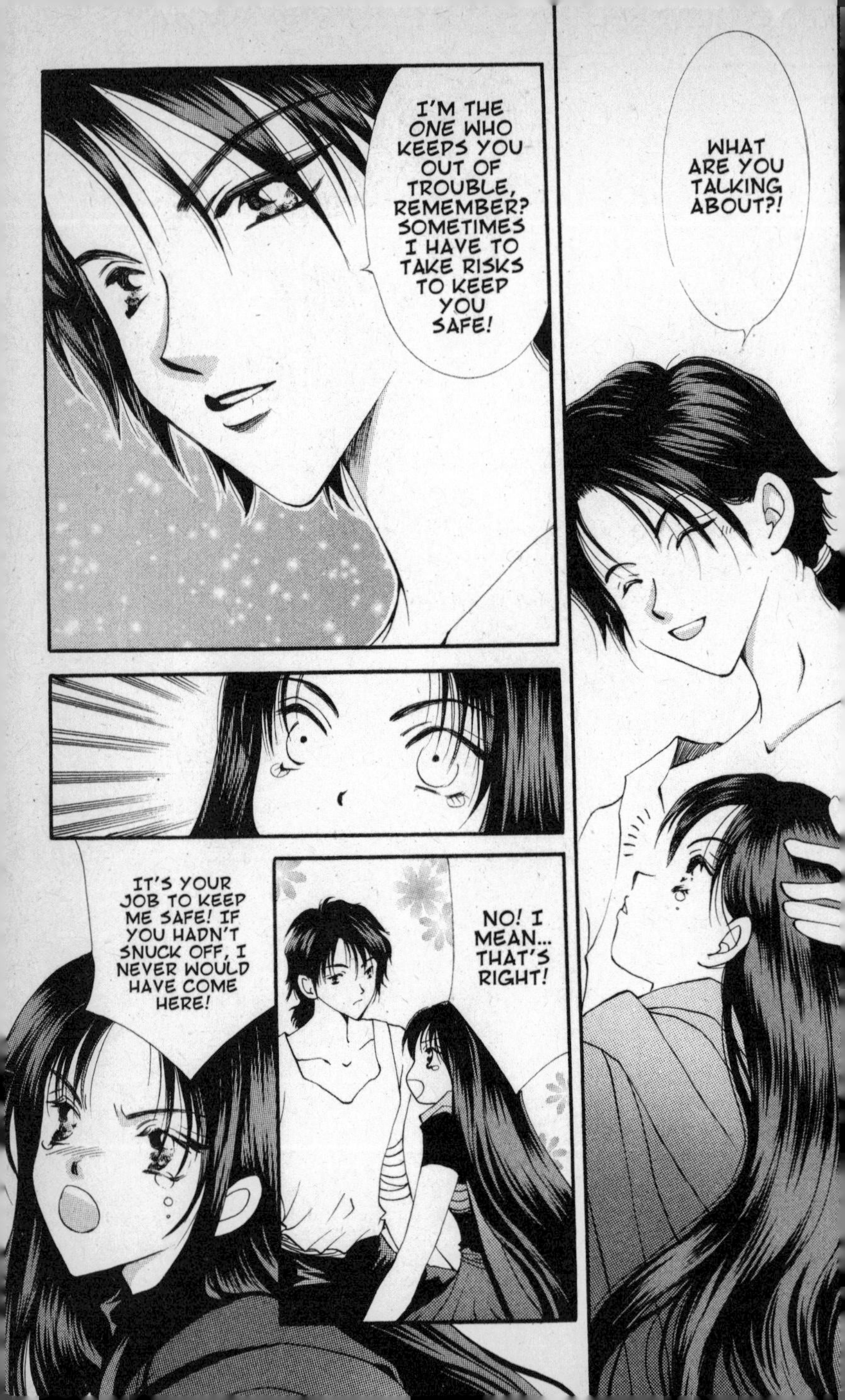
WHAT ARE YOU TALKING ABOUT?!
I'M THE ONE WHO KEEPS YOU OUT OF TROUBLE, REMEMBER? SOMETIMES I HAVE TO TAKE RISKS TO KEEP YOU SAFE!
NO! I MEAN... THAT'S RIGHT!
IT'S YOUR JOB TO KEEP ME SAFE! IF YOU HADN'T SNUCK OFF, I NEVER WOULD HAVE COME HERE!

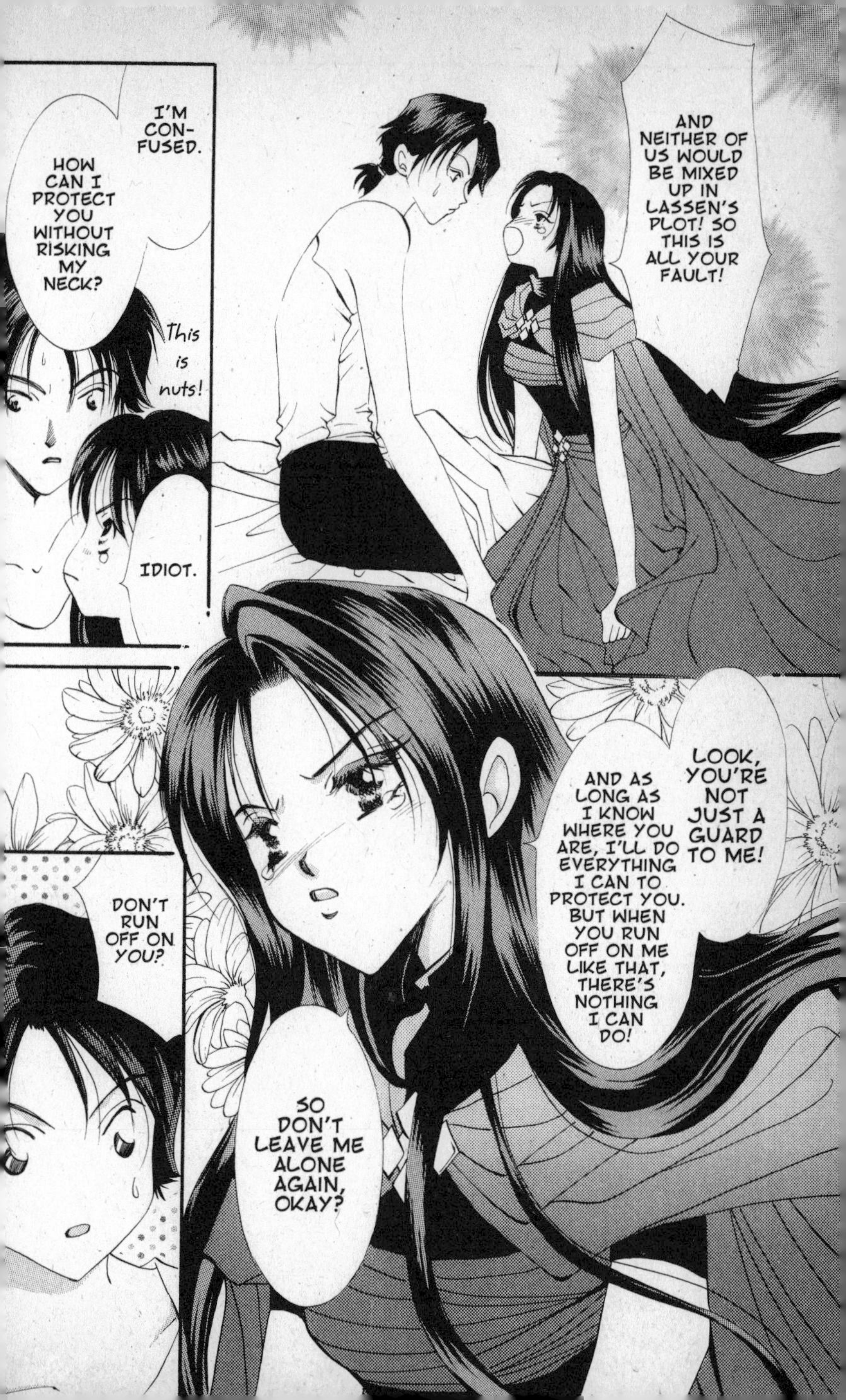
AND NEITHER OF US WOULD BE MIXED UP IN LASSEN'S PLOT! SO THIS IS ALL YOUR FAULT!
I'M CON-FUSED.
HOW CAN I PROTECT YOU WITHOUT RISKING MY NECK?
This is nuts!
IDIOT.
LOOK, YOU'RE NOT JUST A GUARD TO ME!
AND AS LONG AS I KNOW WHERE YOU ARE, I'LL DO EVERYTHING I CAN TO PROTECT YOU. BUT WHEN YOU RUN OFF ON ME LIKE THAT, THERE'S NOTHING I CAN DO!
SO DON'T LEAVE ME ALONE AGAIN, OKAY?
DON'T RUN OFF ON YOU?

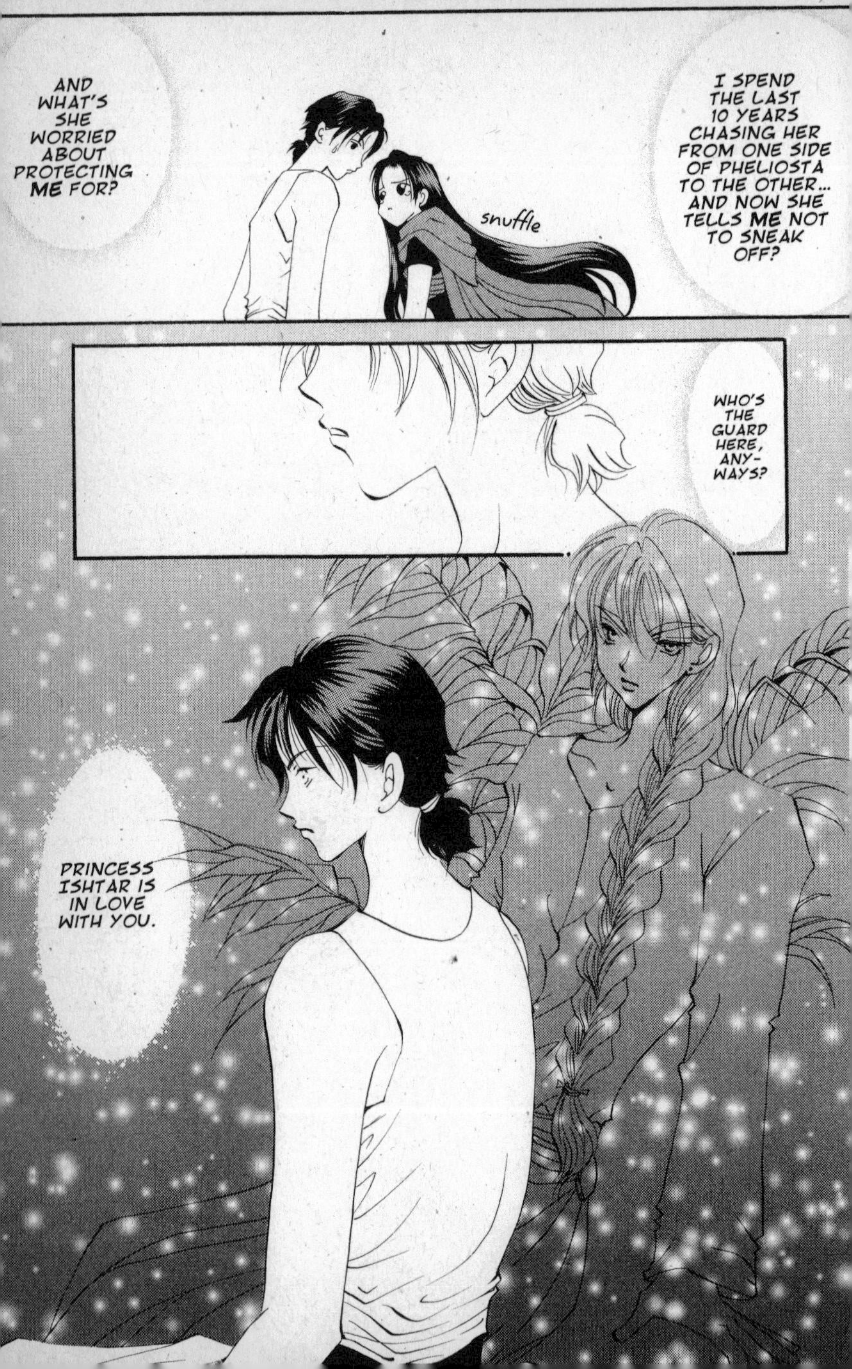
I SPEND THE LAST 10 YEARS CHASING HER FROM ONE SIDE OF PHELIOSTA TO THE OTHER... AND NOW SHE TELLS ME NOT TO SNEAK OFF?
snuffle
AND WHAT'S SHE WORRIED ABOUT PROTECTING ME FOR?
WHO'S THE GUARD HERE, ANY-WAYS?
PRINCESS ISHTAR IS IN LOVE WITH YOU.

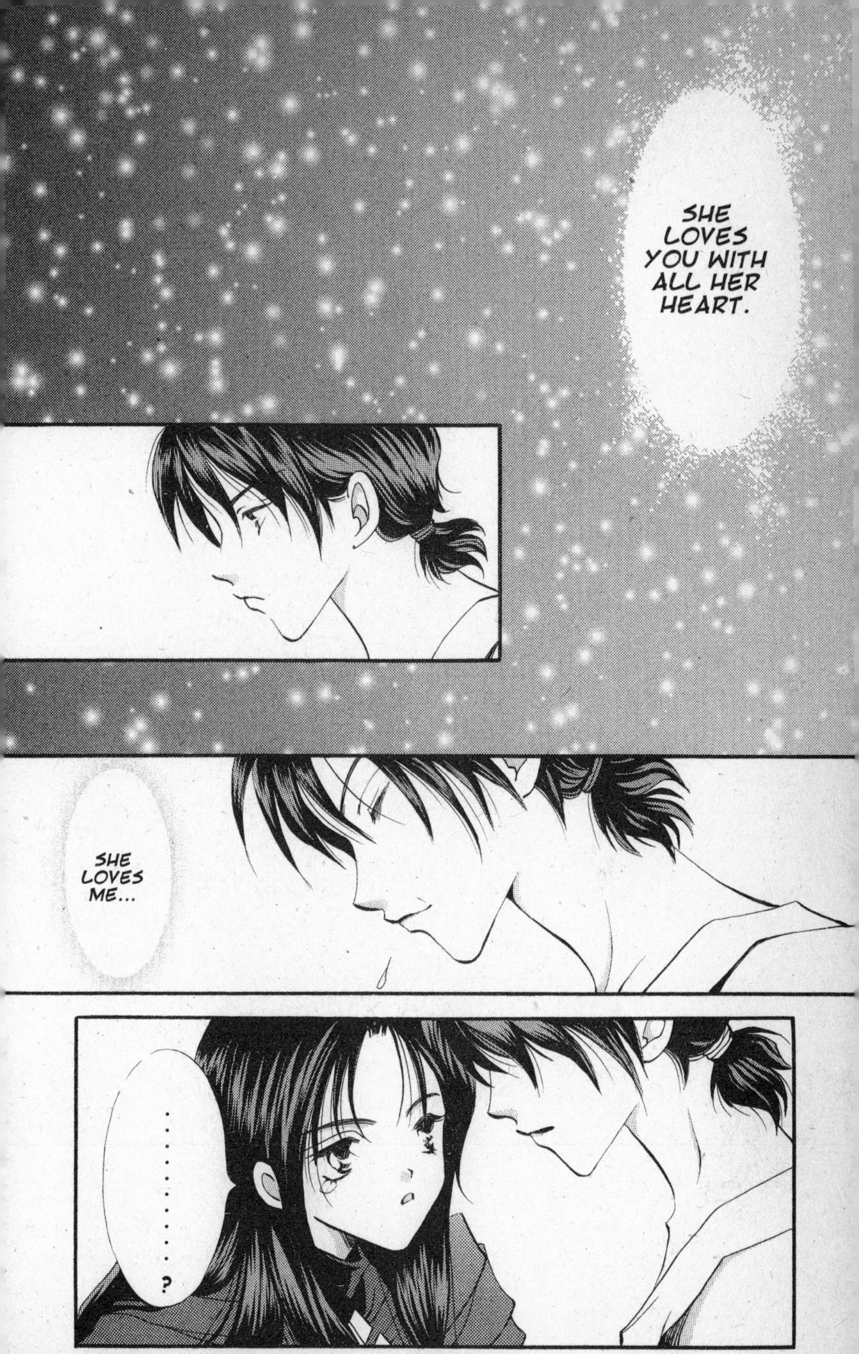
SHE LOVES YOU WITH ALL HER HEART.
SHE LOVES ME...
..........?

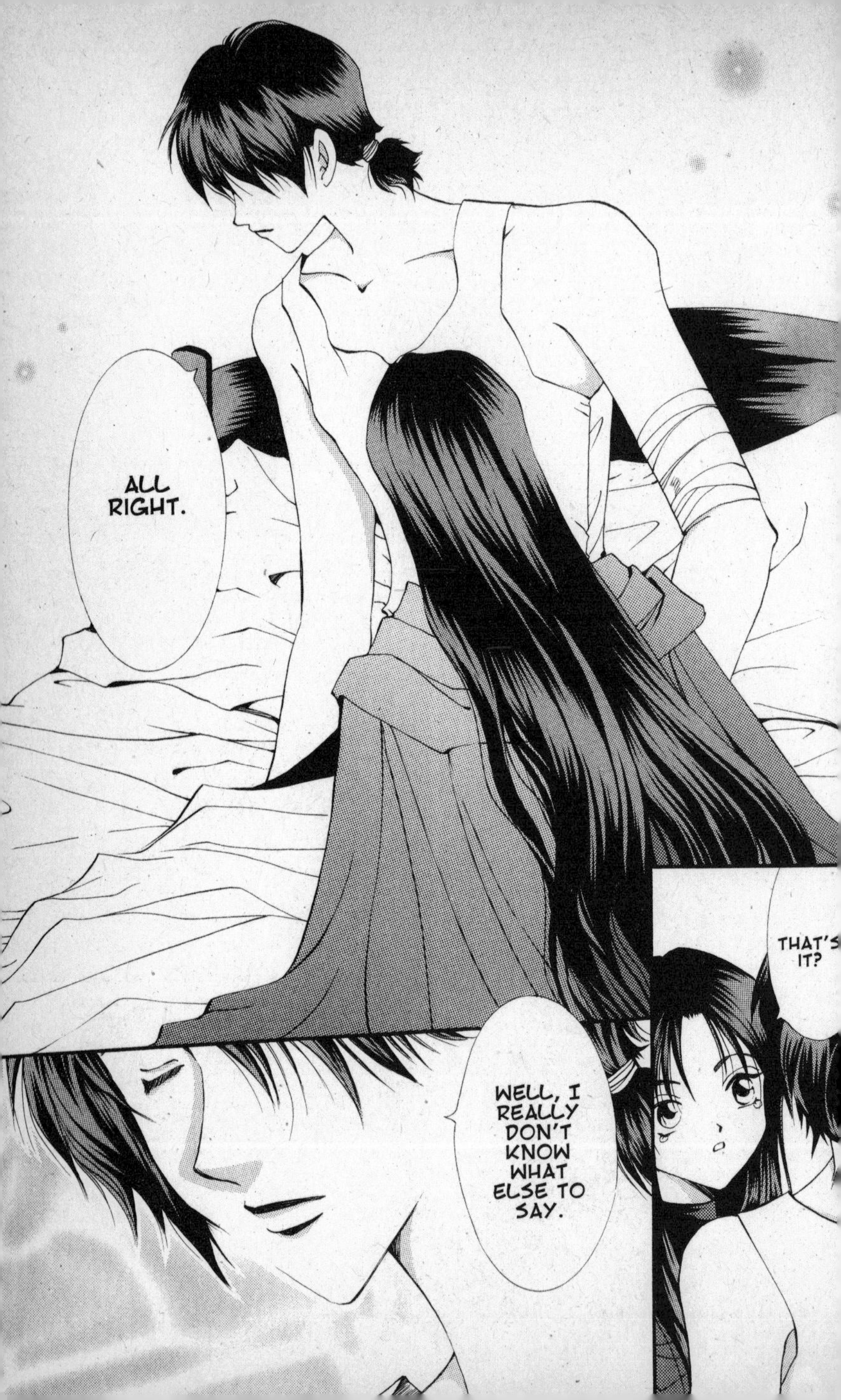
ALL RIGHT.
THAT'S IT?
WELL, I REALLY DON'T KNOW WHAT ELSE TO SAY.

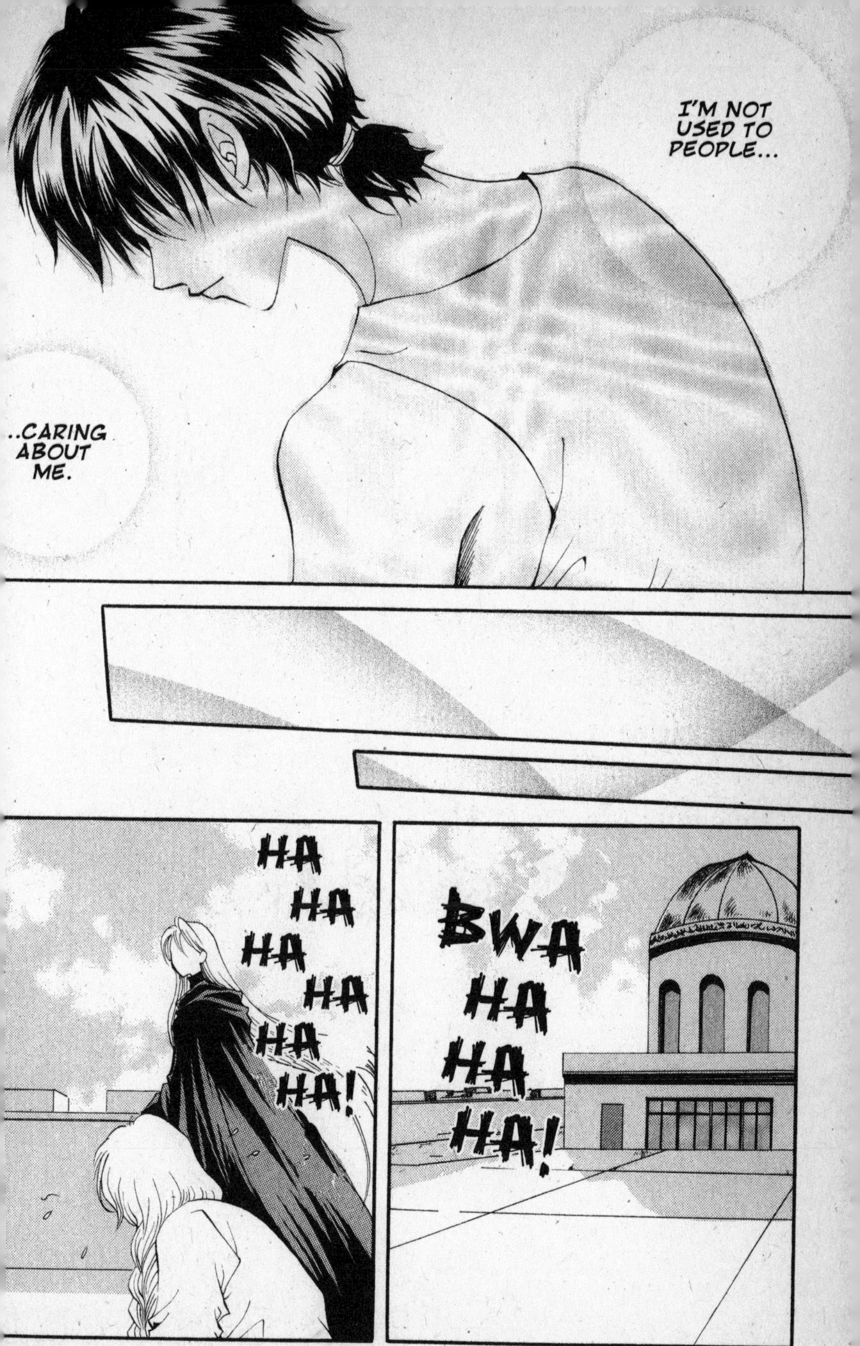
I'M NOT USED TO PEOPLE...
..CARING ABOUT ME.
BWA HA HA HA HA!
HA HA HA HA HA HA!

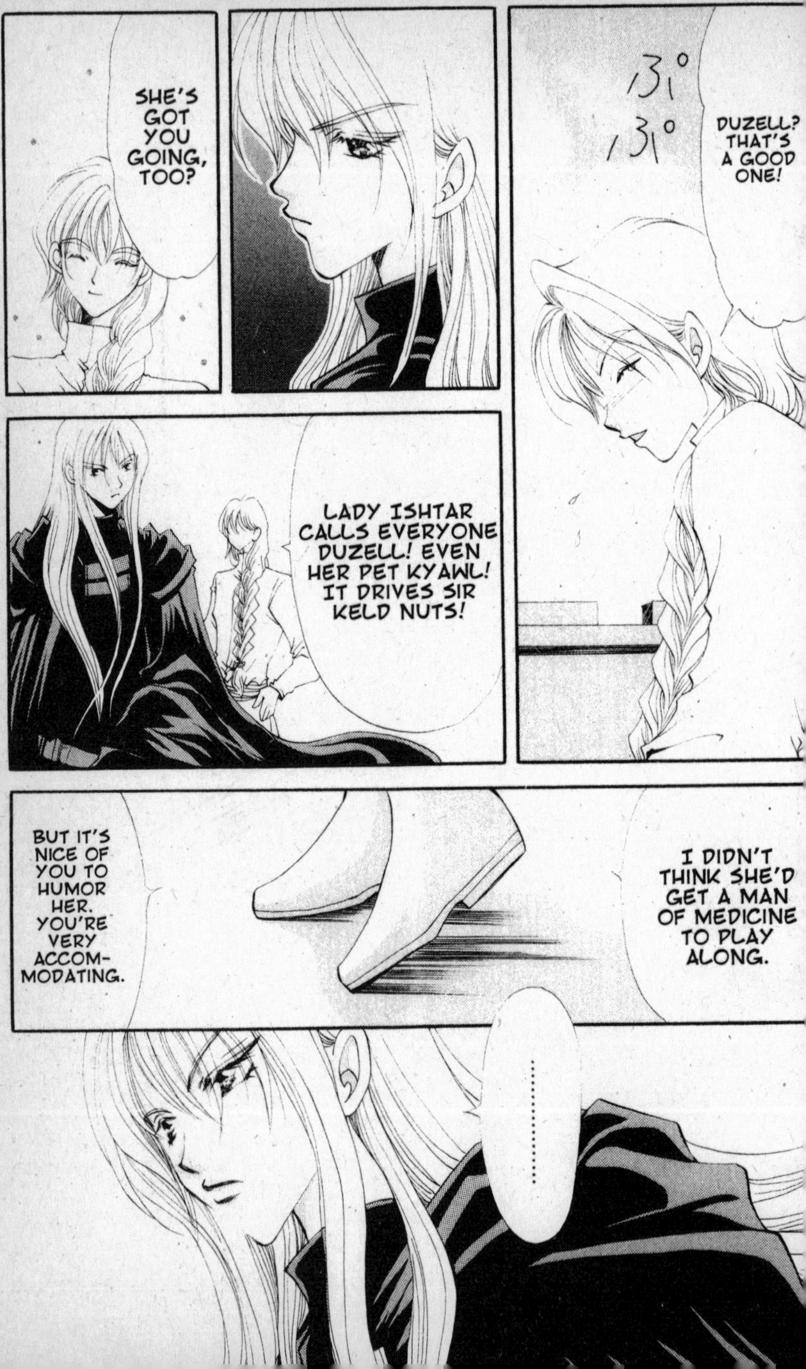
DUZELL? THAT'S A GOOD ONE!
SHE'S GOT YOU GOING, TOO?
LADY ISHTAR CALLS EVERYONE DUZELL! EVEN HER PET KYAWL! IT DRIVES SIR KELD NUTS!
I DIDN'T THINK SHE'D GET A MAN OF MEDICINE TO PLAY ALONG.
BUT IT'S NICE OF YOU TO HUMOR HER. YOU'RE VERY ACCOM-MODATING.
......

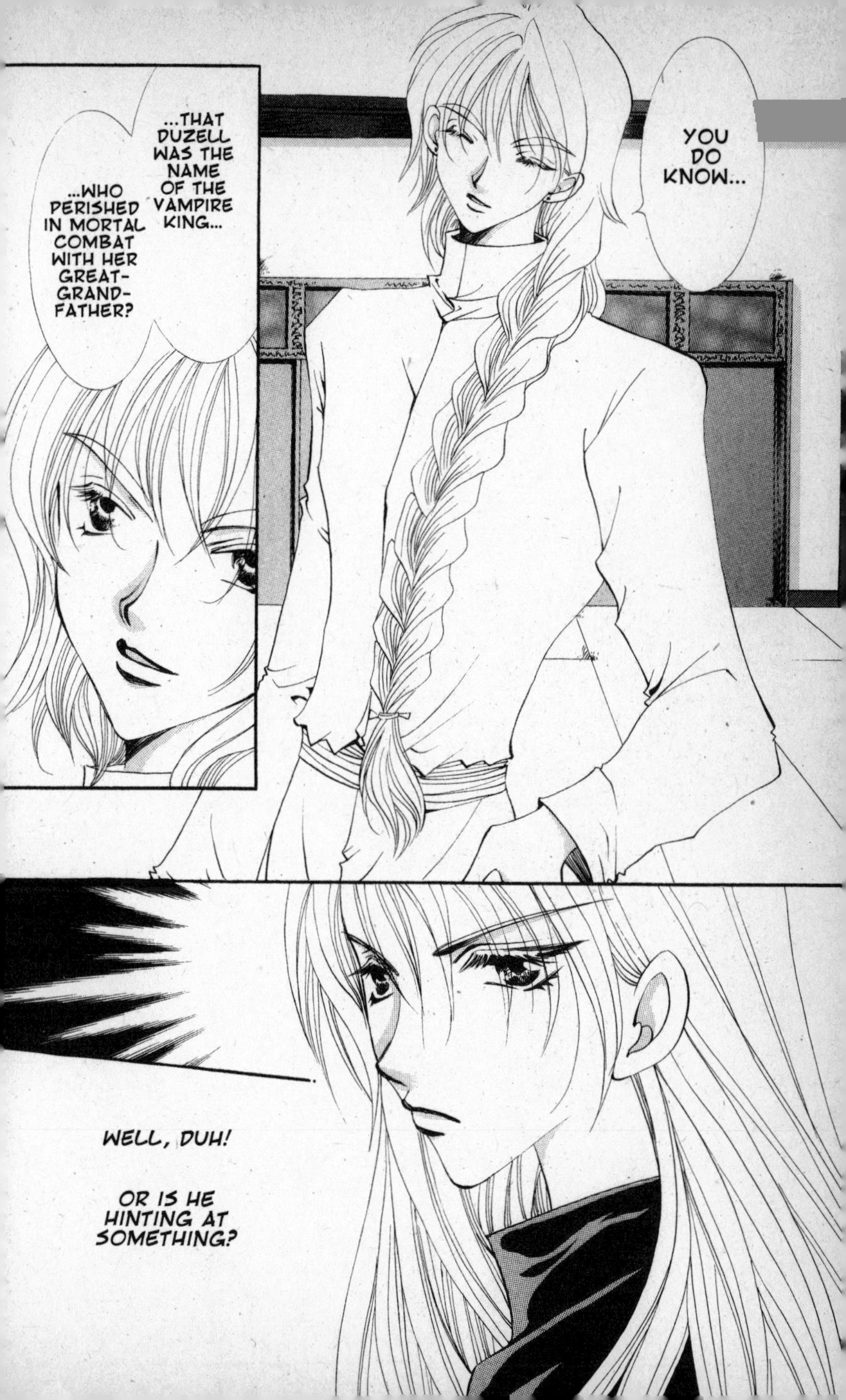

YOU DO KNOW...
...THAT DUZELL WAS THE NAME OF THE VAMPIRE KING...
...WHO PERISHED IN MORTAL COMBAT WITH HER GREAT-GRANDFATHER?
WELL, DUH!
OR IS HE HINTING AT SOMETHING?

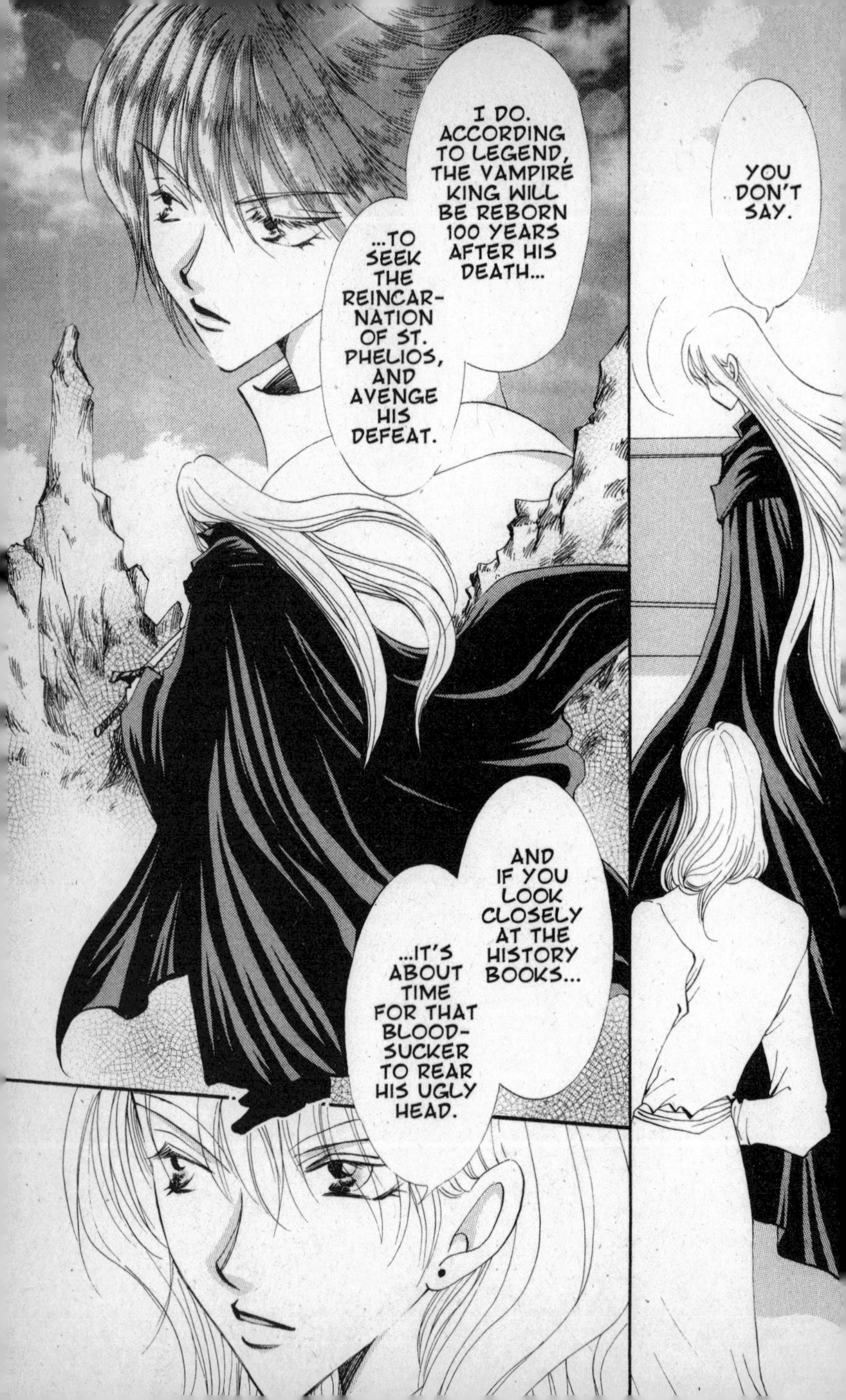
YOU DON'T SAY.
I DO. ACCORDING TO LEGEND, THE VAMPIRE KING WILL BE REBORN 100 YEARS AFTER HIS DEATH...
...TO SEEK THE REINCAR-NATION OF ST. PHELIOS, AND AVENGE HIS DEFEAT.
AND IF YOU LOOK CLOSELY AT THE HISTORY BOOKS...
...IT'S ABOUT TIME FOR THAT BLOOD-SUCKER TO REAR HIS UGLY HEAD.

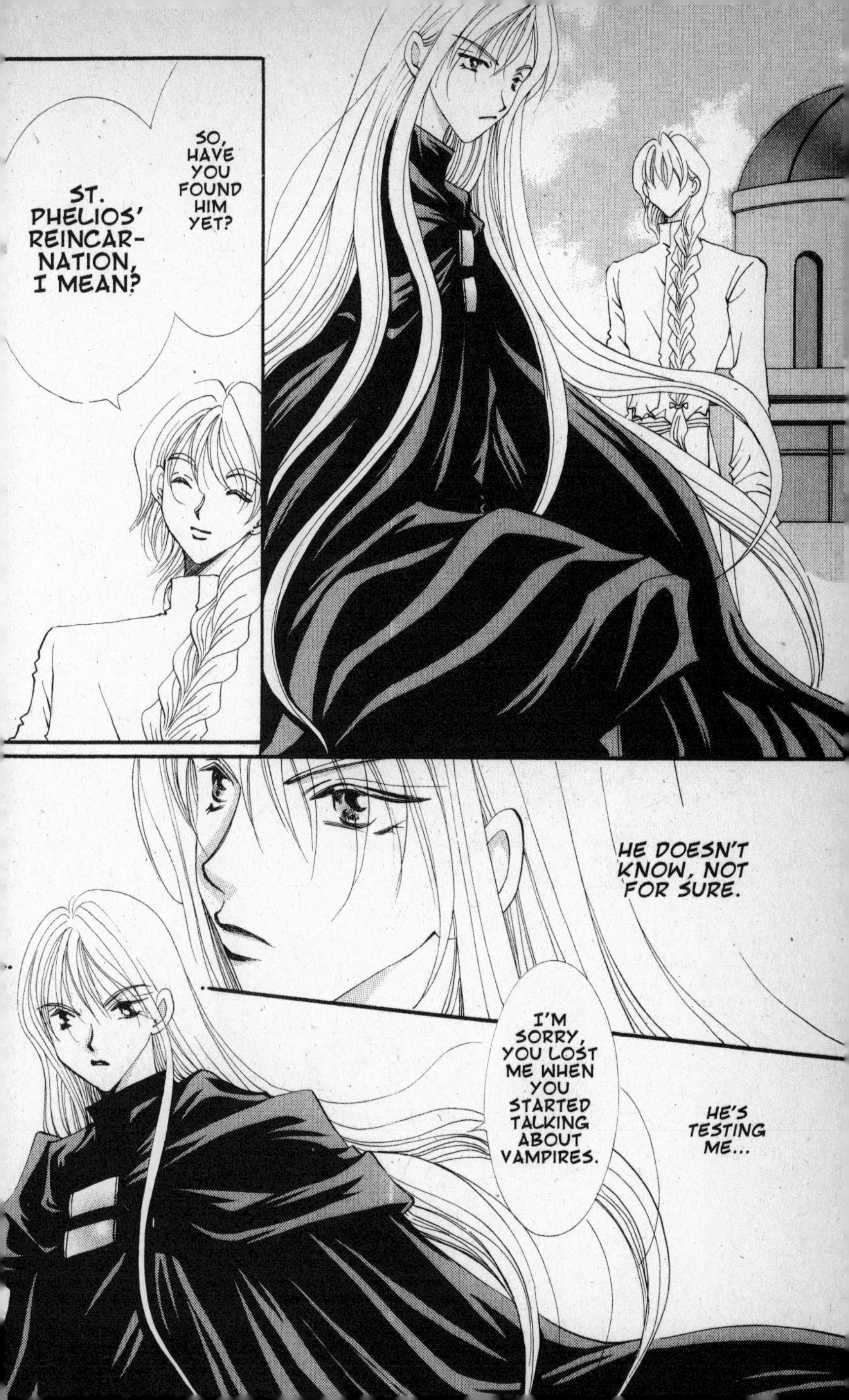
SO, HAVE YOU FOUND HIM YET?
ST. PHELIOS' REINCARNATION, I MEAN?
HE DOESN'T KNOW, NOT FOR SURE.
HE'S TESTING ME...
I'M SORRY, YOU LOST ME WHEN YOU STARTED TALKING ABOUT VAMPIRES.

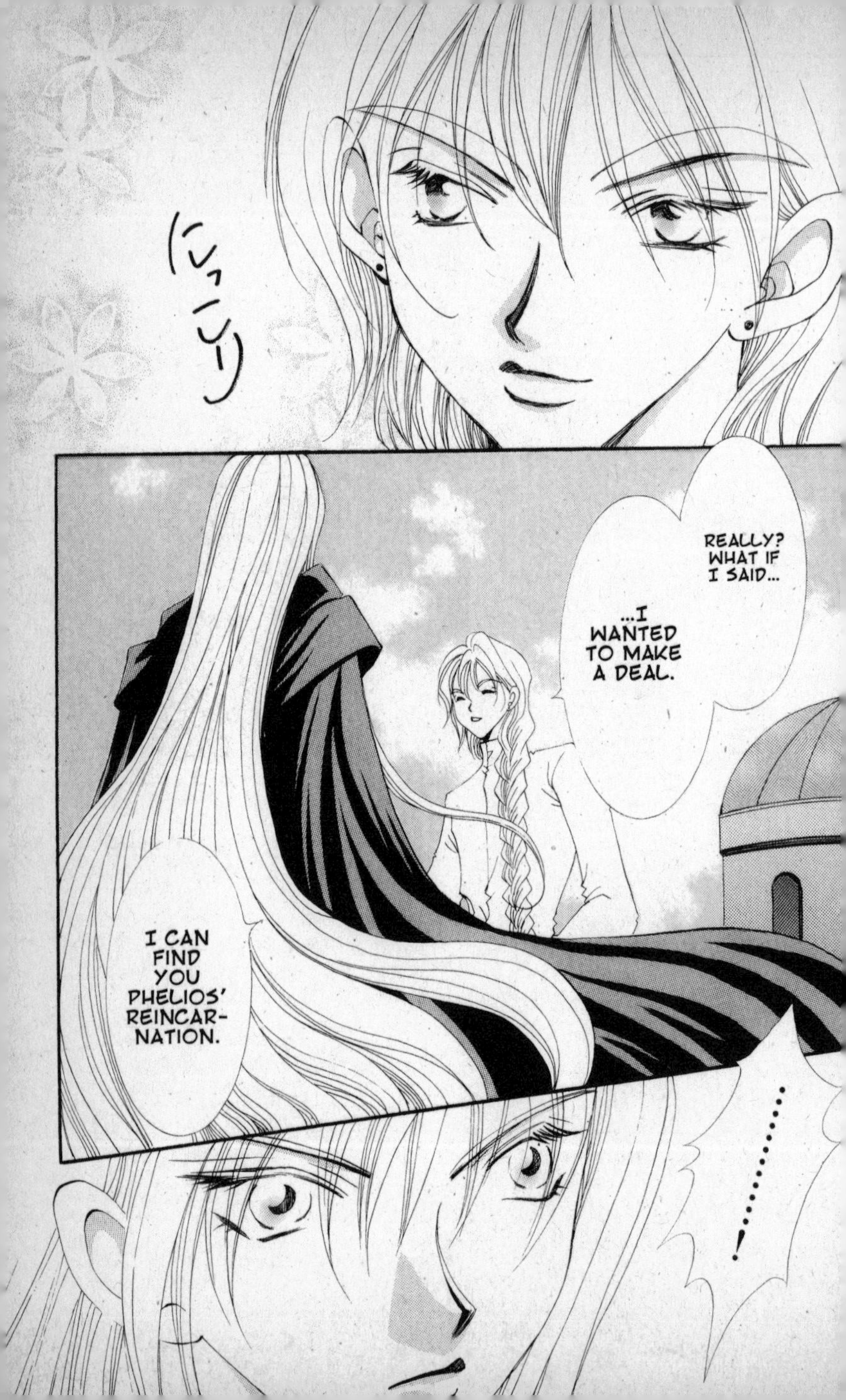
にっこり
REALLY? WHAT IF I SAID...
...I WANTED TO MAKE A DEAL.
I CAN FIND YOU PHELIOS' REINCARNATION.
......!

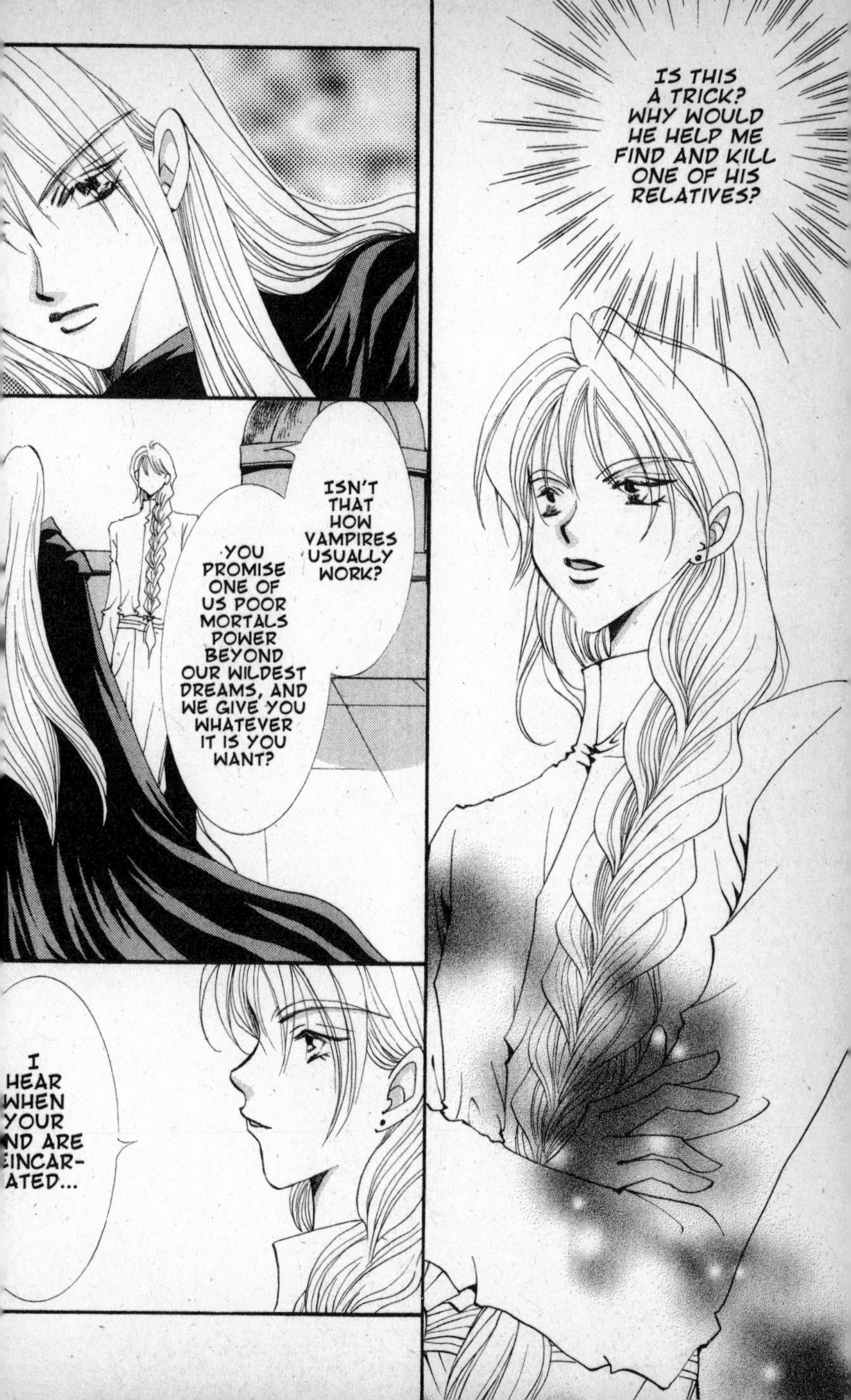
IS THIS A TRICK? WHY WOULD HE HELP ME FIND AND KILL ONE OF HIS RELATIVES?
ISN'T THAT HOW VAMPIRES USUALLY WORK?
YOU PROMISE ONE OF US POOR MORTALS POWER BEYOND OUR WILDEST DREAMS, AND WE GIVE YOU WHATEVER IT IS YOU WANT?
I HEAR WHEN YOUR ND ARE EINCAR-ATED...

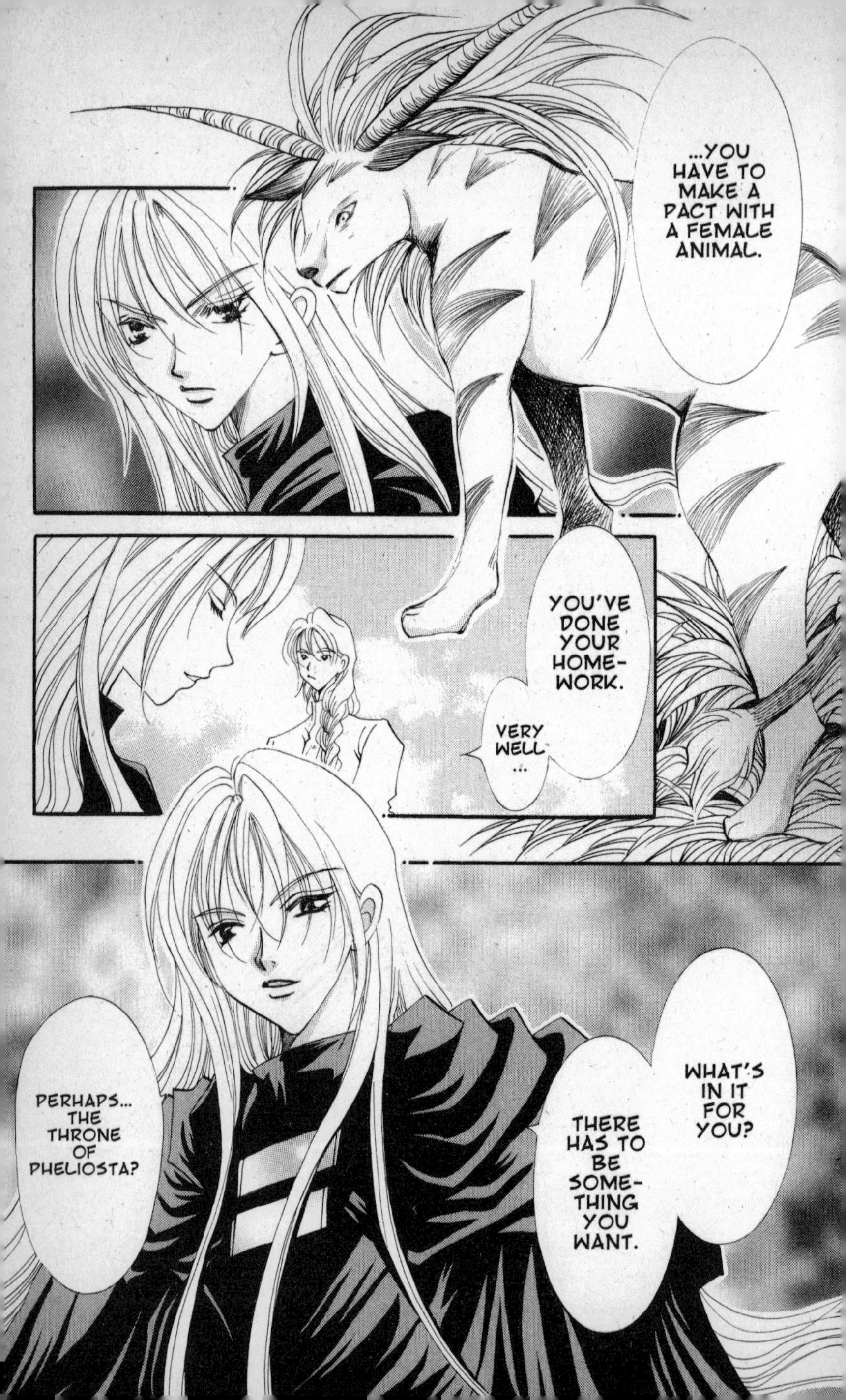
...YOU HAVE TO MAKE A PACT WITH A FEMALE ANIMAL.
YOU'VE DONE YOUR HOME-WORK.
VERY WELL ...
WHAT'S IN IT FOR YOU?
THERE HAS TO BE SOME-THING YOU WANT.
PERHAPS... THE THRONE OF PHELIOSTA?

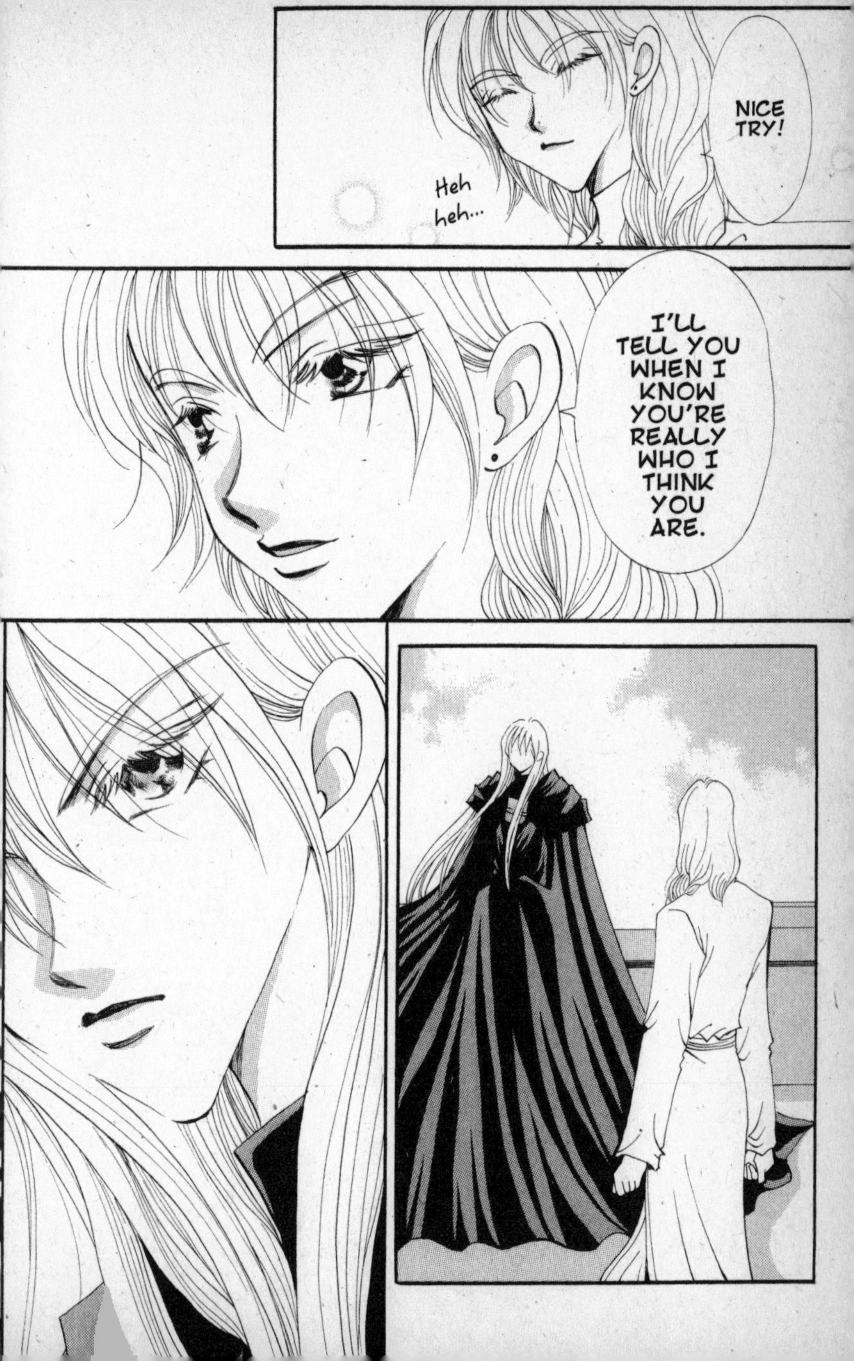
NICE TRY!
Heh heh...
I'LL TELL YOU WHEN I KNOW YOU'RE REALLY WHO I THINK YOU ARE.

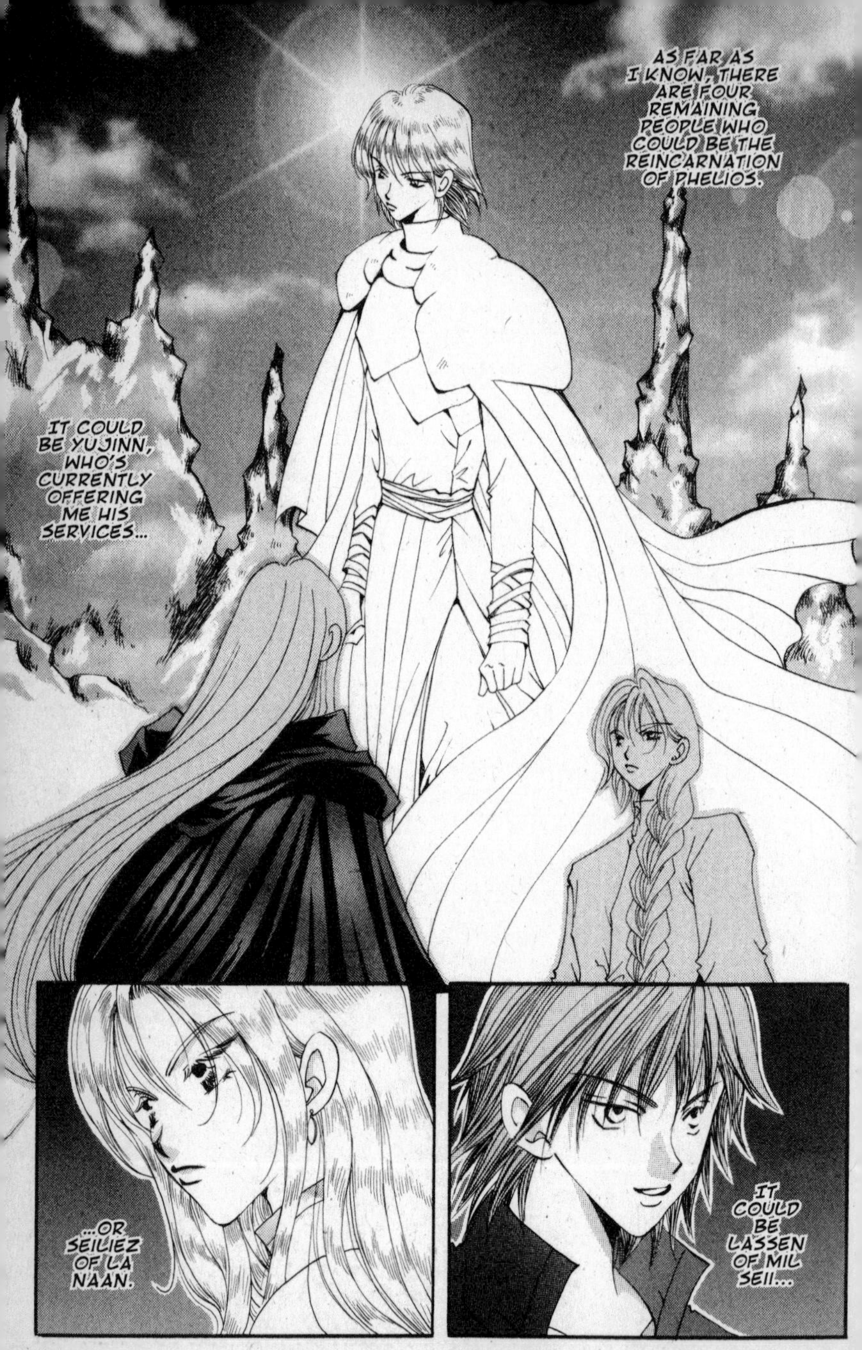
AS FAR AS I KNOW, THERE ARE FOUR REMAINING PEOPLE WHO COULD BE THE REINCARNATION OF PHELIOS.
IT COULD BE YUJINN, WHO'S CURRENTLY OFFERING ME HIS SERVICES...
IT COULD BE LASSEN OF MIL SEII...
...OR SEILIEZ OF LA NAAN.

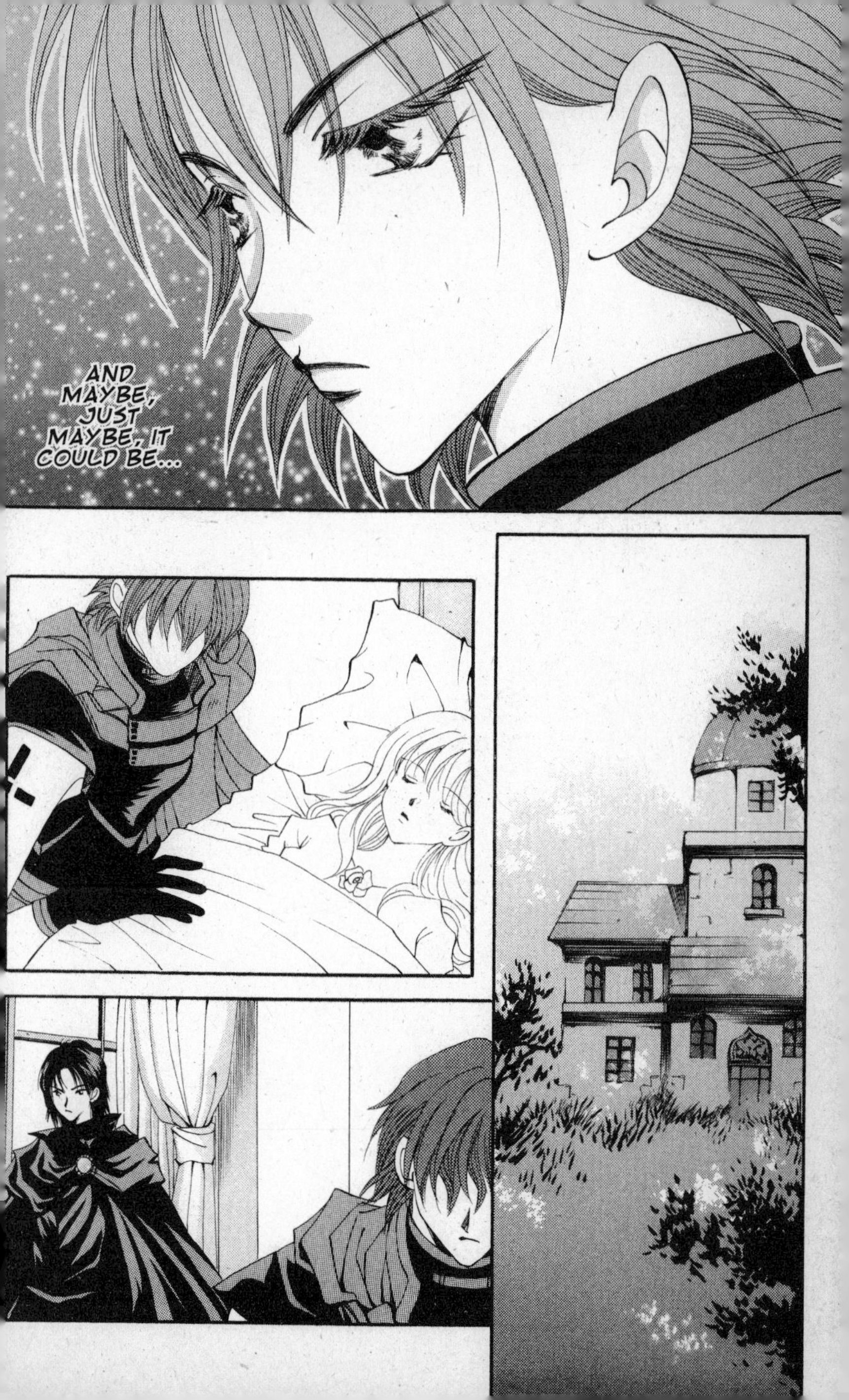
AND MAYBE, JUST MAYBE, IT COULD BE...

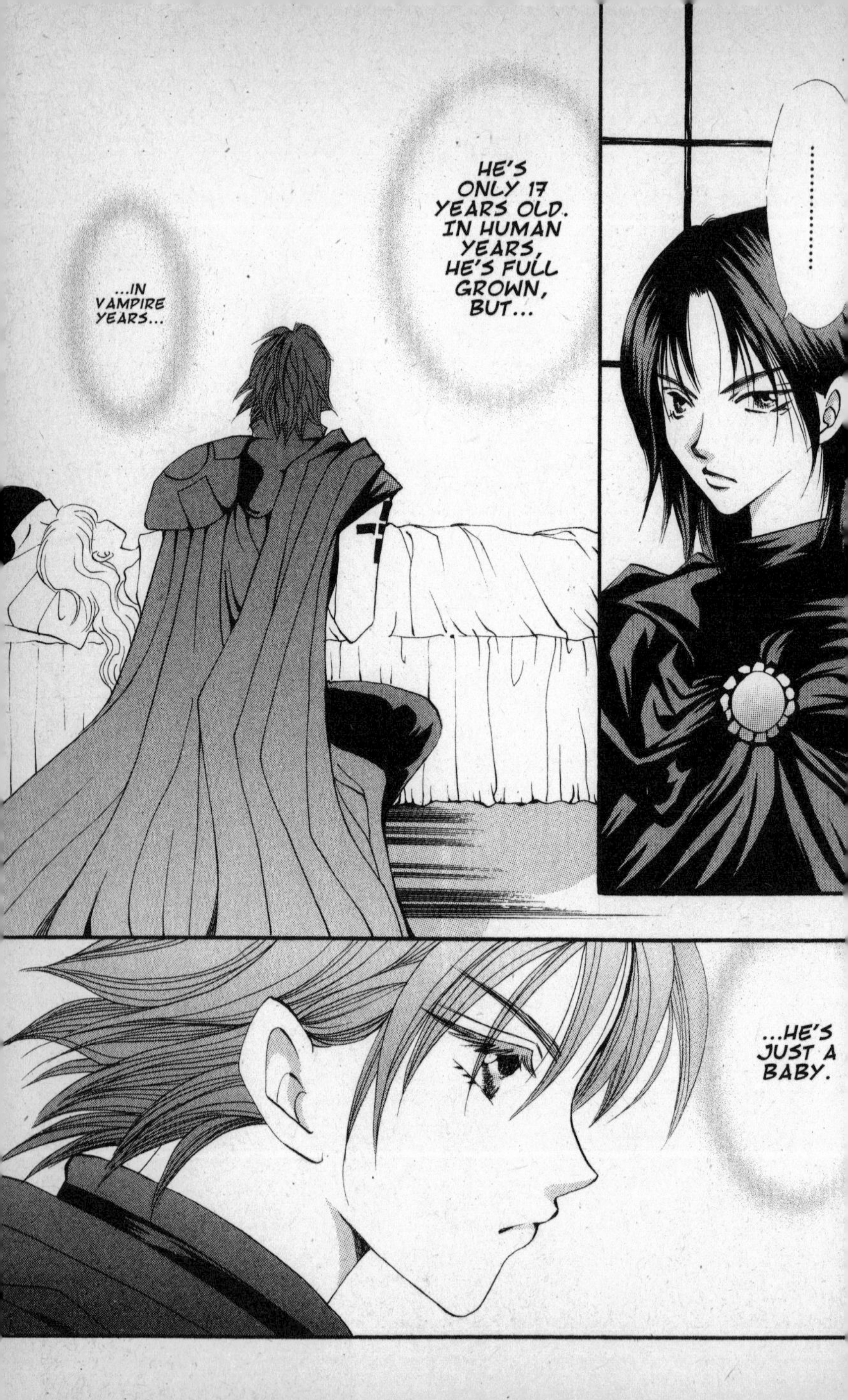
......
HE'S ONLY 17 YEARS OLD. IN HUMAN YEARS, HE'S FULL GROWN, BUT...
...IN VAMPIRE YEARS...
...HE'S JUST A BABY.

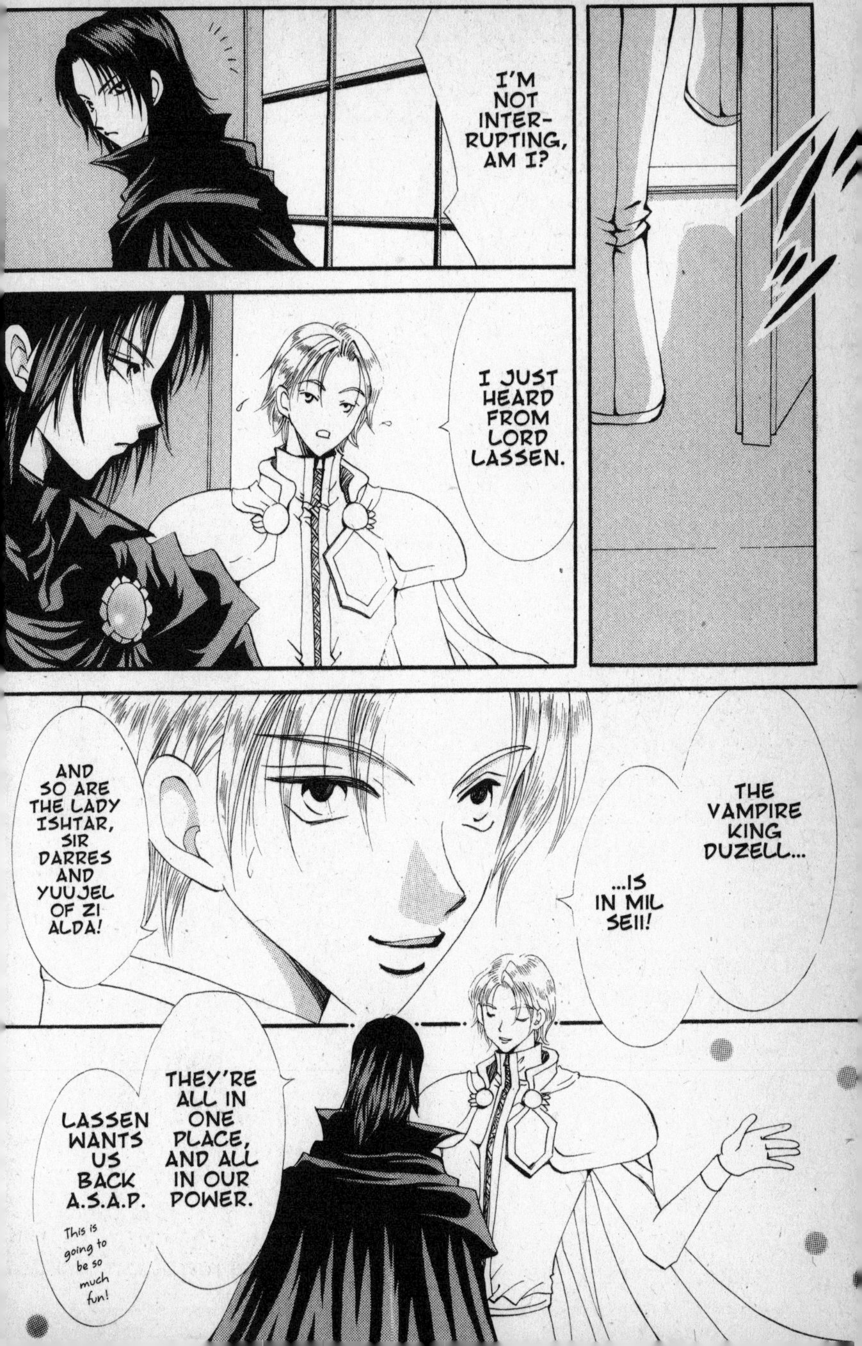
I'M NOT INTERRUPTING, AM I?
I JUST HEARD FROM LORD LASSEN.
THE VAMPIRE KING DUZELL...
...IS IN MIL SEII!
AND SO ARE THE LADY ISHTAR, SIR DARRES AND YUUJEL OF ZI ALDA!
THEY'RE ALL IN ONE PLACE, AND ALL IN OUR POWER.
LASSEN WANTS US BACK A.S.A.P.
This is going to be so much fun!

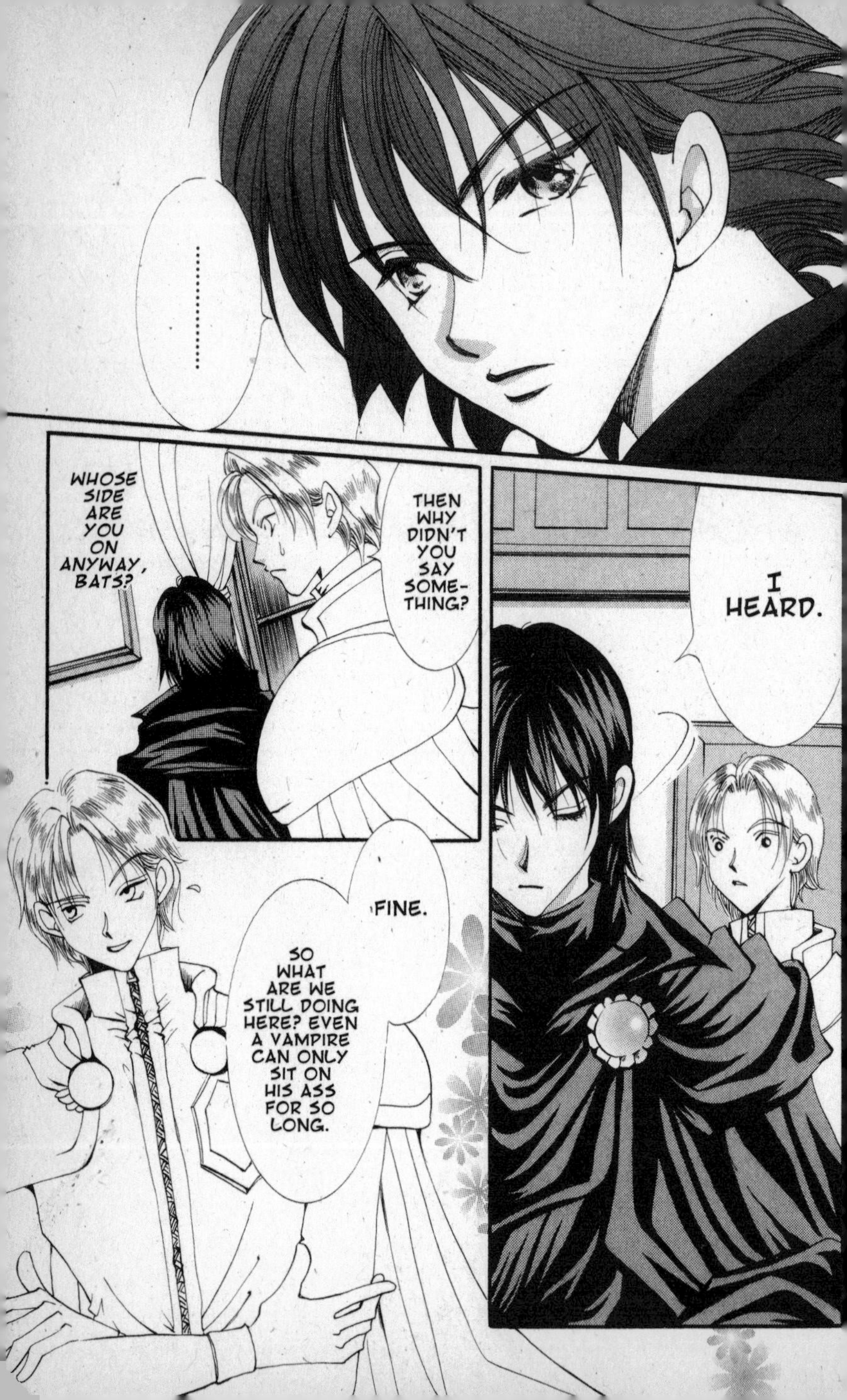
……
I HEARD.
THEN WHY DIDN'T YOU SAY SOMETHING?
WHOSE SIDE ARE YOU ON ANYWAY, BATS?
FINE.
SO WHAT ARE WE STILL DOING HERE? EVEN A VAMPIRE CAN ONLY SIT ON HIS ASS FOR SO LONG.

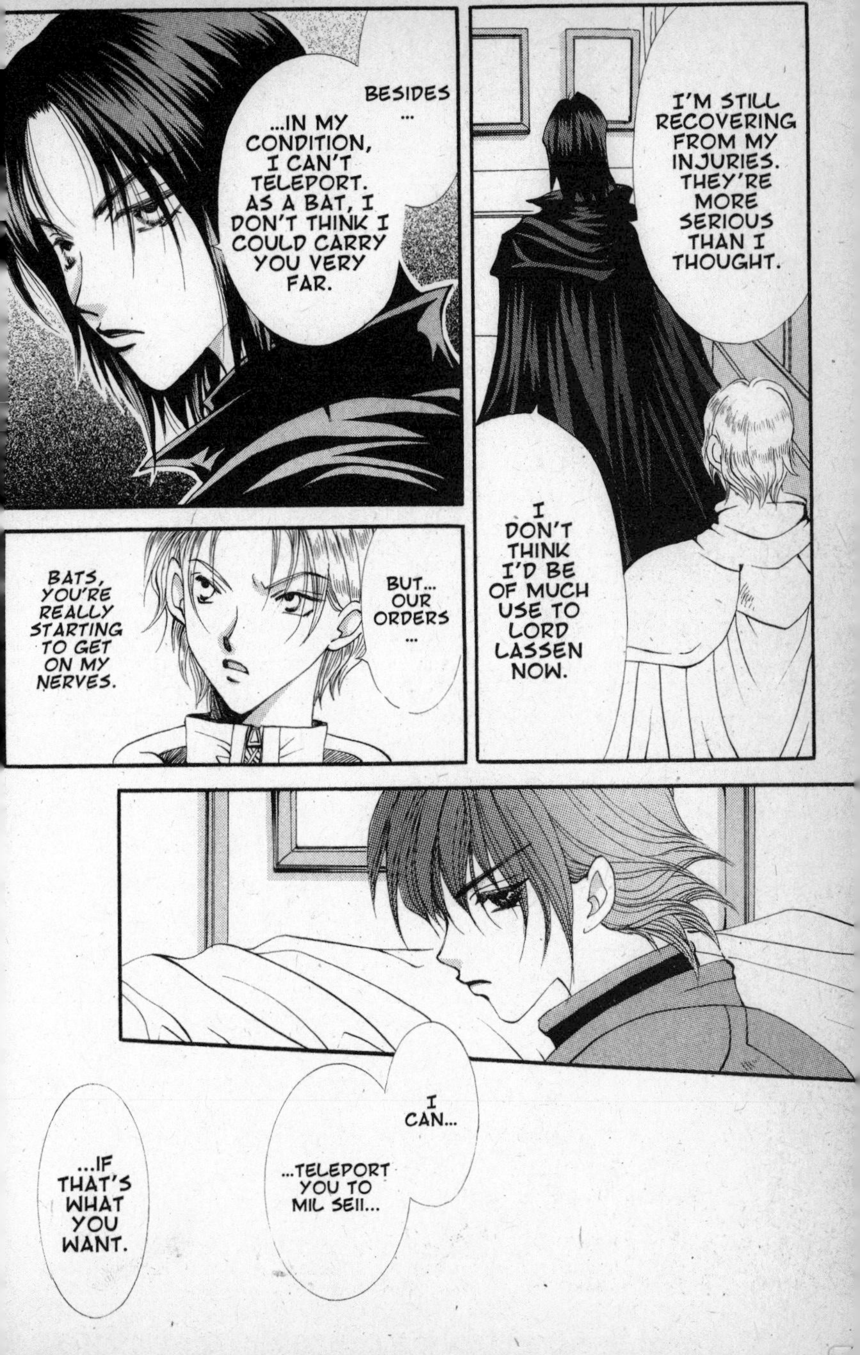
I'M STILL RECOVERING FROM MY INJURIES. THEY'RE MORE SERIOUS THAN I THOUGHT.
I DON'T THINK I'D BE OF MUCH USE TO LORD LASSEN NOW.
BESIDES...
...IN MY CONDITION, I CAN'T TELEPORT. AS A BAT, I DON'T THINK I COULD CARRY YOU VERY FAR.
BUT... OUR ORDERS...
BATS, YOU'RE REALLY STARTING TO GET ON MY NERVES.
I CAN...
...TELEPORT YOU TO MIL SEII...
...IF THAT'S WHAT YOU WANT.

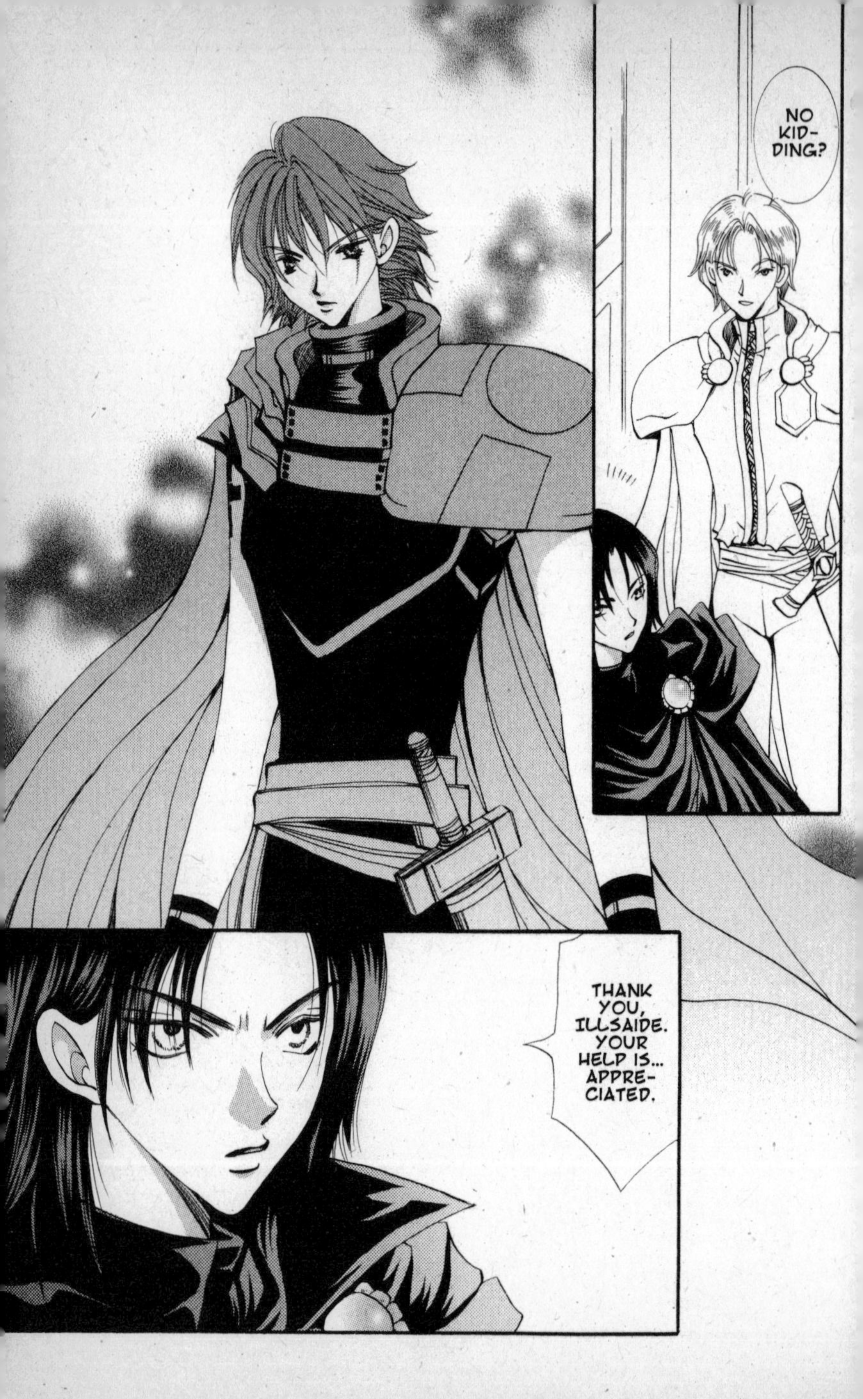
NO KID-DING?
THANK YOU, ILLSAIDE. YOUR HELP IS... APPRE-CIATED.

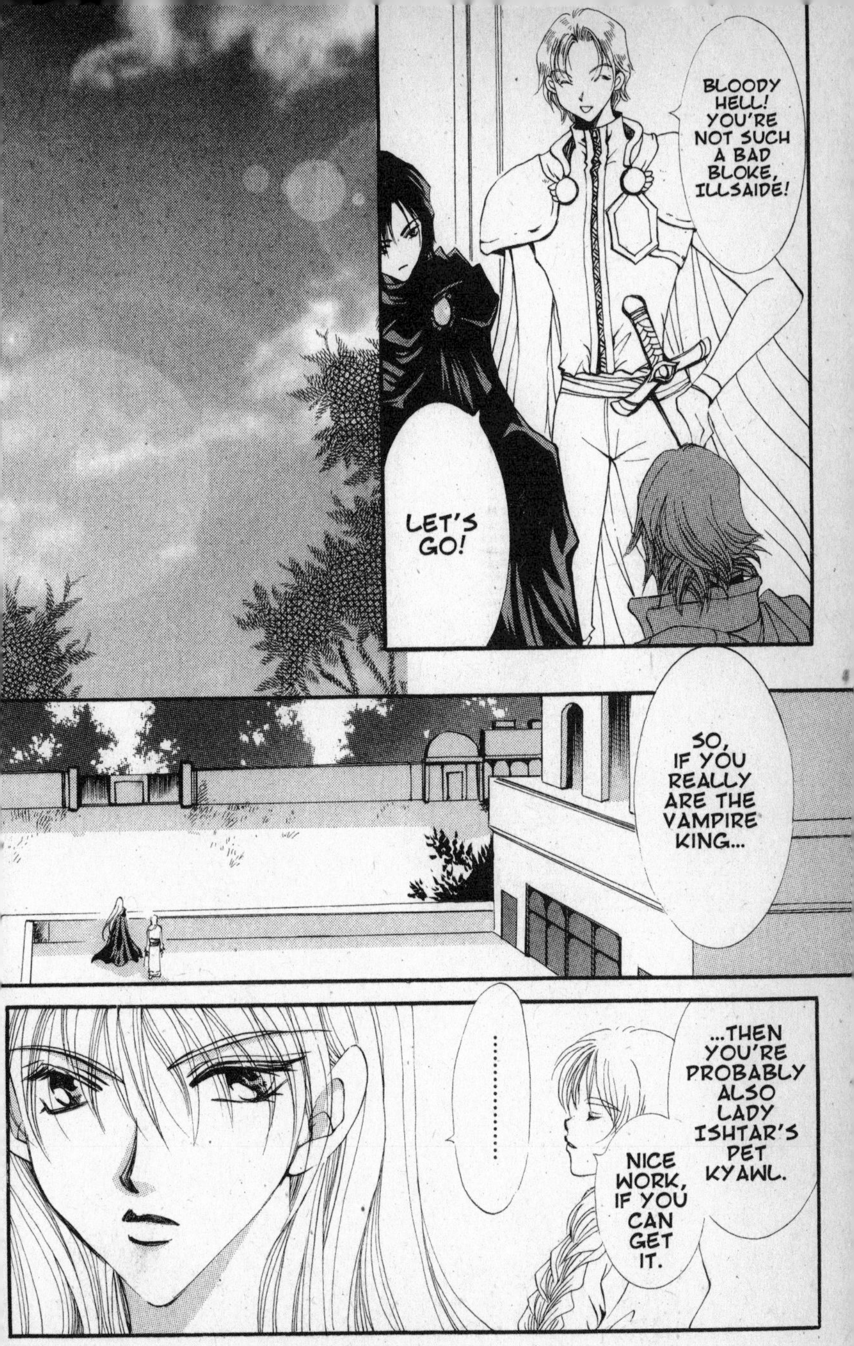
BLOODY HELL! YOU'RE NOT SUCH A BAD BLOKE, ILLSAIDE!
LET'S GO!
SO, IF YOU REALLY ARE THE VAMPIRE KING...
...THEN YOU'RE PROBABLY ALSO LADY ISHTAR'S PET KYAWL.
NICE WORK, IF YOU CAN GET IT.
......

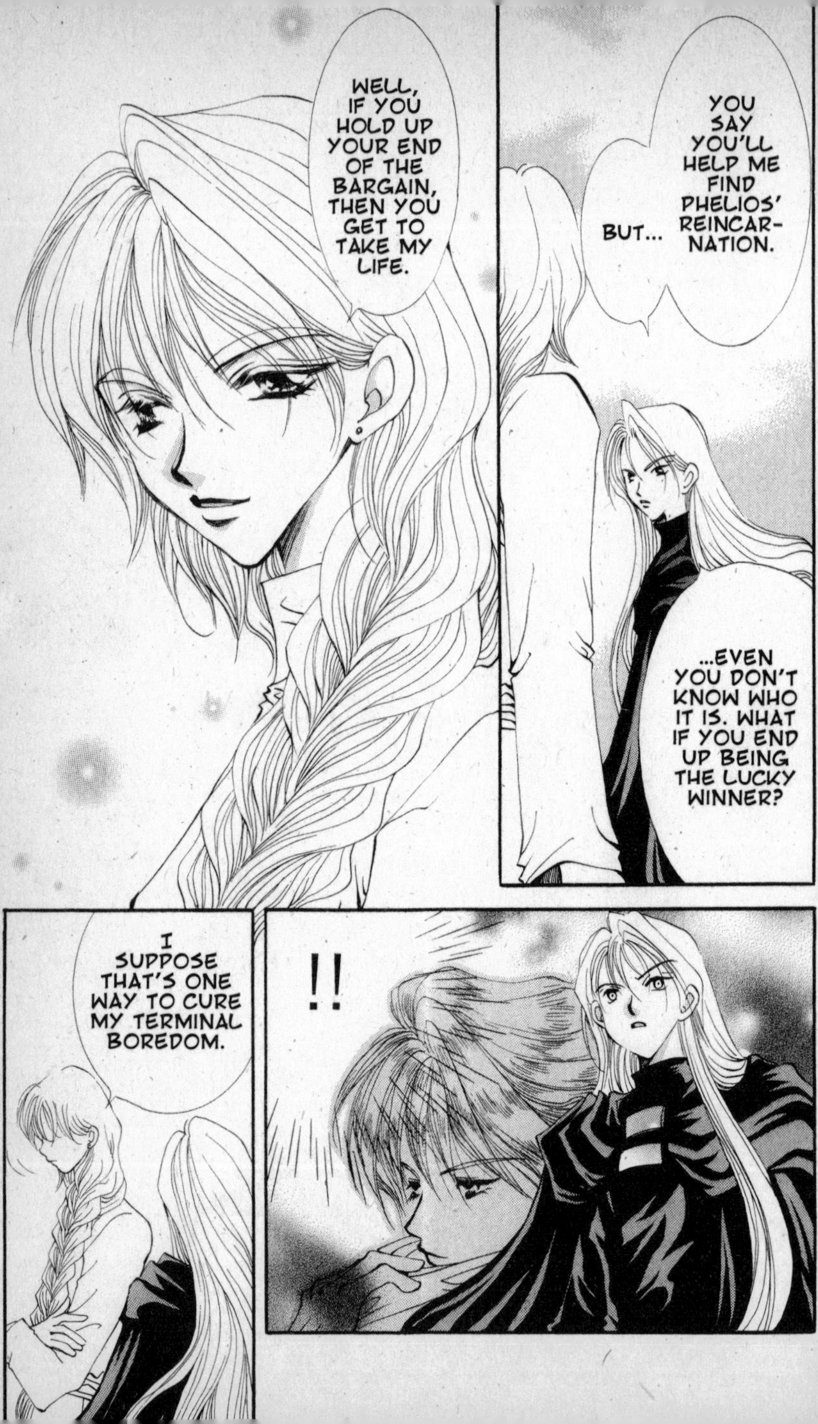
YOU SAY YOU'LL HELP ME FIND PHELIOS' REINCARNATION.
BUT...
...EVEN YOU DON'T KNOW WHO IT IS. WHAT IF YOU END UP BEING THE LUCKY WINNER?
WELL, IF YOU HOLD UP YOUR END OF THE BARGAIN, THEN YOU GET TO TAKE MY LIFE.
!!
I SUPPOSE THAT'S ONE WAY TO CURE MY TERMINAL BOREDOM.

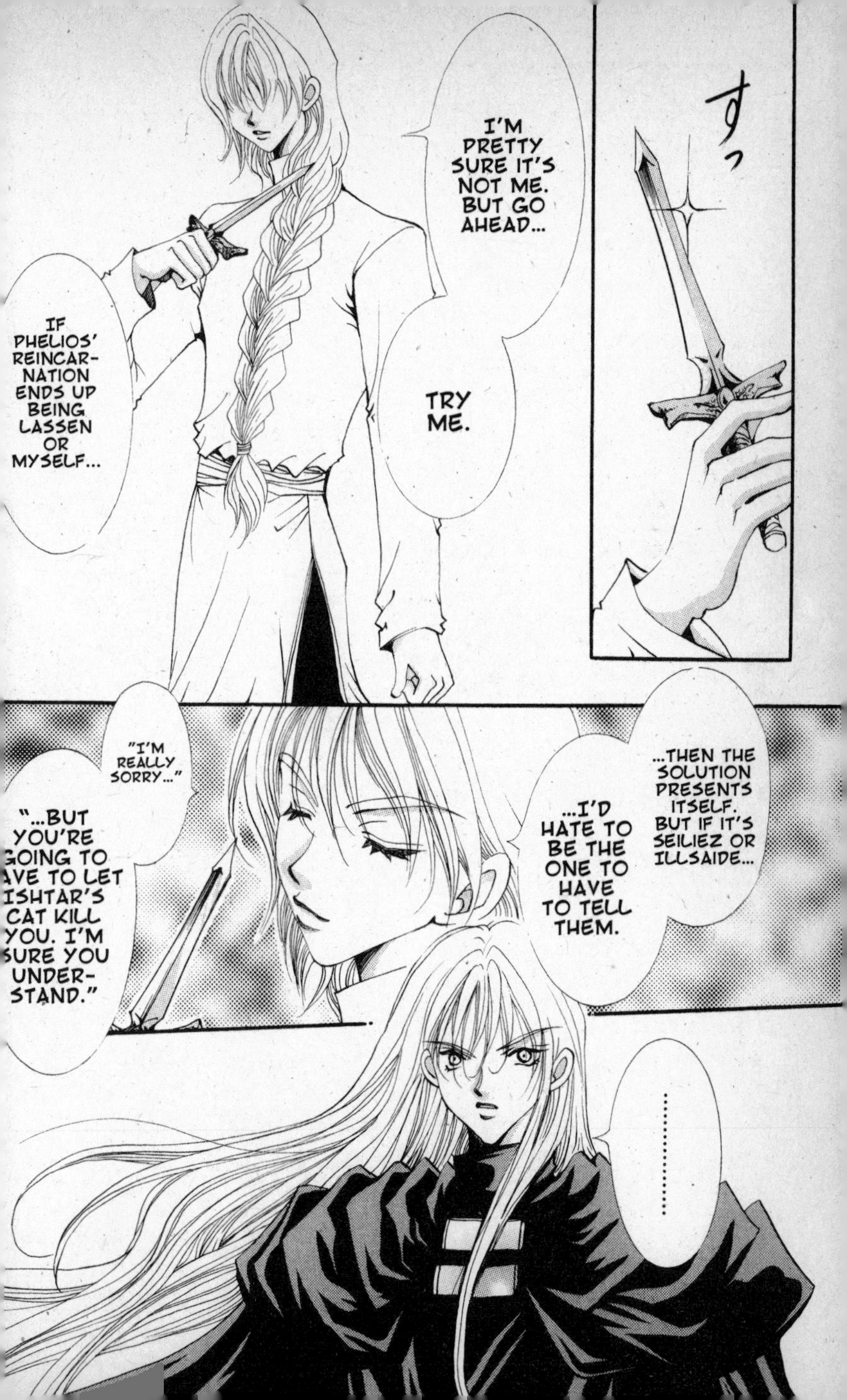
すっ
I'M PRETTY SURE IT'S NOT ME. BUT GO AHEAD...
TRY ME.
IF PHELIOS' REINCARNATION ENDS UP BEING LASSEN OR MYSELF...
...THEN THE SOLUTION PRESENTS ITSELF. BUT IF IT'S SEILIEZ OR ILLSAIDE...
...I'D HATE TO BE THE ONE TO HAVE TO TELL THEM.
"I'M REALLY SORRY..."
"...BUT YOU'RE GOING TO AVE TO LET ISHTAR'S CAT KILL YOU. I'M URE YOU UNDERSTAND."
......

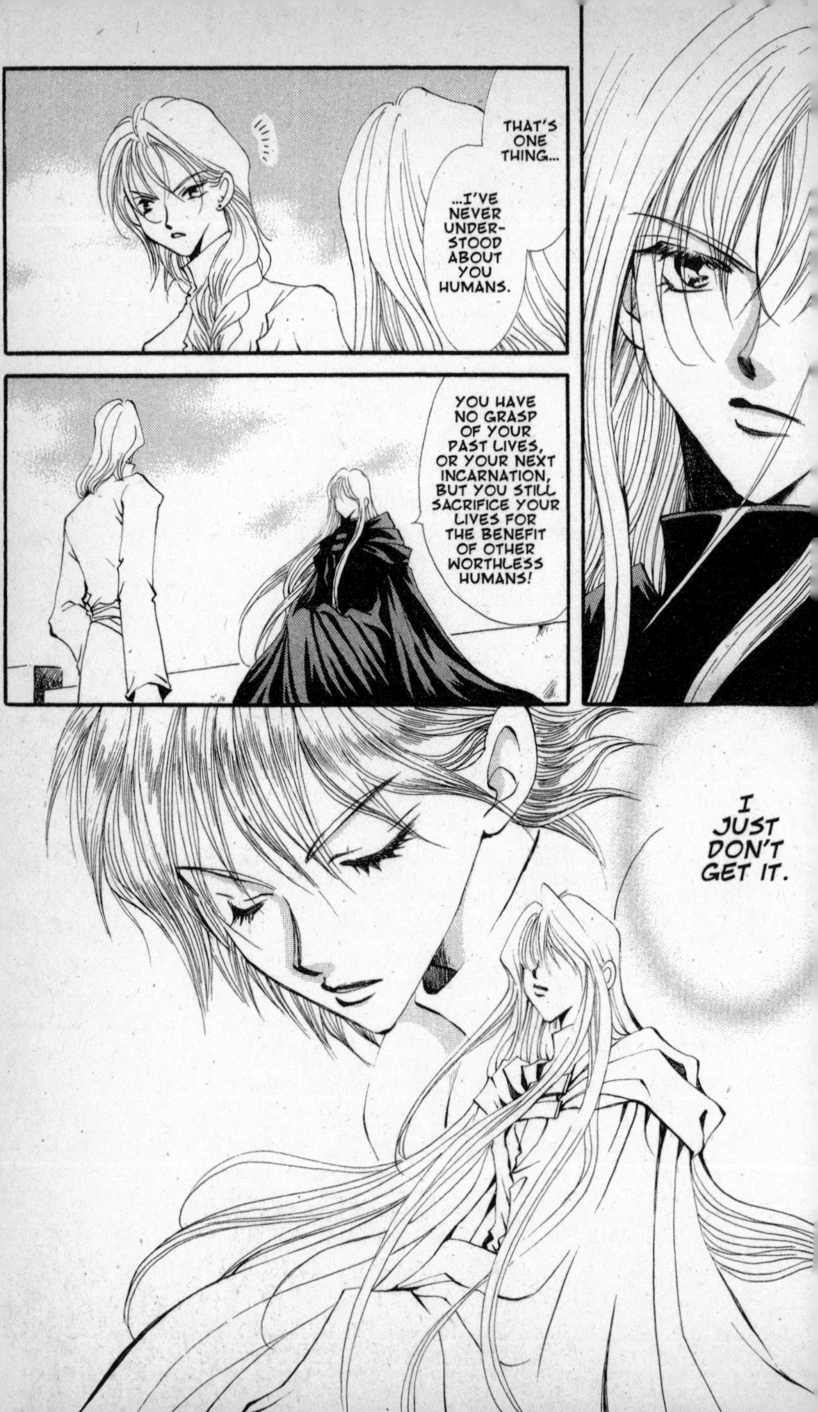
THAT'S ONE THING...
...I'VE NEVER UNDER-STOOD ABOUT YOU HUMANS.
YOU HAVE NO GRASP OF YOUR PAST LIVES, OR YOUR NEXT INCARNATION, BUT YOU STILL SACRIFICE YOUR LIVES FOR THE BENEFIT OF OTHER WORTHLESS HUMANS!
I JUST DON'T GET IT.

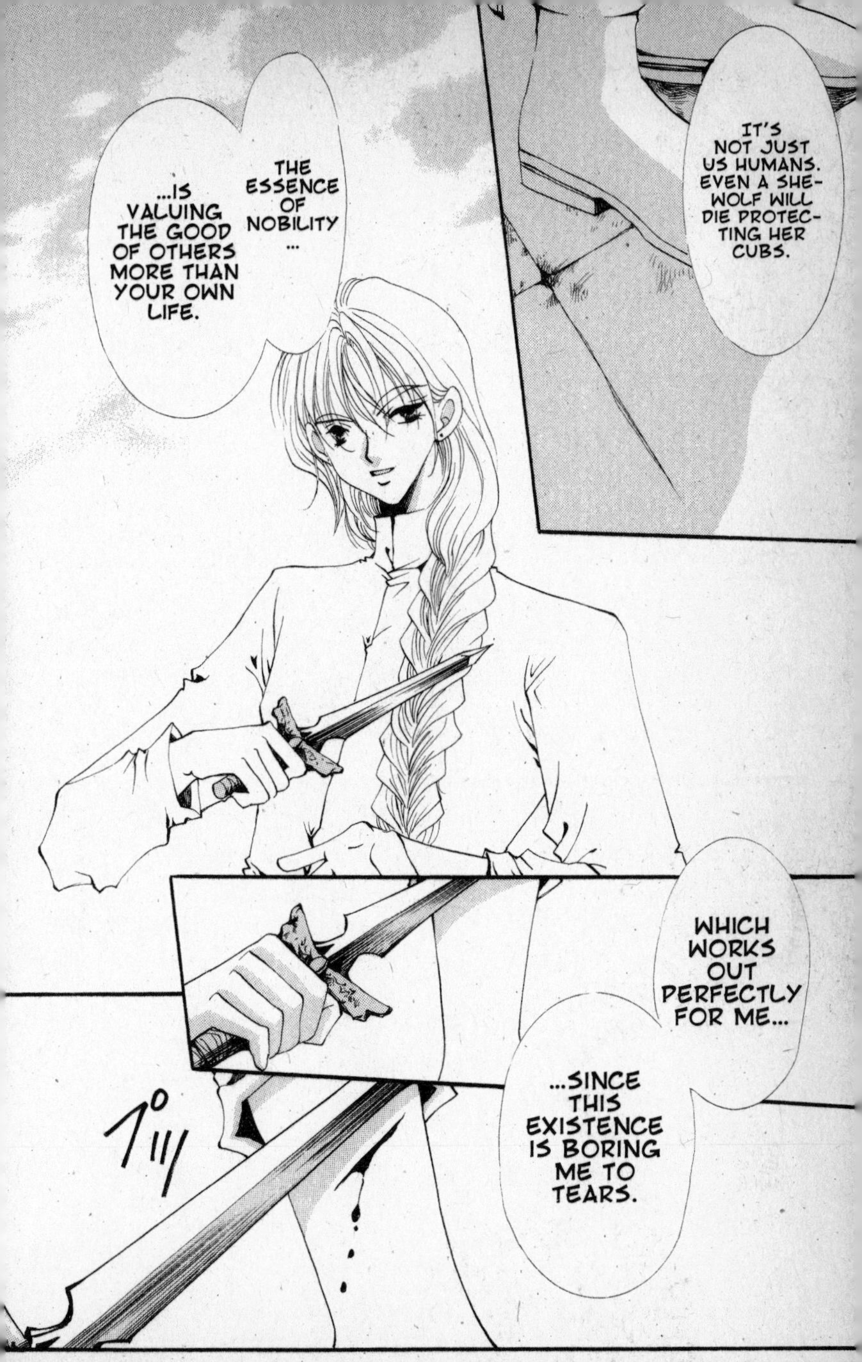
IT'S NOT JUST US HUMANS. EVEN A SHE-WOLF WILL DIE PROTECTING HER CUBS.
THE ESSENCE OF NOBILITY...
...IS VALUING THE GOOD OF OTHERS MORE THAN YOUR OWN LIFE.
WHICH WORKS OUT PERFECTLY FOR ME...
...SINCE THIS EXISTENCE IS BORING ME TO TEARS.
プツ

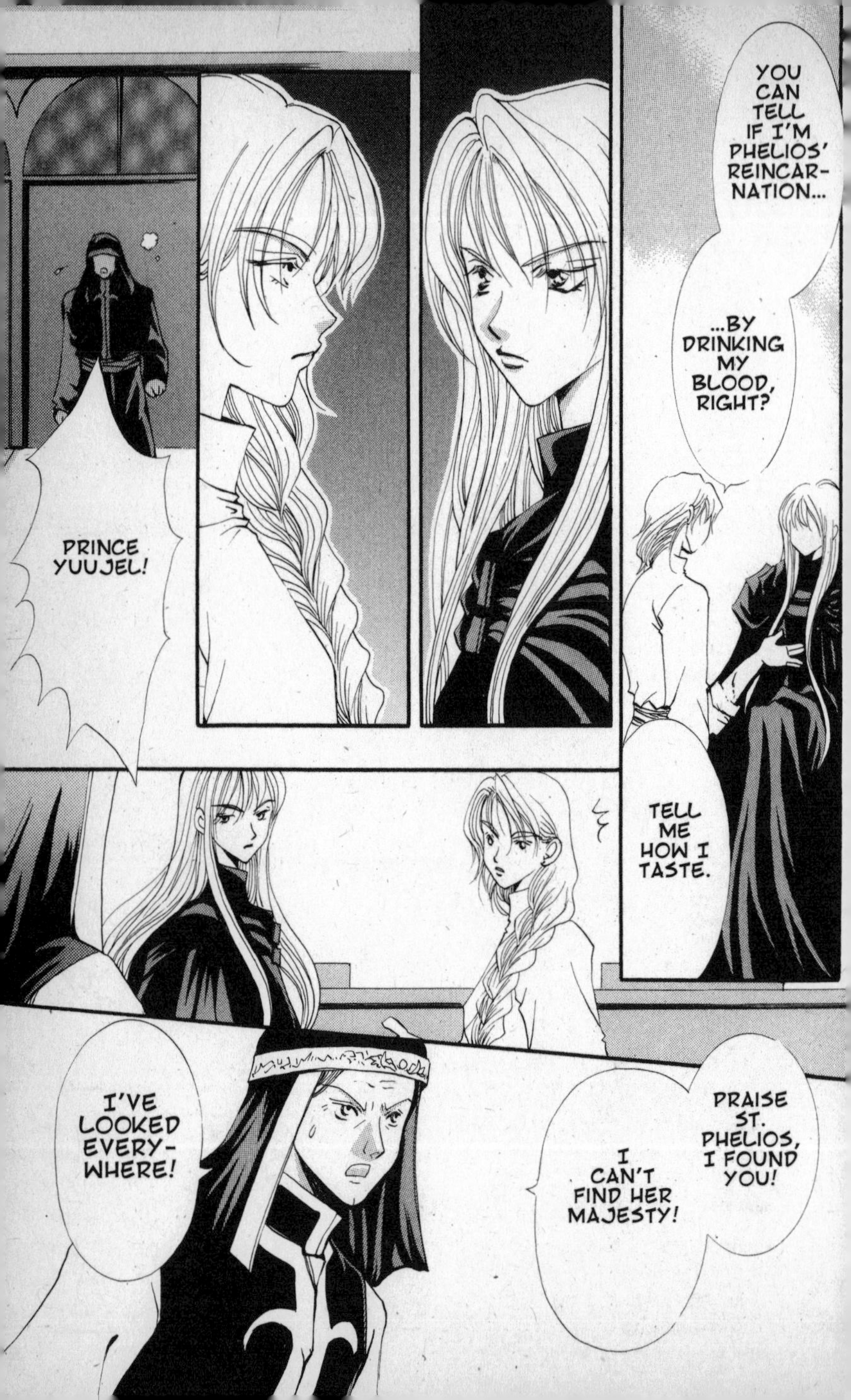
YOU CAN TELL IF I'M PHELIOS' REINCARNATION...
...BY DRINKING MY BLOOD, RIGHT?
TELL ME HOW I TASTE.
PRINCE YUUJEL!
PRAISE ST. PHELIOS, I FOUND YOU!
I CAN'T FIND HER MAJESTY!
I'VE LOOKED EVERYWHERE!

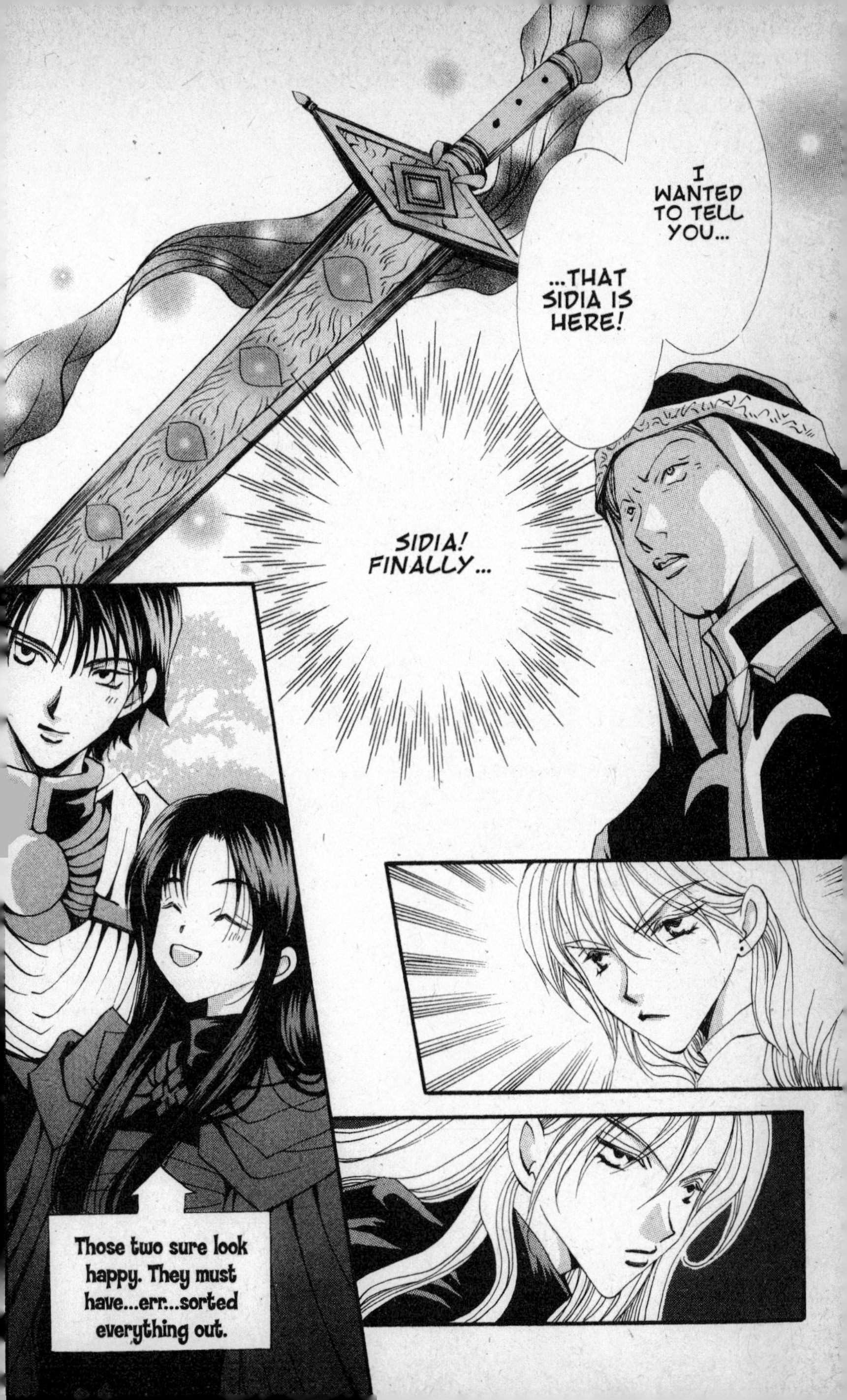
I WANTED TO TELL YOU...
...THAT SIDIA IS HERE!
SIDIA! FINALLY...
Those two sure look happy. They must have...err...sorted everything out.

北領篇
Act.13

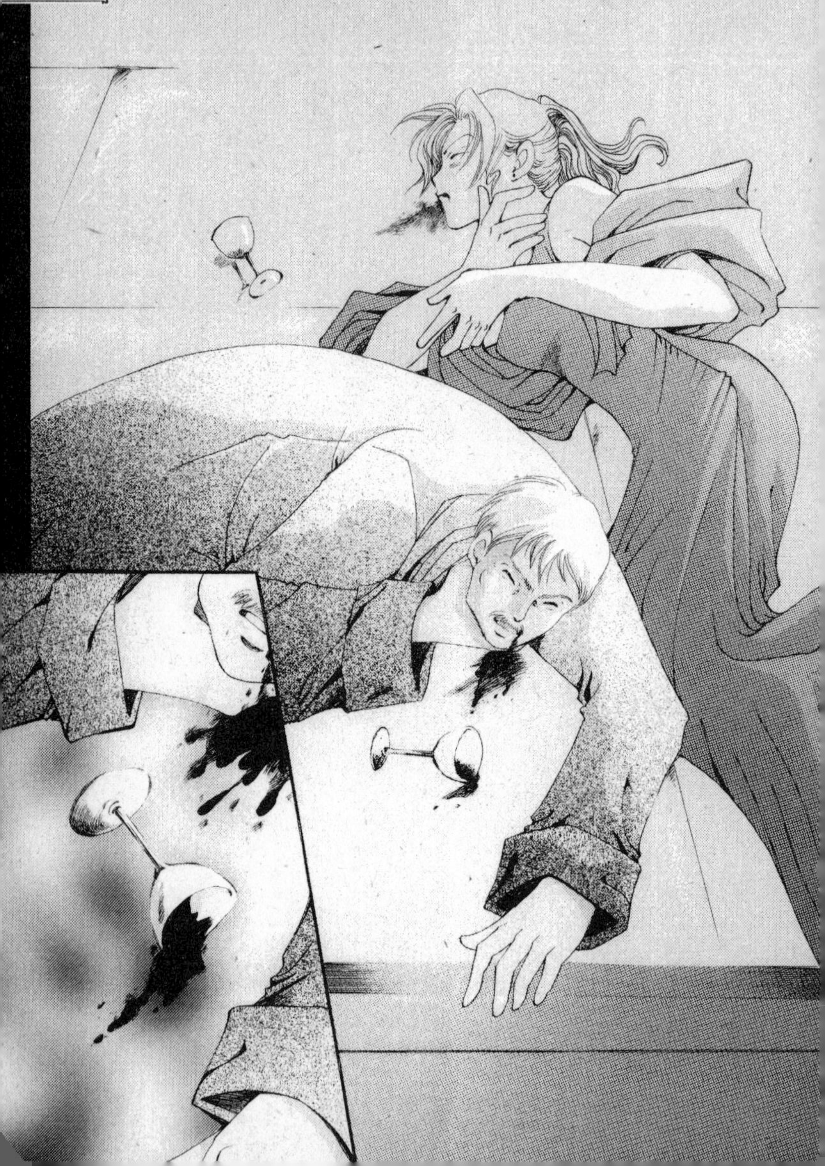

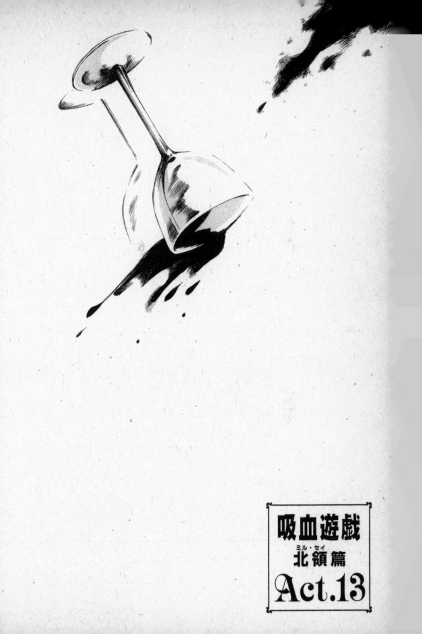

吸血遊戯
北領篇
ミル・セイ
Act.13

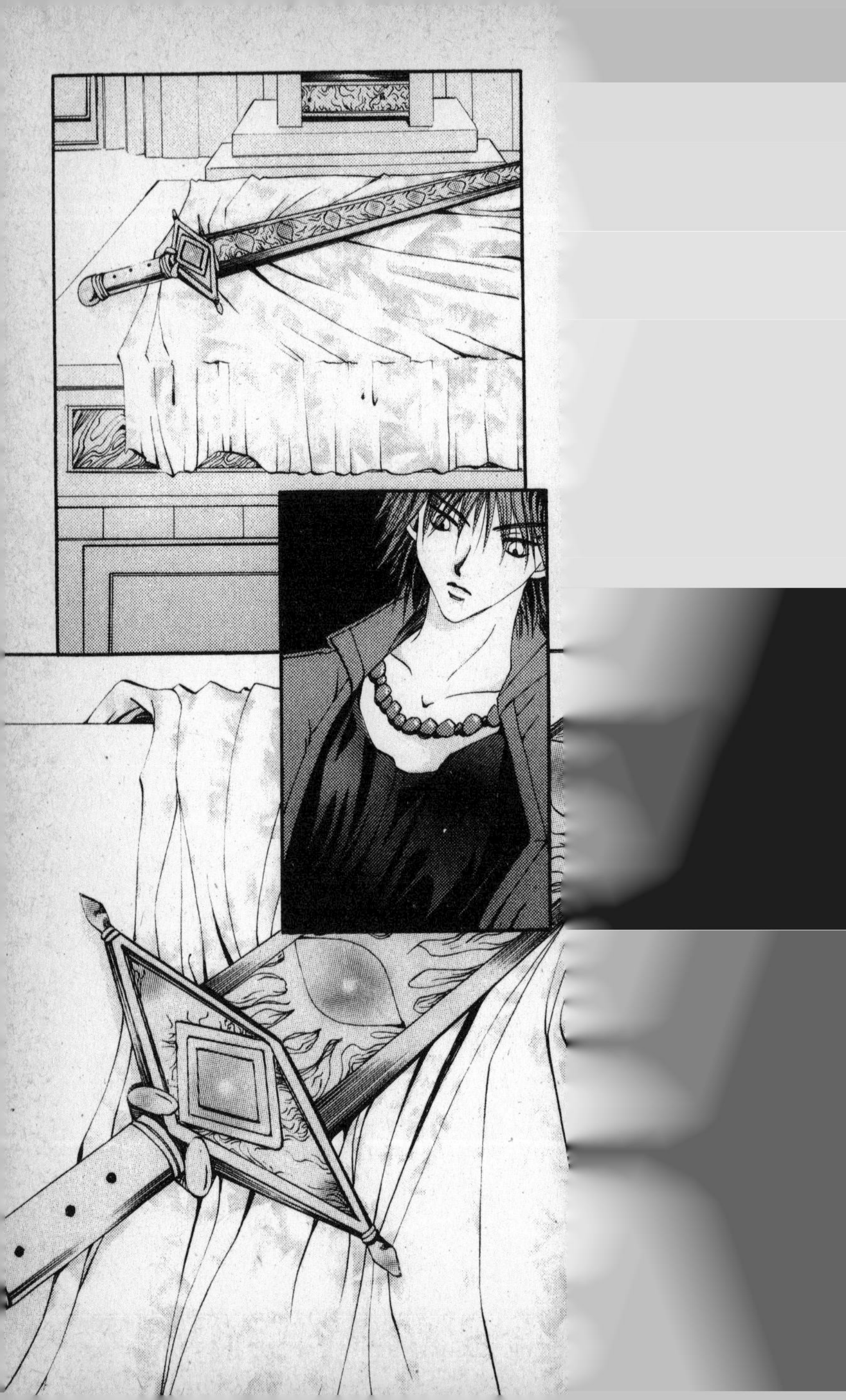

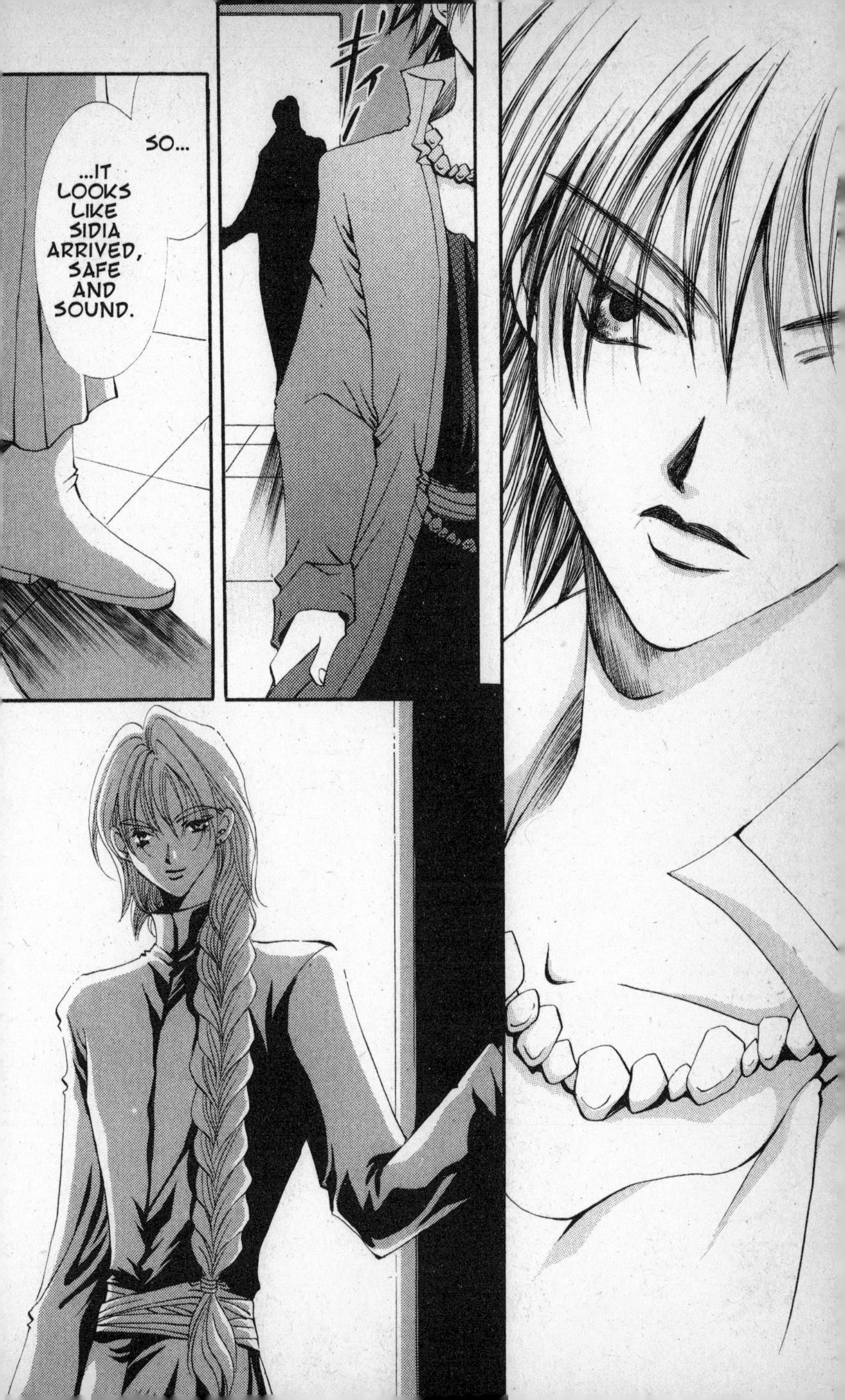
SO...
...IT LOOKS LIKE SIDIA ARRIVED, SAFE AND SOUND.

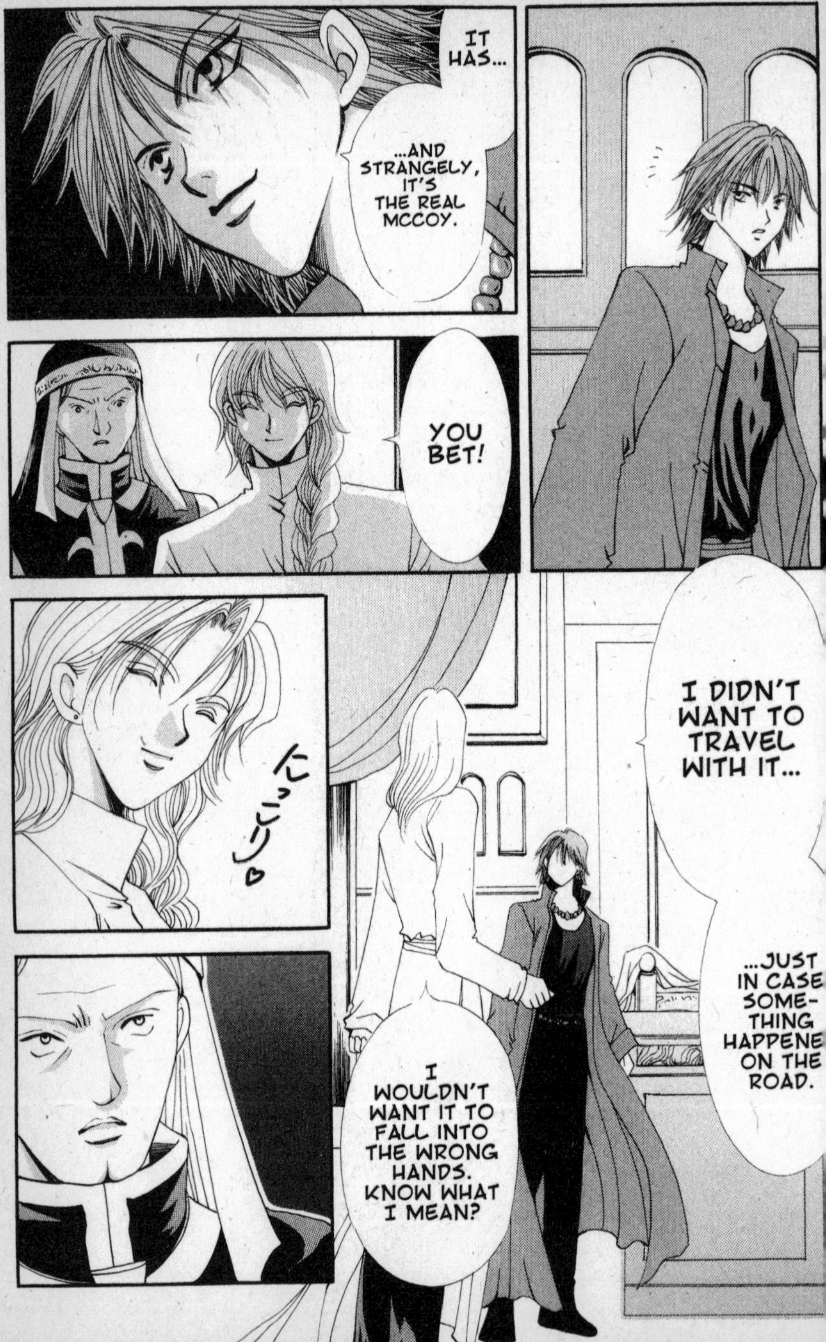
IT HAS...
...AND STRANGELY, IT'S THE REAL MCCOY.
YOU BET!
I DIDN'T WANT TO TRAVEL WITH IT...
...JUST IN CASE SOME-THING HAPPENE ON THE ROAD.
I WOULDN'T WANT IT TO FALL INTO THE WRONG HANDS. KNOW WHAT I MEAN?
にっこり♥

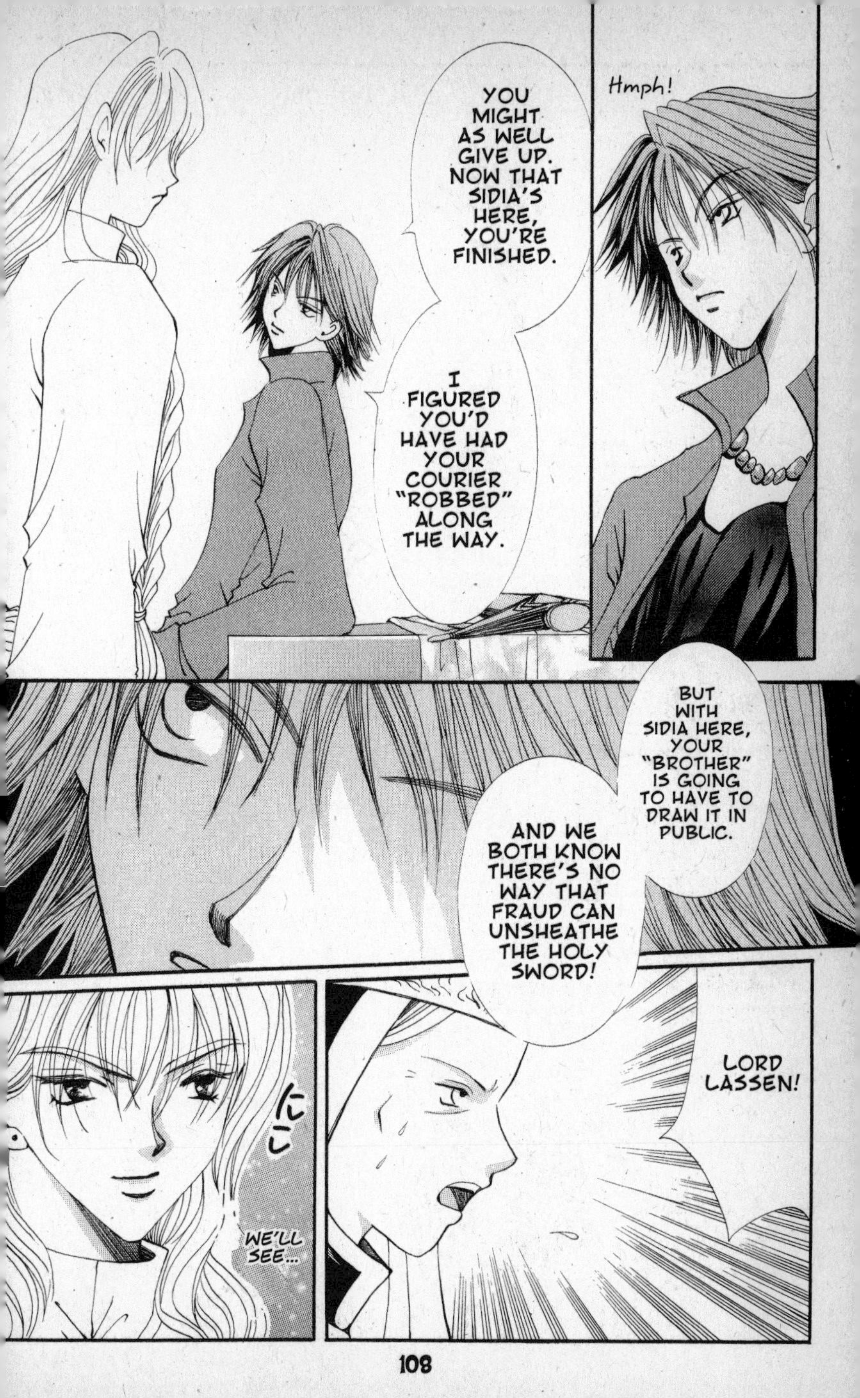
Hmph!
YOU MIGHT AS WELL GIVE UP. NOW THAT SIDIA'S HERE, YOU'RE FINISHED.
I FIGURED YOU'D HAVE HAD YOUR COURIER "ROBBED" ALONG THE WAY.
BUT WITH SIDIA HERE, YOUR "BROTHER" IS GOING TO HAVE TO DRAW IT IN PUBLIC.
AND WE BOTH KNOW THERE'S NO WAY THAT FRAUD CAN UNSHEATHE THE HOLY SWORD!
LORD LASSEN!
にこ
WE'LL SEE...

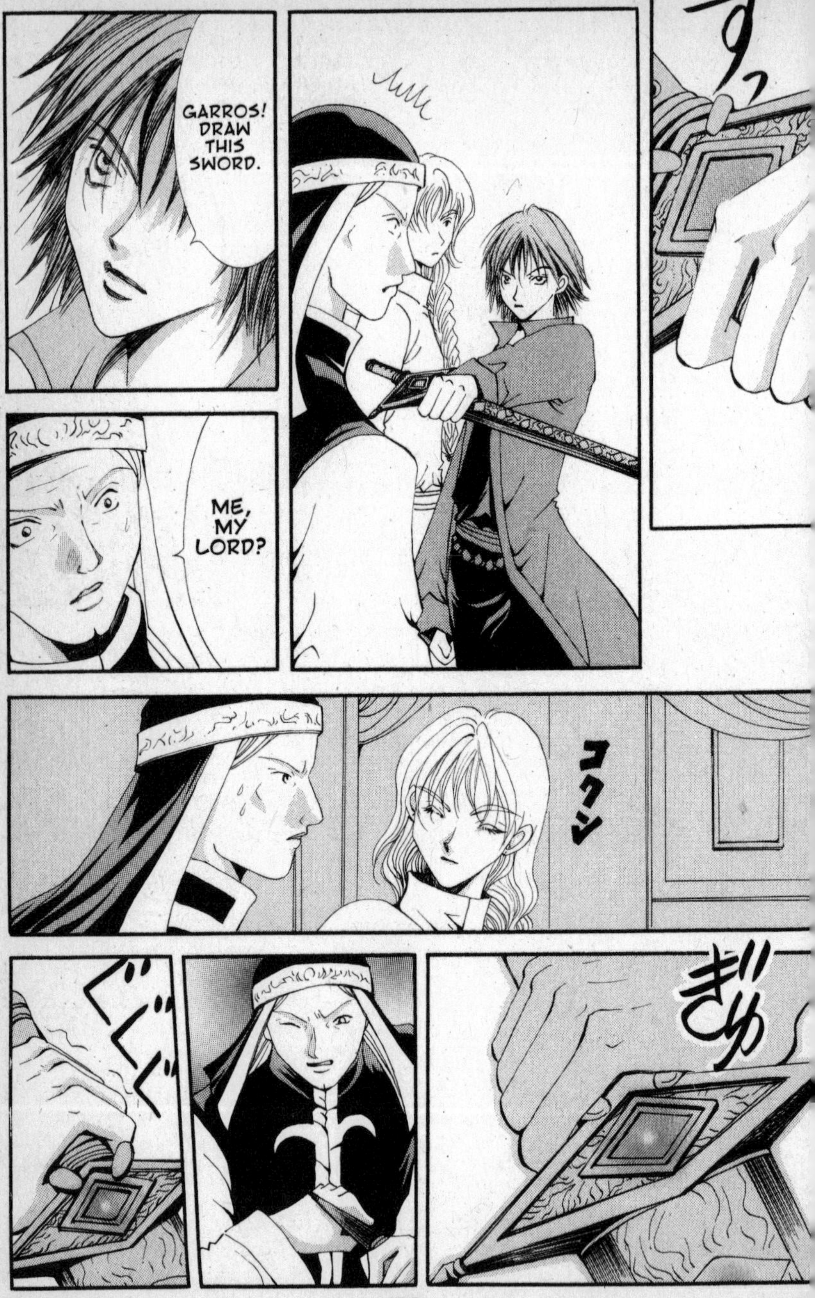
すっ
GARROS! DRAW THIS SWORD.
ME, MY LORD?
コクン
ぎゅ
ぐぐぐ

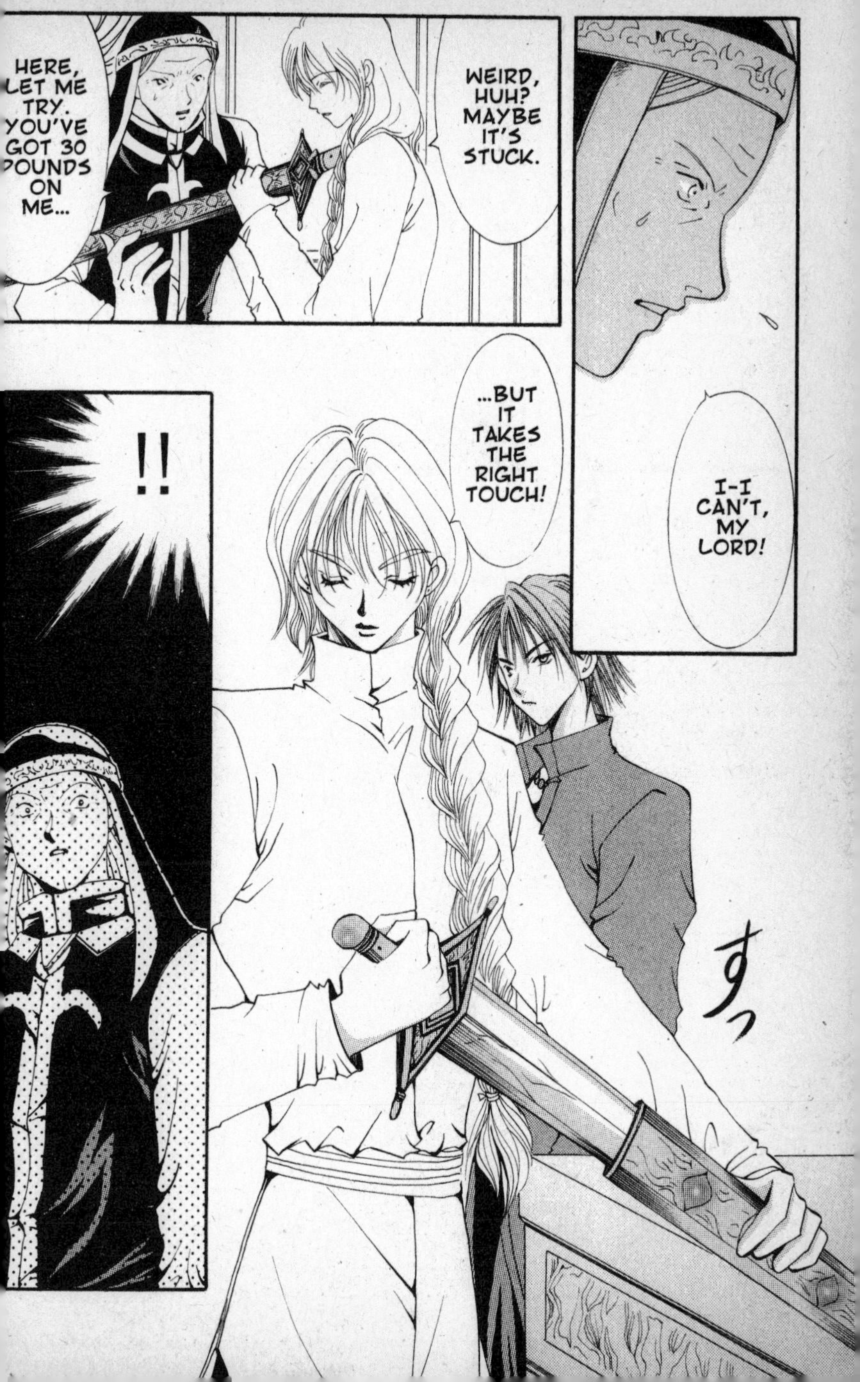
I-I CAN'T, MY LORD!
WEIRD, HUH? MAYBE IT'S STUCK.
HERE, LET ME TRY. YOU'VE GOT 30 POUNDS ON ME...
...BUT IT TAKES THE RIGHT TOUCH!
すっ
!!

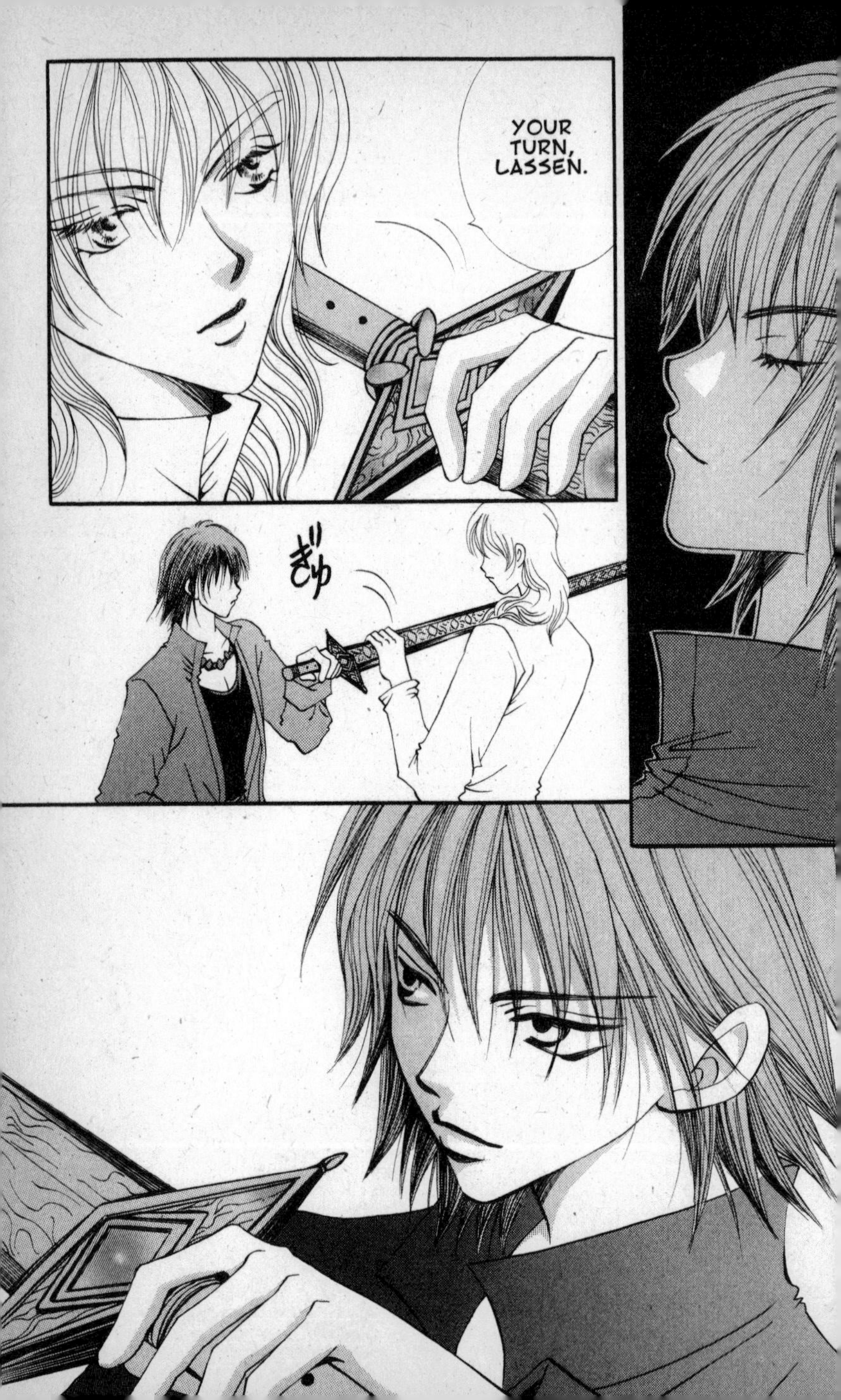
YOUR TURN, LASSEN.
ぎゅ

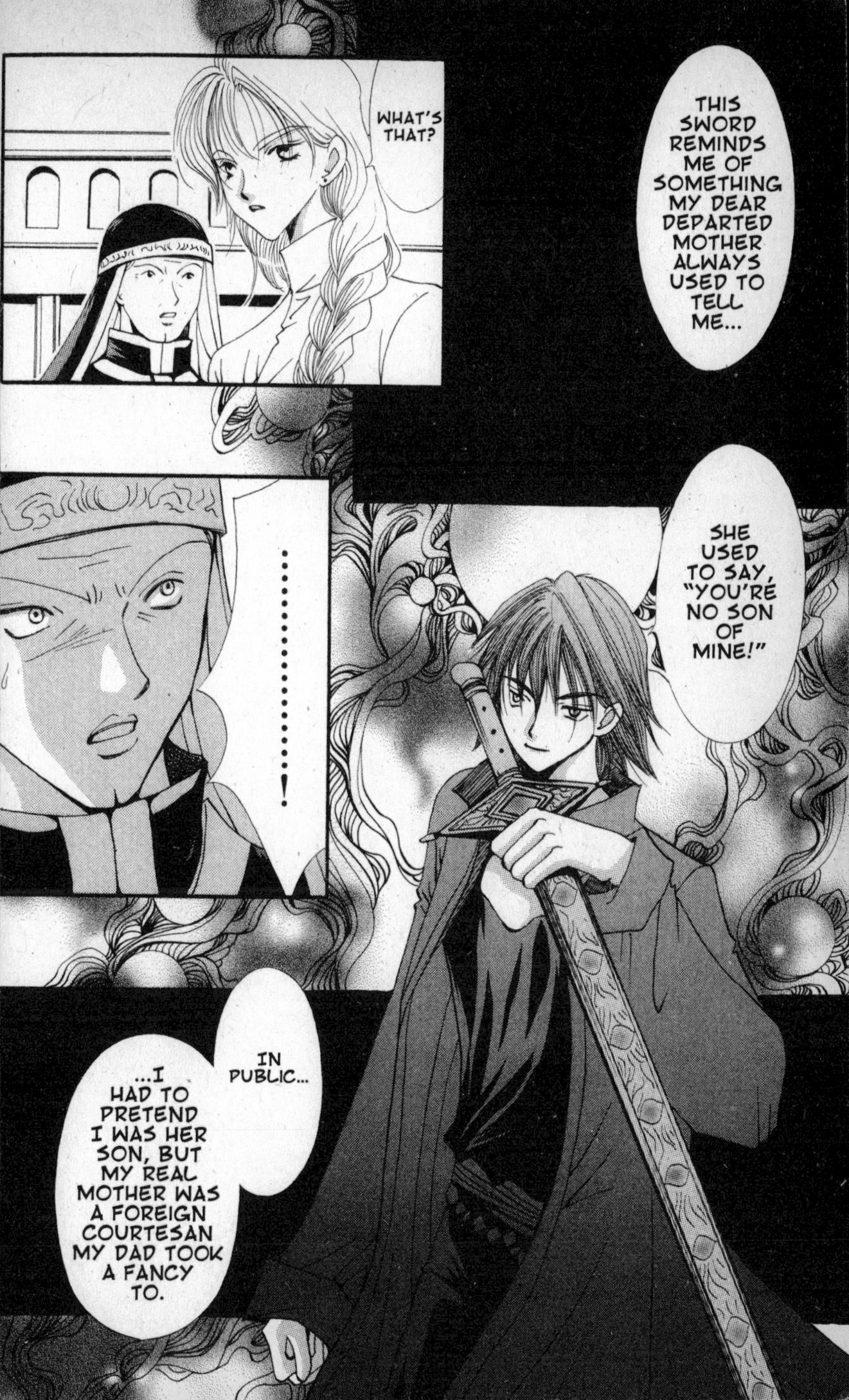
THIS SWORD REMINDS ME OF SOMETHING MY DEAR DEPARTED MOTHER ALWAYS USED TO TELL ME...
WHAT'S THAT?
SHE USED TO SAY, "YOU'RE NO SON OF MINE!"
......!
IN PUBLIC...
...I HAD TO PRETEND I WAS HER SON, BUT MY REAL MOTHER WAS A FOREIGN COURTESAN MY DAD TOOK A FANCY TO.

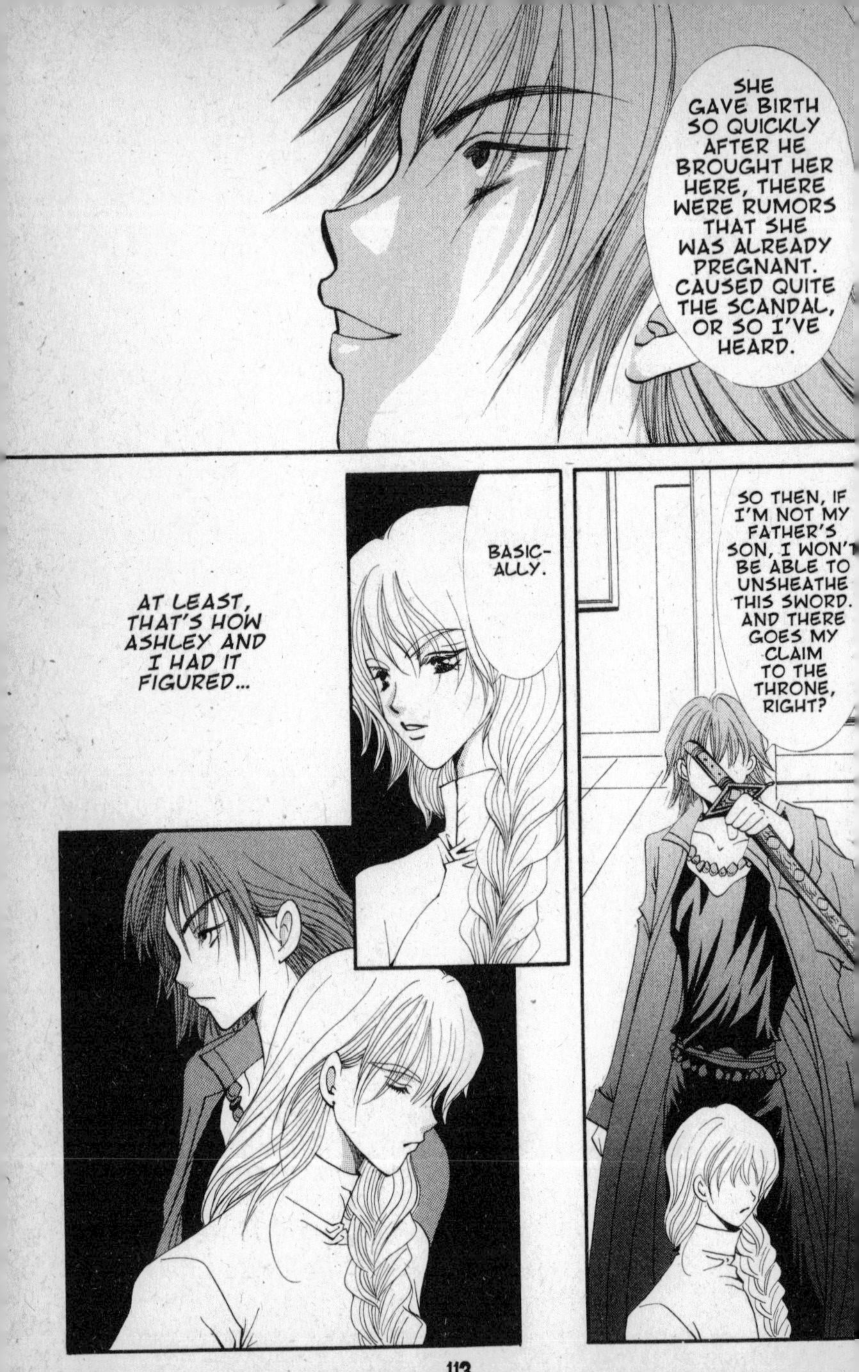
SHE GAVE BIRTH SO QUICKLY AFTER HE BROUGHT HER HERE, THERE WERE RUMORS THAT SHE WAS ALREADY PREGNANT. CAUSED QUITE THE SCANDAL, OR SO I'VE HEARD.
SO THEN, IF I'M NOT MY FATHER'S SON, I WON'T BE ABLE TO UNSHEATHE THIS SWORD. AND THERE GOES MY CLAIM TO THE THRONE, RIGHT?
BASIC-ALLY.
AT LEAST, THAT'S HOW ASHLEY AND I HAD IT FIGURED...

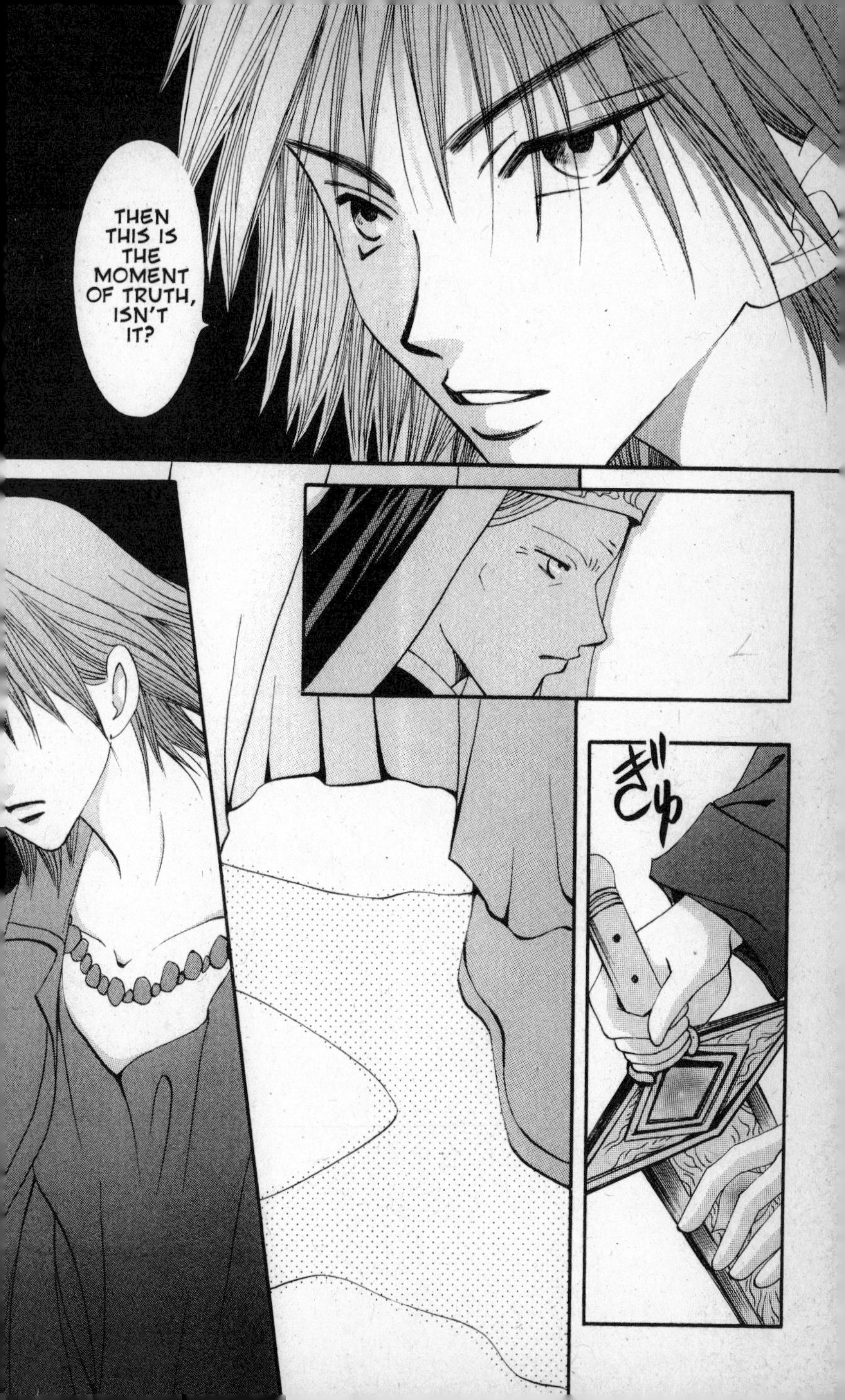

THEN THIS IS THE MOMENT OF TRUTH, ISN'T IT?
ぎゅ

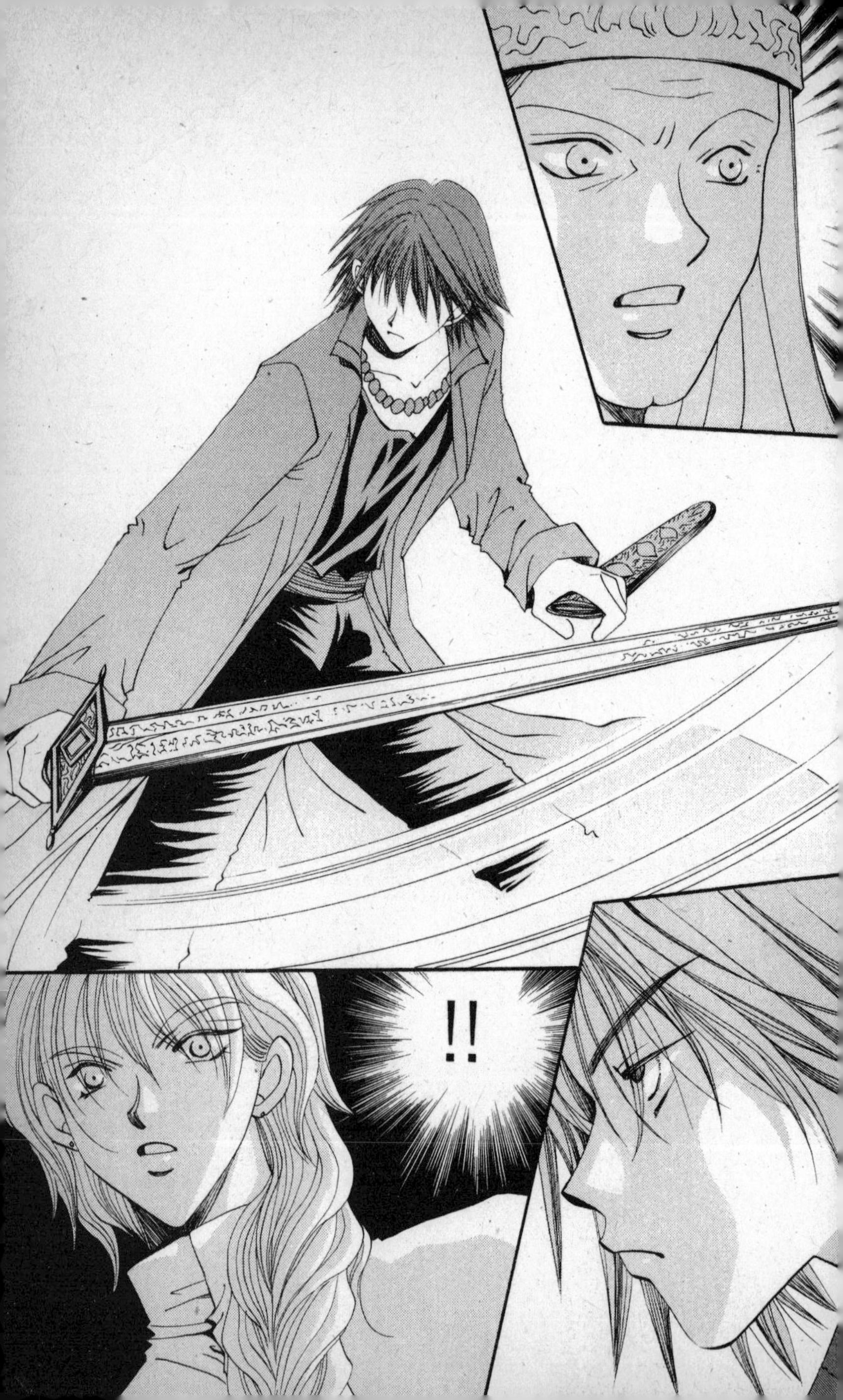
!!

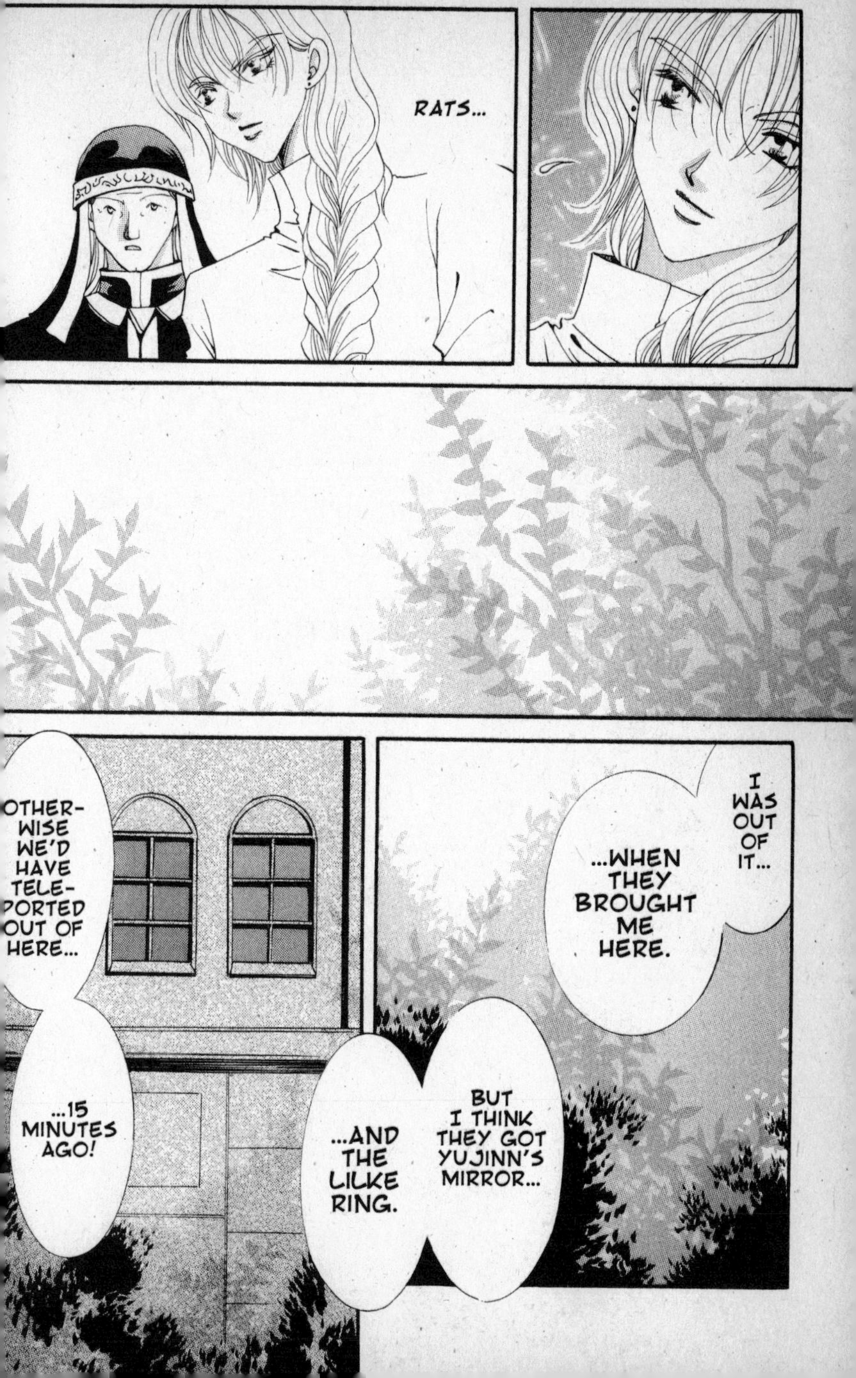
RATS...
I WAS OUT OF IT...
...WHEN THEY BROUGHT ME HERE.
BUT I THINK THEY GOT YUJINN'S MIRROR...
...AND THE LILKE RING.
OTHER-WISE WE'D HAVE TELE-PORTED OUT OF HERE...
...15 MINUTES AGO!

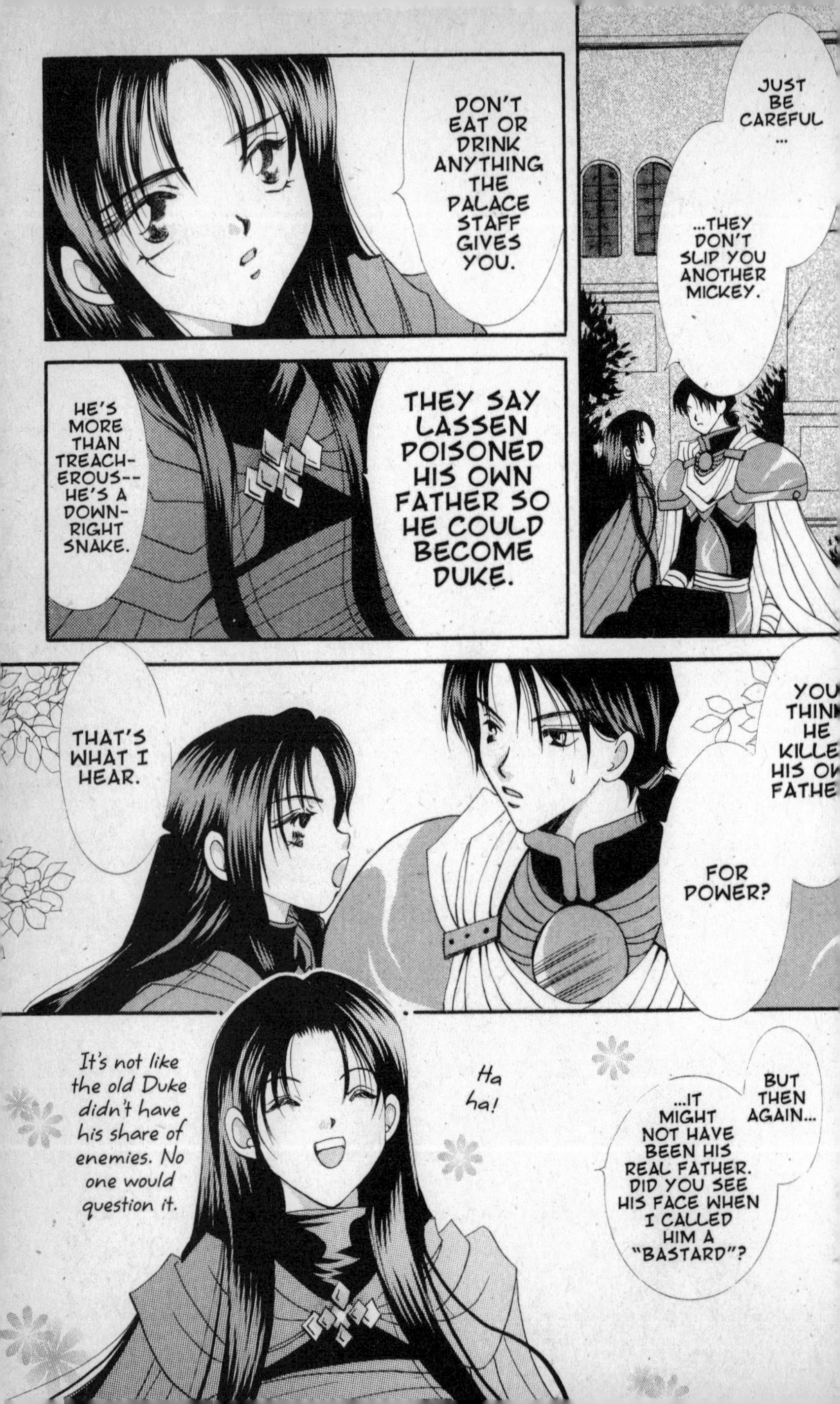
JUST BE CAREFUL ...
...THEY DON'T SLIP YOU ANOTHER MICKEY.
DON'T EAT OR DRINK ANYTHING THE PALACE STAFF GIVES YOU.
THEY SAY LASSEN POISONED HIS OWN FATHER SO HE COULD BECOME DUKE.
HE'S MORE THAN TREACH-EROUS-- HE'S A DOWN-RIGHT SNAKE.
YOU THIN HE KILLE HIS OW FATHE
FOR POWER?
THAT'S WHAT I HEAR.
BUT THEN AGAIN...
...IT MIGHT NOT HAVE BEEN HIS REAL FATHER. DID YOU SEE HIS FACE WHEN I CALLED HIM A "BASTARD"?
Ha ha!
It's not like the old Duke didn't have his share of enemies. No one would question it.

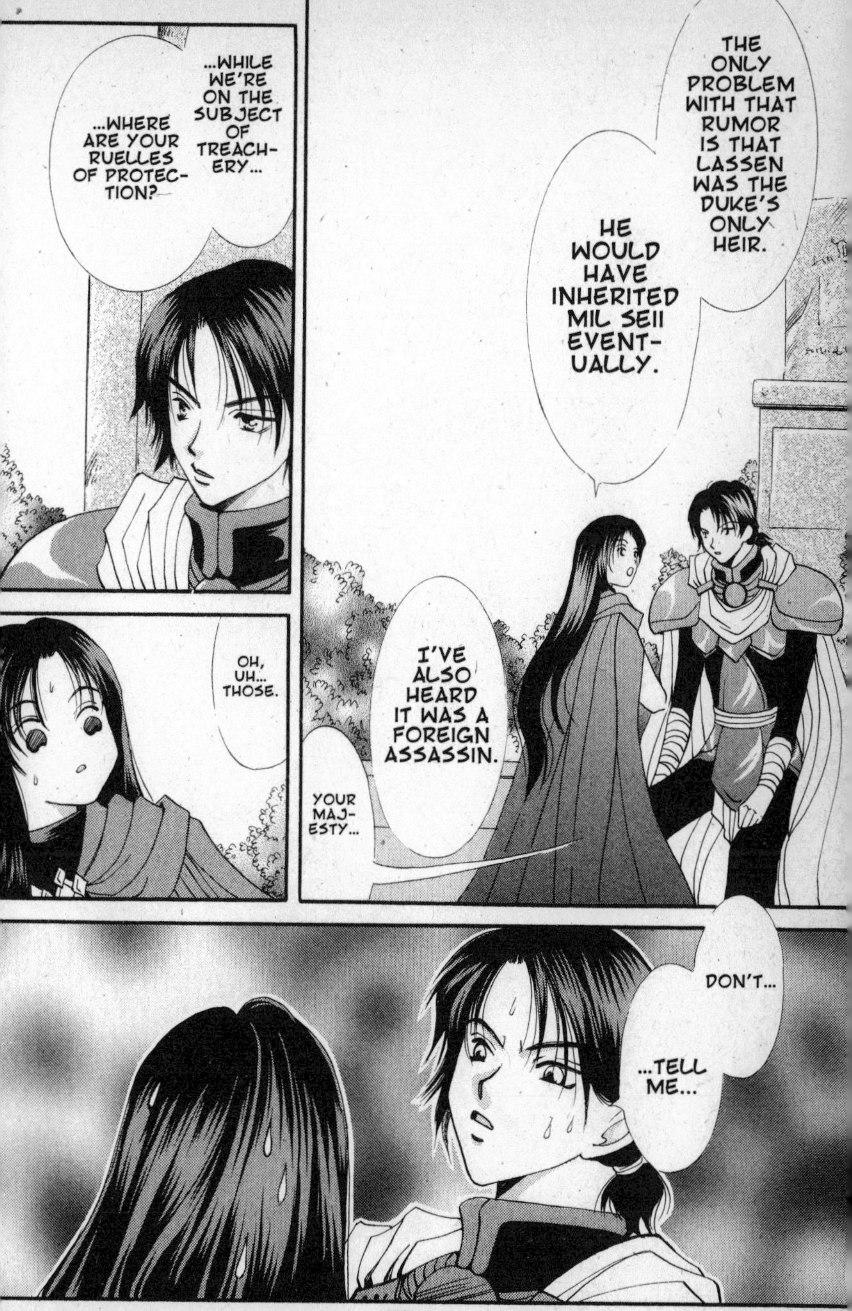
THE ONLY PROBLEM WITH THAT RUMOR IS THAT LASSEN WAS THE DUKE'S ONLY HEIR.
HE WOULD HAVE INHERITED MIL SEII EVENT-UALLY.
I'VE ALSO HEARD IT WAS A FOREIGN ASSASSIN.
YOUR MAJ-ESTY...
...WHILE WE'RE ON THE SUBJECT OF TREACH-ERY...
...WHERE ARE YOUR RUELLES OF PROTEC-TION?
OH, UH... THOSE.
DON'T...
...TELL ME...

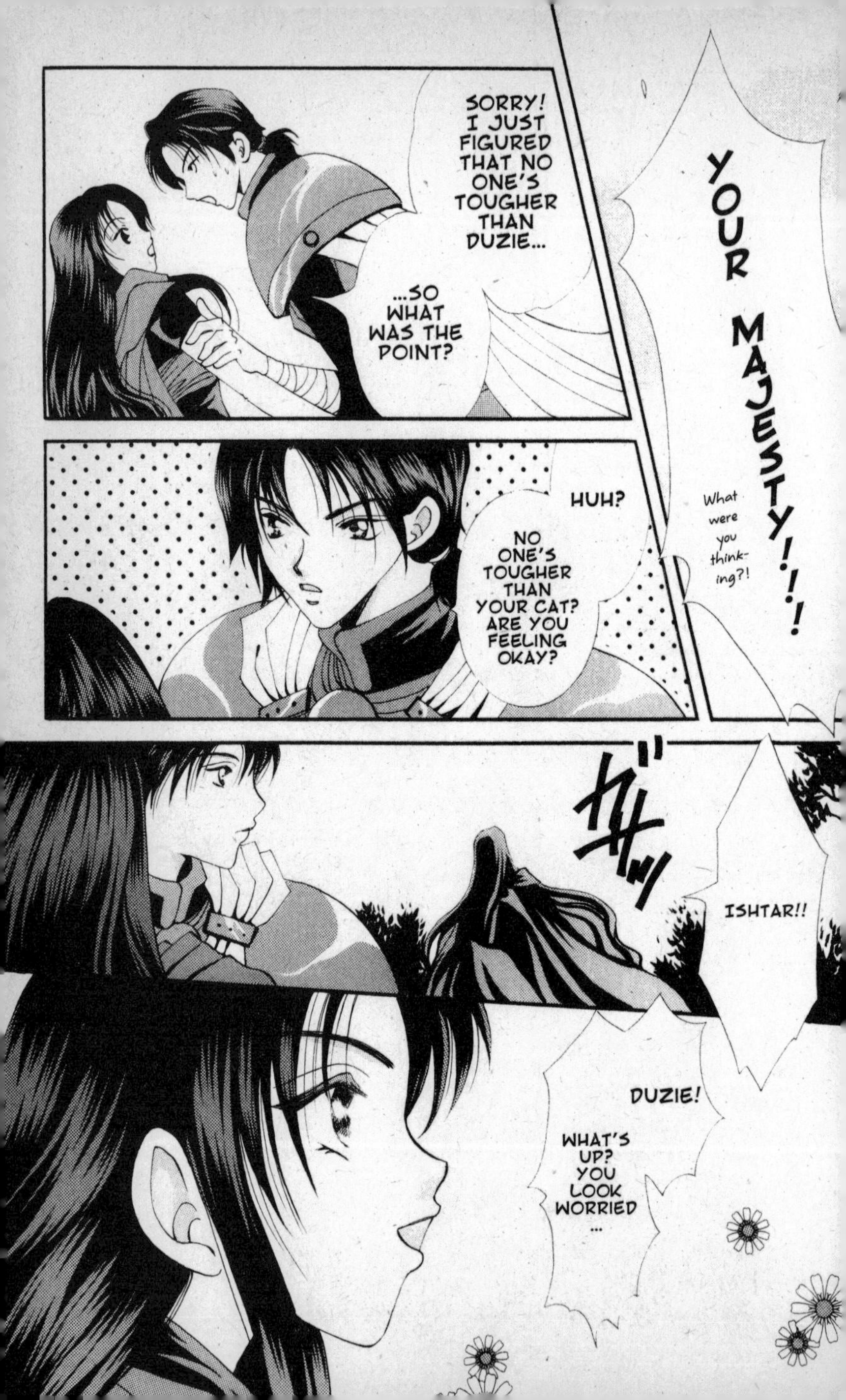
YOUR MAJESTY!!!
What were you thinking?!
SORRY! I JUST FIGURED THAT NO ONE'S TOUGHER THAN DUZIE...
...SO WHAT WAS THE POINT?
HUH?
NO ONE'S TOUGHER THAN YOUR CAT? ARE YOU FEELING OKAY?
ガサッ
ISHTAR!!
DUZIE!
WHAT'S UP? YOU LOOK WORRIED ...

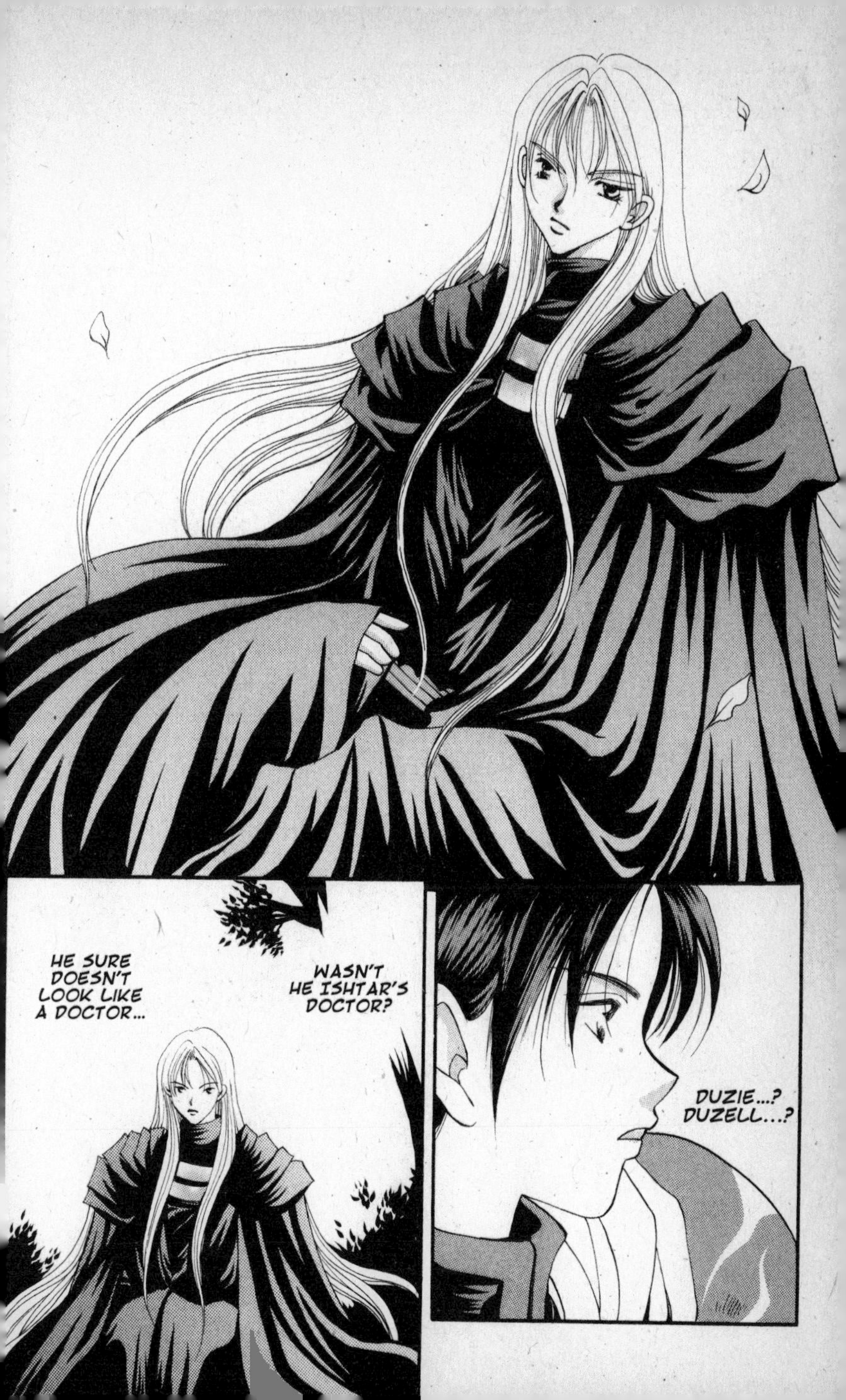
DUZIE...? DUZELL...?
WASN'T HE ISHTAR'S DOCTOR?
HE SURE DOESN'T LOOK LIKE A DOCTOR...

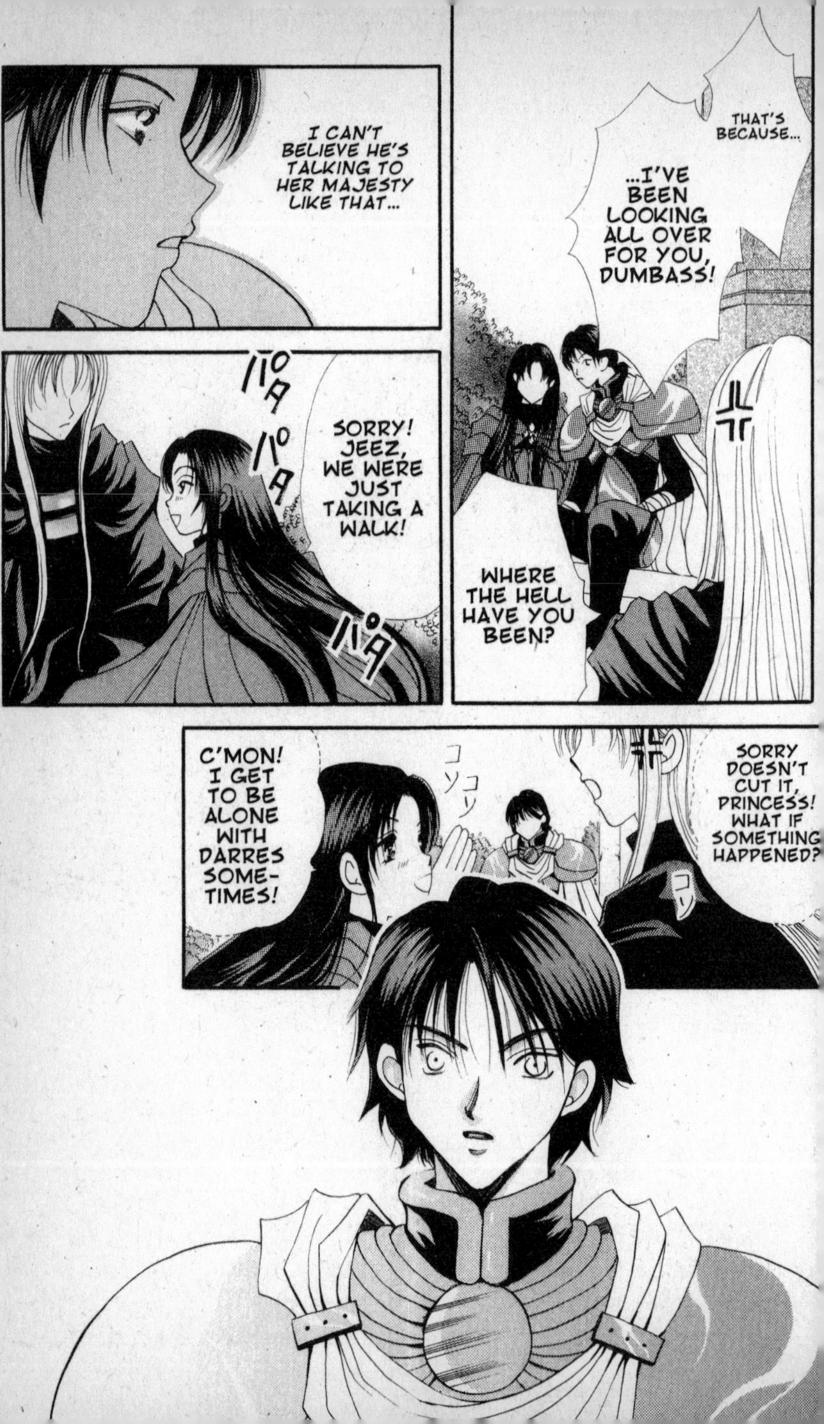
THAT'S BECAUSE...
...I'VE BEEN LOOKING ALL OVER FOR YOU, DUMBASS!
WHERE THE HELL HAVE YOU BEEN?
I CAN'T BELIEVE HE'S TALKING TO HER MAJESTY LIKE THAT...
パタ
パタ
SORRY! JEEZ, WE WERE JUST TAKING A WALK!
パタ
SORRY DOESN'T CUT IT, PRINCESS! WHAT IF SOMETHING HAPPENED?
コソコソ
C'MON! I GET TO BE ALONE WITH DARRES SOME-TIMES!

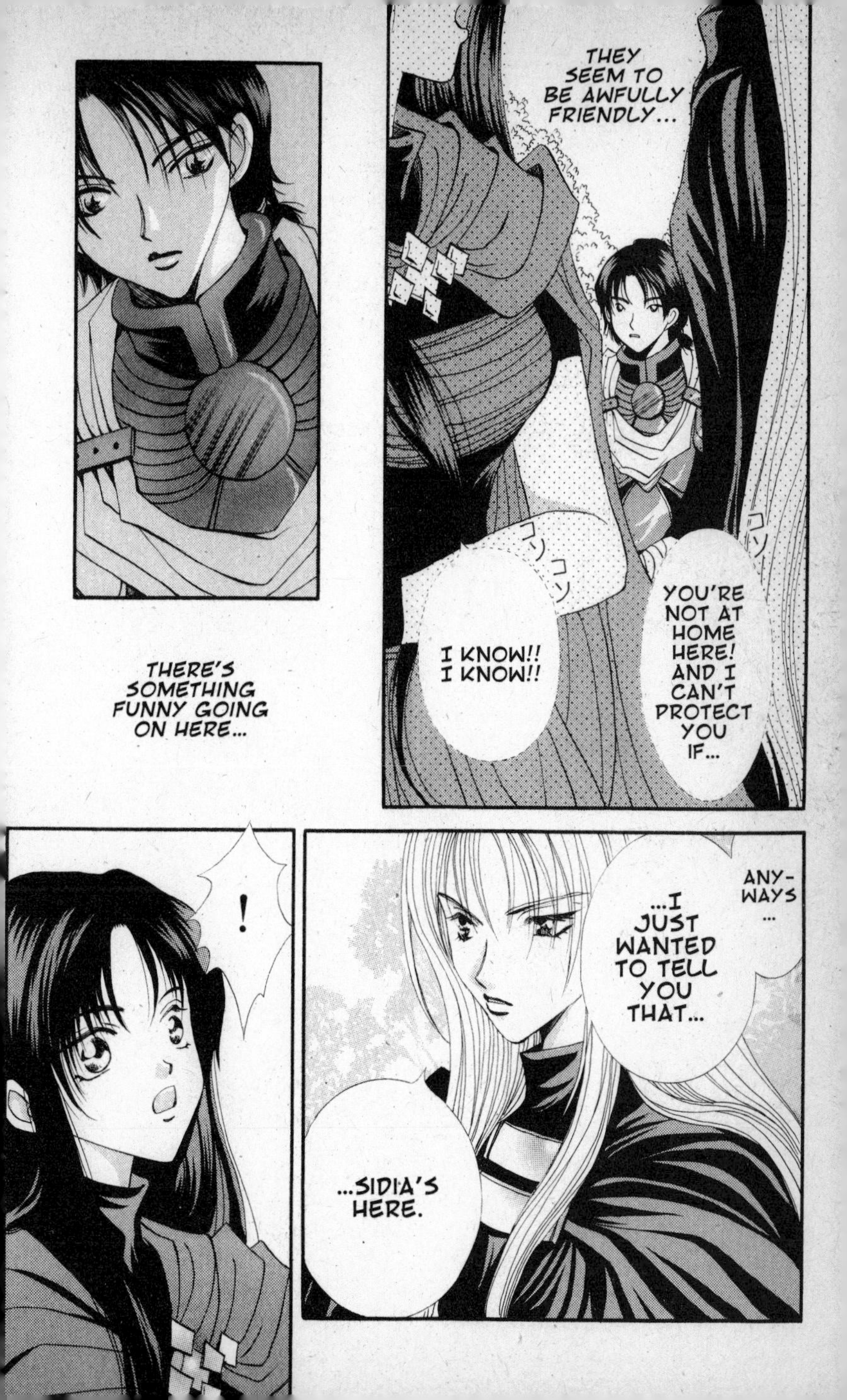

THEY SEEM TO BE AWFULLY FRIENDLY...
コソ
YOU'RE NOT AT HOME HERE! AND I CAN'T PROTECT YOU IF...
コソコソ
I KNOW!! I KNOW!!
THERE'S SOMETHING FUNNY GOING ON HERE...
ANY-WAYS...
...I JUST WANTED TO TELL YOU THAT...
...SIDIA'S HERE.
!

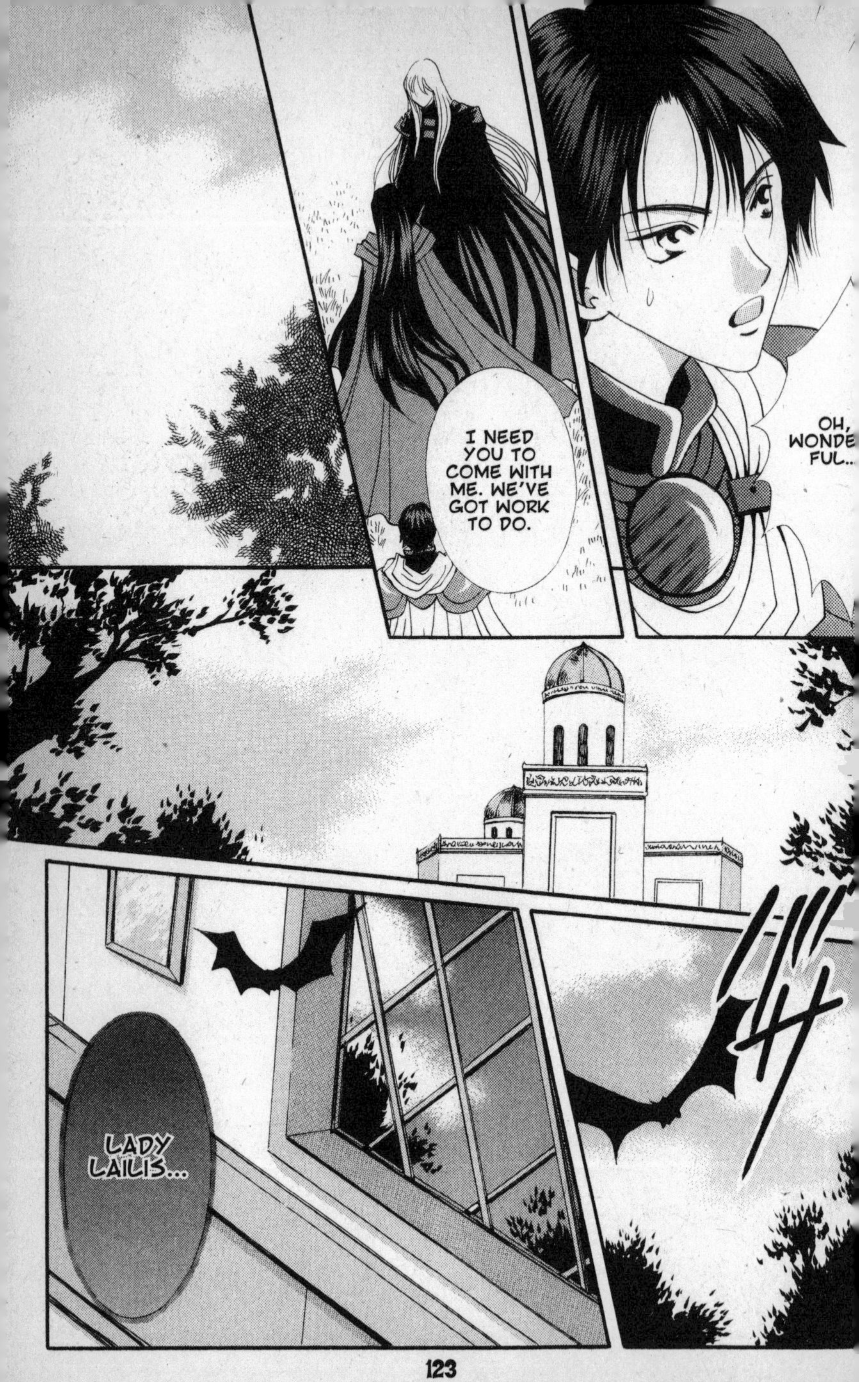
OH, WONDE FUL...
I NEED YOU TO COME WITH ME. WE'VE GOT WORK TO DO.
LADY LAILIS...

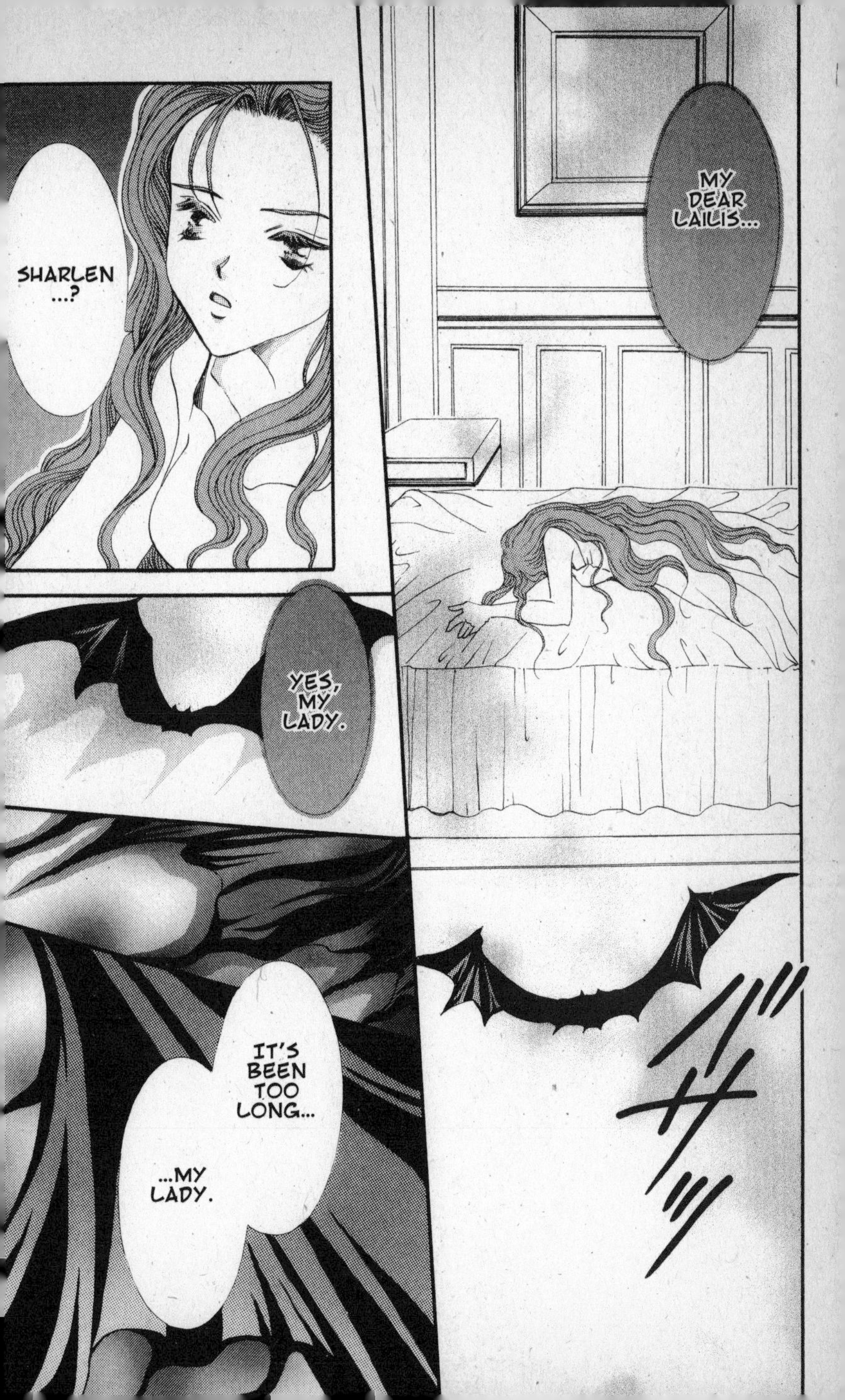
MY DEAR LAILIS...
SHARLEN ...?
YES, MY LADY.
IT'S BEEN TOO LONG...
...MY LADY.

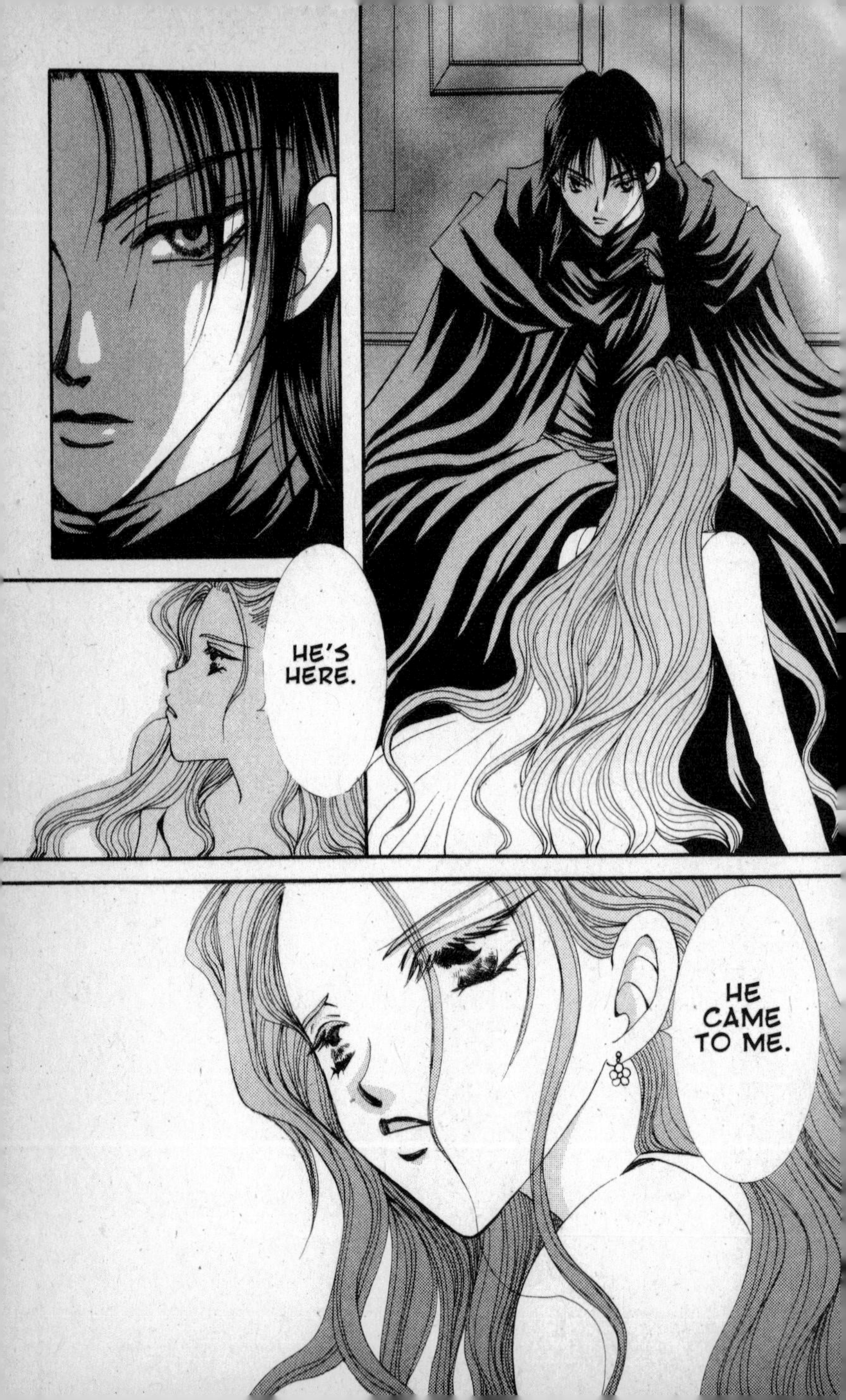
HE'S HERE.
HE CAME TO ME.

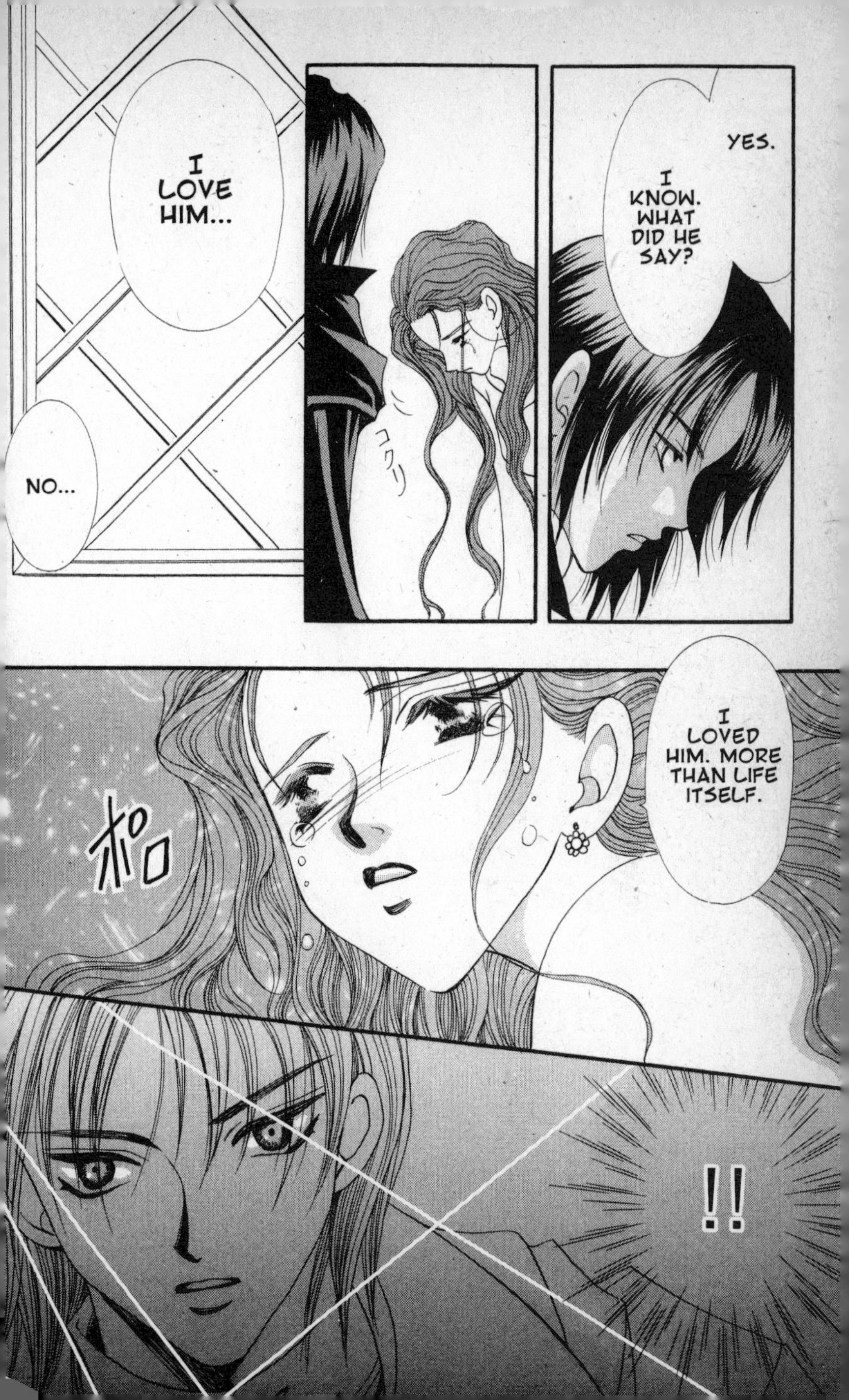
YES.
I KNOW. WHAT DID HE SAY?
コクリ
I LOVE HIM...
NO...
I LOVED HIM. MORE THAN LIFE ITSELF.
ポロ
!!

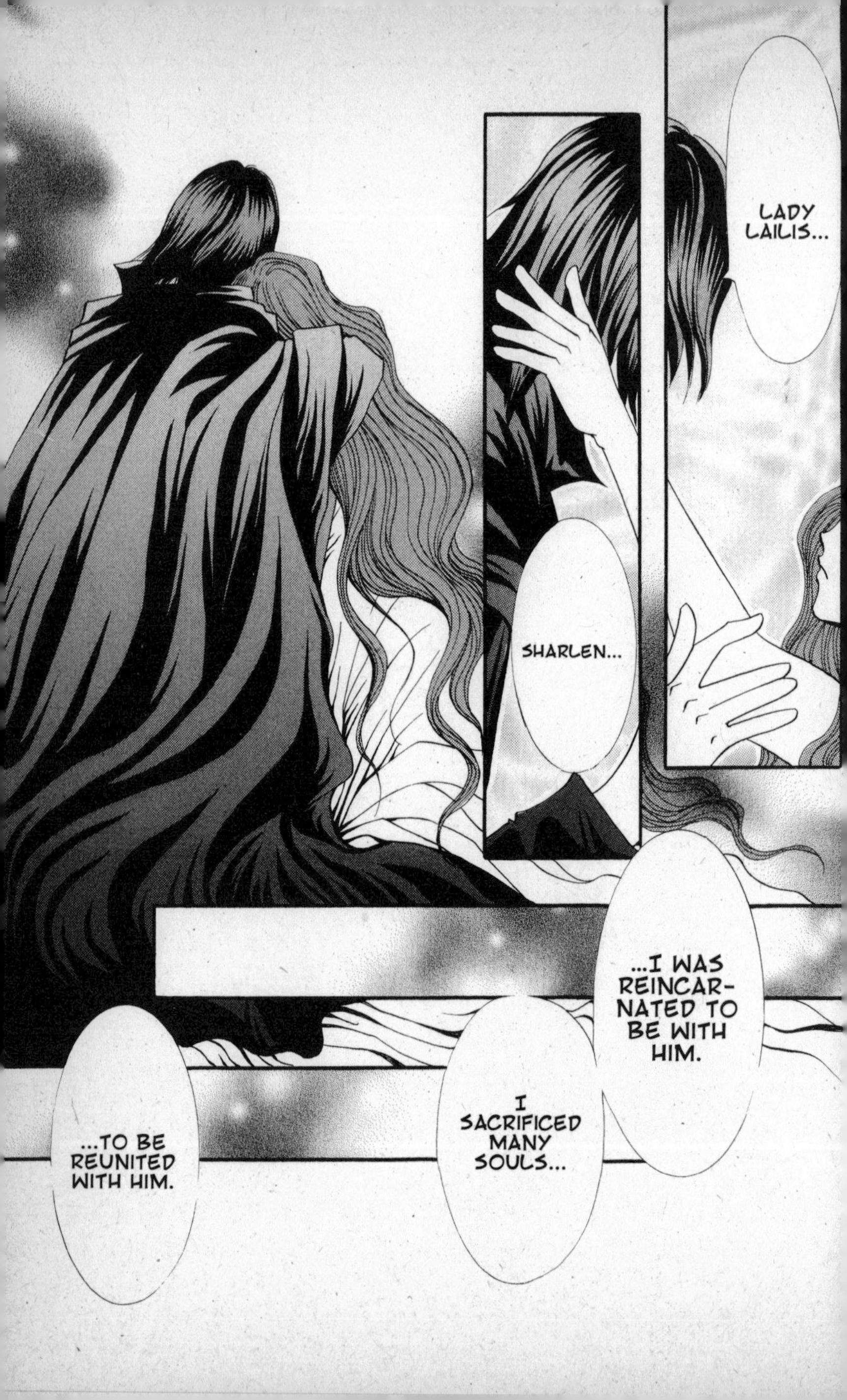
LADY LAILIS...
SHARLEN...
...I WAS REINCARNATED TO BE WITH HIM.
I SACRIFICED MANY SOULS...
...TO BE REUNITED WITH HIM.

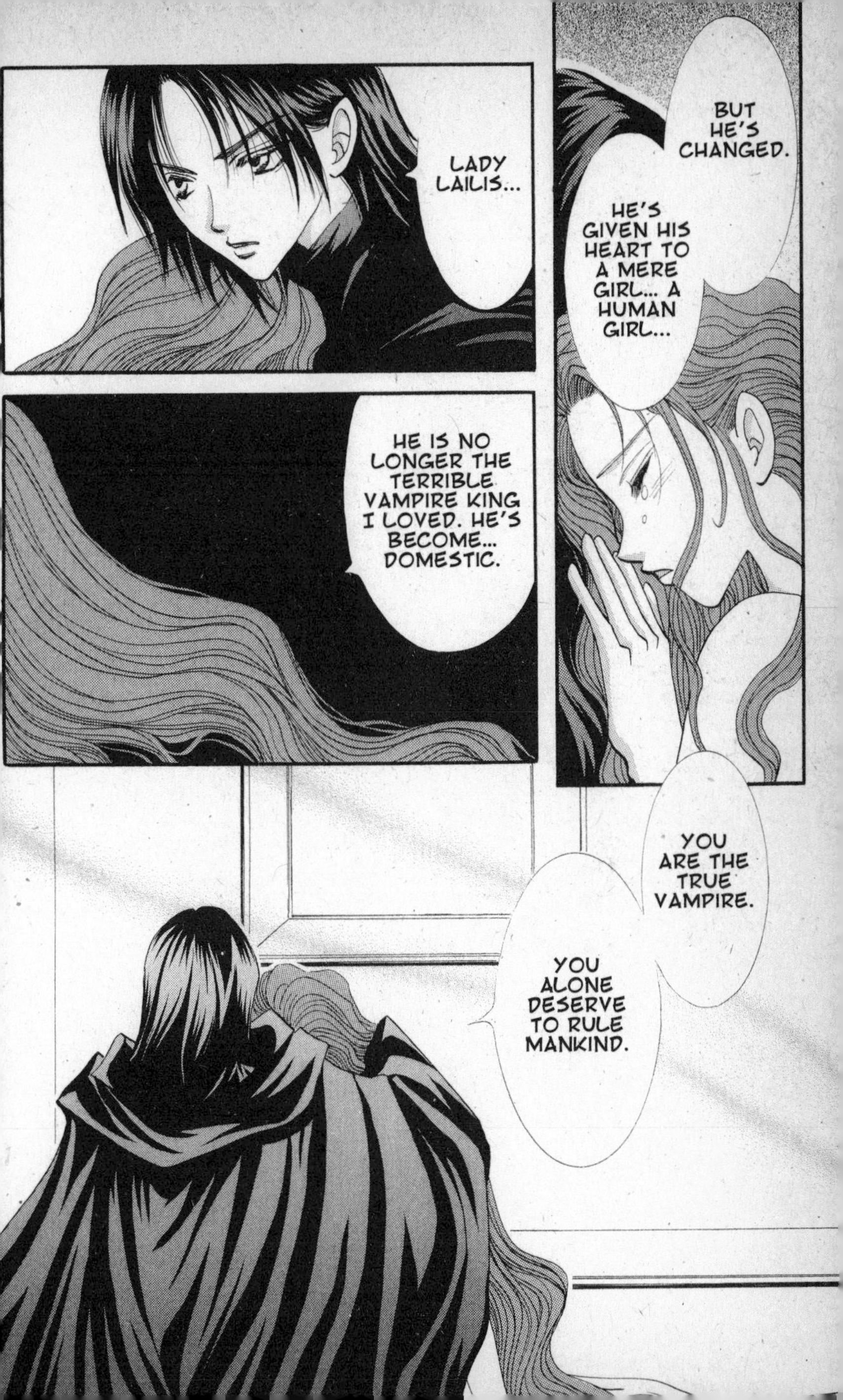
BUT HE'S CHANGED.
HE'S GIVEN HIS HEART TO A MERE GIRL... A HUMAN GIRL...
LADY LAILIS...
HE IS NO LONGER THE TERRIBLE VAMPIRE KING I LOVED. HE'S BECOME... DOMESTIC.
YOU ARE THE TRUE VAMPIRE.
YOU ALONE DESERVE TO RULE MANKIND.

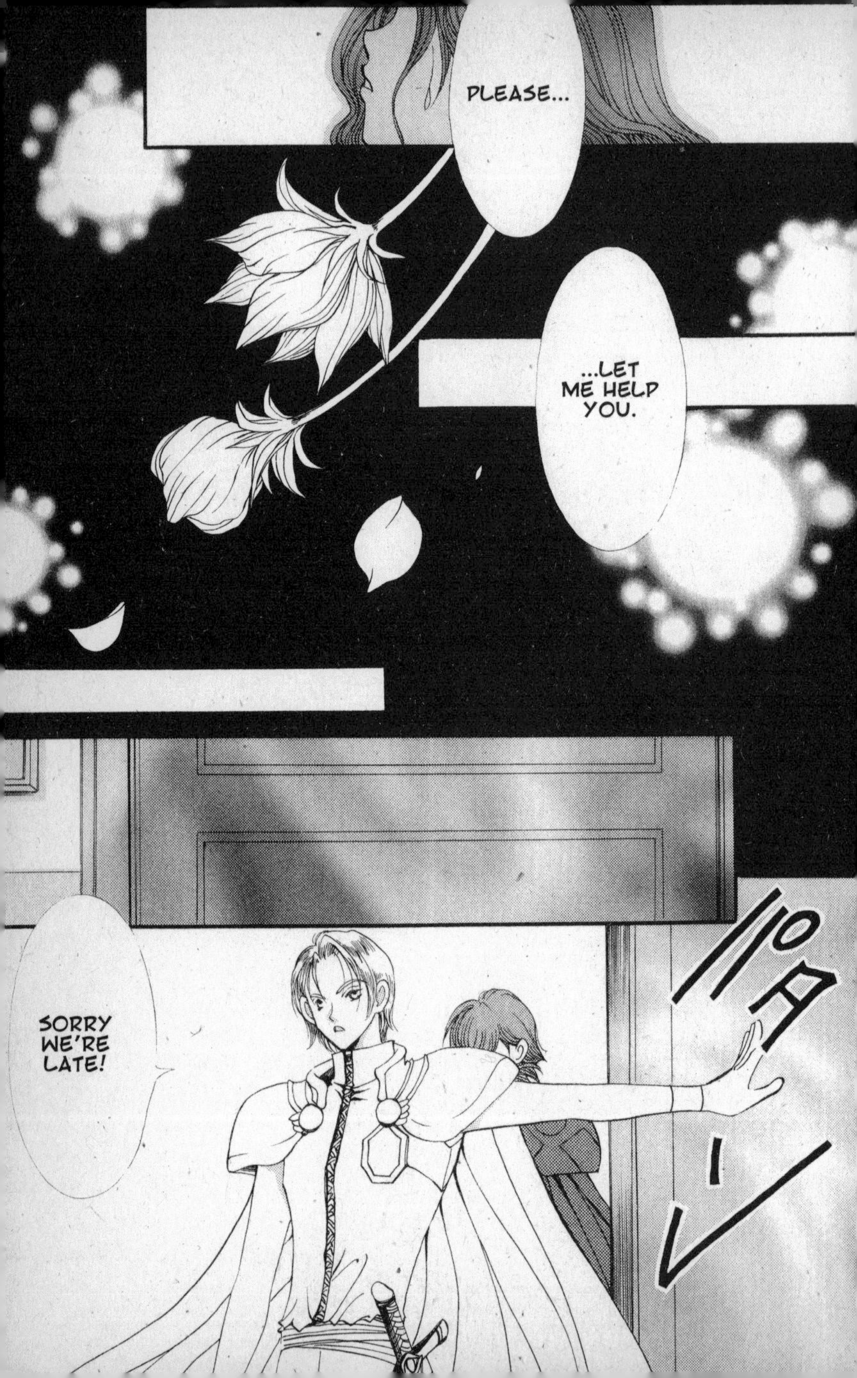
PLEASE...
...LET ME HELP YOU.
SORRY WE'RE LATE!

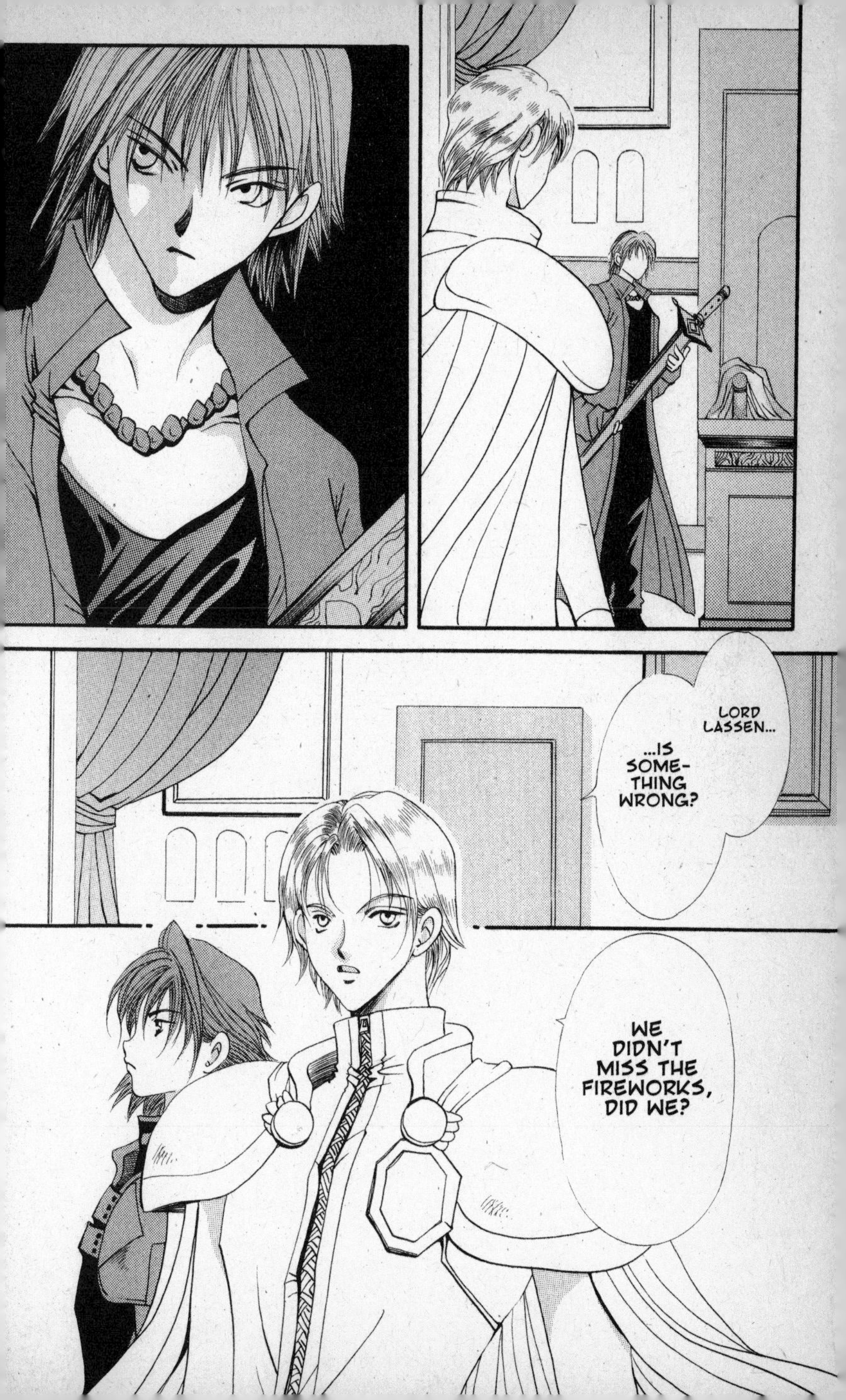
LORD LASSEN...
...IS SOMETHING WRONG?
WE DIDN'T MISS THE FIREWORKS, DID WE?

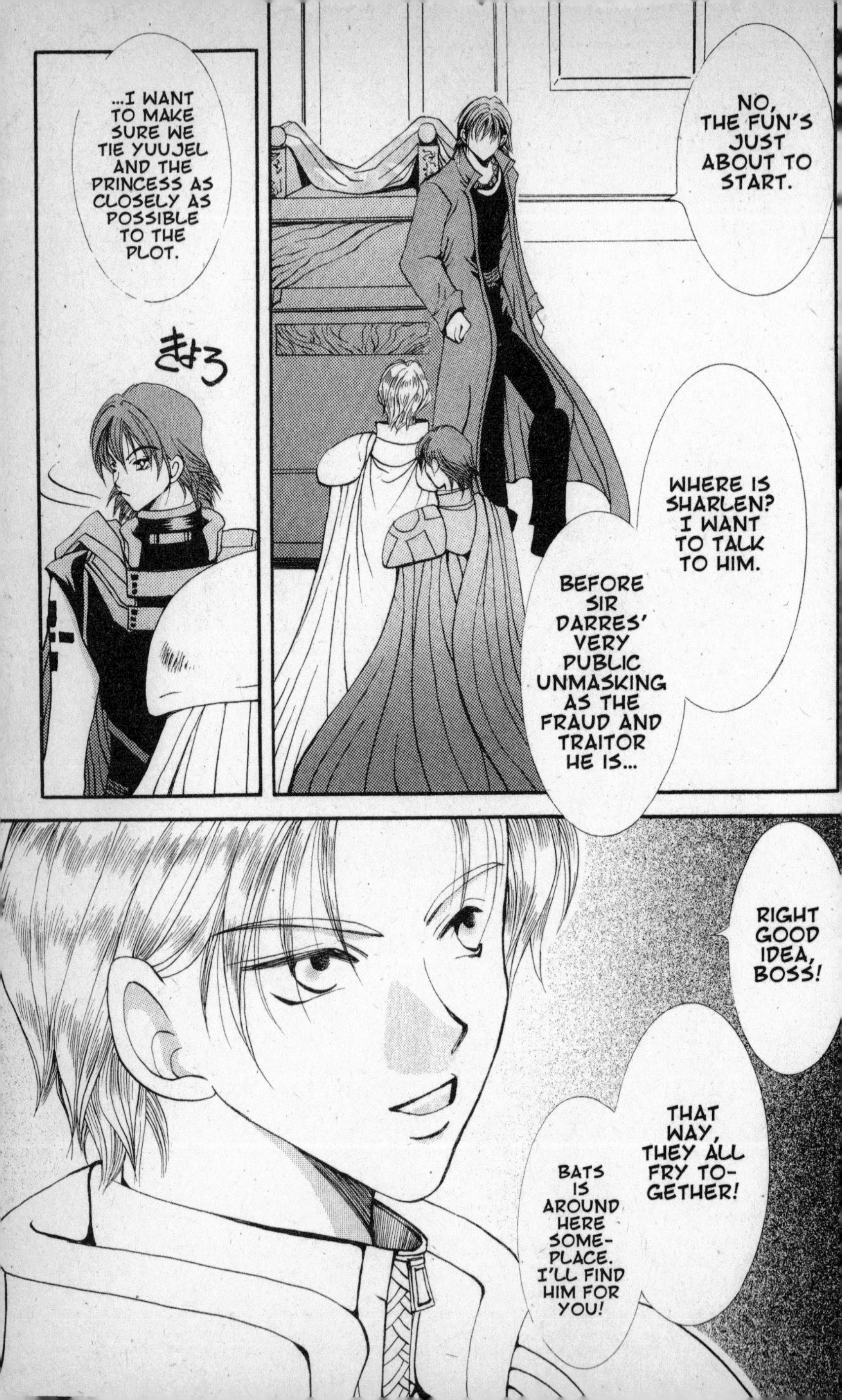
NO, THE FUN'S JUST ABOUT TO START.
WHERE IS SHARLEN? I WANT TO TALK TO HIM.
BEFORE SIR DARRES' VERY PUBLIC UNMASKING AS THE FRAUD AND TRAITOR HE IS...
...I WANT TO MAKE SURE WE TIE YUUJEL AND THE PRINCESS AS CLOSELY AS POSSIBLE TO THE PLOT.
きょろ
RIGHT GOOD IDEA, BOSS!
THAT WAY, THEY ALL FRY TO-GETHER!
BATS IS AROUND HERE SOME-PLACE. I'LL FIND HIM FOR YOU!

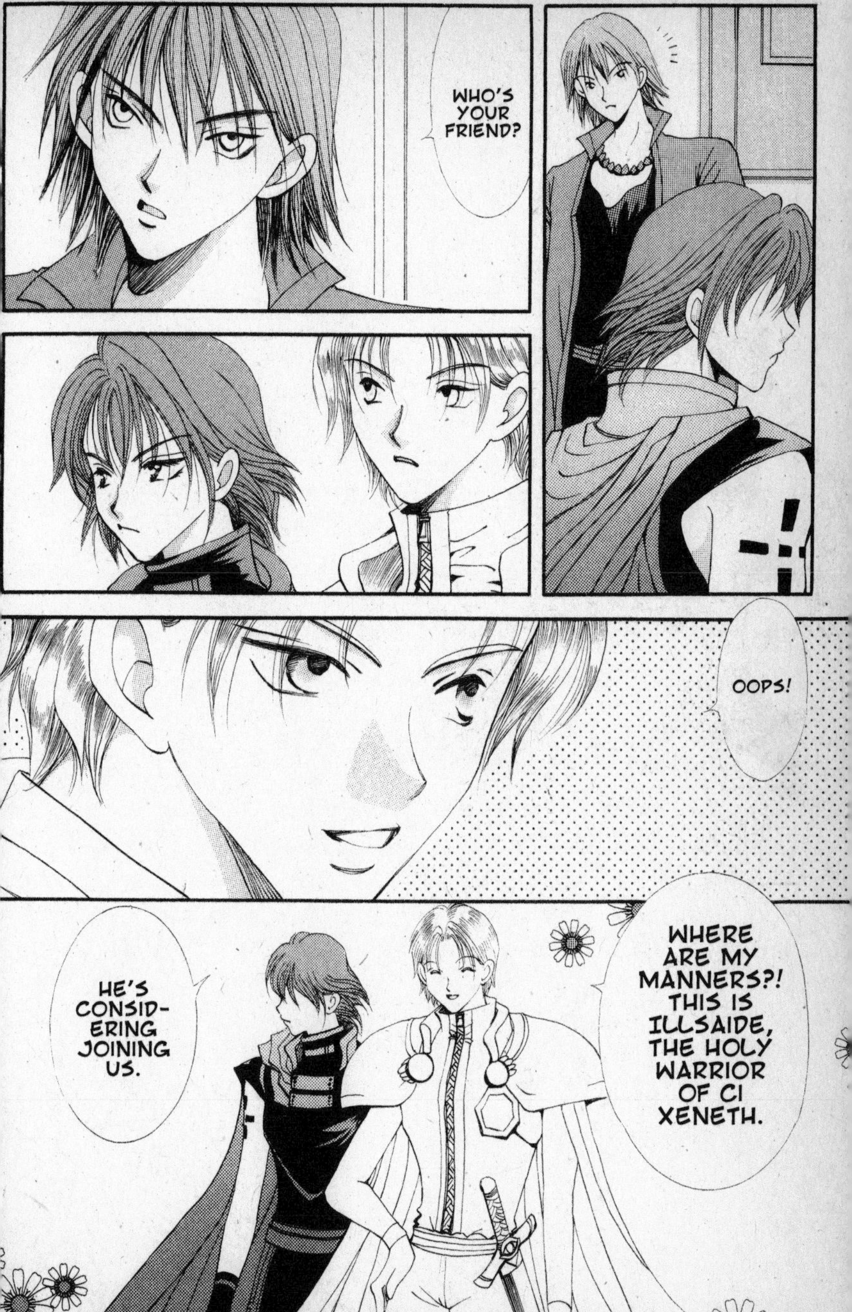
WHO'S YOUR FRIEND?
OOPS!
WHERE ARE MY MANNERS?! THIS IS ILLSAIDE, THE HOLY WARRIOR OF CI XENETH.
HE'S CONSID-ERING JOINING US.

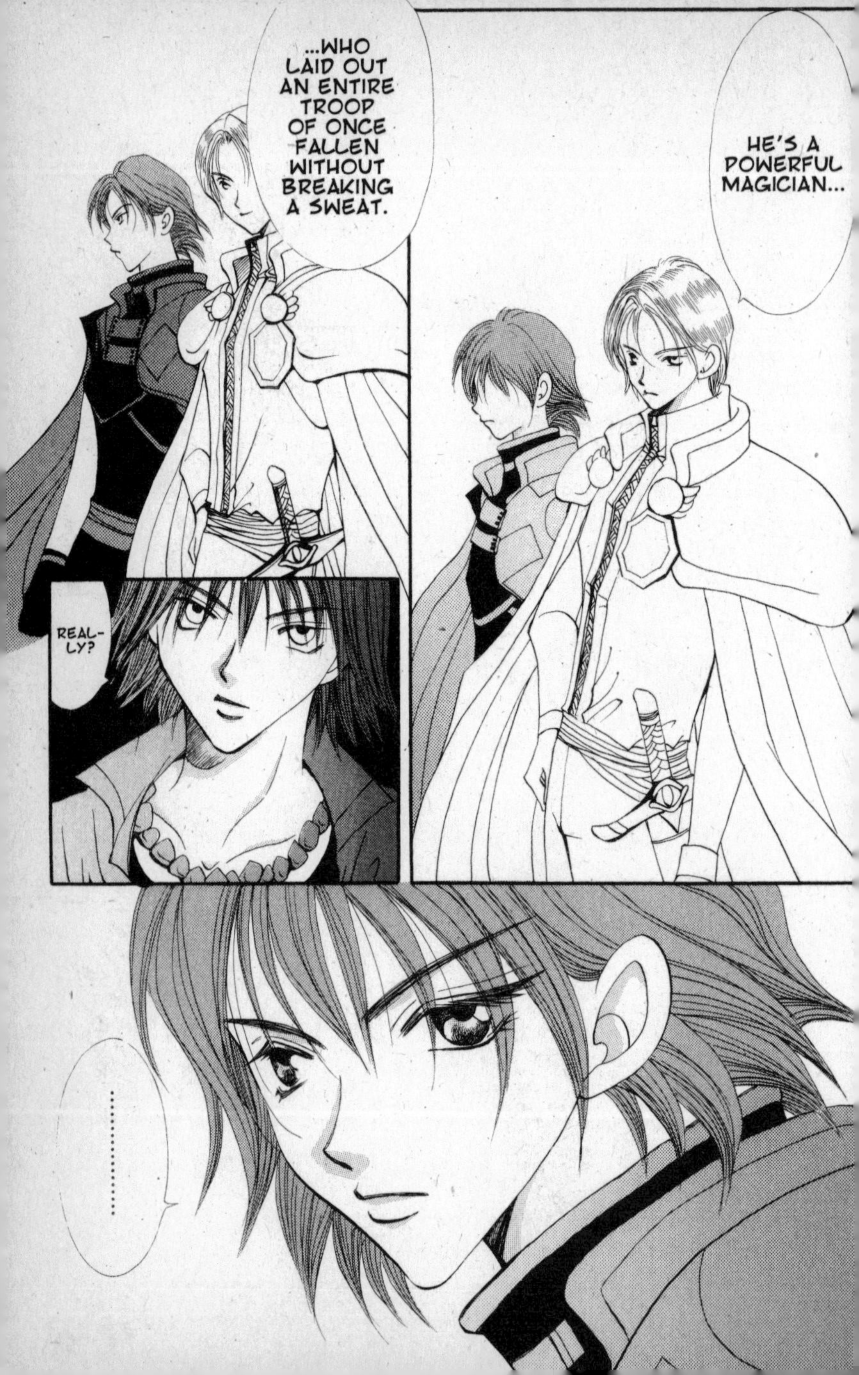
HE'S A POWERFUL MAGICIAN...
...WHO LAID OUT AN ENTIRE TROOP OF ONCE FALLEN WITHOUT BREAKING A SWEAT.
REAL-LY?
......

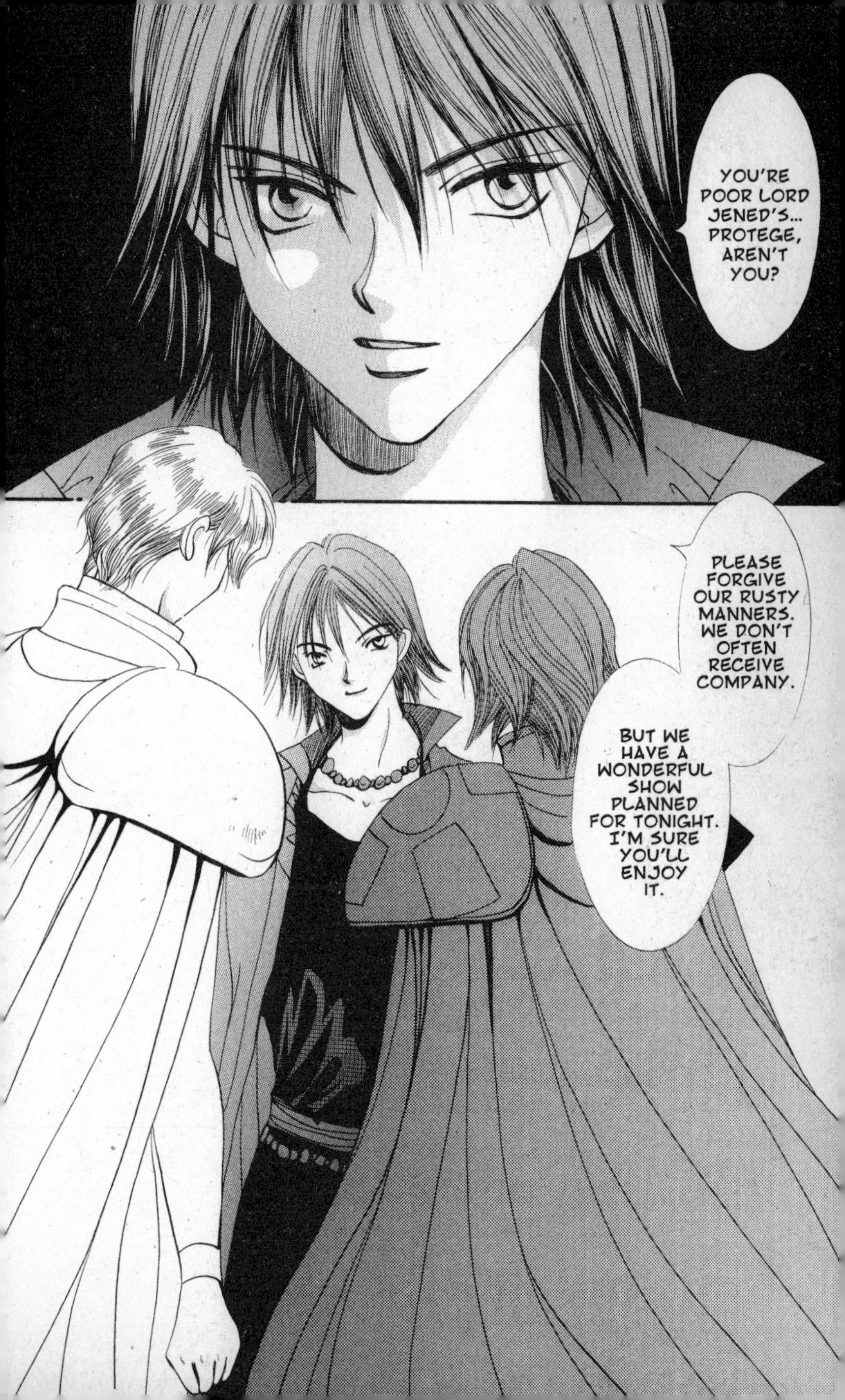
YOU'RE POOR LORD JENED'S... PROTEGE, AREN'T YOU?
PLEASE FORGIVE OUR RUSTY MANNERS. WE DON'T OFTEN RECEIVE COMPANY.
BUT WE HAVE A WONDERFUL SHOW PLANNED FOR TONIGHT. I'M SURE YOU'LL ENJOY IT.

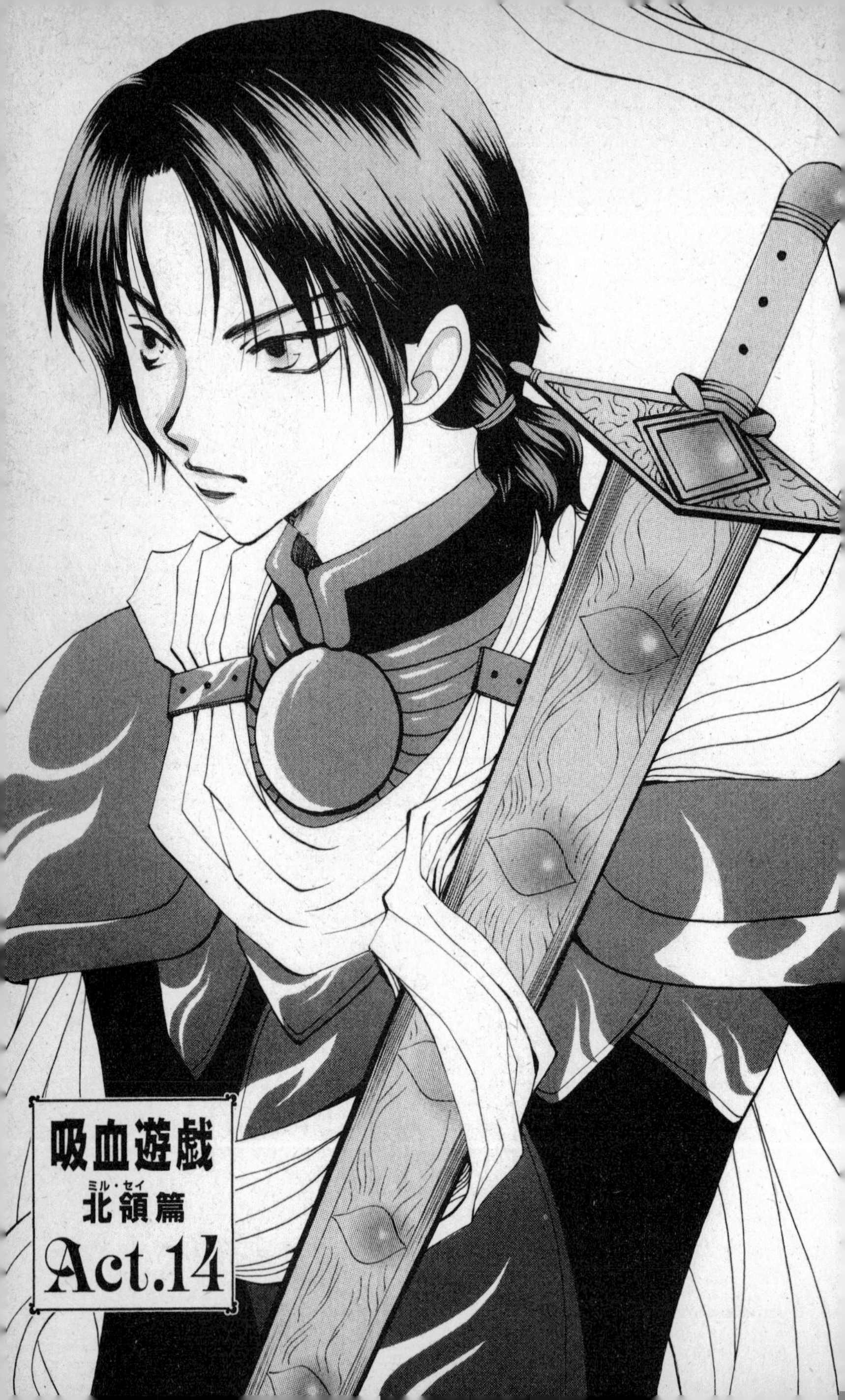

吸血遊戯
北領篇
ミル・セイ
Act.14

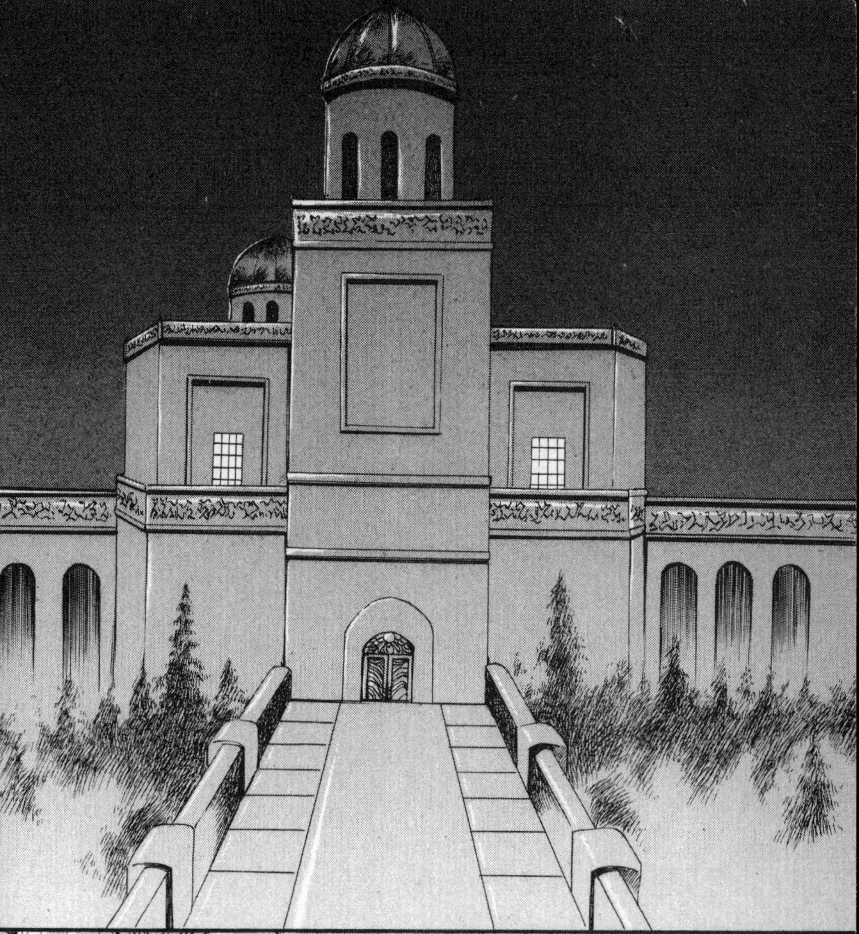
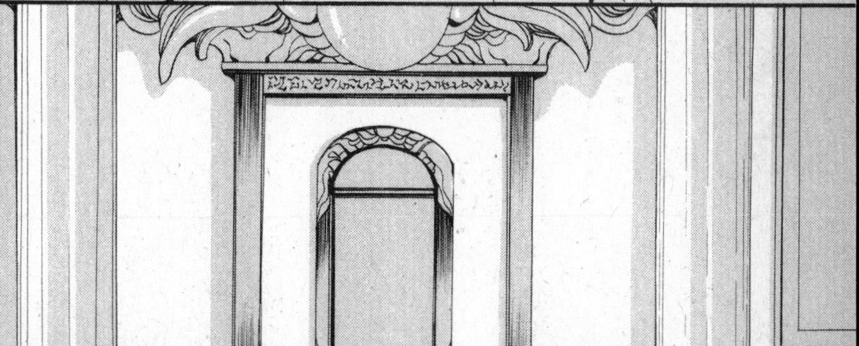

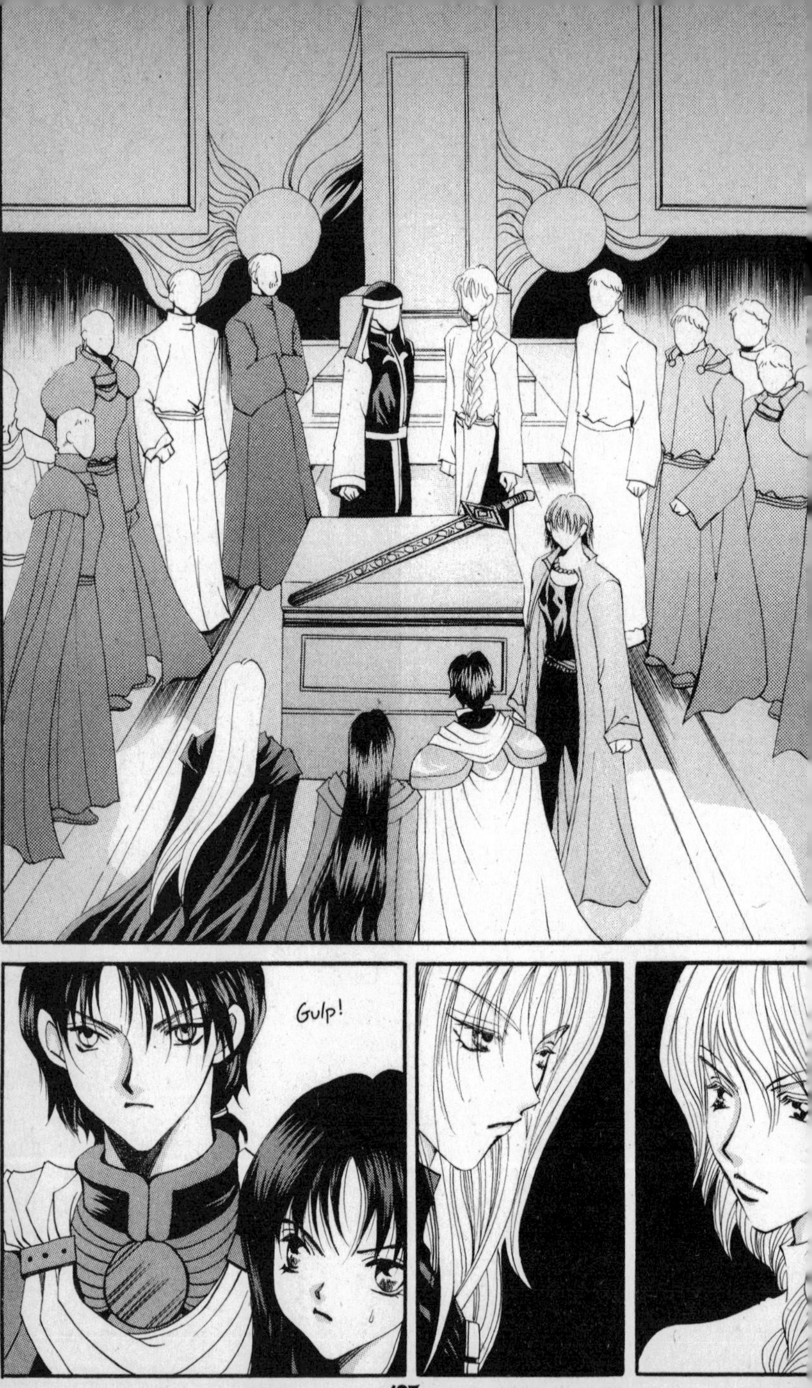
Gulp!

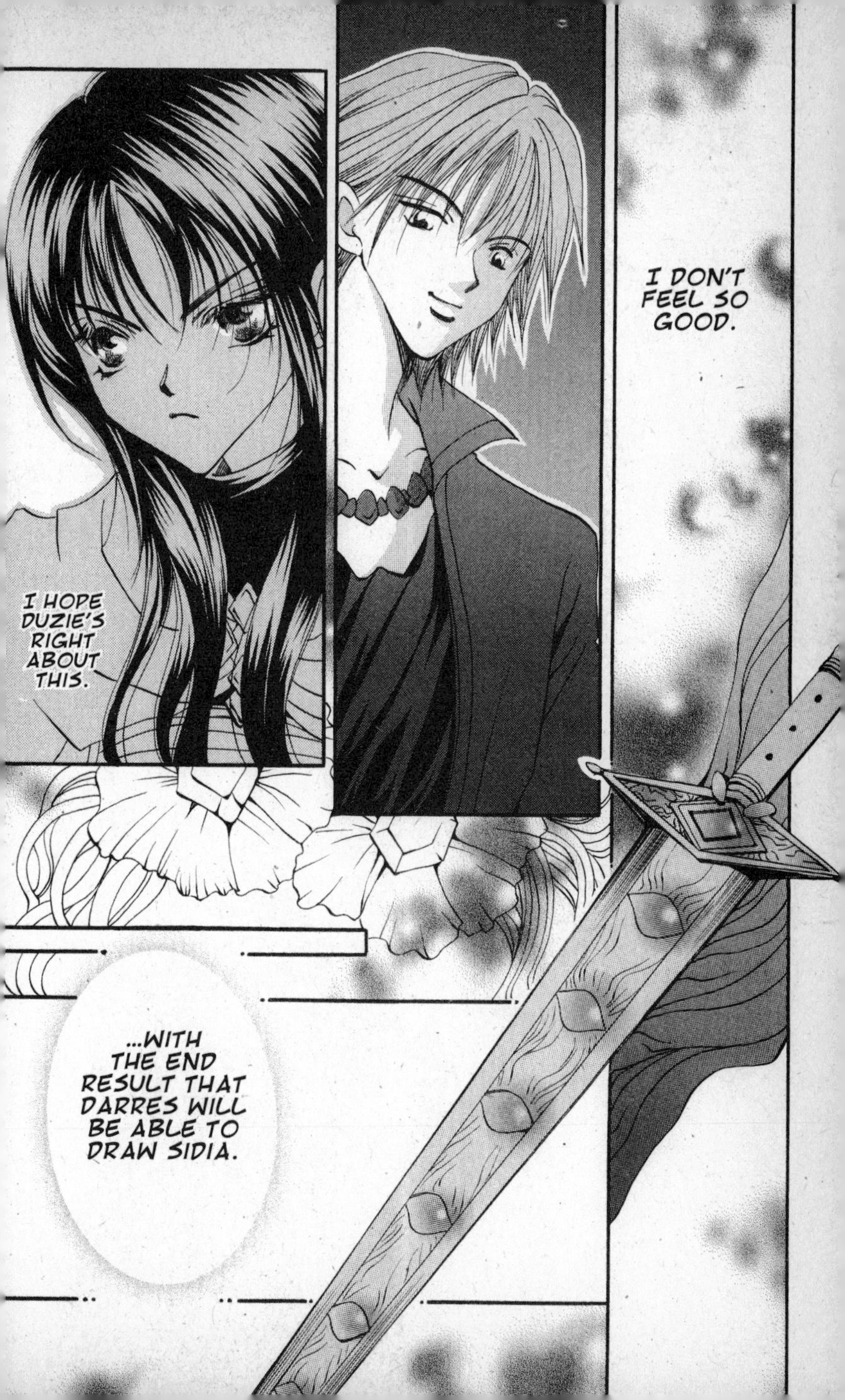
I DON'T FEEL SO GOOD.
I HOPE DUZIE'S RIGHT ABOUT THIS.
...WITH THE END RESULT THAT DARRES WILL BE ABLE TO DRAW SIDIA.

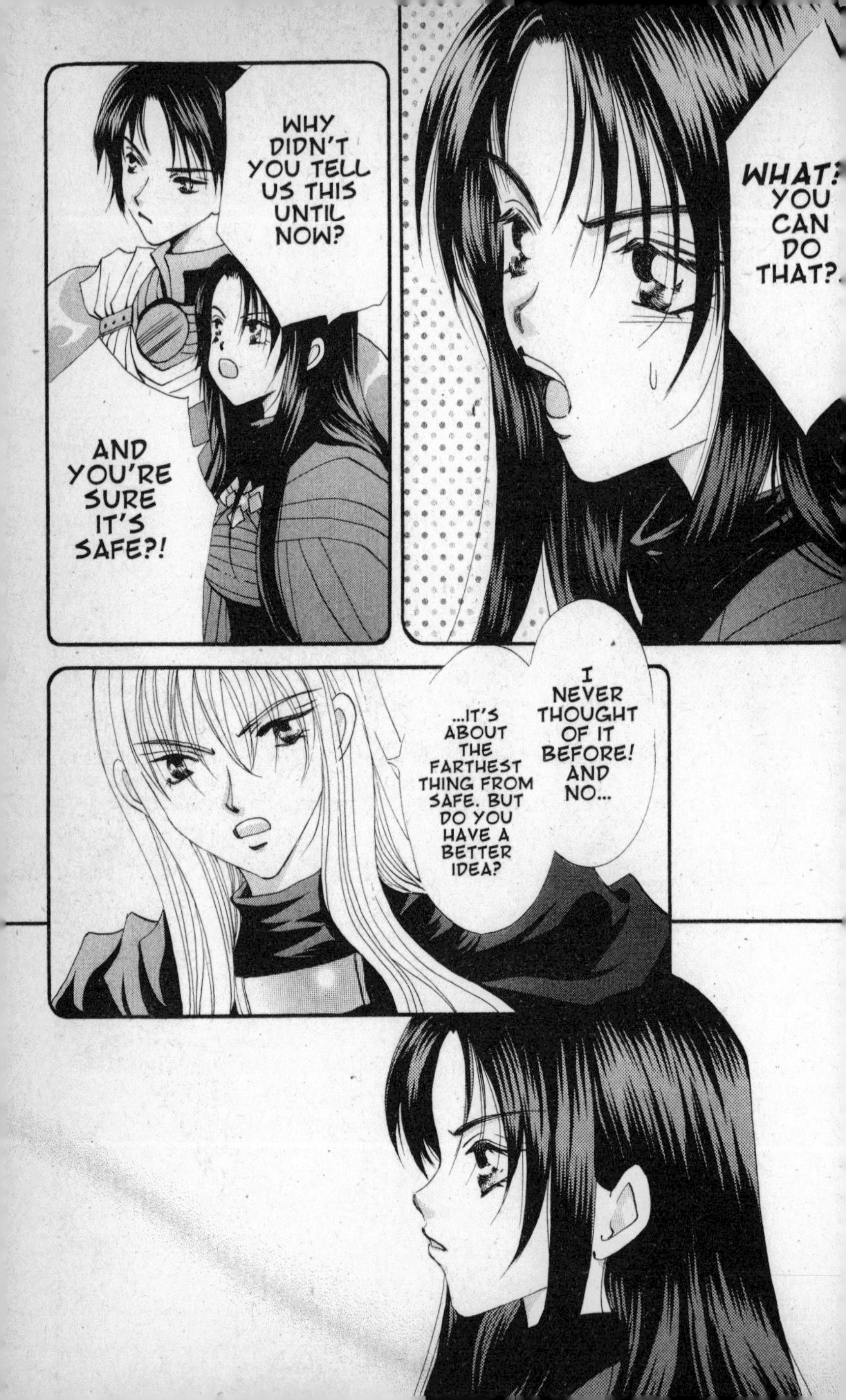
WHAT? YOU CAN DO THAT?
WHY DIDN'T YOU TELL US THIS UNTIL NOW?
AND YOU'RE SURE IT'S SAFE?!
I NEVER THOUGHT OF IT BEFORE! AND NO...
...IT'S ABOUT THE FARTHEST THING FROM SAFE. BUT DO YOU HAVE A BETTER IDEA?

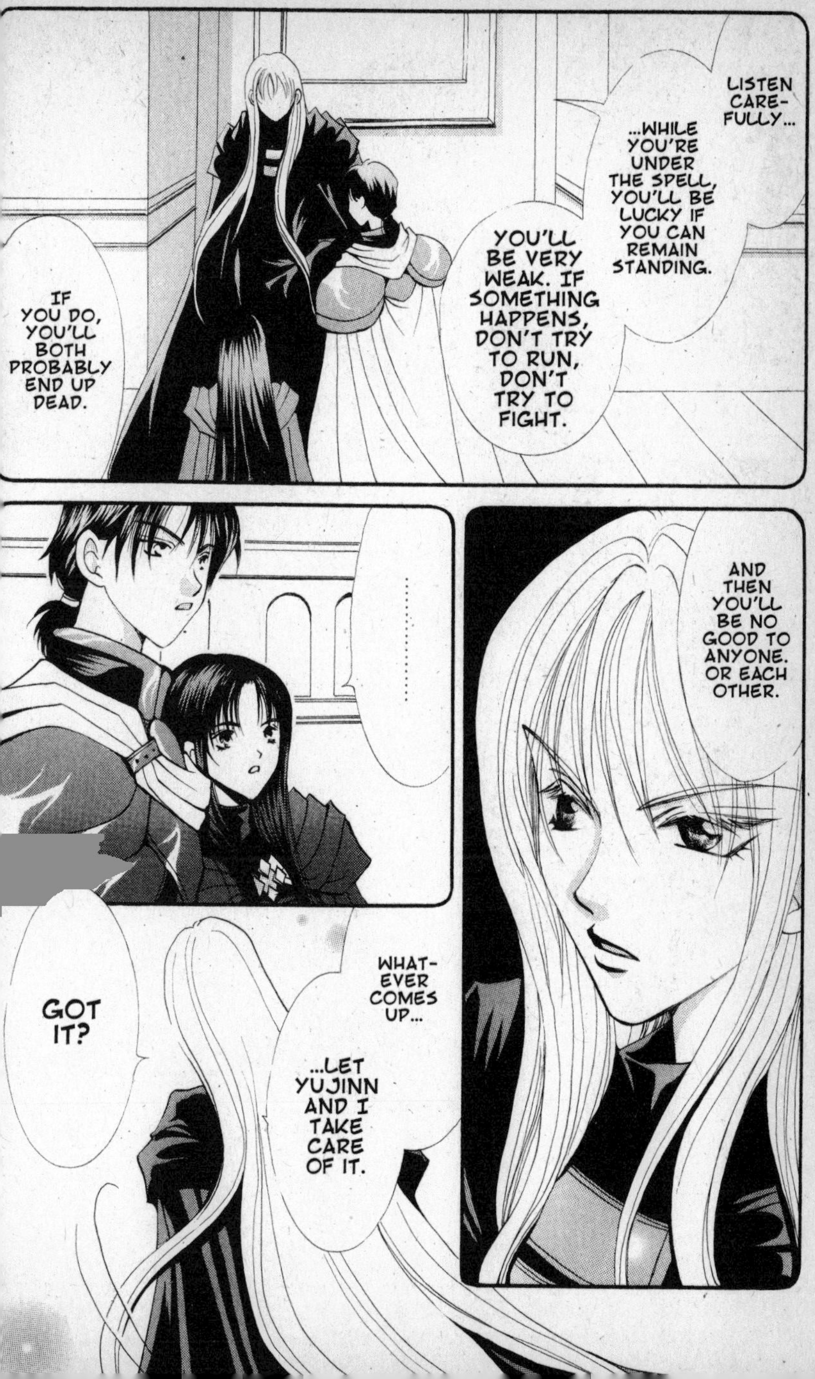
LISTEN CAREFULLY...
...WHILE YOU'RE UNDER THE SPELL, YOU'LL BE LUCKY IF YOU CAN REMAIN STANDING.
YOU'LL BE VERY WEAK. IF SOMETHING HAPPENS, DON'T TRY TO RUN, DON'T TRY TO FIGHT.
IF YOU DO, YOU'LL BOTH PROBABLY END UP DEAD.
AND THEN YOU'LL BE NO GOOD TO ANYONE. OR EACH OTHER.
......
WHATEVER COMES UP...
...LET YUJINN AND I TAKE CARE OF IT.
GOT IT?

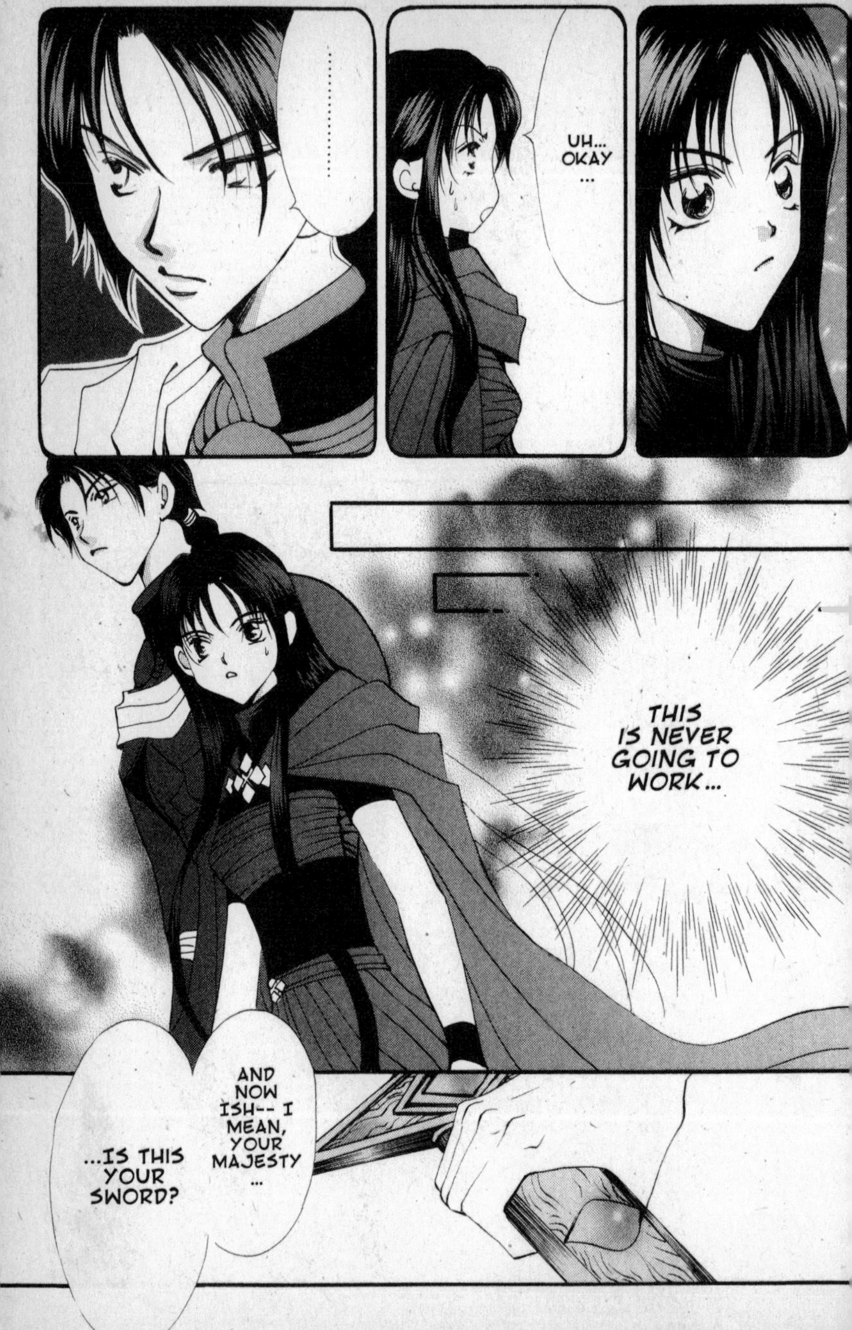
UH... OKAY ...
......
THIS IS NEVER GOING TO WORK...
AND NOW ISH-- I MEAN, YOUR MAJESTY ...
...IS THIS YOUR SWORD?

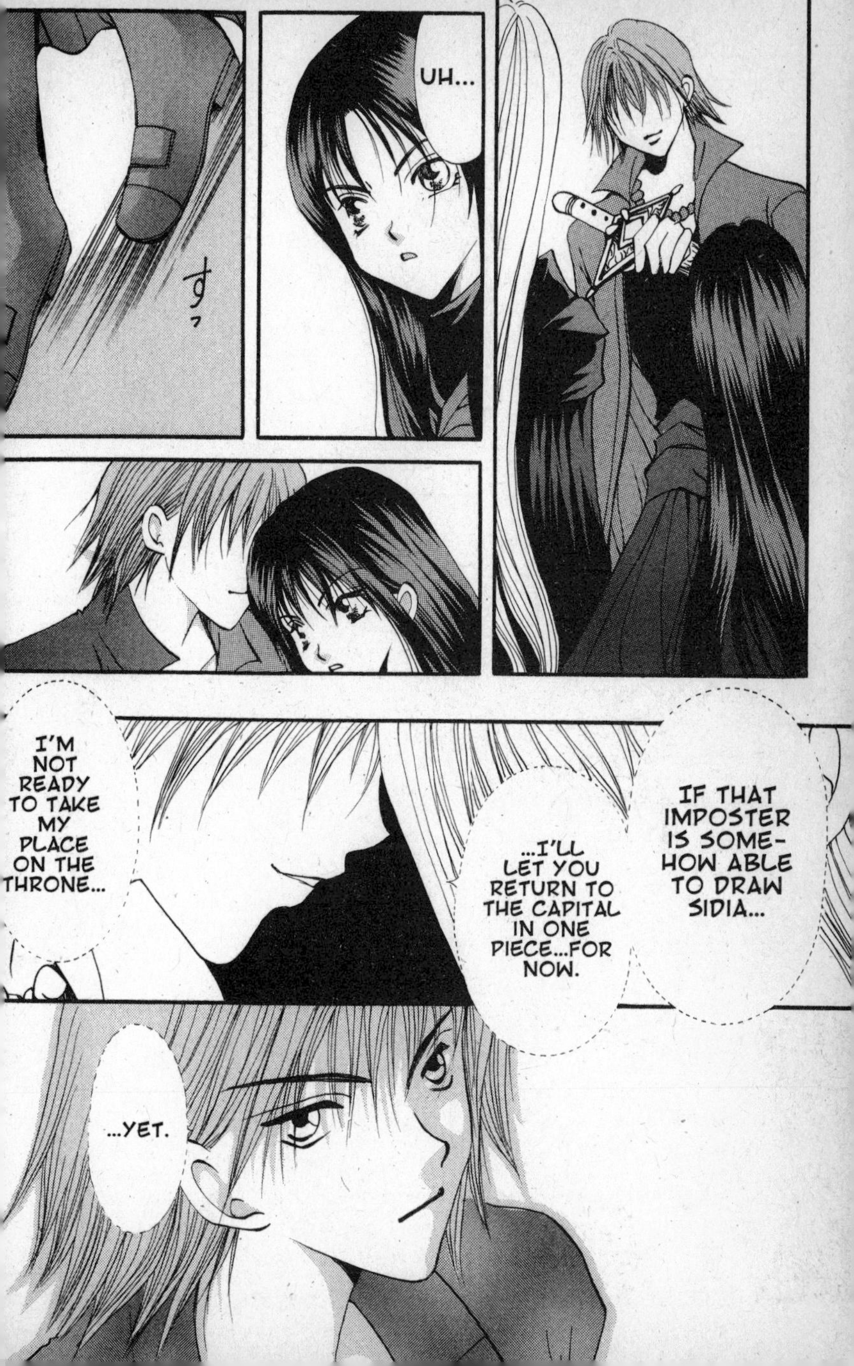
UH...
す
IF THAT IMPOSTER IS SOMEHOW ABLE TO DRAW SIDIA...
...I'LL LET YOU RETURN TO THE CAPITAL IN ONE PIECE...FOR NOW.
I'M NOT READY TO TAKE MY PLACE ON THE THRONE...
...YET.

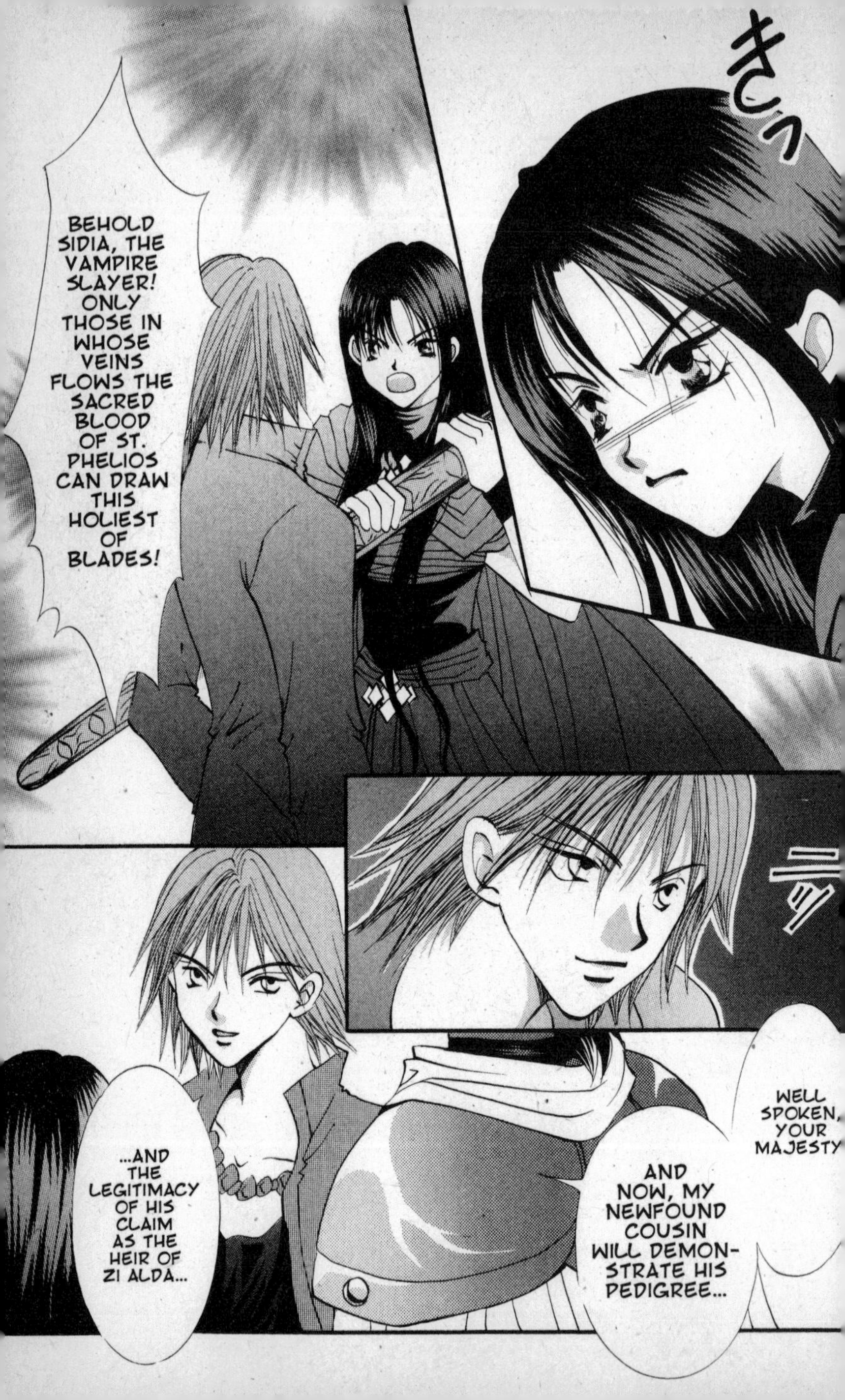
きっ
BEHOLD SIDIA, THE VAMPIRE SLAYER! ONLY THOSE IN WHOSE VEINS FLOWS THE SACRED BLOOD OF ST. PHELIOS CAN DRAW THIS HOLIEST OF BLADES!
ニッ
WELL SPOKEN, YOUR MAJESTY
AND NOW, MY NEWFOUND COUSIN WILL DEMON-STRATE HIS PEDIGREE...
...AND THE LEGITIMACY OF HIS CLAIM AS THE HEIR OF ZI ALDA...

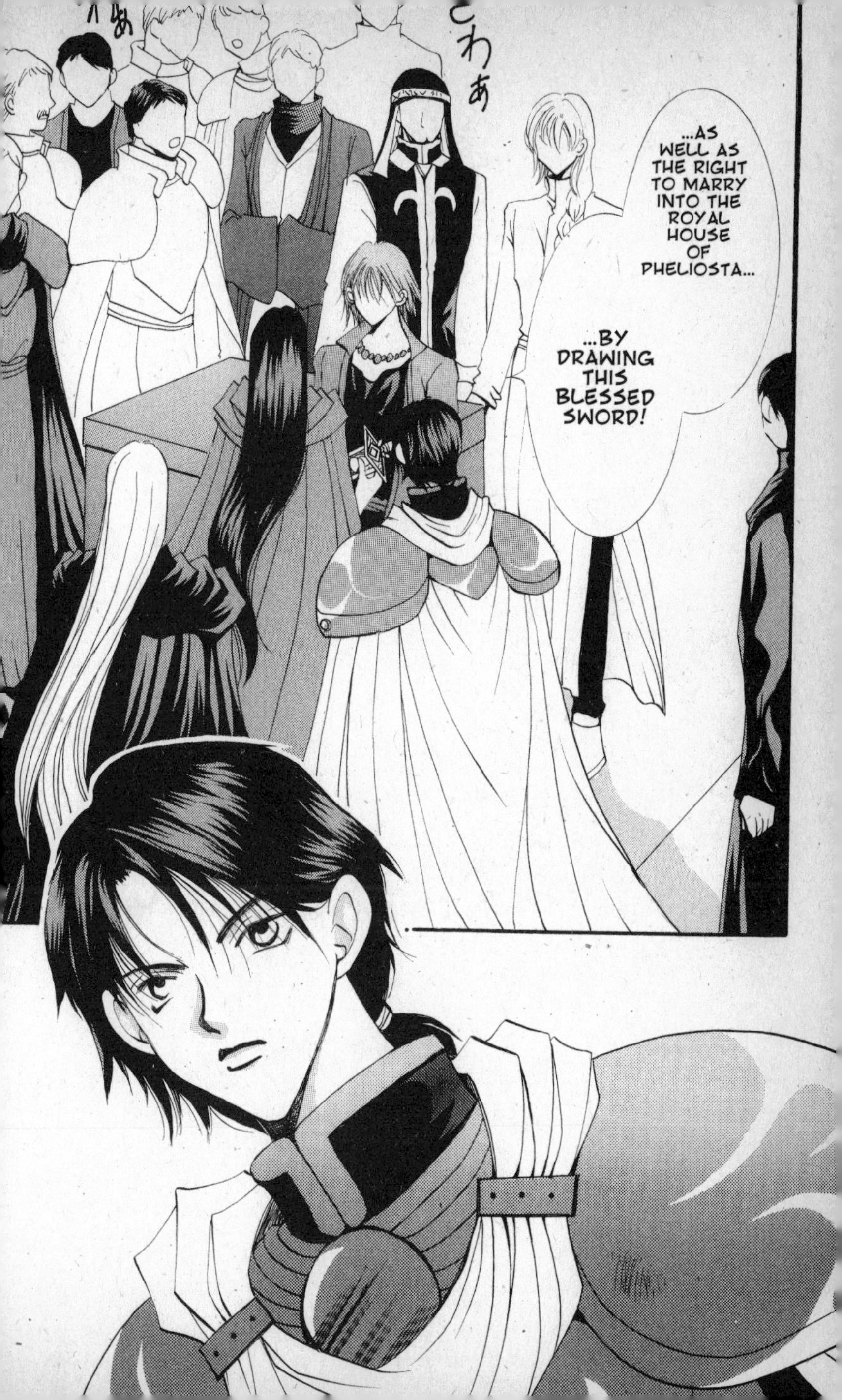
...AS WELL AS THE RIGHT TO MARRY INTO THE ROYAL HOUSE OF PHELIOSTA...
...BY DRAWING THIS BLESSED SWORD!

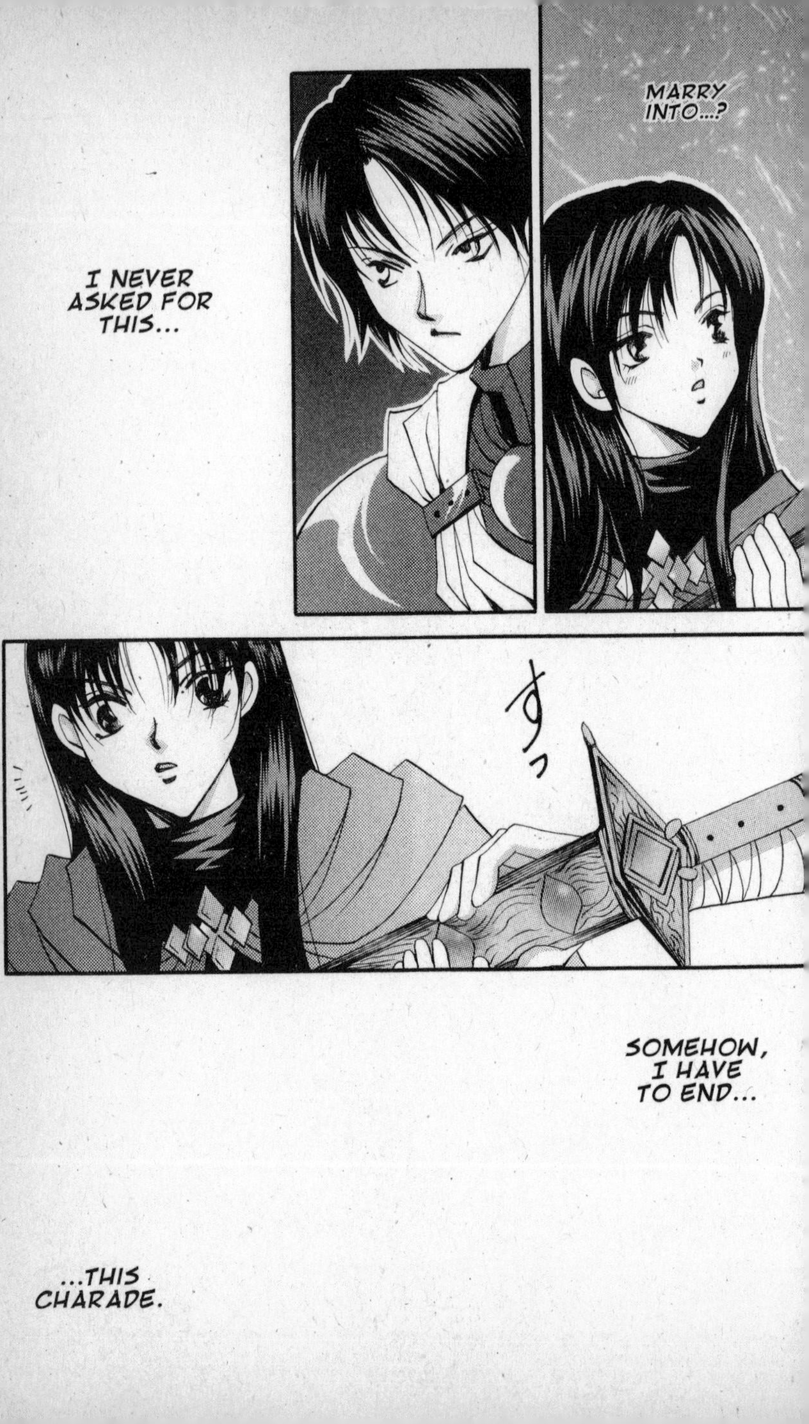
MARRY INTO...?
I NEVER ASKED FOR THIS...
すっ
SOMEHOW, I HAVE TO END...
...THIS CHARADE.

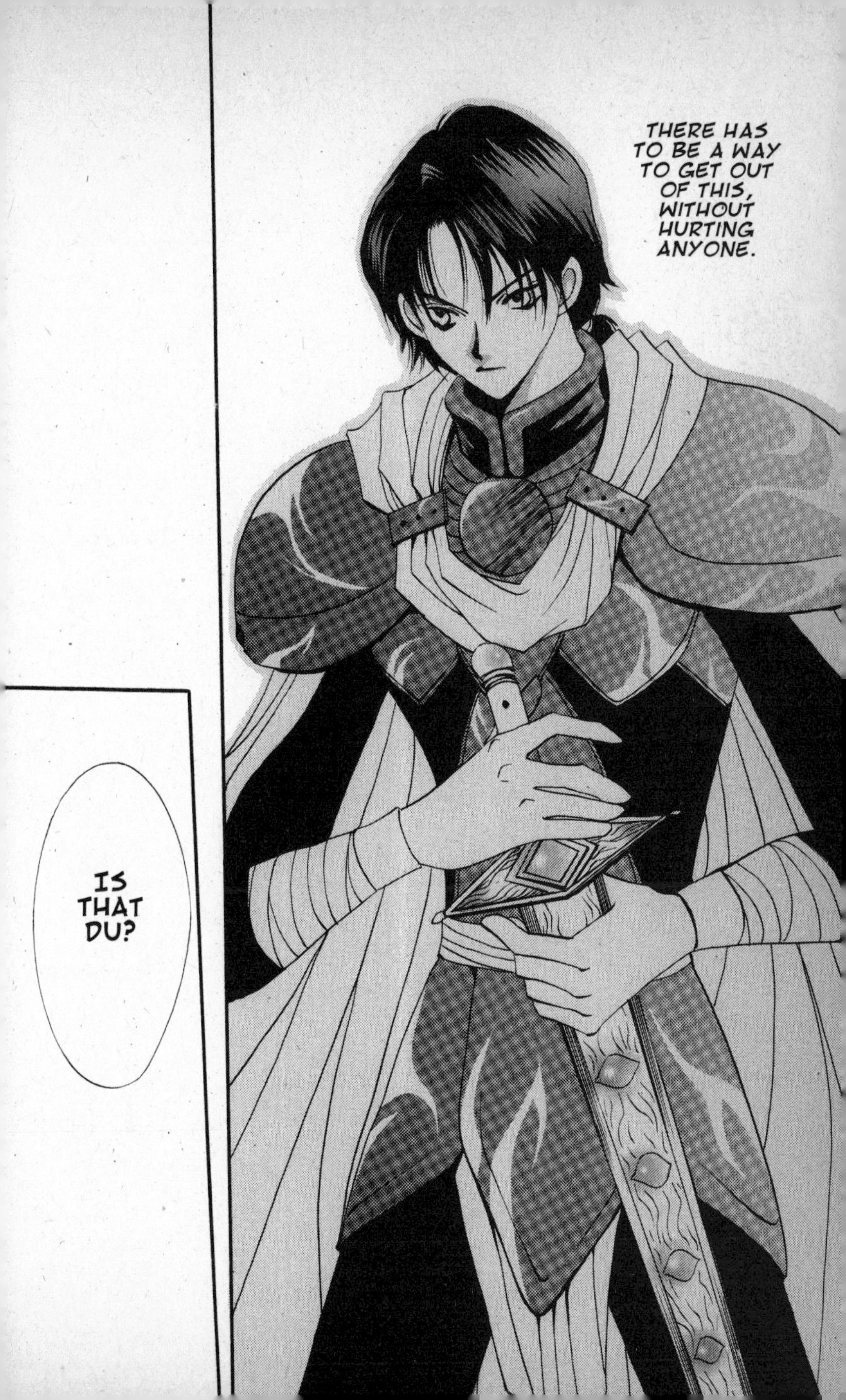
THERE HAS TO BE A WAY TO GET OUT OF THIS, WITHOUT HURTING ANYONE.
IS THAT DU?

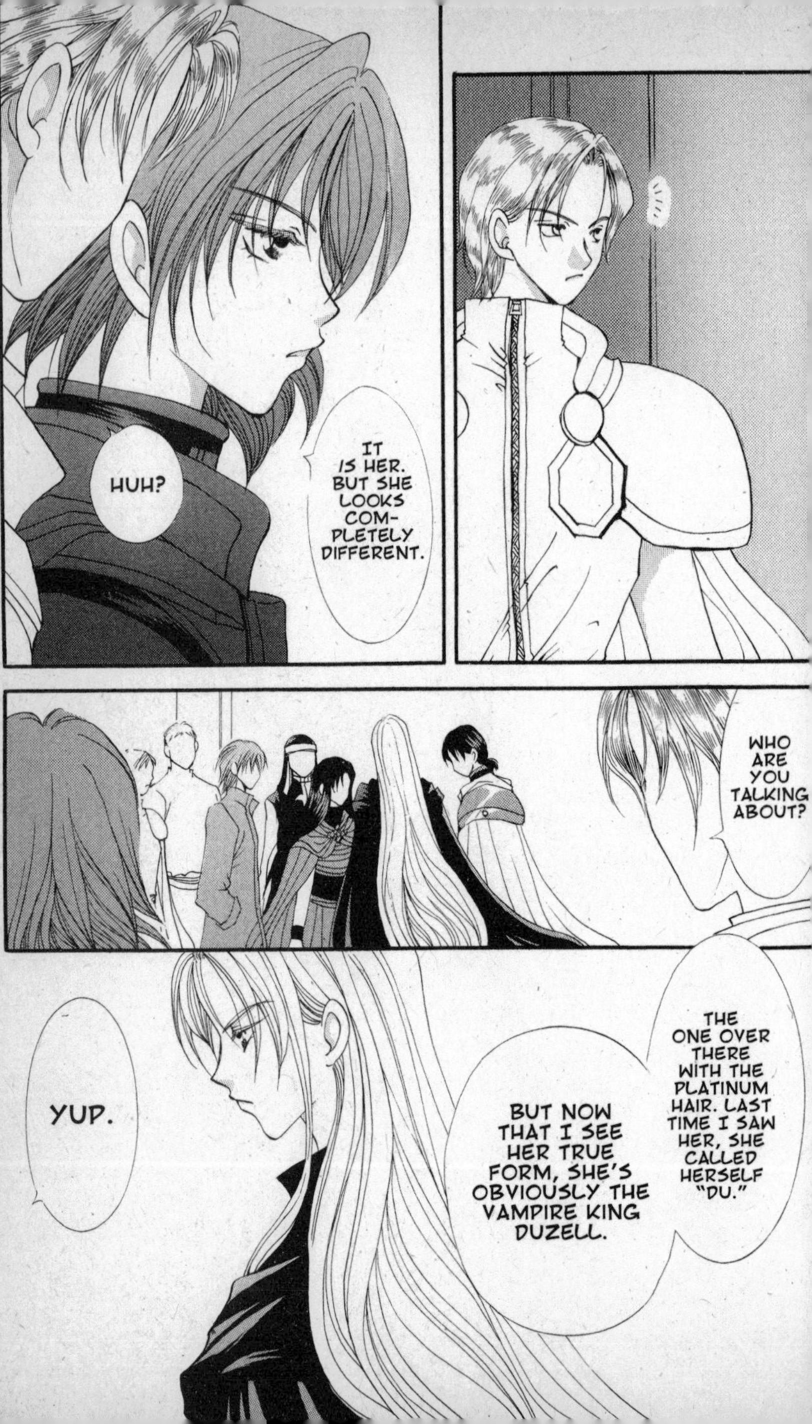
...
IT IS HER. BUT SHE LOOKS COMPLETELY DIFFERENT.
HUH?
WHO ARE YOU TALKING ABOUT?
THE ONE OVER THERE WITH THE PLATINUM HAIR. LAST TIME I SAW HER, SHE CALLED HERSELF "DU."
BUT NOW THAT I SEE HER TRUE FORM, SHE'S OBVIOUSLY THE VAMPIRE KING DUZELL.
YUP.

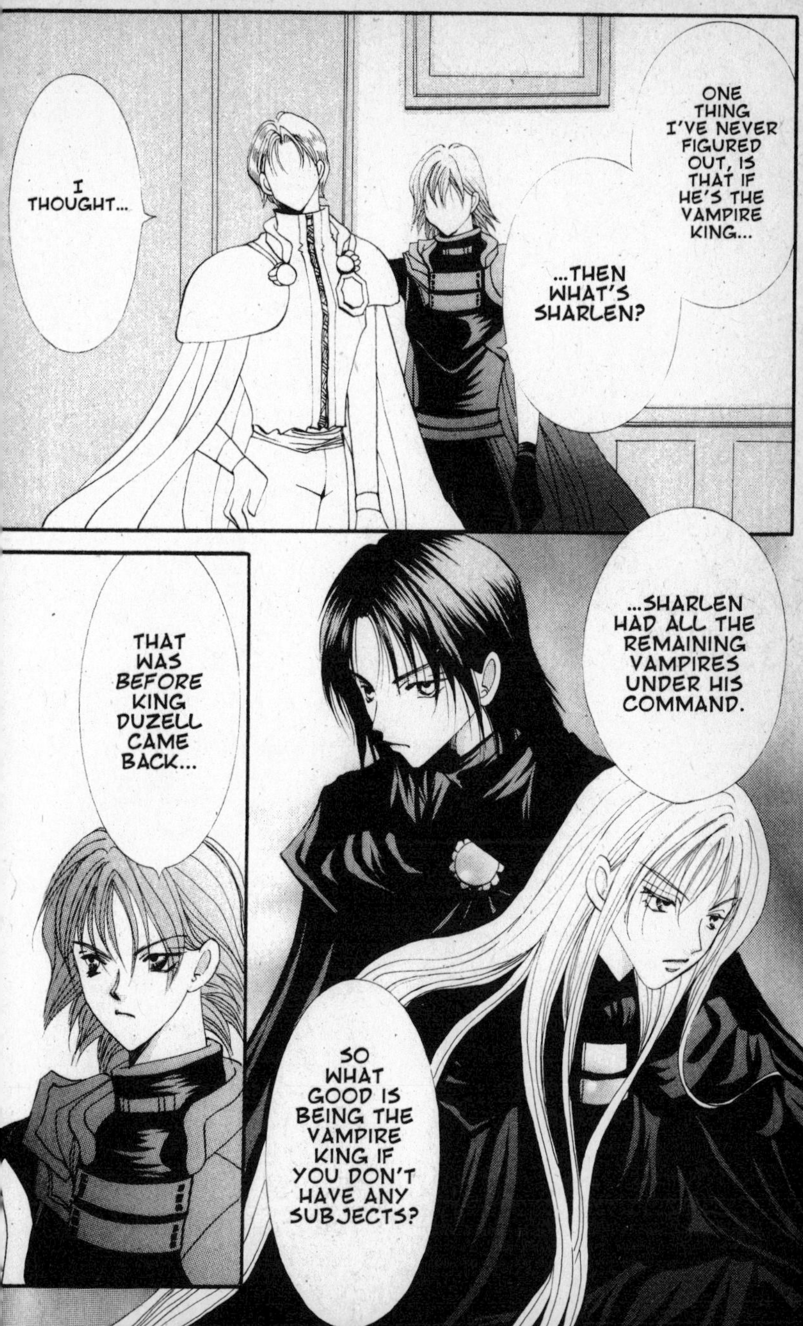
ONE THING I'VE NEVER FIGURED OUT, IS THAT IF HE'S THE VAMPIRE KING...
...THEN WHAT'S SHARLEN?
I THOUGHT...
...SHARLEN HAD ALL THE REMAINING VAMPIRES UNDER HIS COMMAND.
THAT WAS BEFORE KING DUZELL CAME BACK...
SO WHAT GOOD IS BEING THE VAMPIRE KING IF YOU DON'T HAVE ANY SUBJECTS?

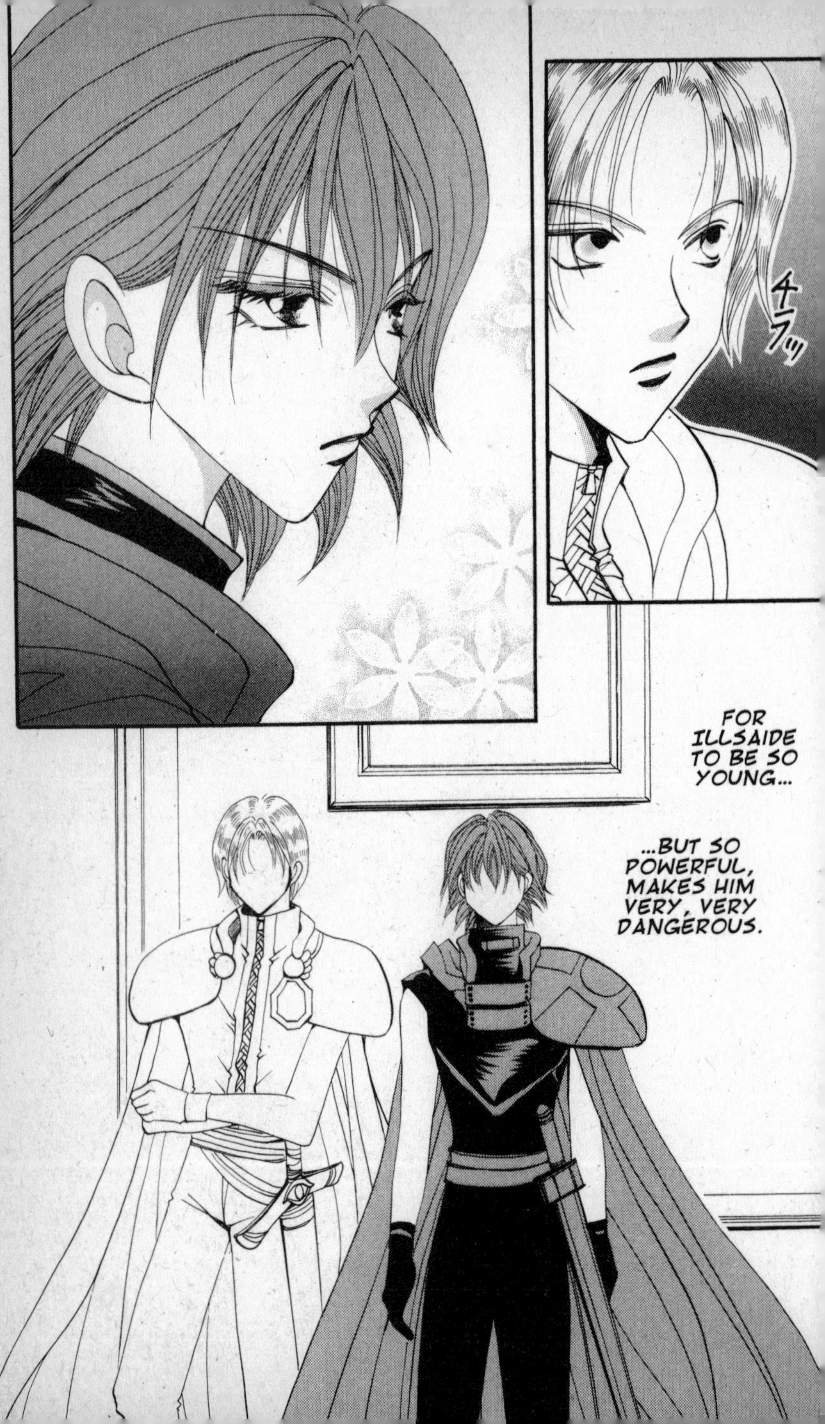

チーフッ
FOR ILLSAIDE TO BE SO YOUNG...
...BUT SO POWERFUL, MAKES HIM VERY, VERY DANGEROUS.

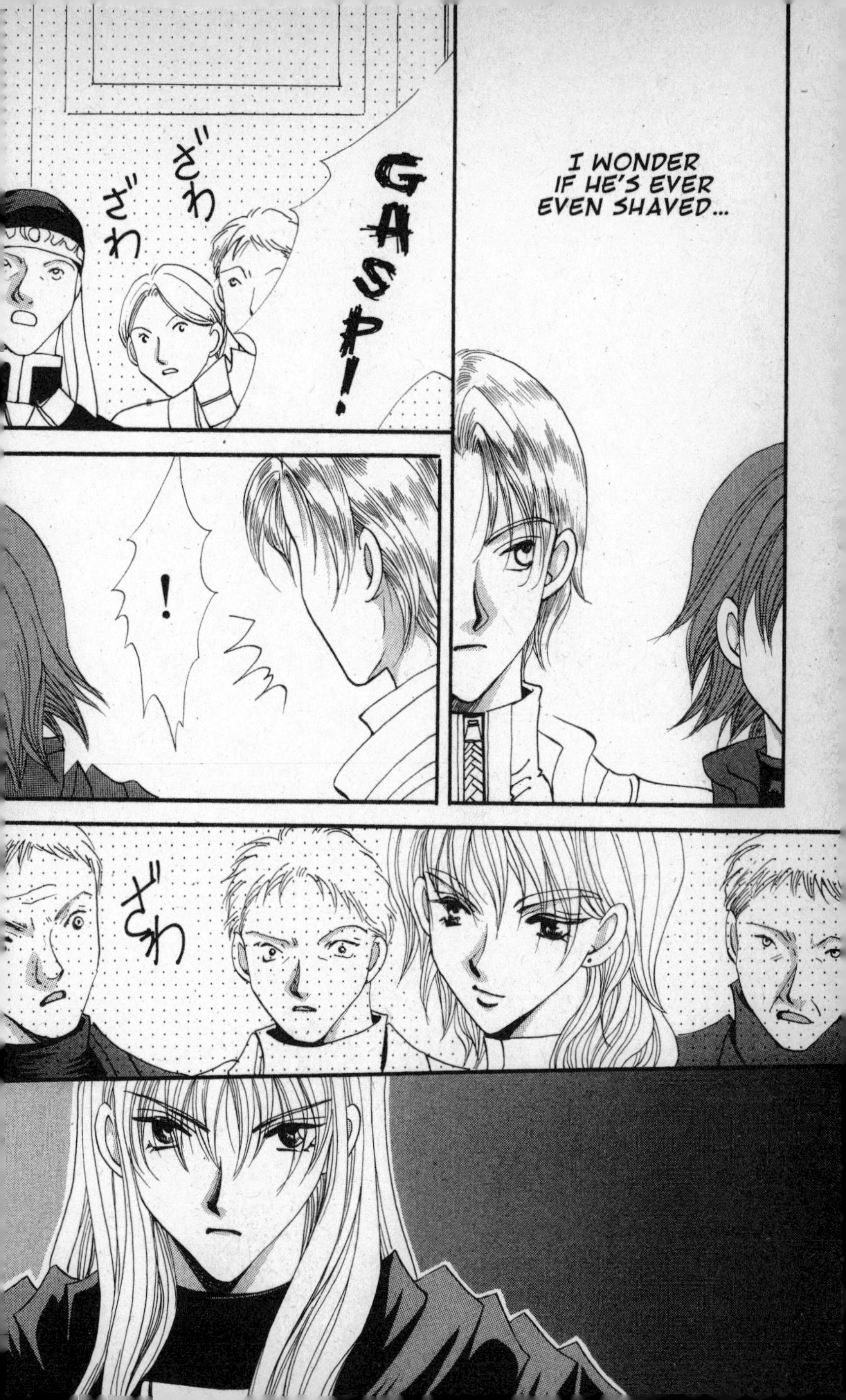

I WONDER IF HE'S EVER EVEN SHAVED...
GASP!
ざわ
ざわ
!
ざわ

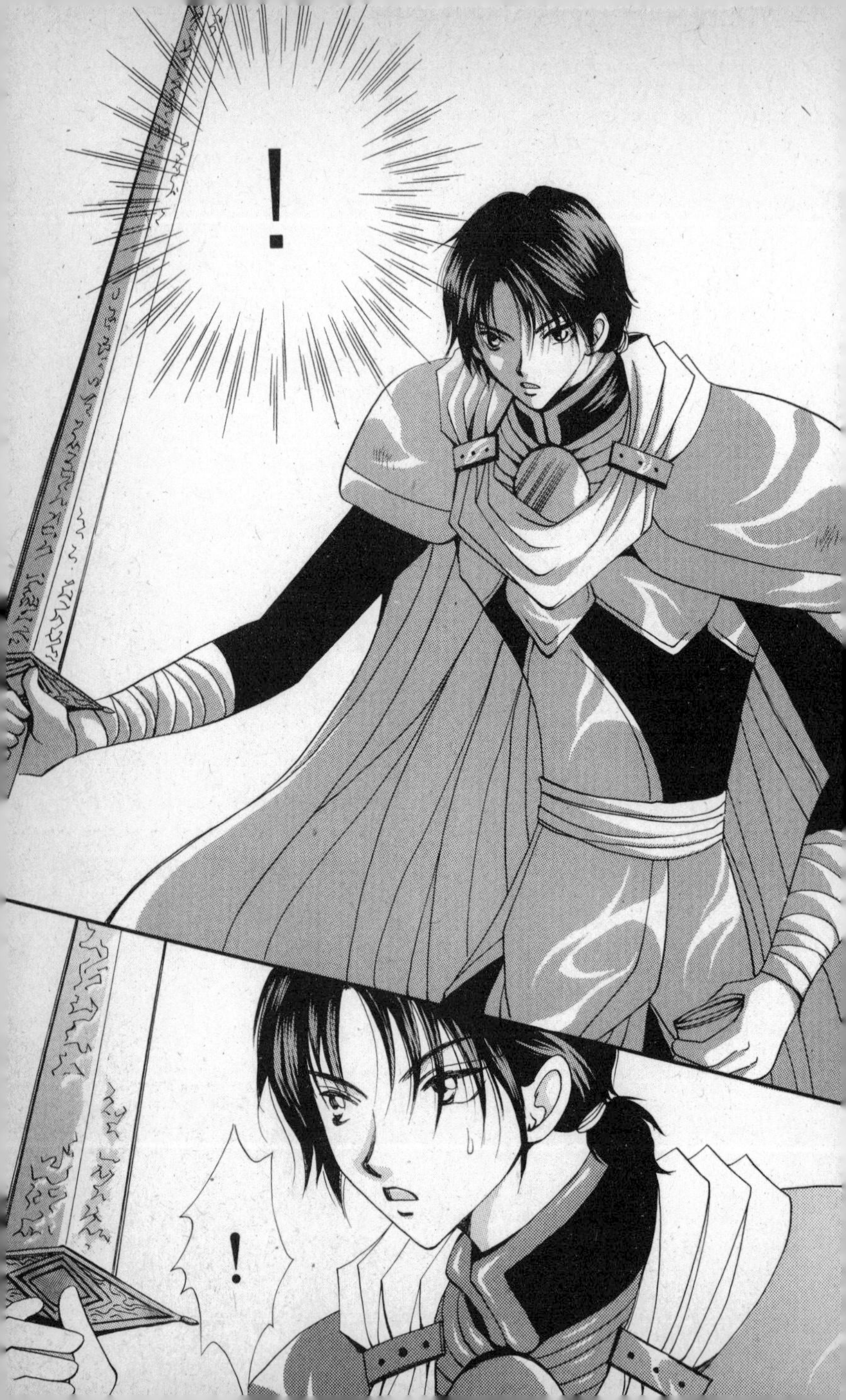
!
!

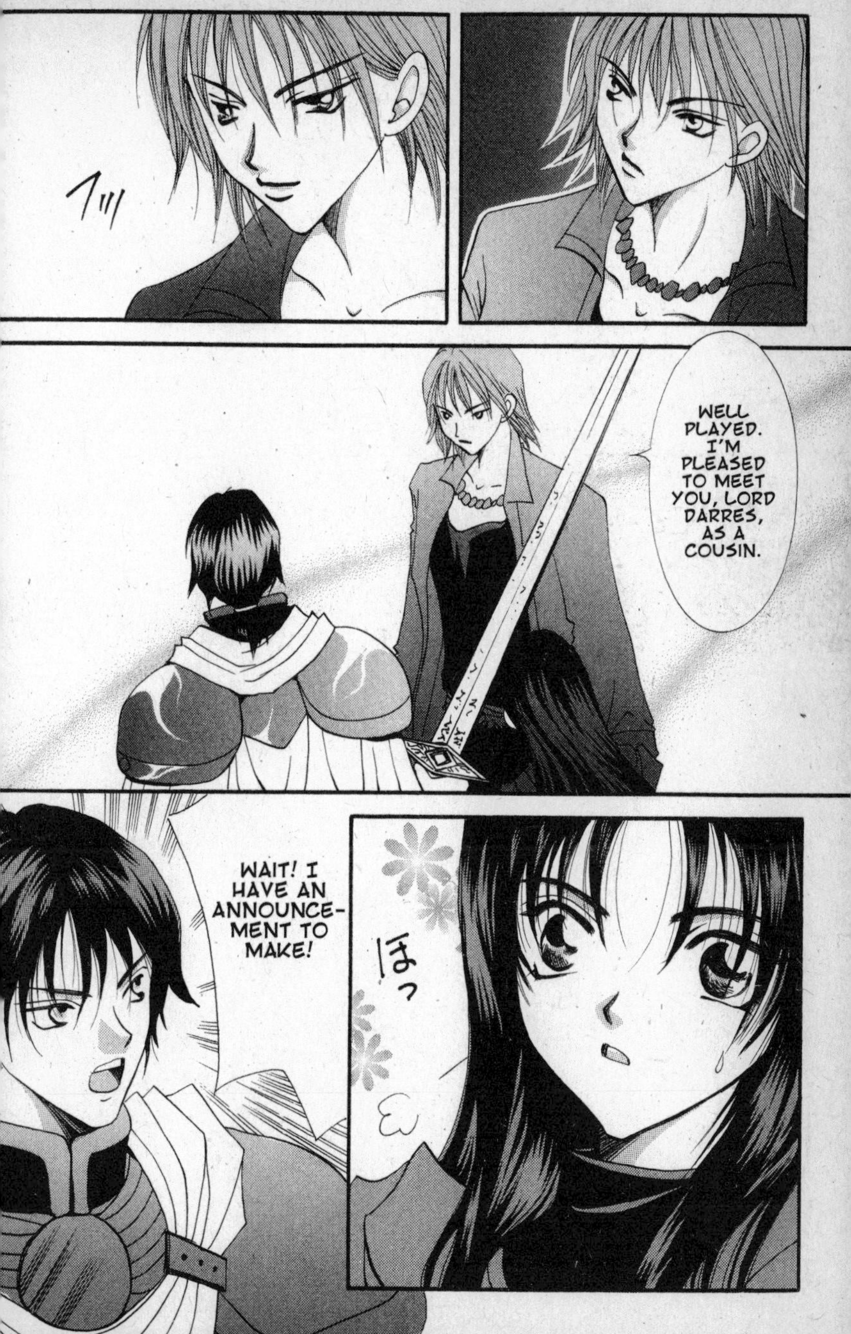
フッ
WELL PLAYED. I'M PLEASED TO MEET YOU, LORD DARRES, AS A COUSIN.
ほっ
WAIT! I HAVE AN ANNOUNCEMENT TO MAKE!

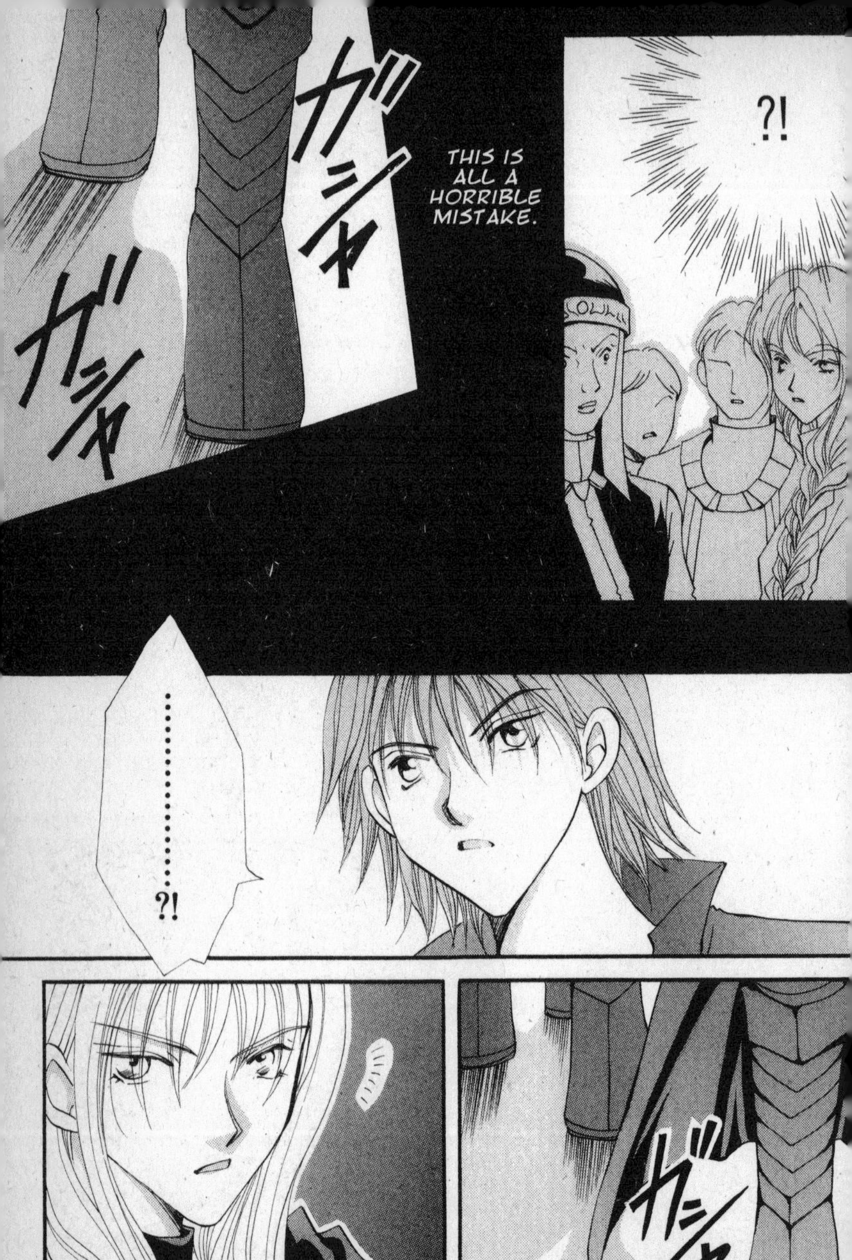

?!
THIS IS ALL A HORRIBLE MISTAKE.
ガシャ
ガシャ
……?!
ガシャ

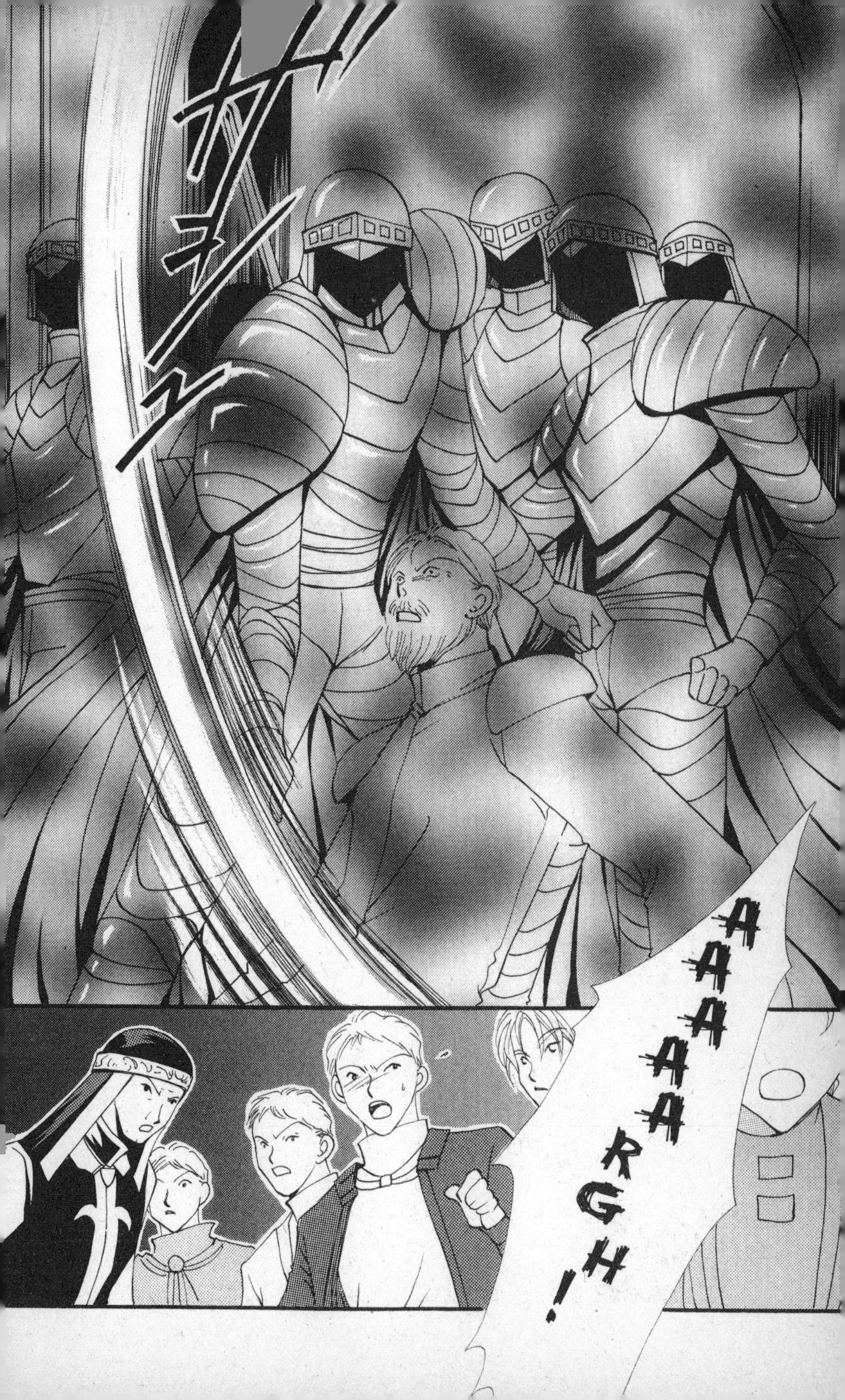
AAAAARGH!

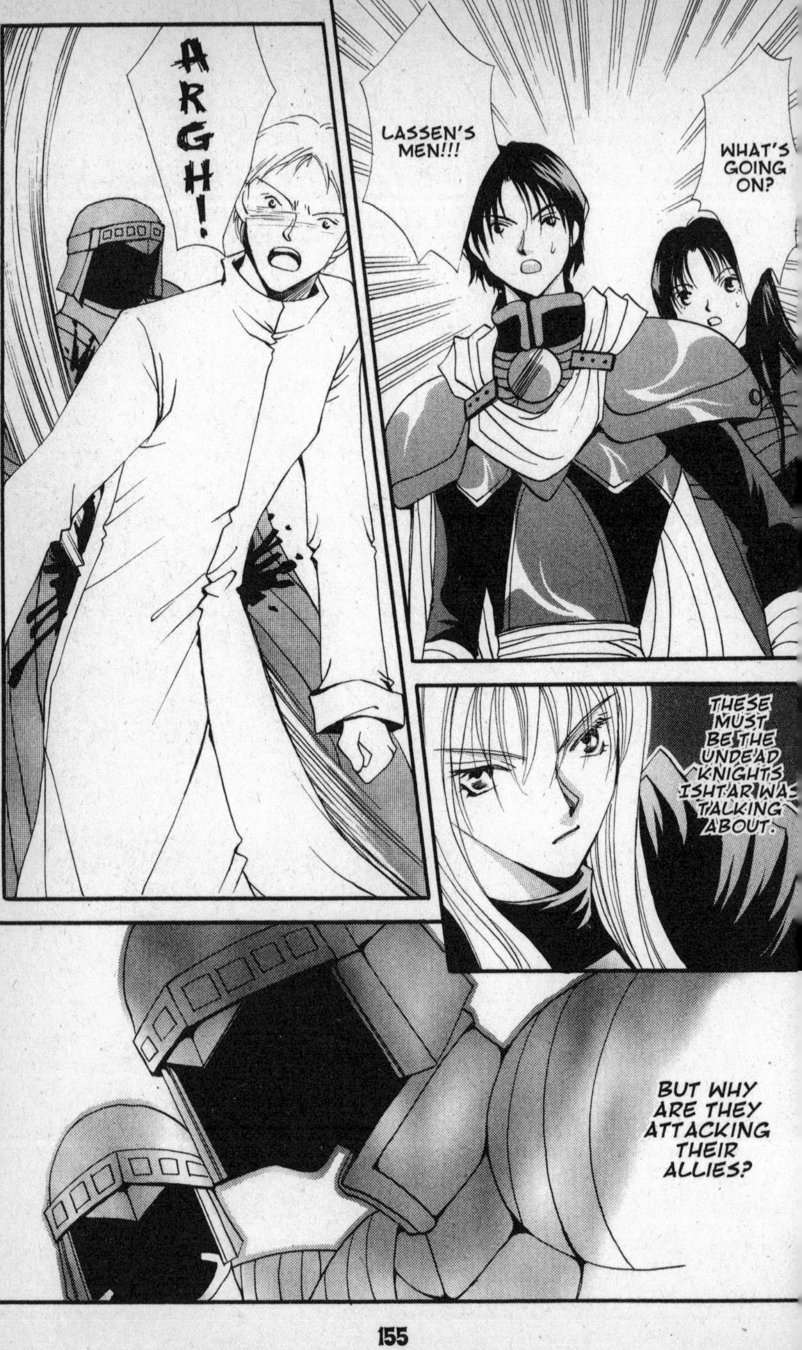
WHAT'S GOING ON?
LASSEN'S MEN!!!
THESE MUST BE THE UNDEAD KNIGHTS ISHTAR WAS TALKING ABOUT.
ARGH!
BUT WHY ARE THEY ATTACKING THEIR ALLIES?

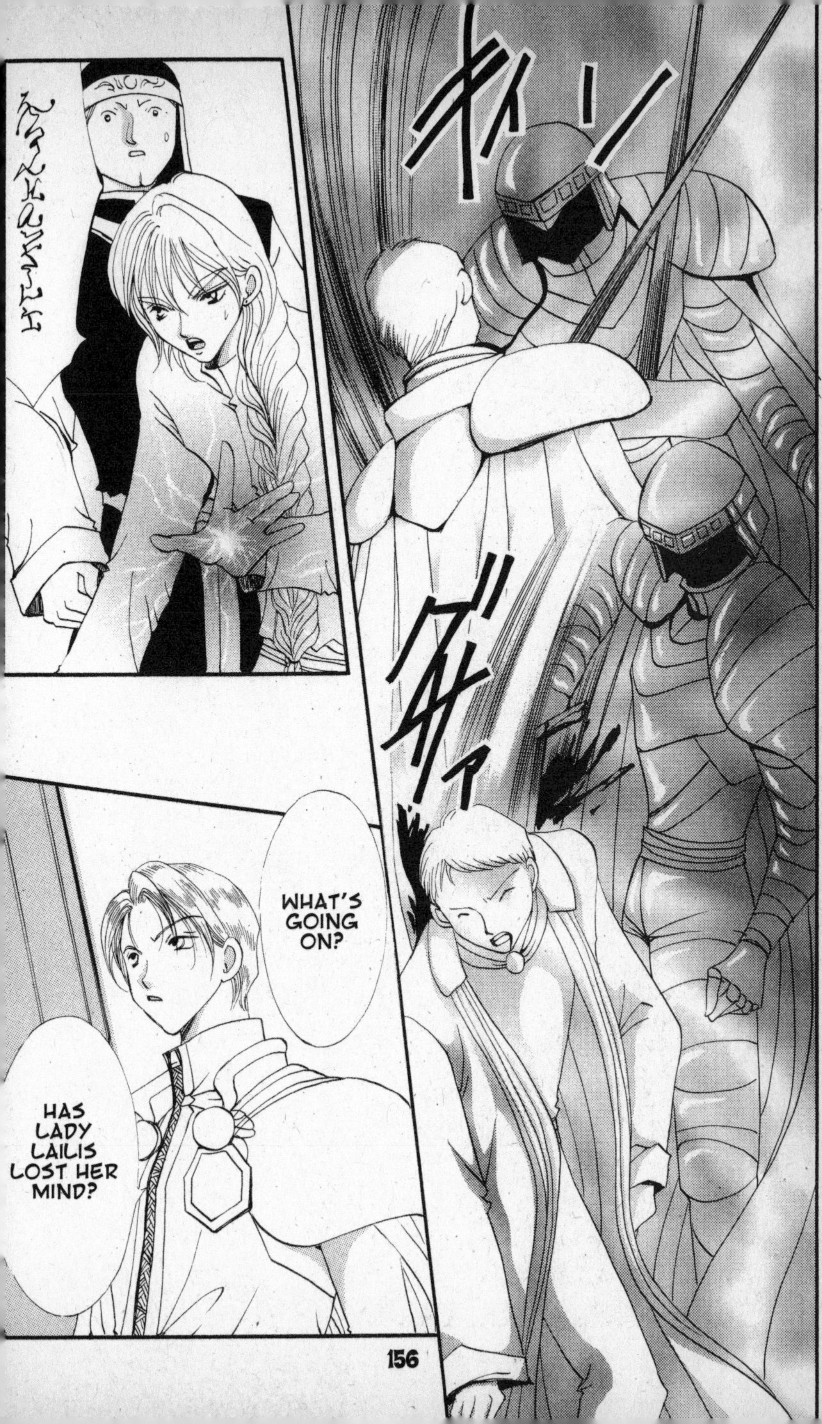
WHAT'S GOING ON?
HAS LADY LAILIS LOST HER MIND?

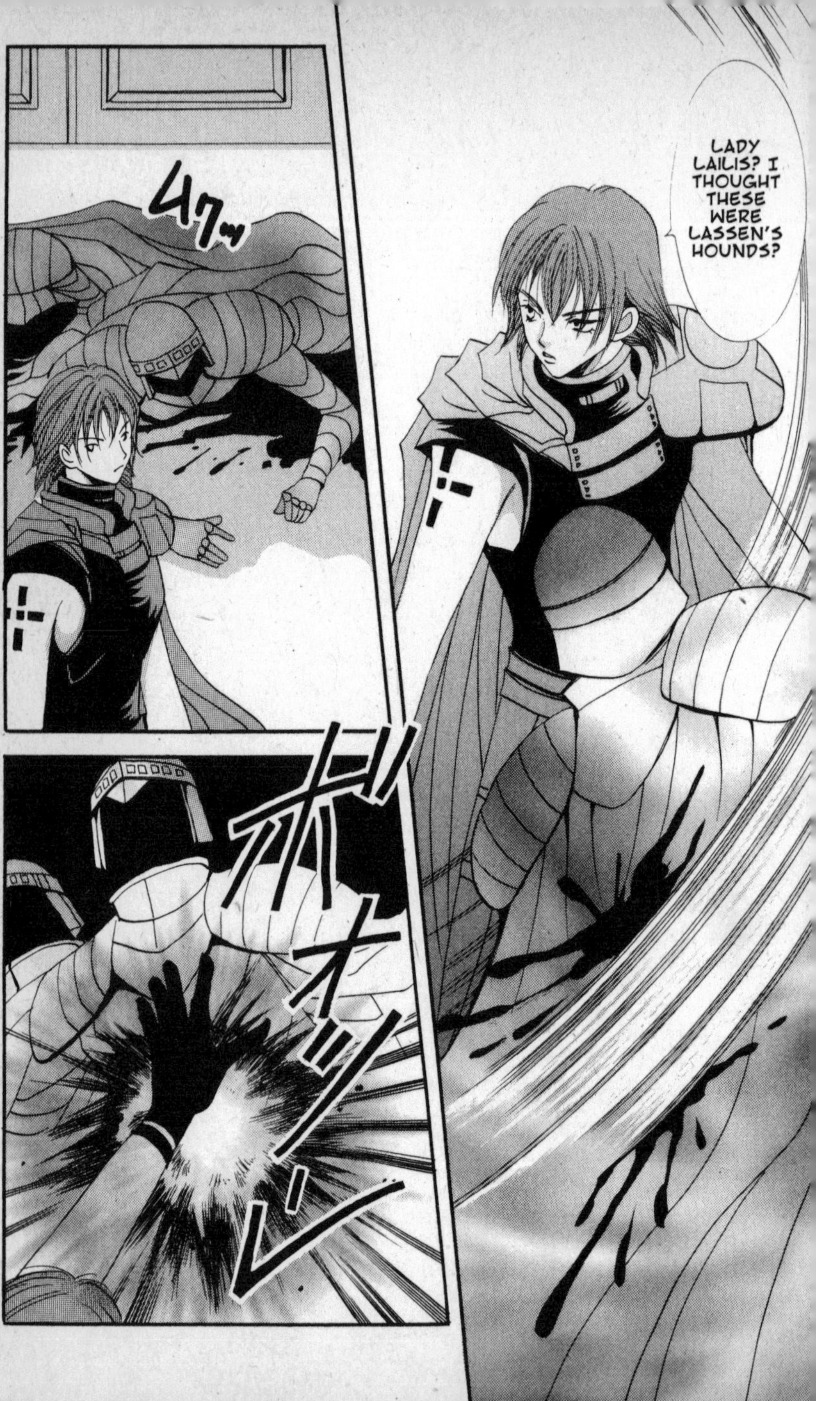
LADY LAILIS? I THOUGHT THESE WERE LASSEN'S HOUNDS?

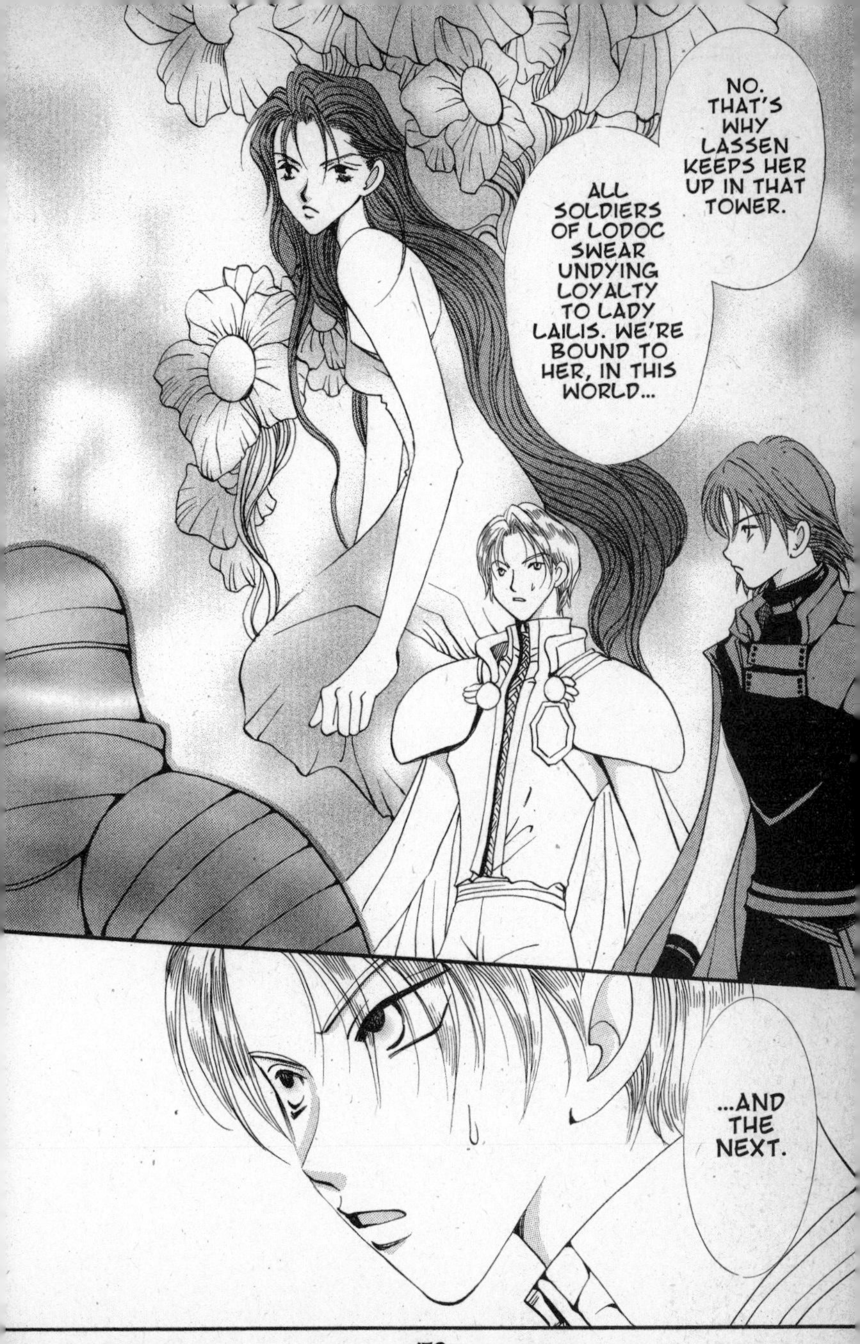
NO. THAT'S WHY LASSEN KEEPS HER UP IN THAT TOWER.
ALL SOLDIERS OF LODOC SWEAR UNDYING LOYALTY TO LADY LAILIS. WE'RE BOUND TO HER, IN THIS WORLD...
...AND THE NEXT.

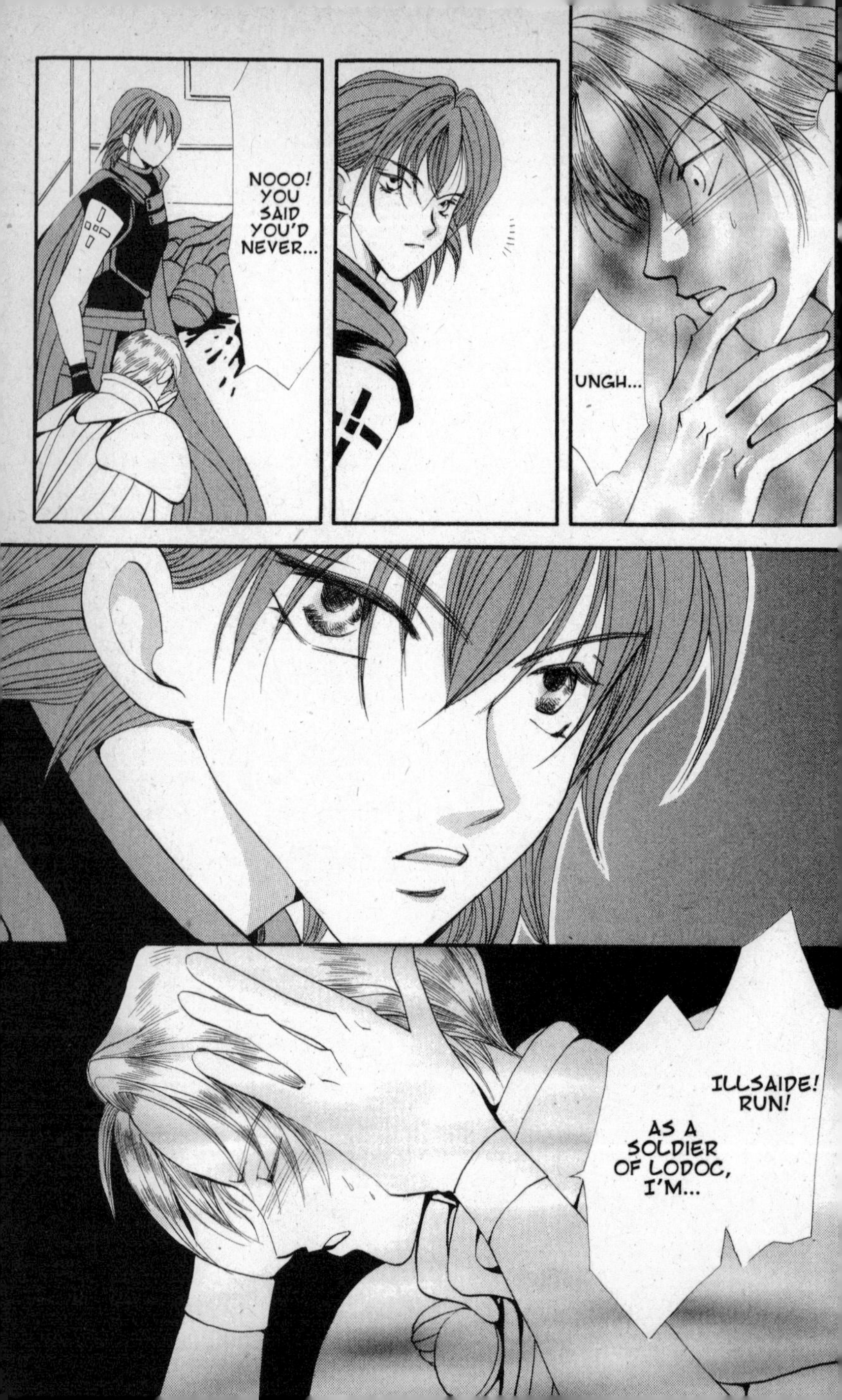
UNGH...
NOOO! YOU SAID YOU'D NEVER...
ILLSAIDE! RUN!
AS A SOLDIER OF LODOC, I'M...

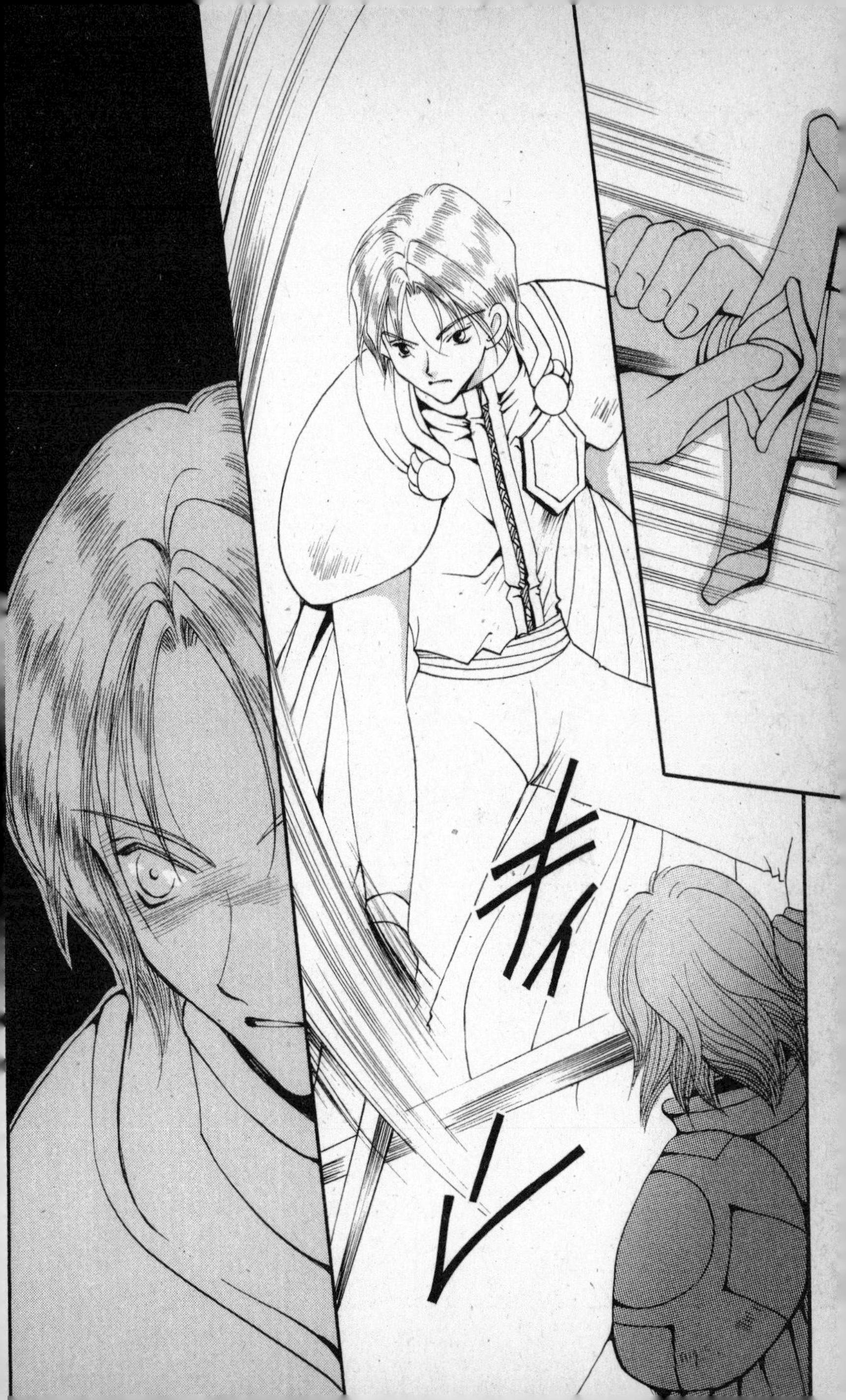
キィン

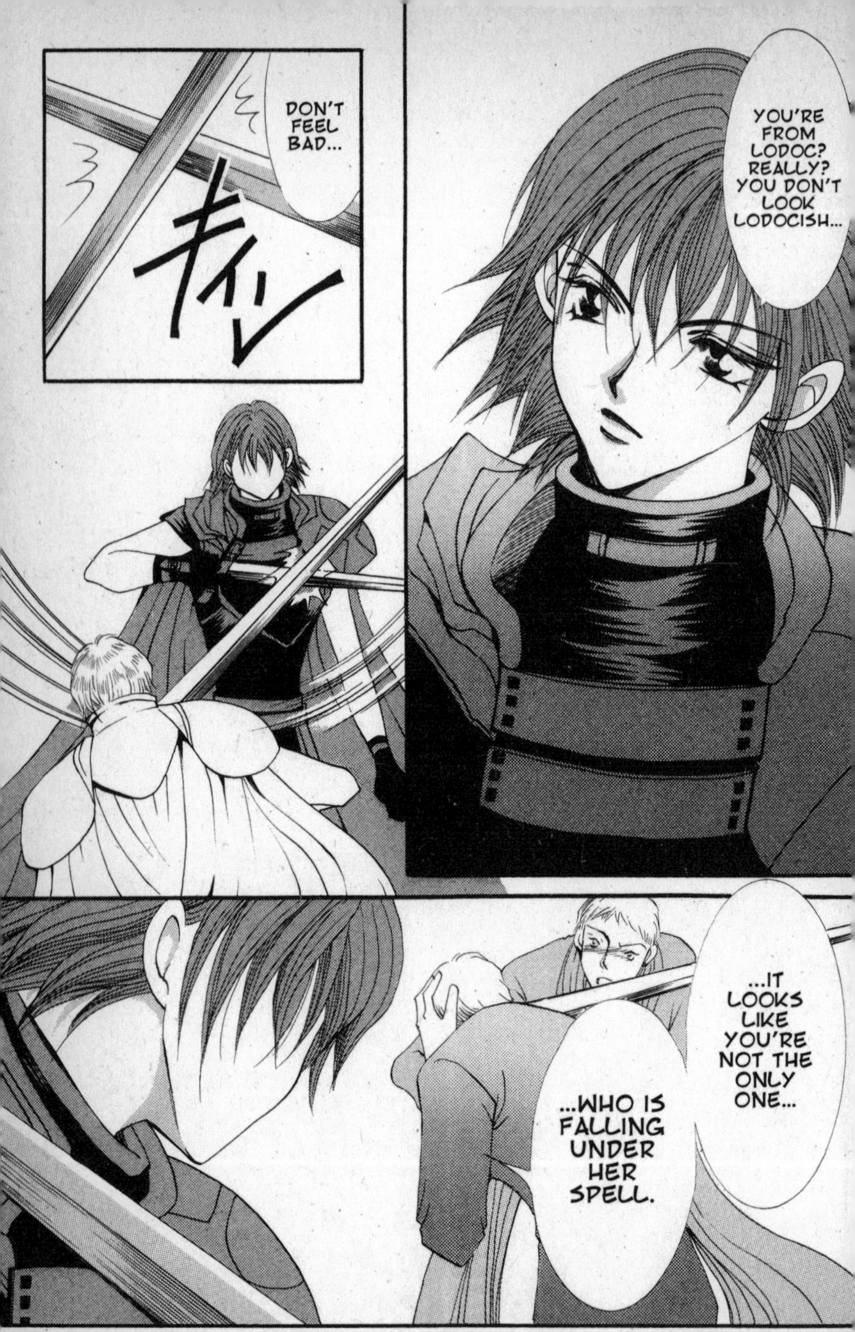
YOU'RE FROM LODOC? REALLY? YOU DON'T LOOK LODOCISH...
DON'T FEEL BAD...
キィン
...IT LOOKS LIKE YOU'RE NOT THE ONLY ONE...
...WHO IS FALLING UNDER HER SPELL.

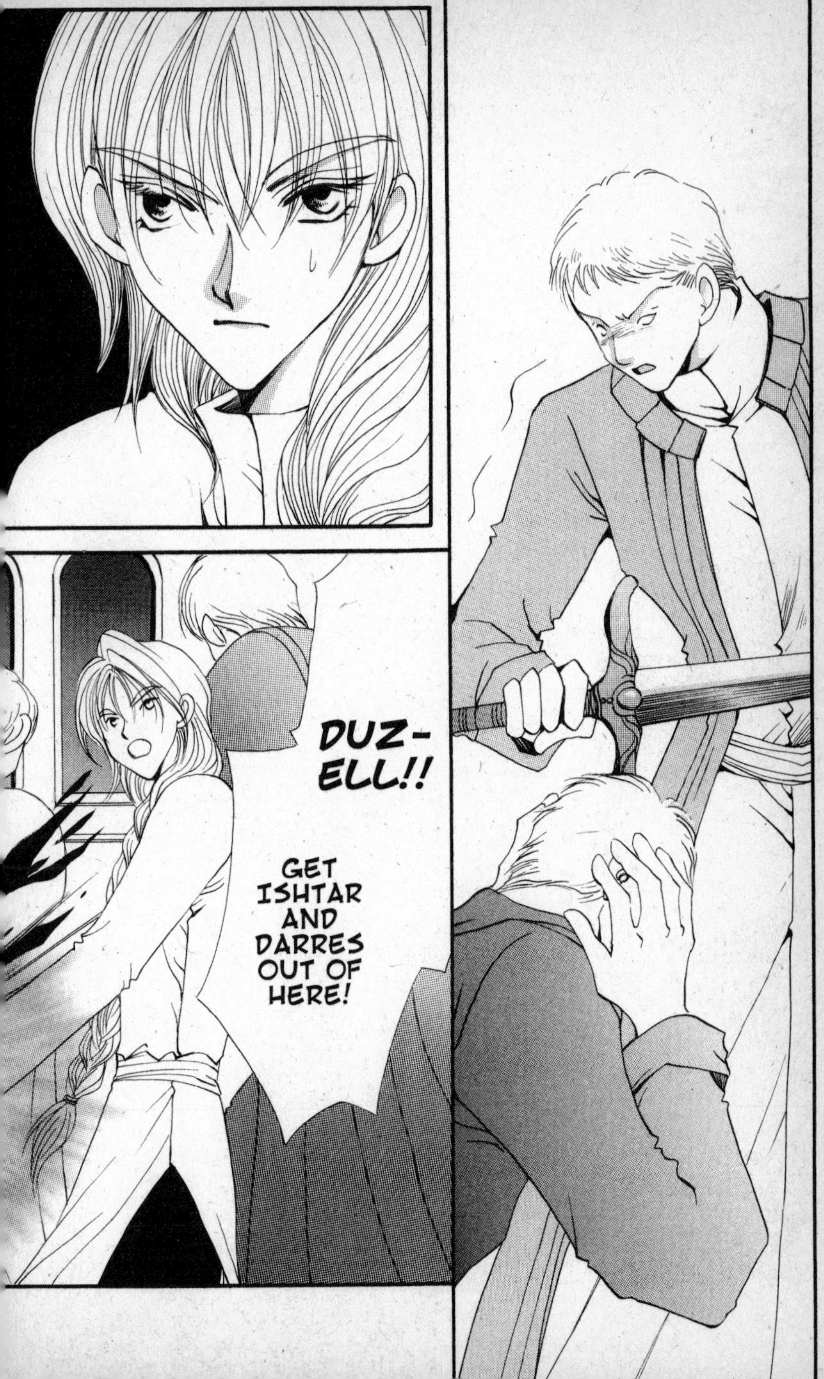
DUZ-ELL!!
GET ISHTAR AND DARRES OUT OF HERE!

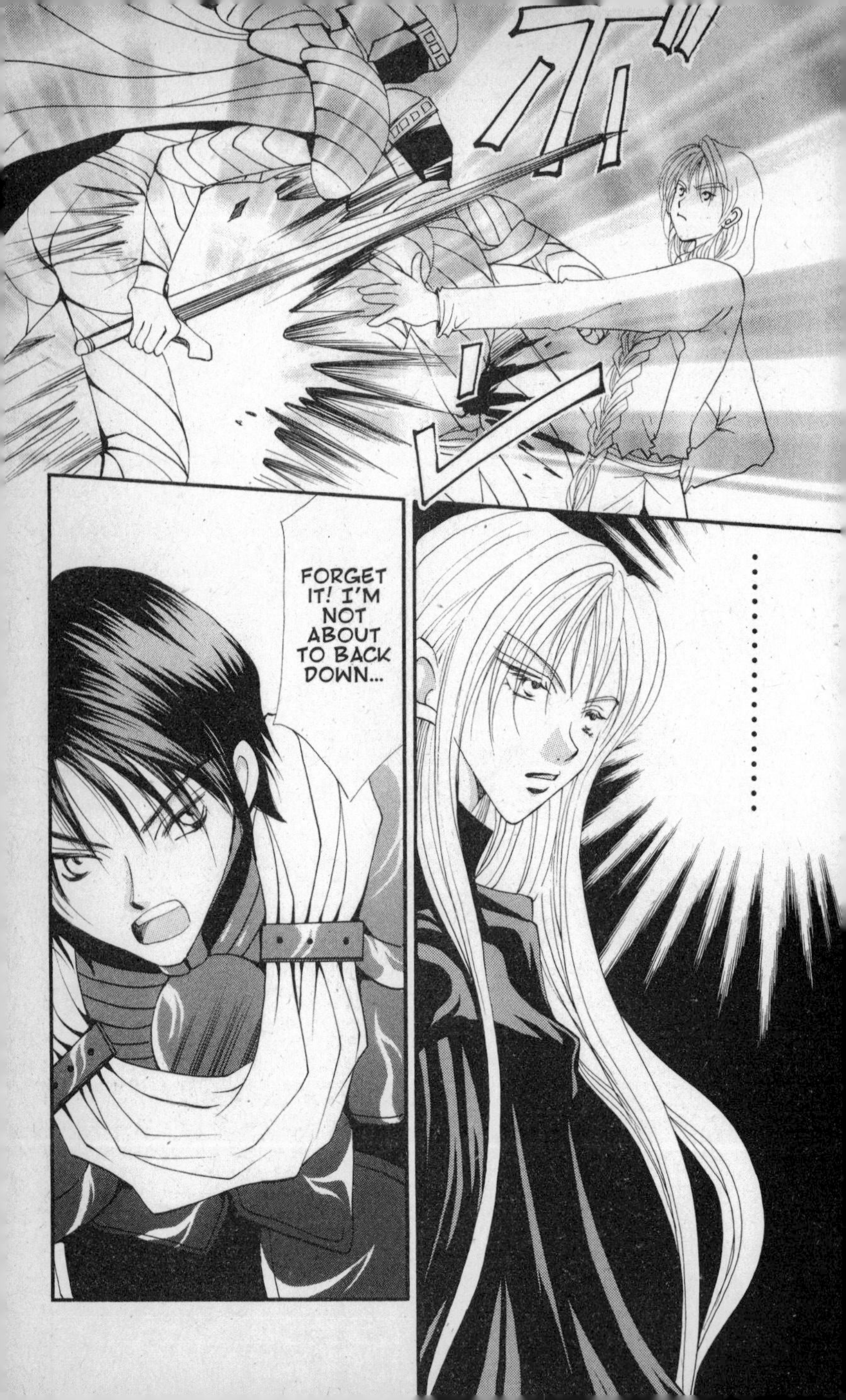
....
FORGET IT! I'M NOT ABOUT TO BACK DOWN...

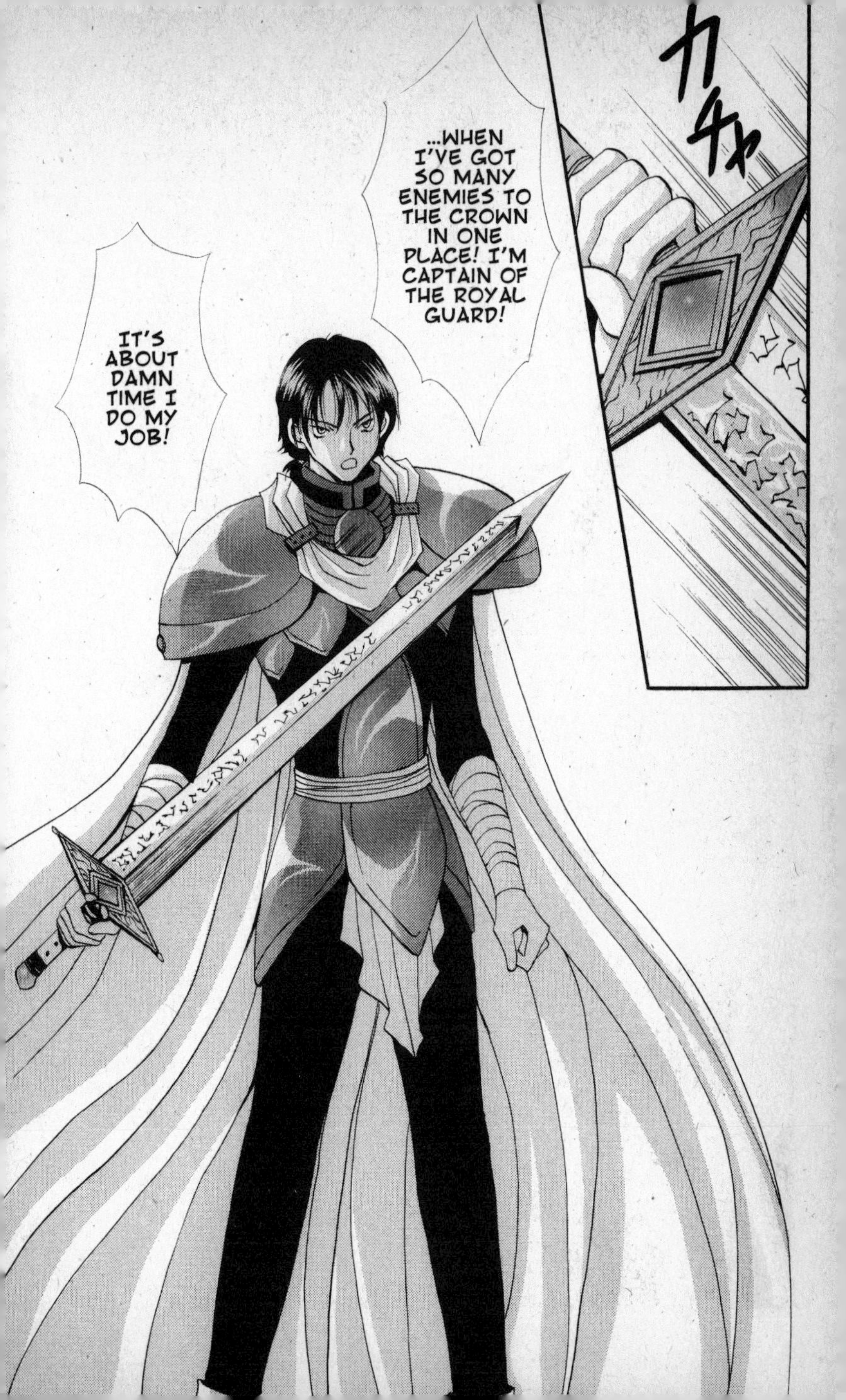
カチャ
...WHEN I'VE GOT SO MANY ENEMIES TO THE CROWN IN ONE PLACE! I'M CAPTAIN OF THE ROYAL GUARD!
IT'S ABOUT DAMN TIME I DO MY JOB!

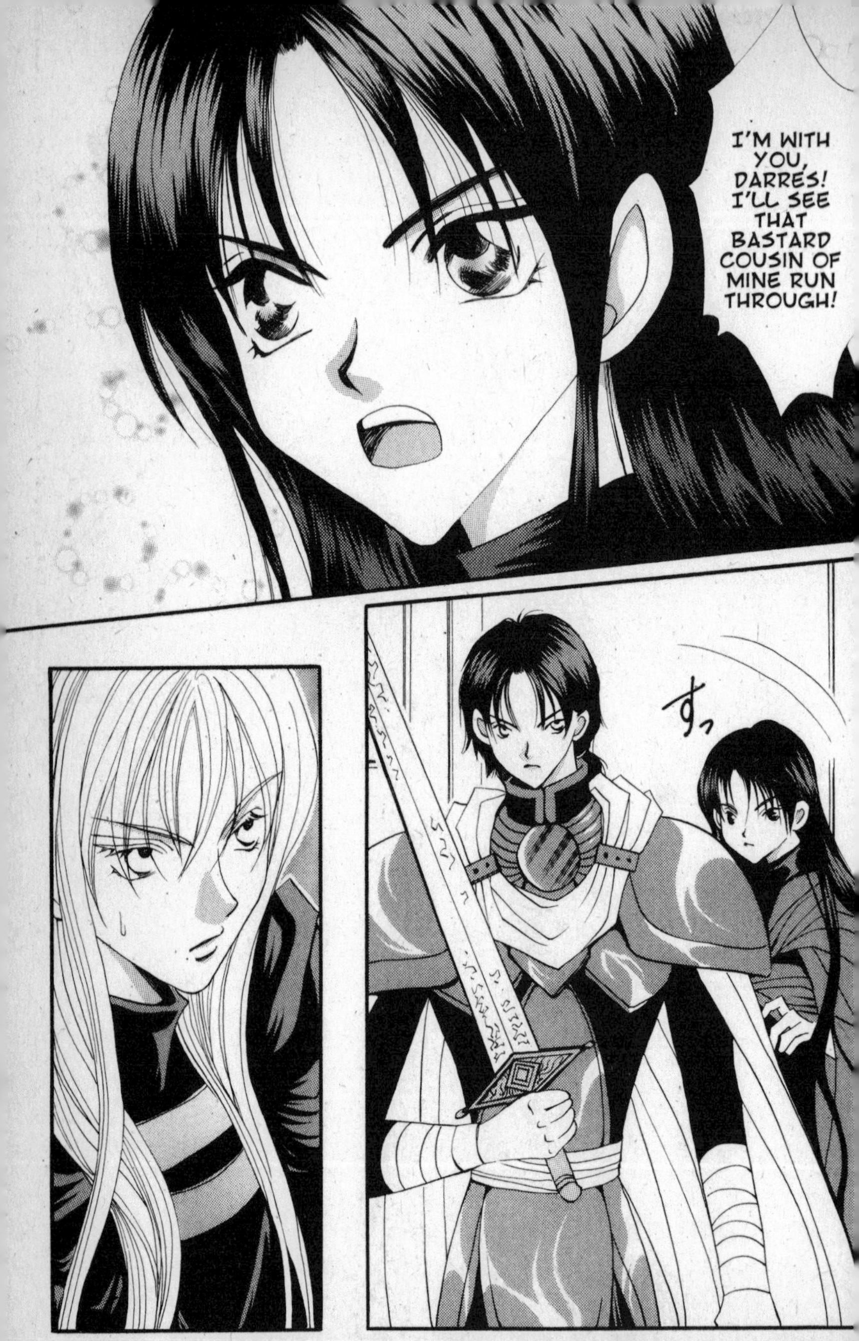
I'M WITH YOU, DARRES! I'LL SEE THAT BASTARD COUSIN OF MINE RUN THROUGH!
すっ

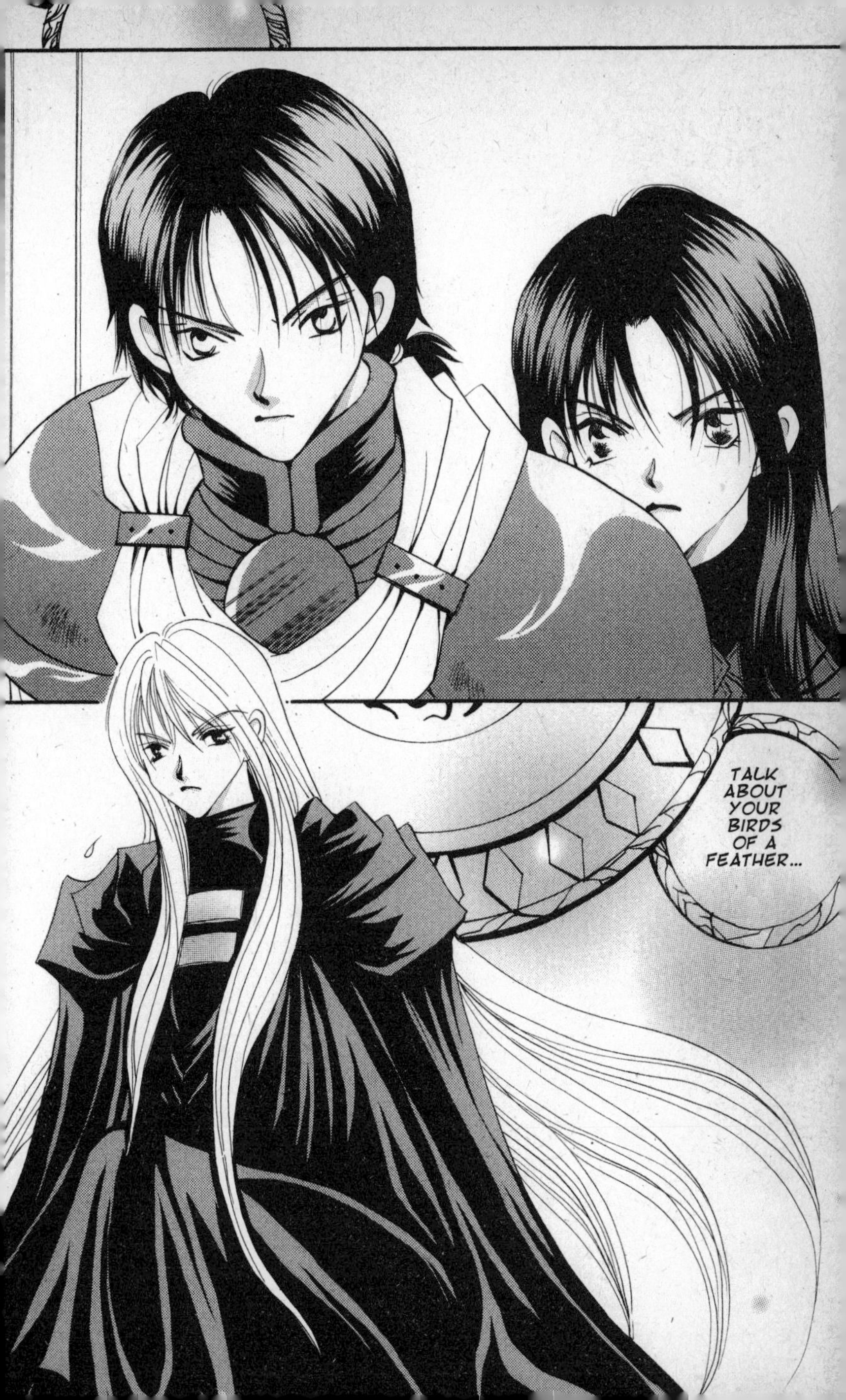
TALK ABOUT YOUR BIRDS OF A FEATHER...

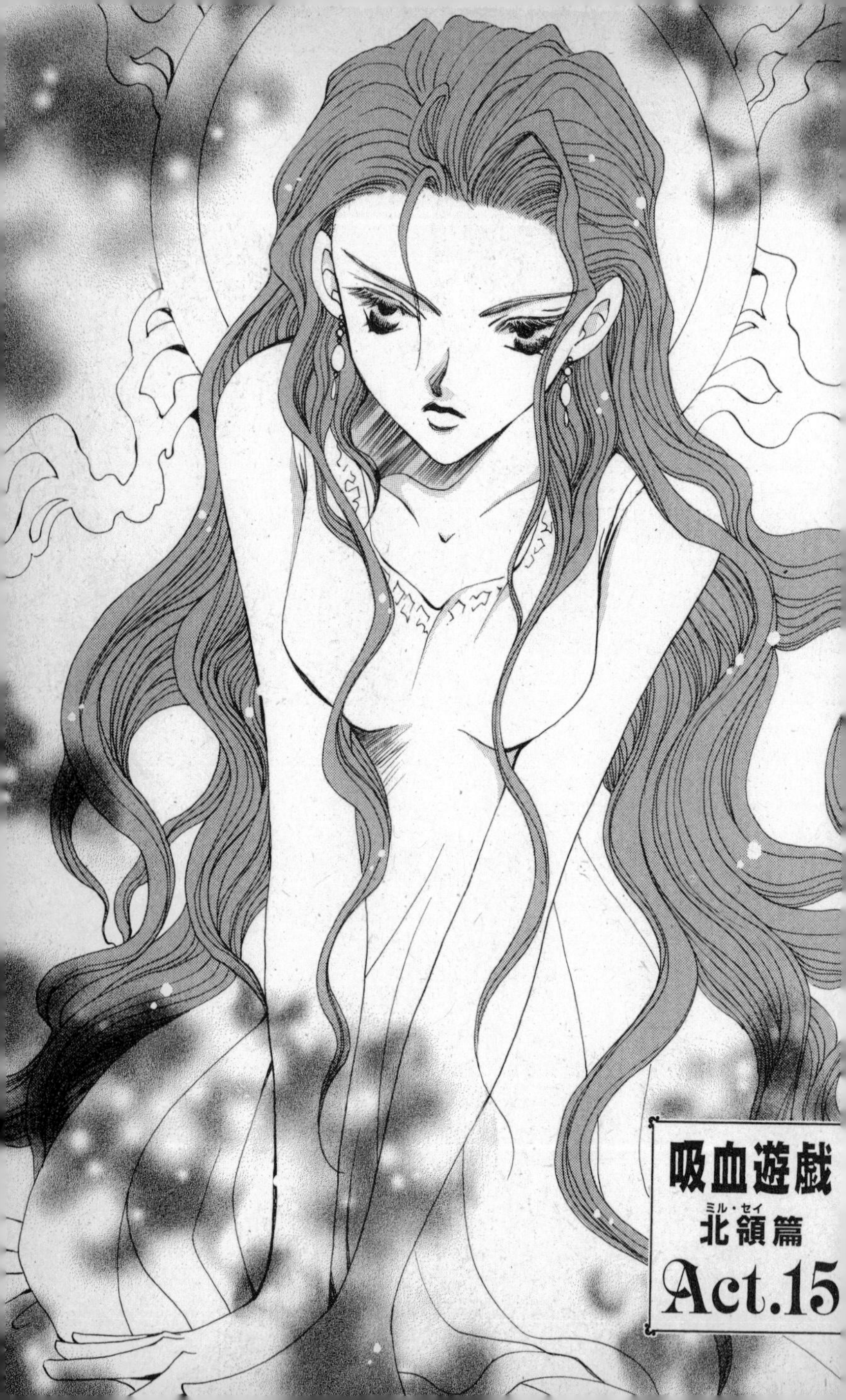
吸血遊戯
北領篇 (ミル・セイ)
Act.15

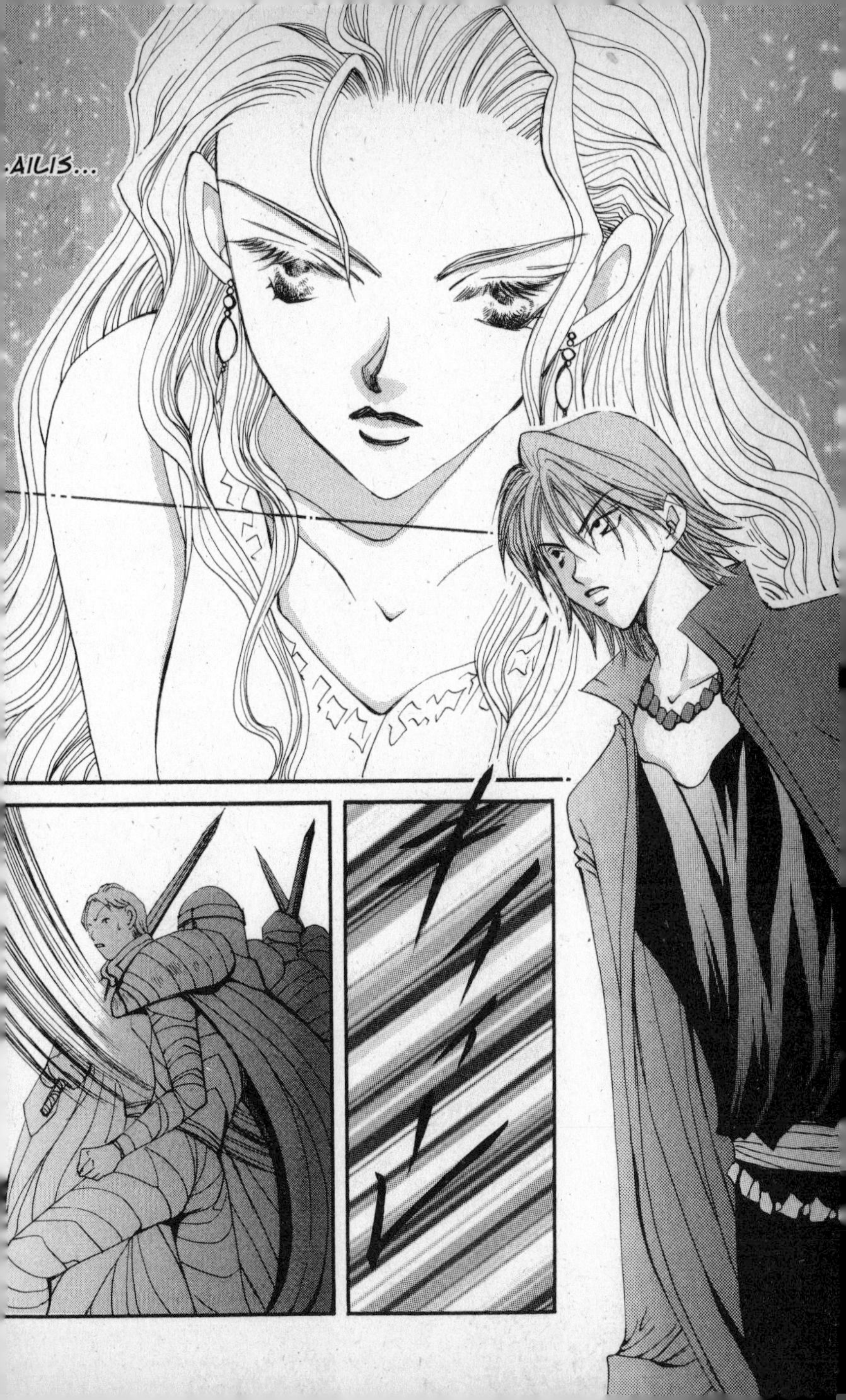
.AILIS...

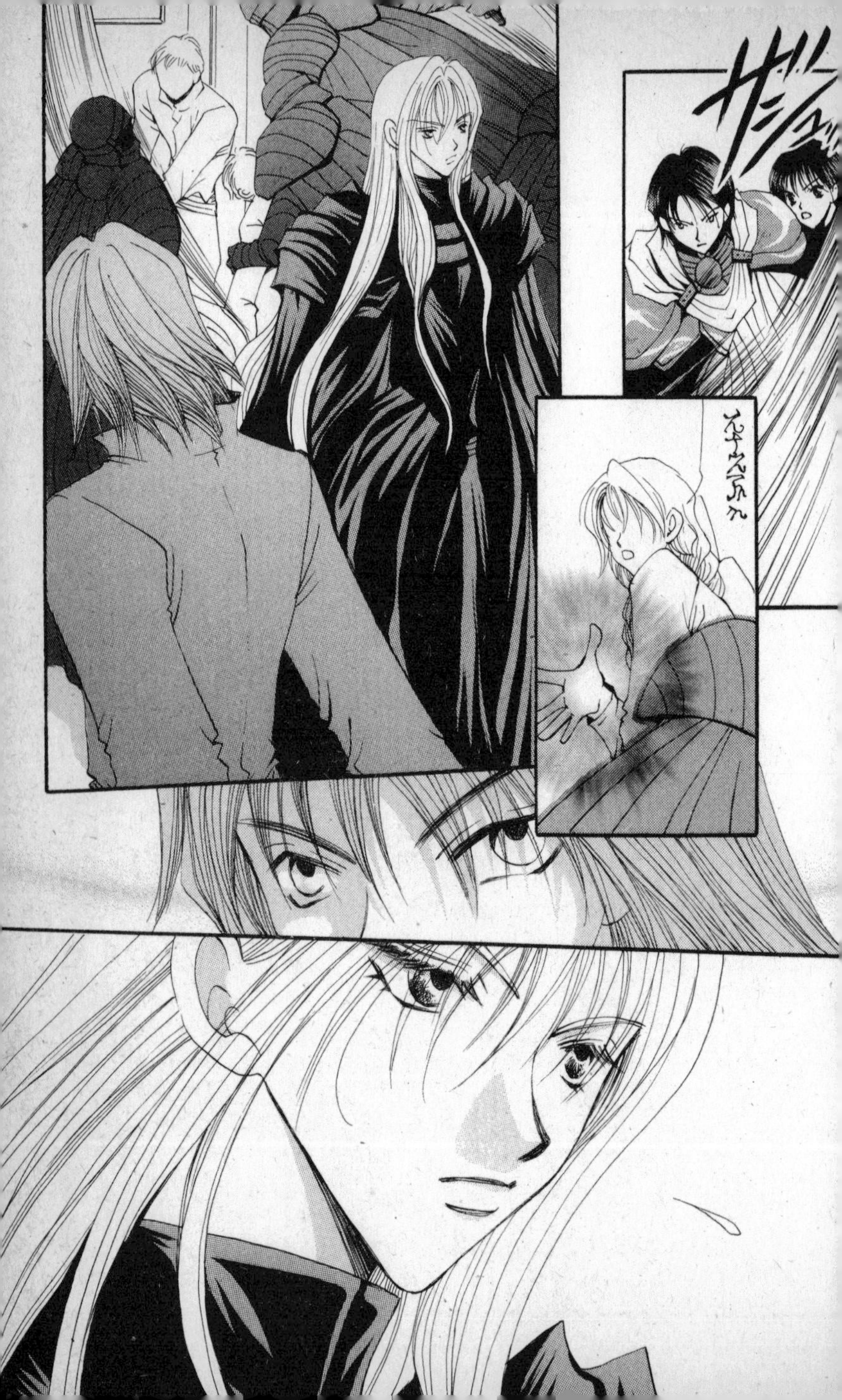
ザシュッ

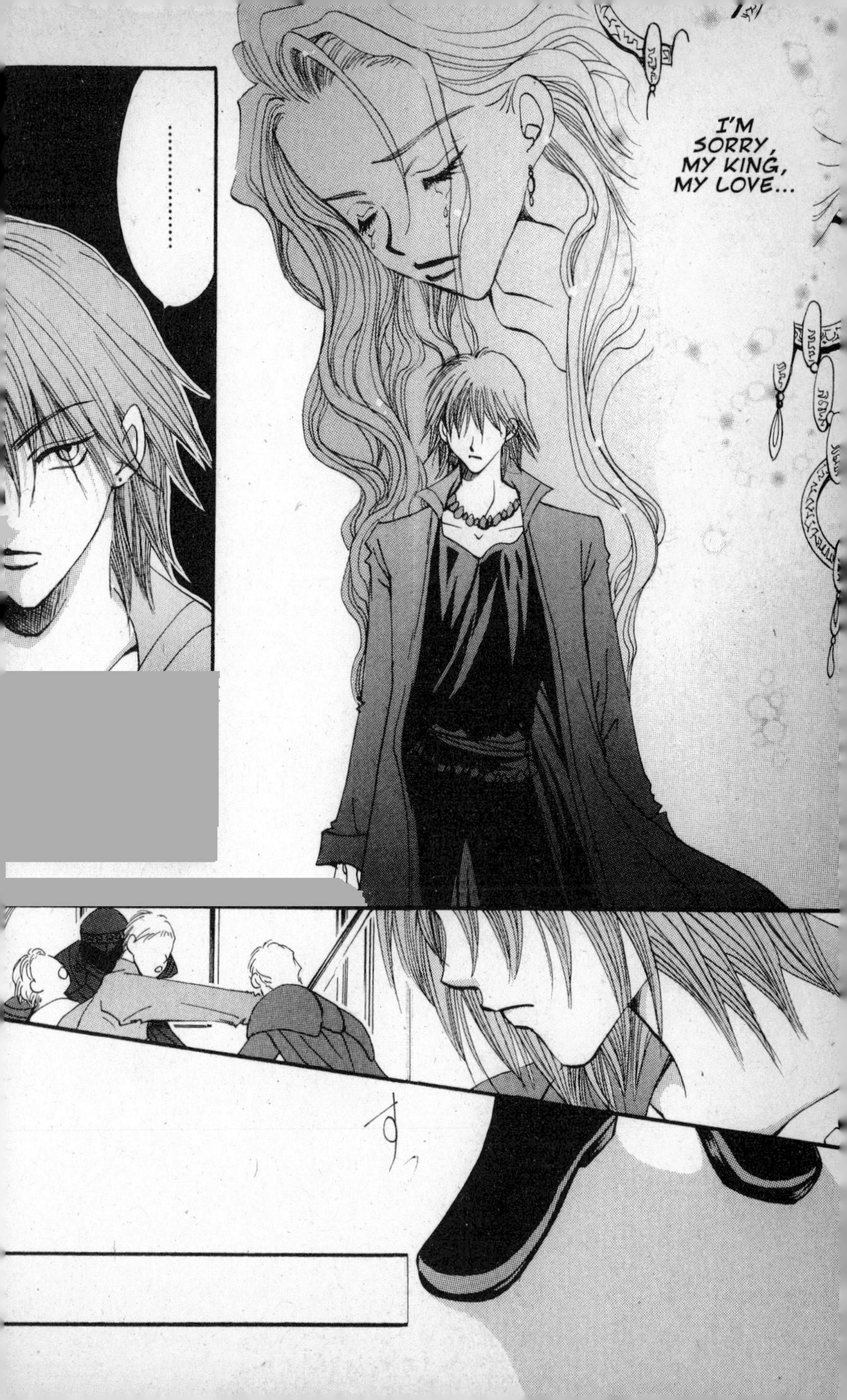
I'M SORRY, MY KING, MY LOVE...
......

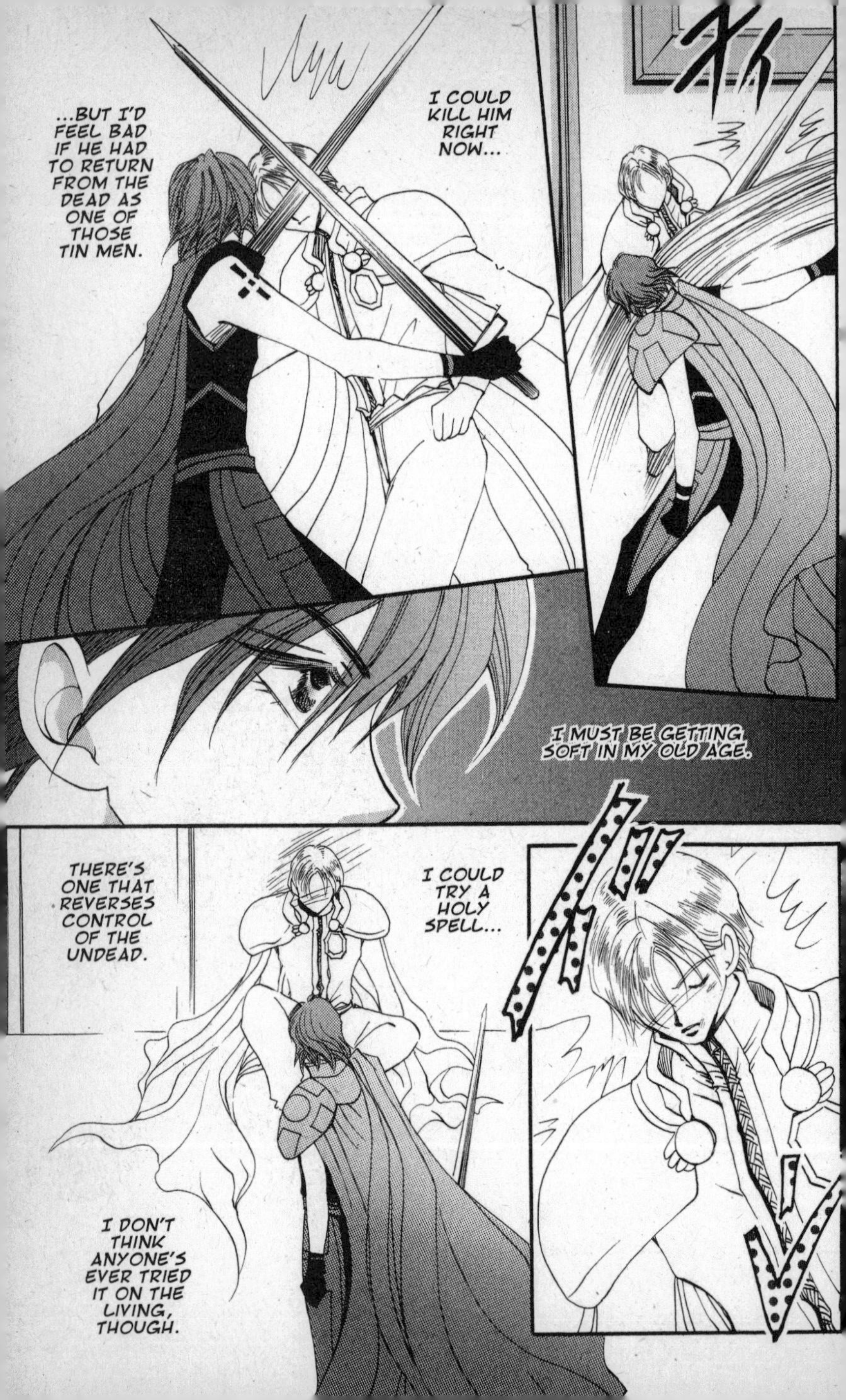
I COULD KILL HIM RIGHT NOW...
...BUT I'D FEEL BAD IF HE HAD TO RETURN FROM THE DEAD AS ONE OF THOSE TIN MEN.
I MUST BE GETTING SOFT IN MY OLD AGE.
I COULD TRY A HOLY SPELL...
THERE'S ONE THAT REVERSES CONTROL OF THE UNDEAD.
I DON'T THINK ANYONE'S EVER TRIED IT ON THE LIVING, THOUGH.

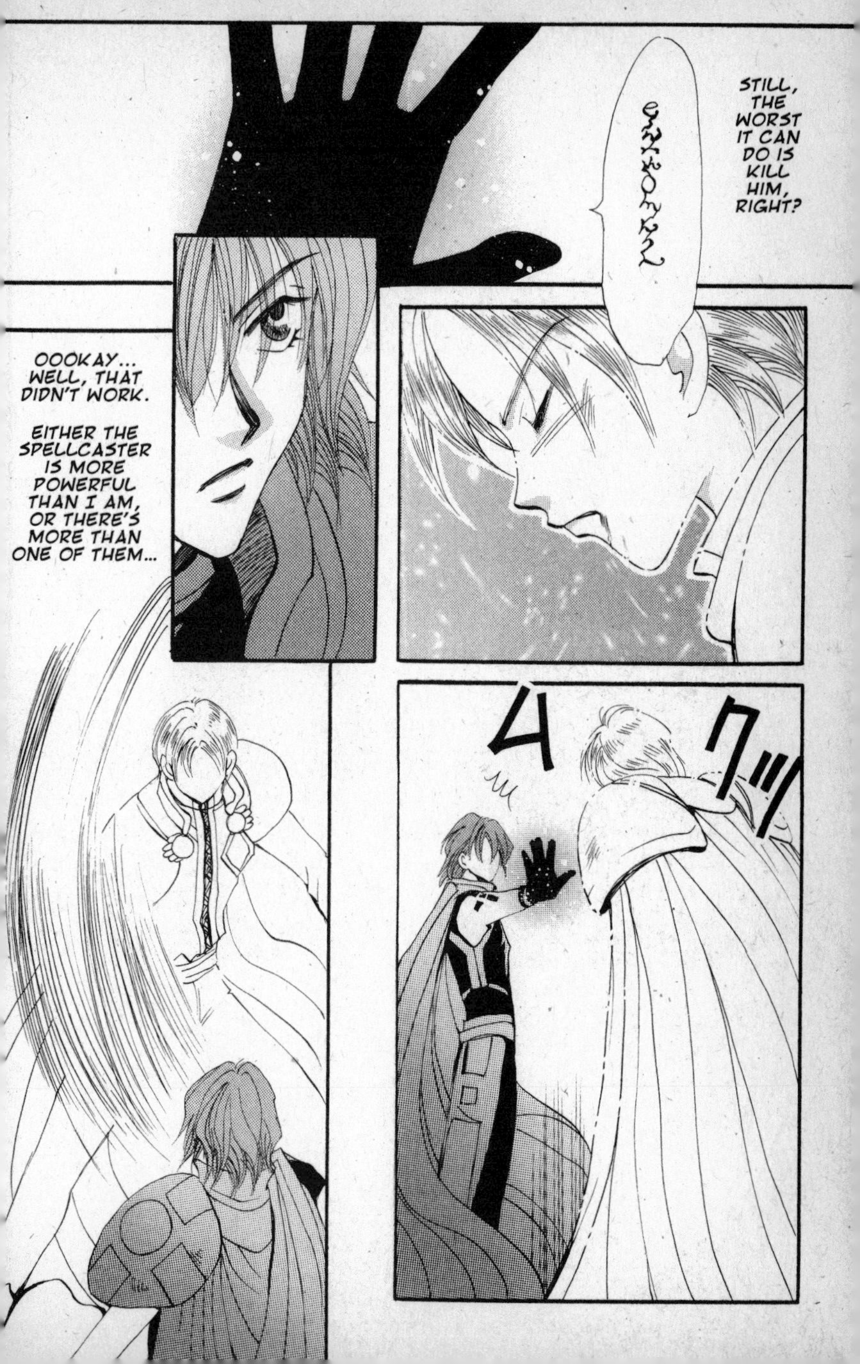
STILL, THE WORST IT CAN DO IS KILL HIM, RIGHT?
OOOKAY... WELL, THAT DIDN'T WORK.
EITHER THE SPELLCASTER IS MORE POWERFUL THAN I AM, OR THERE'S MORE THAN ONE OF THEM...
ム クッ

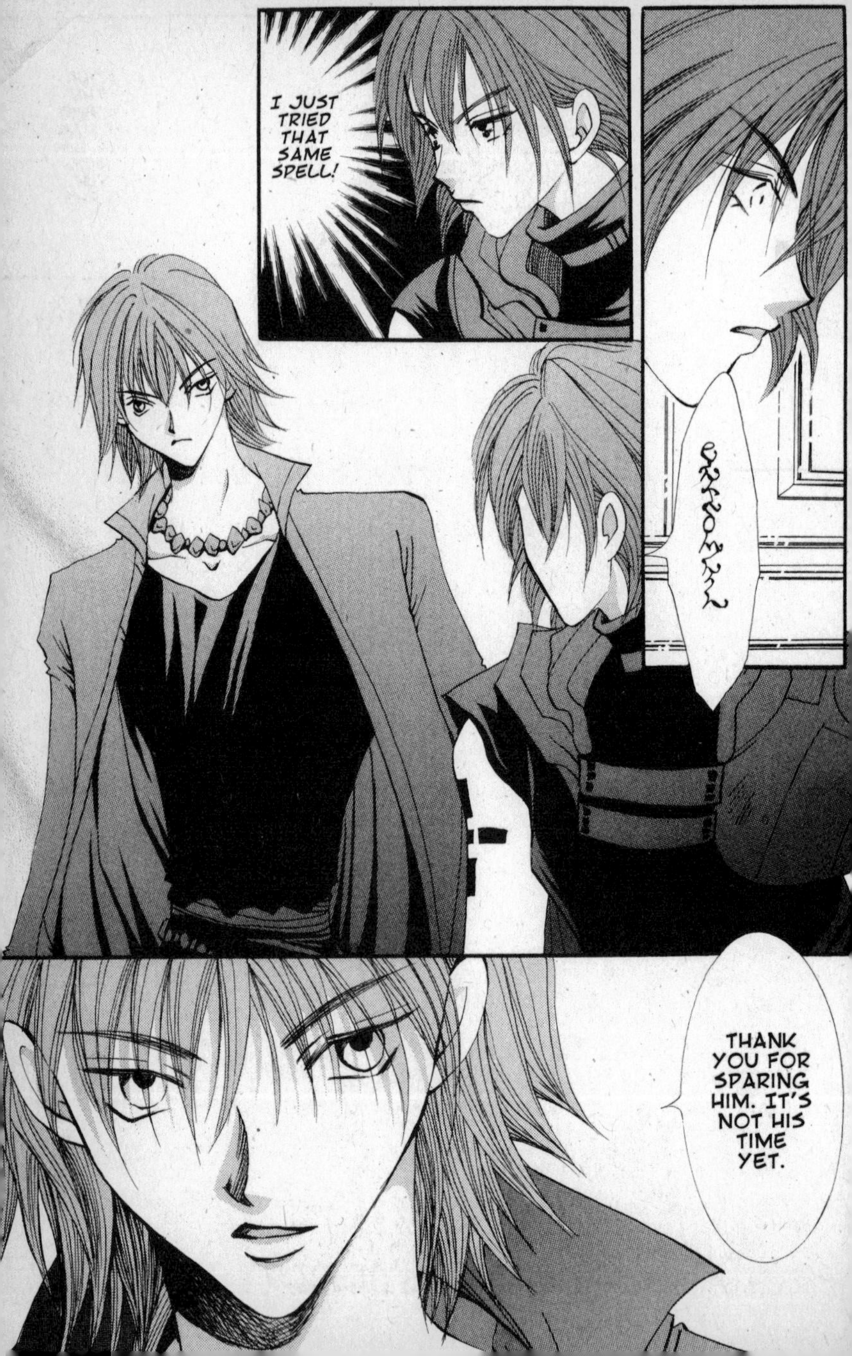

I JUST TRIED THAT SAME SPELL!
THANK YOU FOR SPARING HIM. IT'S NOT HIS TIME YET.

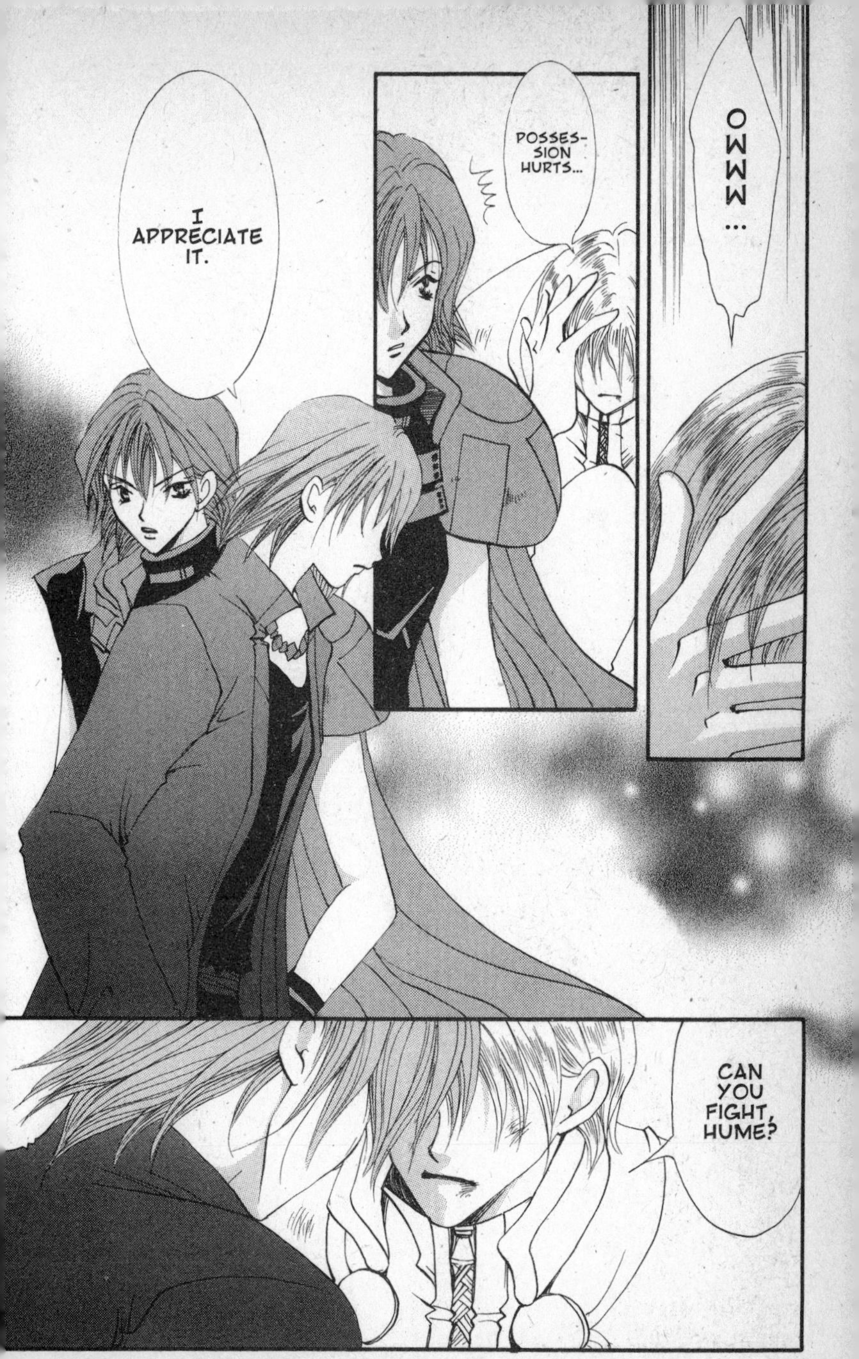
OWWW...
POSSES-SION HURTS...
I APPRECIATE IT.
CAN YOU FIGHT, HUME?

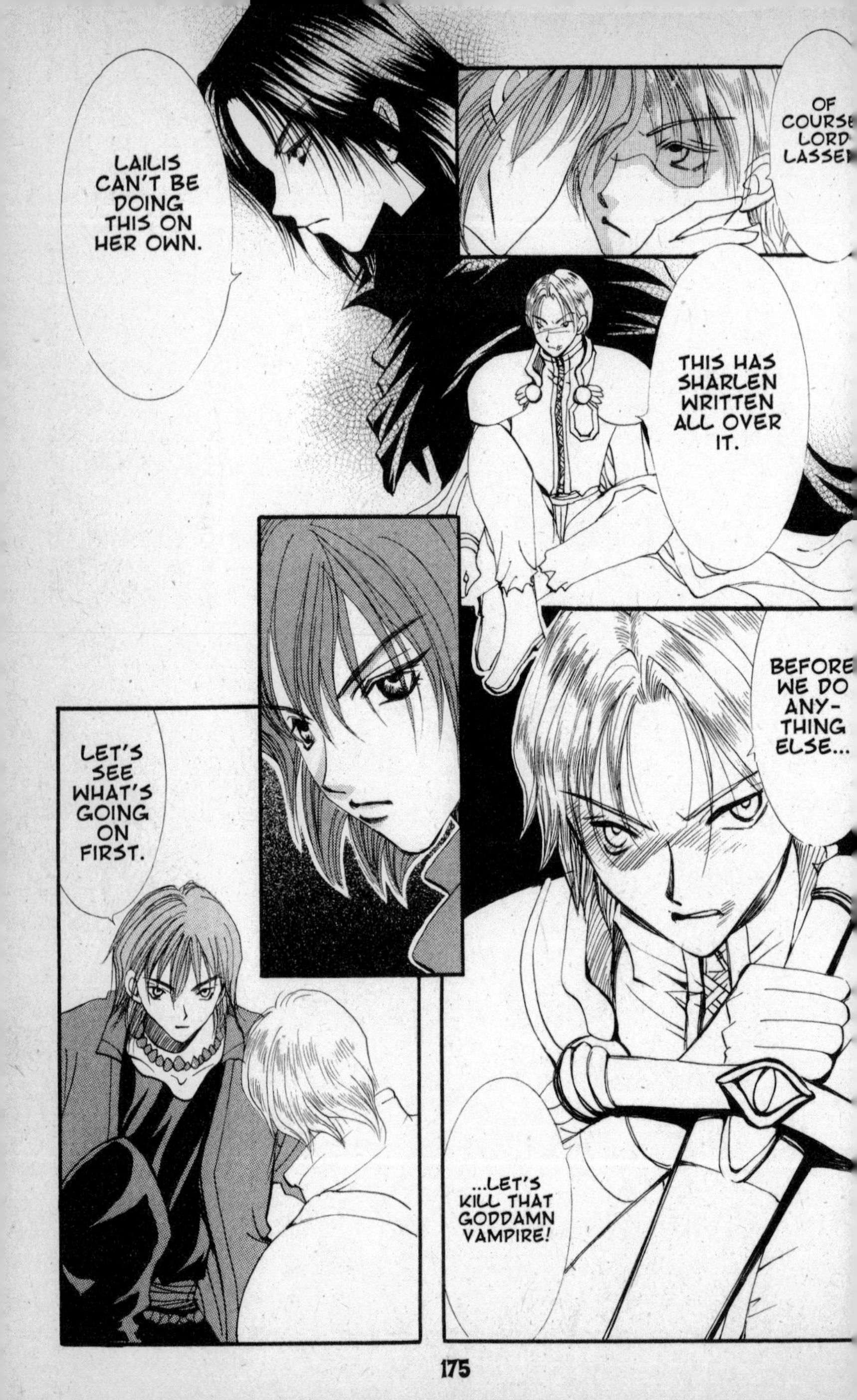
OF COURSE LORD LASSE
THIS HAS SHARLEN WRITTEN ALL OVER IT.
LAILIS CAN'T BE DOING THIS ON HER OWN.
BEFORE WE DO ANY-THING ELSE...
...LET'S KILL THAT GODDAMN VAMPIRE!
LET'S SEE WHAT'S GOING ON FIRST.

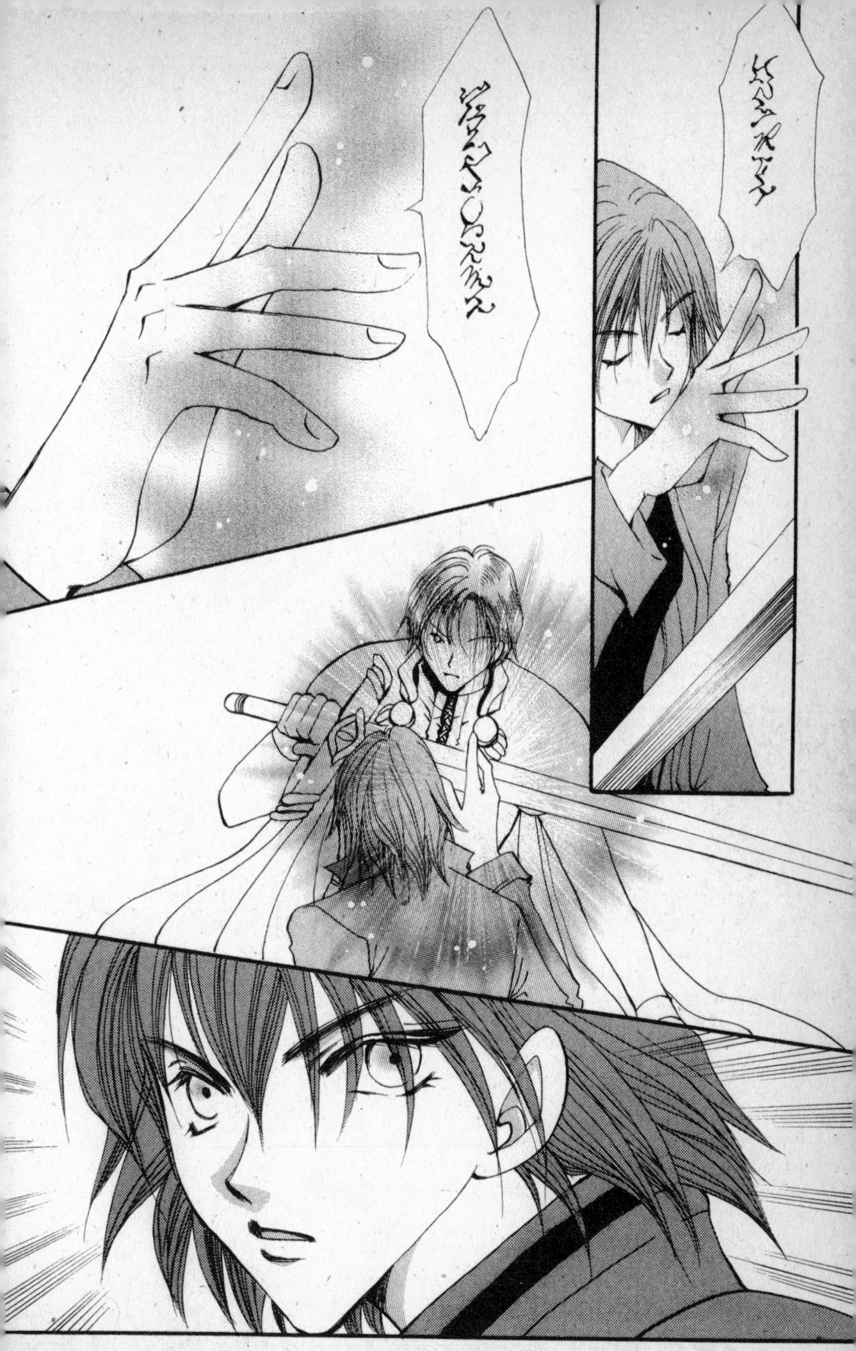

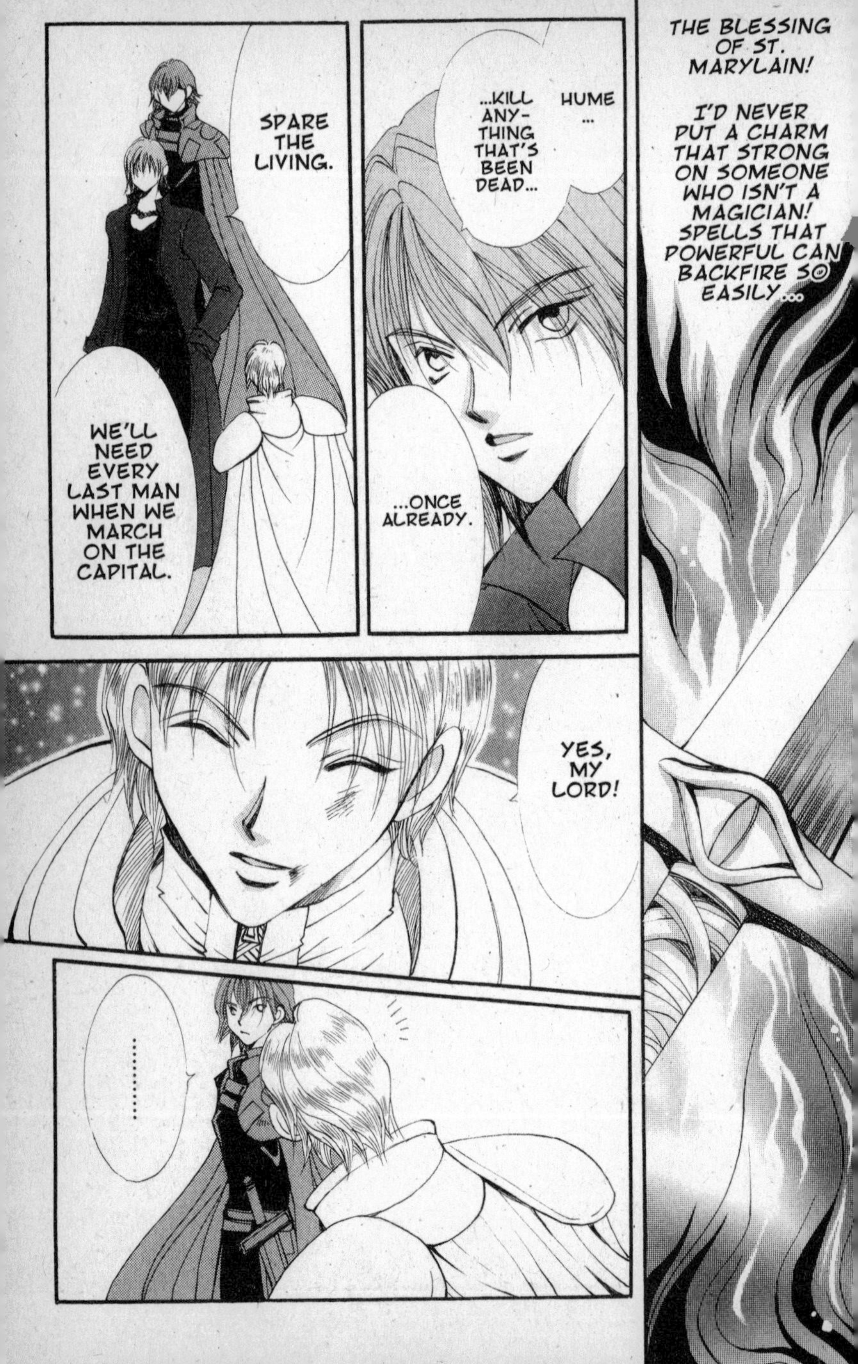
THE BLESSING OF ST. MARYLAIN!
I'D NEVER PUT A CHARM THAT STRONG ON SOMEONE WHO ISN'T A MAGICIAN! SPELLS THAT POWERFUL CAN BACKFIRE SO EASILY...
HUME ...
...KILL ANY-THING THAT'S BEEN DEAD...
...ONCE ALREADY.
SPARE THE LIVING.
WE'LL NEED EVERY LAST MAN WHEN WE MARCH ON THE CAPITAL.
YES, MY LORD!
....

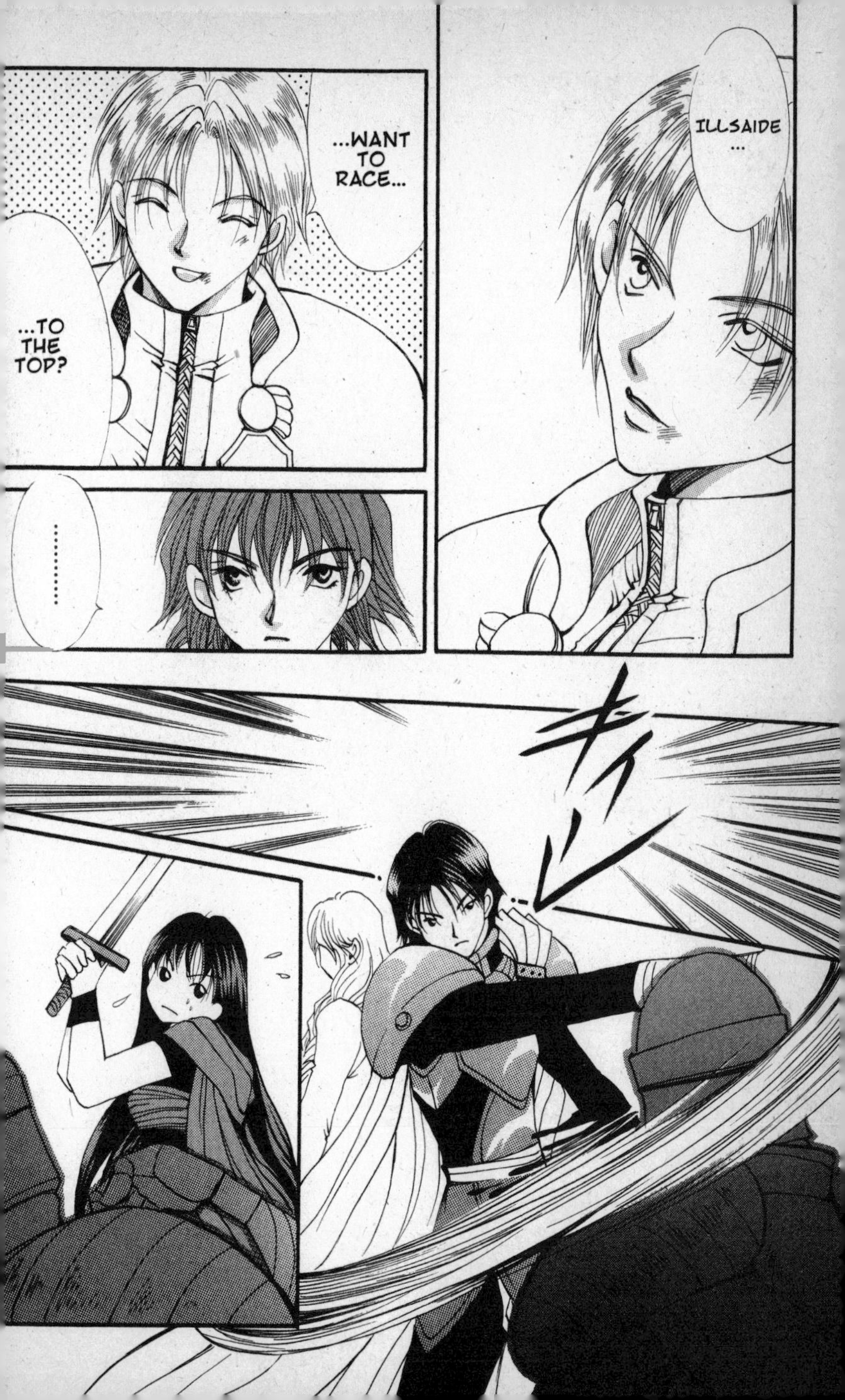
ILLSAIDE ...
...WANT TO RACE...
...TO THE TOP?
......

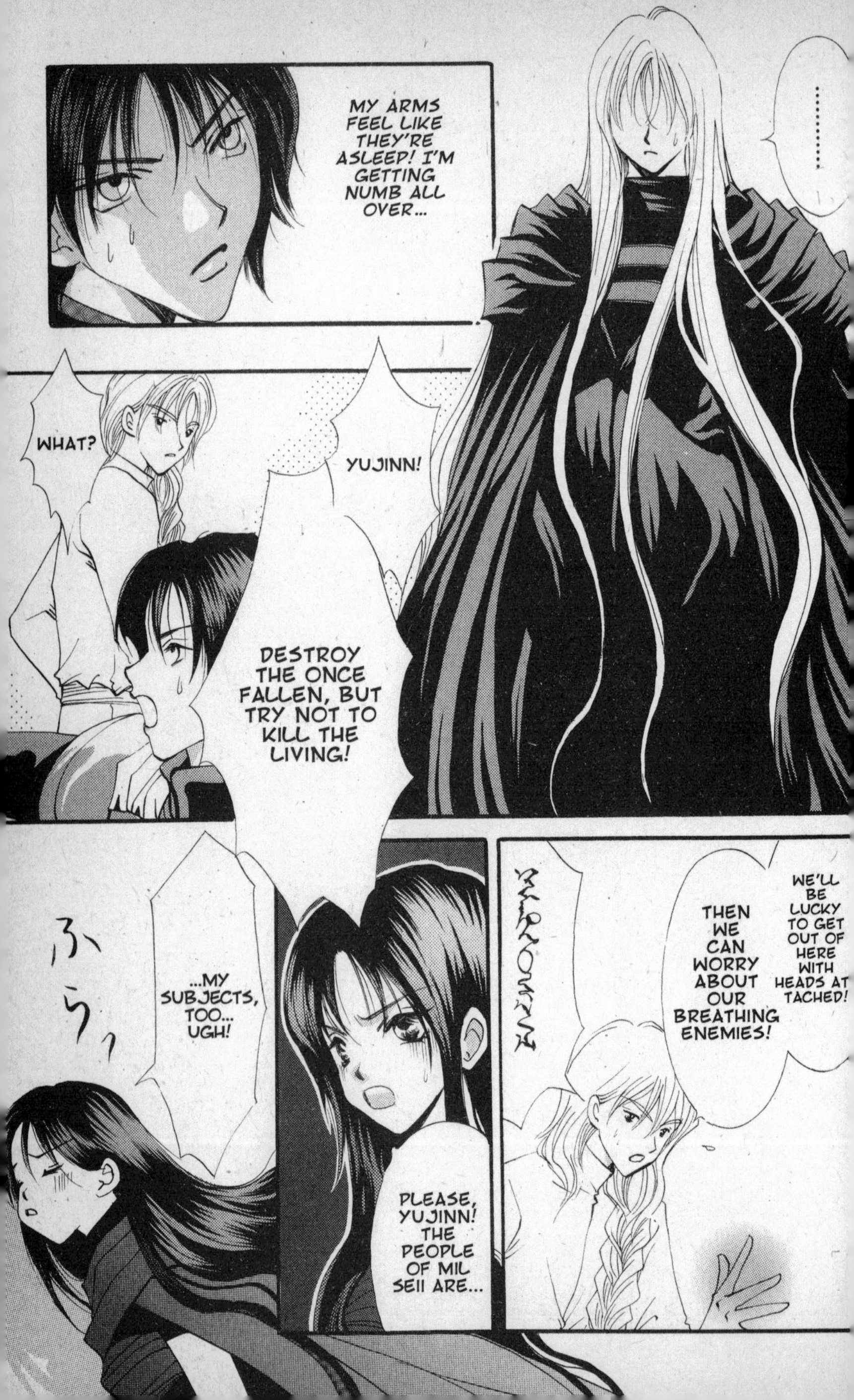
......
MY ARMS FEEL LIKE THEY'RE ASLEEP! I'M GETTING NUMB ALL OVER...
YUJINN!
WHAT?
DESTROY THE ONCE FALLEN, BUT TRY NOT TO KILL THE LIVING!
WE'LL BE LUCKY TO GET OUT OF HERE WITH HEADS ATTACHED!
THEN WE CAN WORRY ABOUT OUR BREATHING ENEMIES!
PLEASE, YUJINN! THE PEOPLE OF MIL SEII ARE...
ふら
...MY SUBJECTS, TOO... UGH!

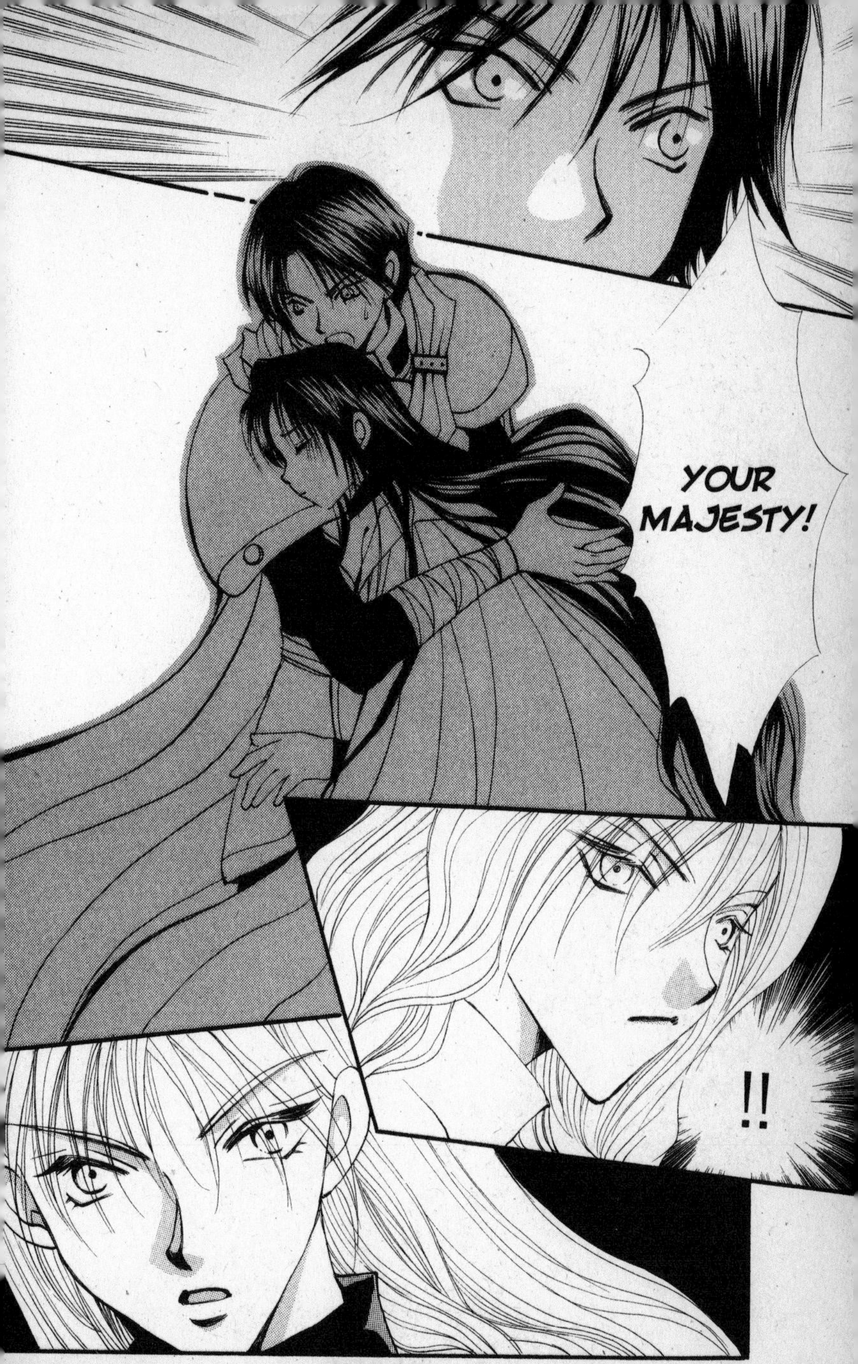
YOUR MAJESTY!
!!

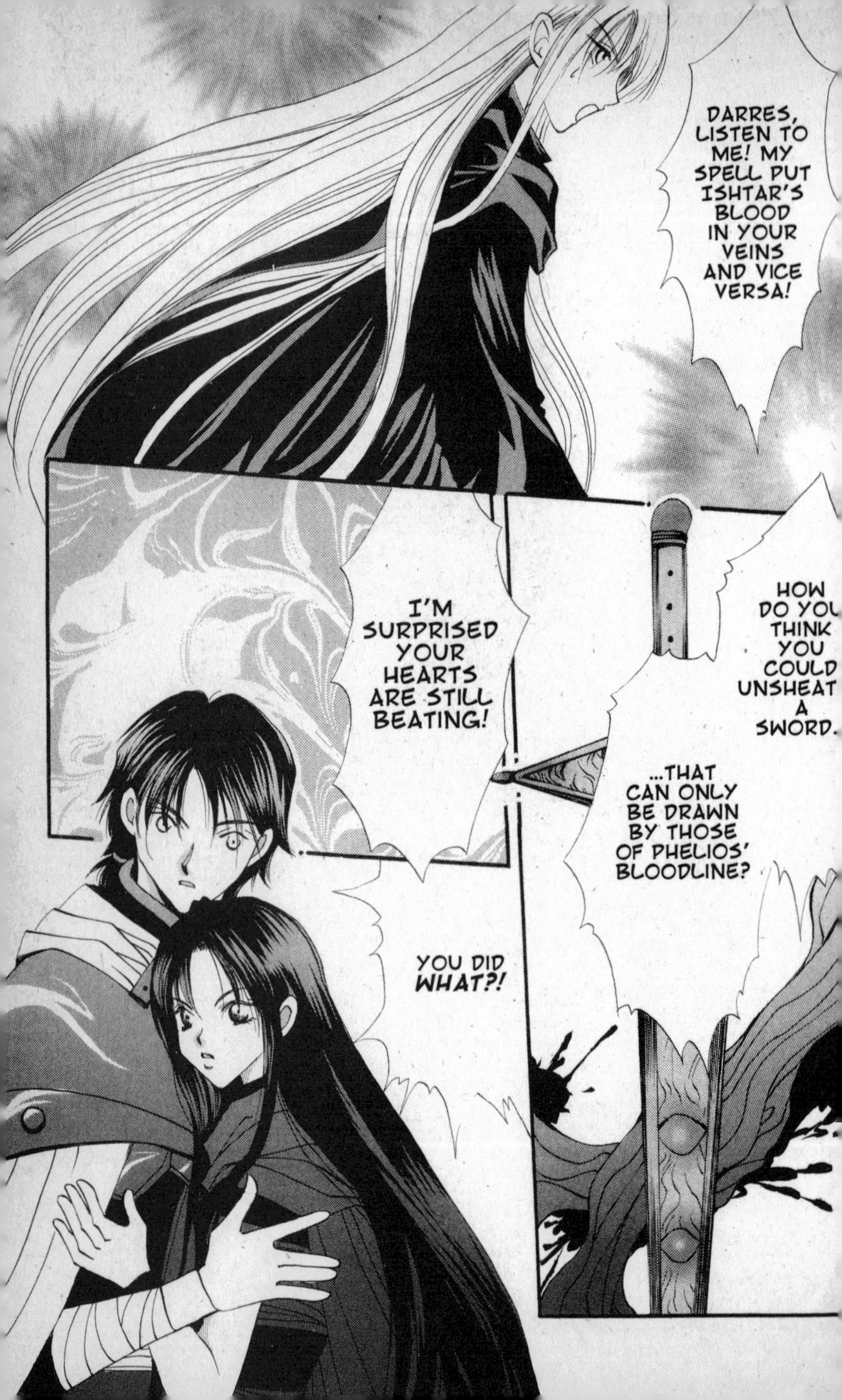
DARRES, LISTEN TO ME! MY SPELL PUT ISHTAR'S BLOOD IN YOUR VEINS AND VICE VERSA!
HOW DO YOU THINK YOU COULD UNSHEAT A SWORD...
...THAT CAN ONLY BE DRAWN BY THOSE OF PHELIOS' BLOODLINE?
I'M SURPRISED YOUR HEARTS ARE STILL BEATING!
YOU DID WHAT?!

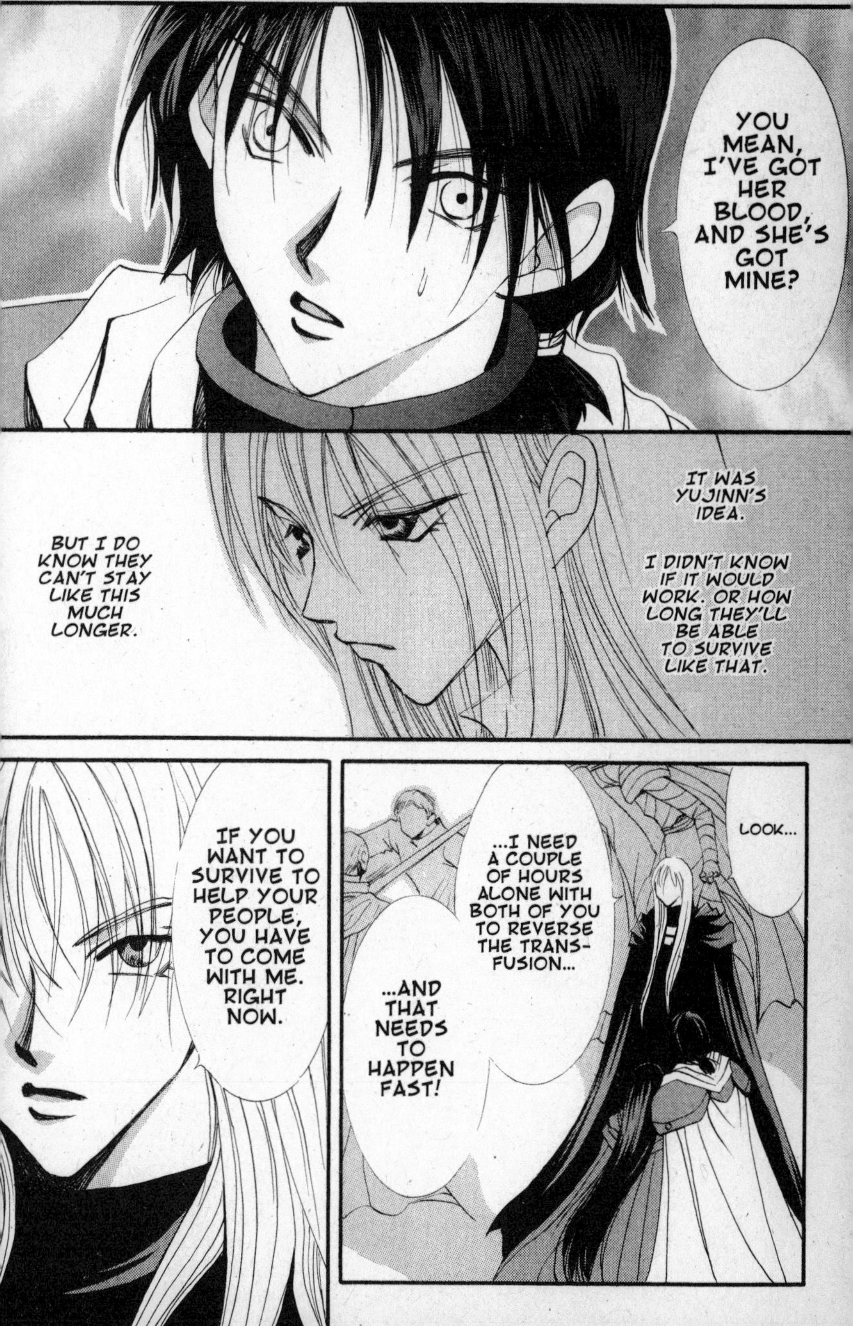
YOU MEAN, I'VE GOT HER BLOOD, AND SHE'S GOT MINE?
IT WAS YUJINN'S IDEA.
I DIDN'T KNOW IF IT WOULD WORK. OR HOW LONG THEY'LL BE ABLE TO SURVIVE LIKE THAT.
BUT I DO KNOW THEY CAN'T STAY LIKE THIS MUCH LONGER.
LOOK...
...I NEED A COUPLE OF HOURS ALONE WITH BOTH OF YOU TO REVERSE THE TRANS-FUSION...
...AND THAT NEEDS TO HAPPEN FAST!
IF YOU WANT TO SURVIVE TO HELP YOUR PEOPLE, YOU HAVE TO COME WITH ME. RIGHT NOW.

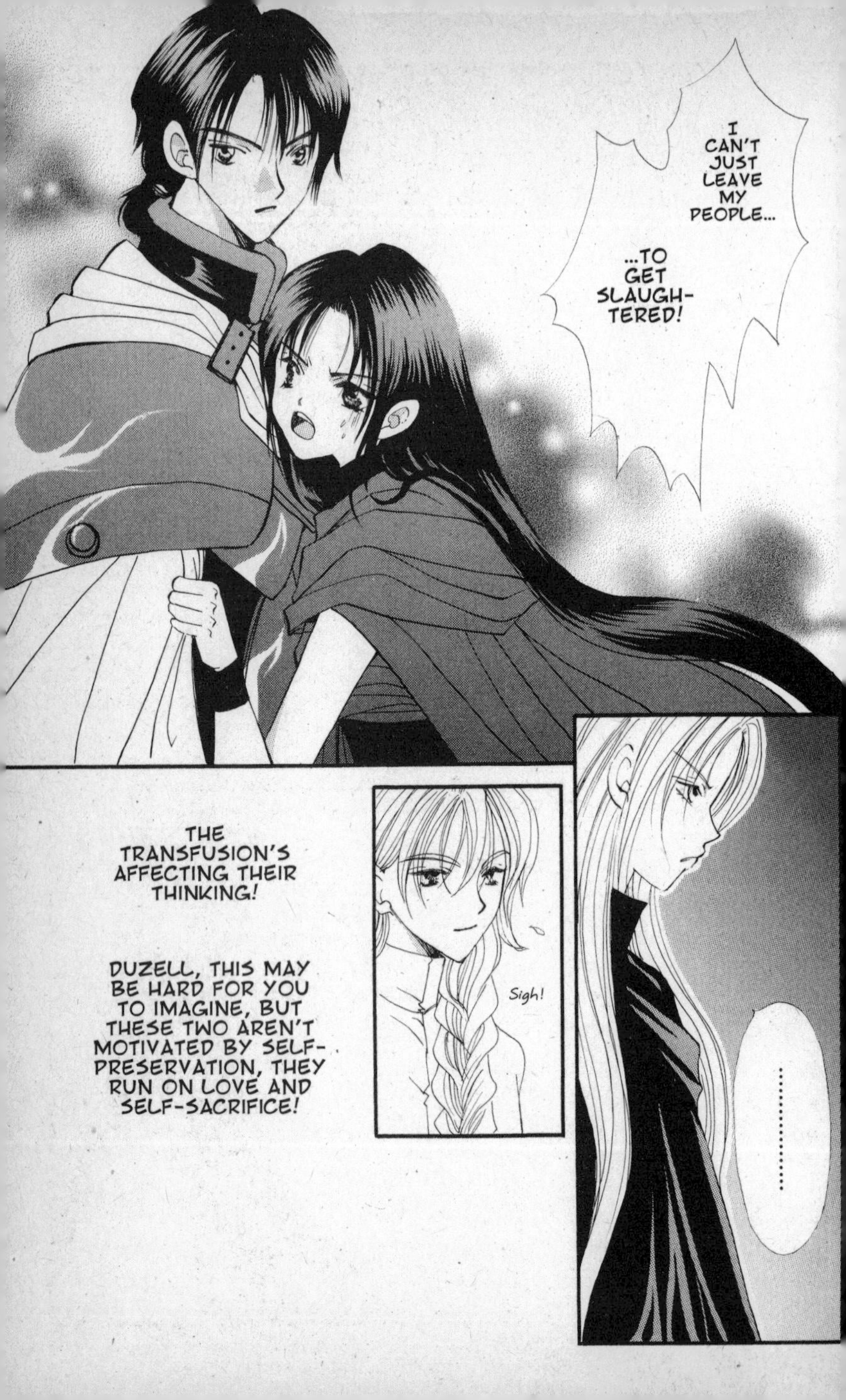
I CAN'T JUST LEAVE MY PEOPLE...
...TO GET SLAUGHTERED!
......
Sigh!
THE TRANSFUSION'S AFFECTING THEIR THINKING!
DUZELL, THIS MAY BE HARD FOR YOU TO IMAGINE, BUT THESE TWO AREN'T MOTIVATED BY SELF-PRESERVATION, THEY RUN ON LOVE AND SELF-SACRIFICE!

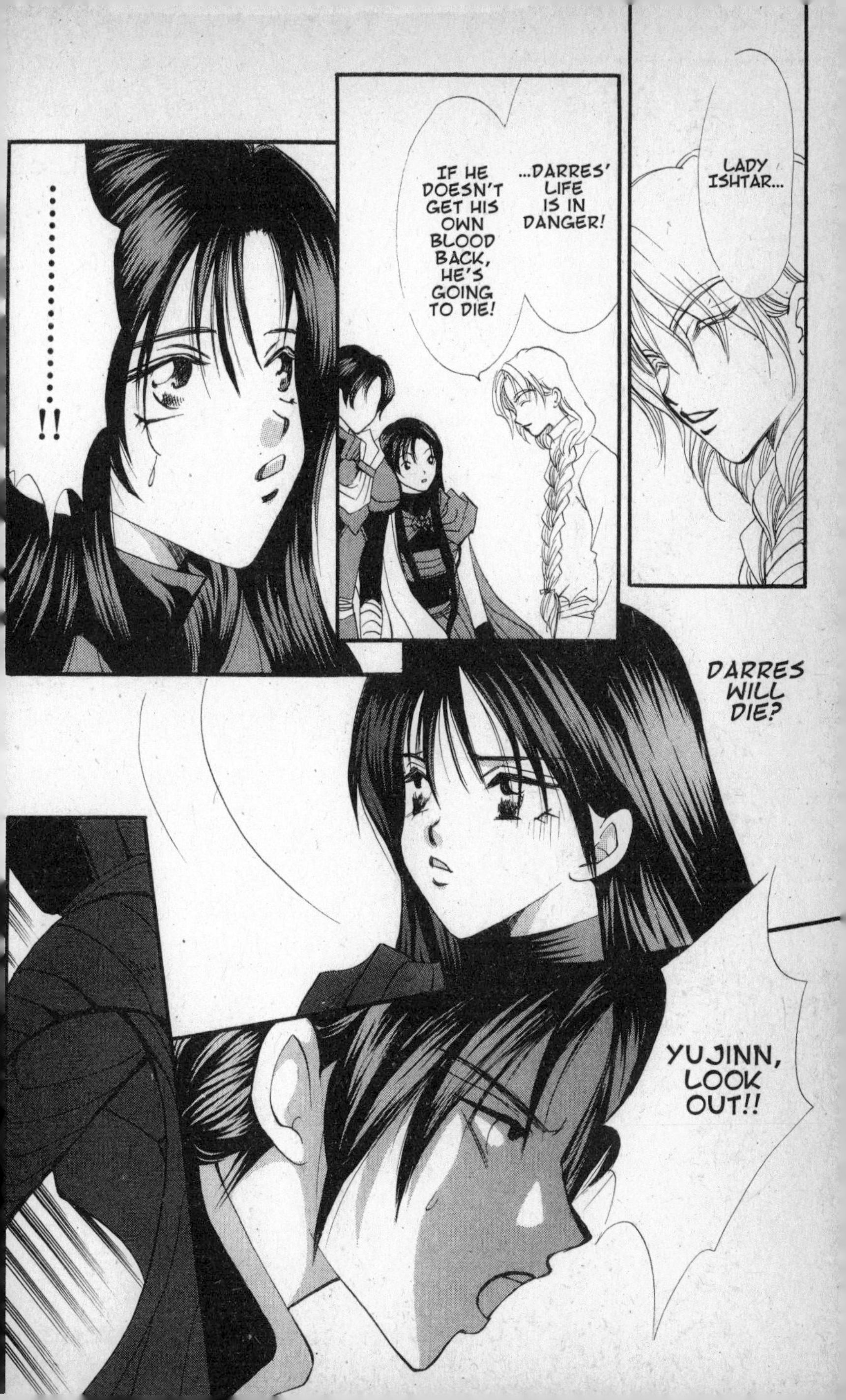
LADY ISHTAR...
...DARRES' LIFE IS IN DANGER!
IF HE DOESN'T GET HIS OWN BLOOD BACK, HE'S GOING TO DIE!
......!!
DARRES WILL DIE?
YUJINN, LOOK OUT!!

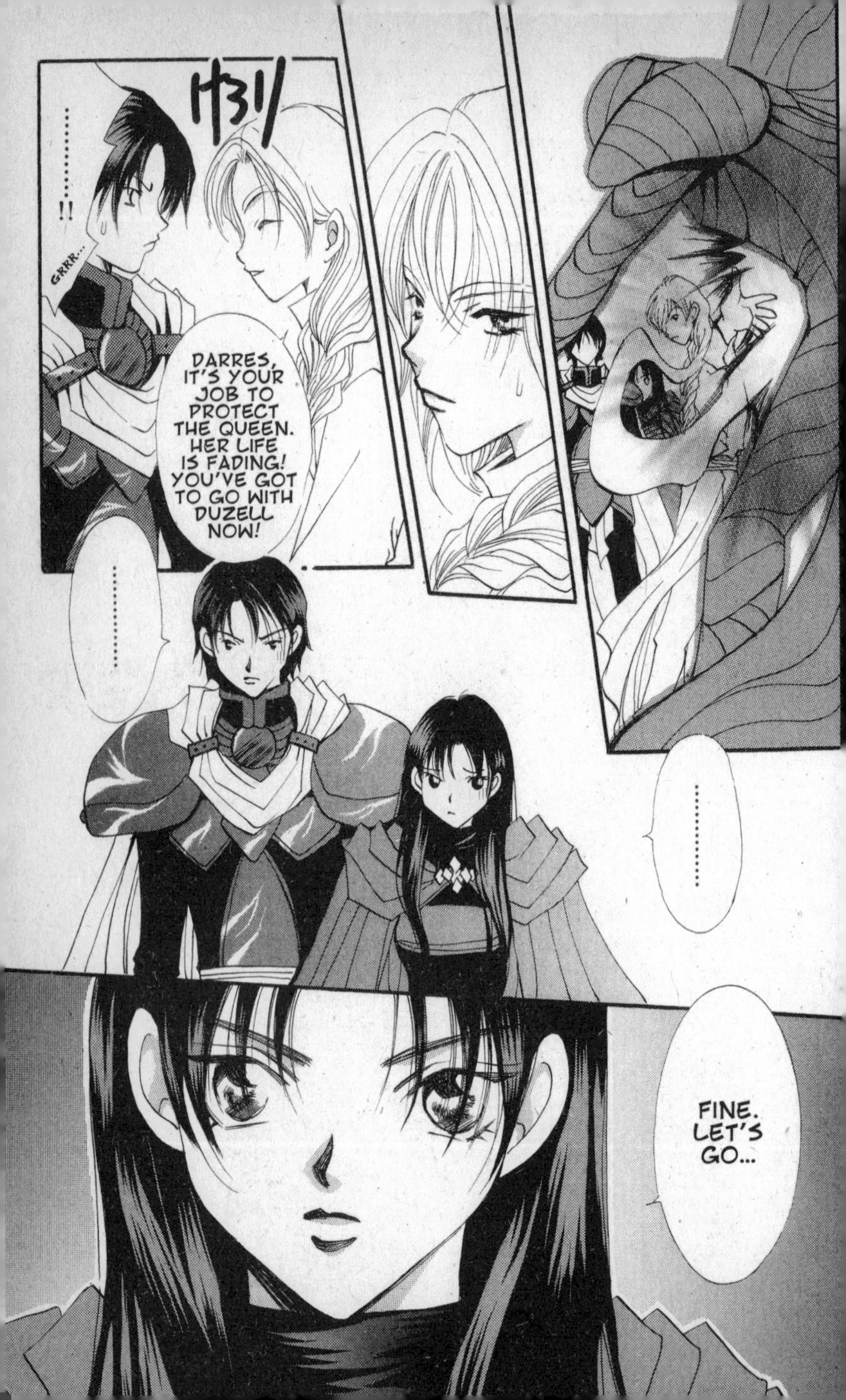

DARRES, IT'S YOUR JOB TO PROTECT THE QUEEN. HER LIFE IS FADING! YOU'VE GOT TO GO WITH DUZELL NOW!
......!!
GRRR...
......
......
FINE. LET'S GO...

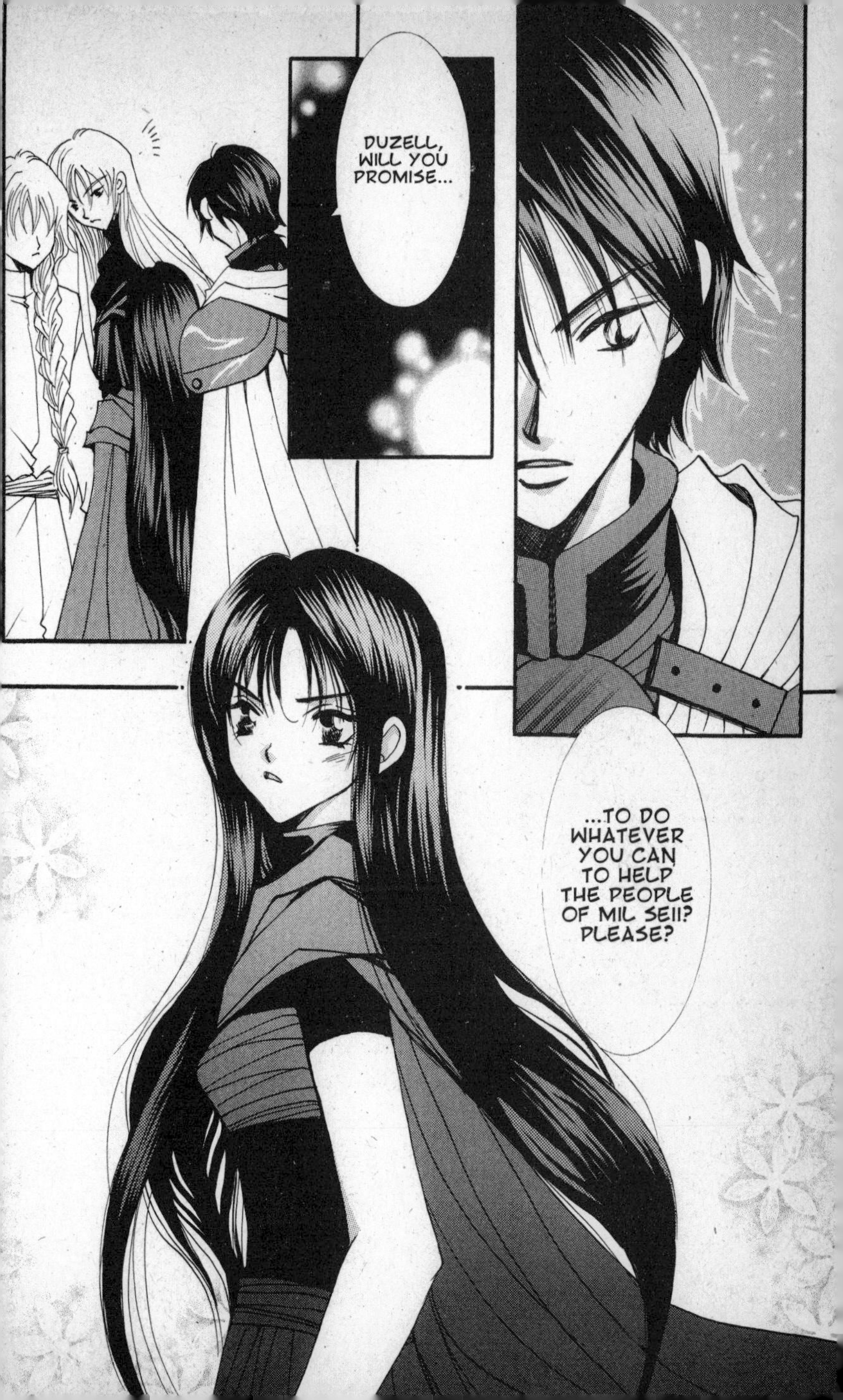
DUZELL, WILL YOU PROMISE...
...TO DO WHATEVER YOU CAN TO HELP THE PEOPLE OF MIL SEII? PLEASE?

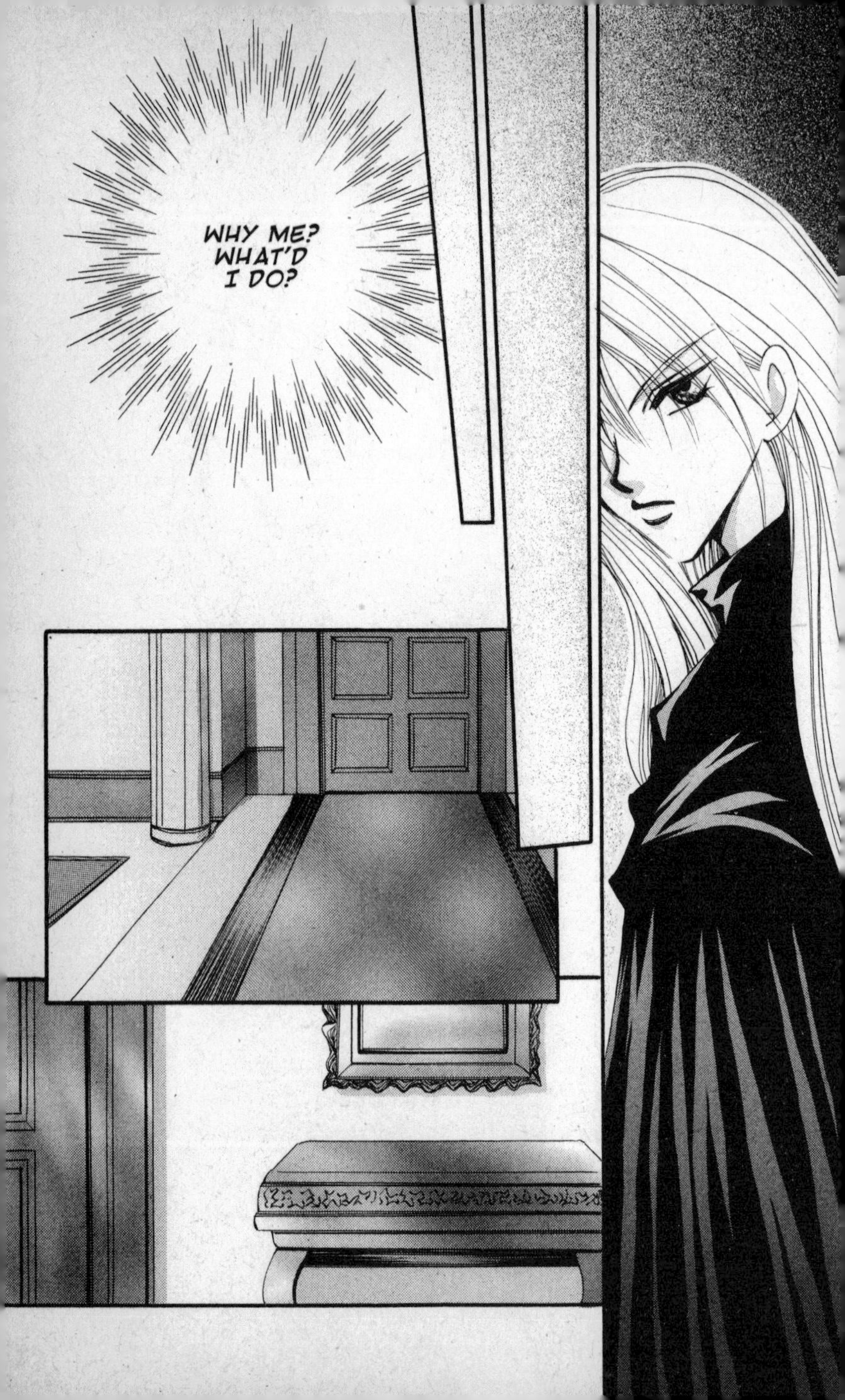
WHY ME? WHAT'D I DO?

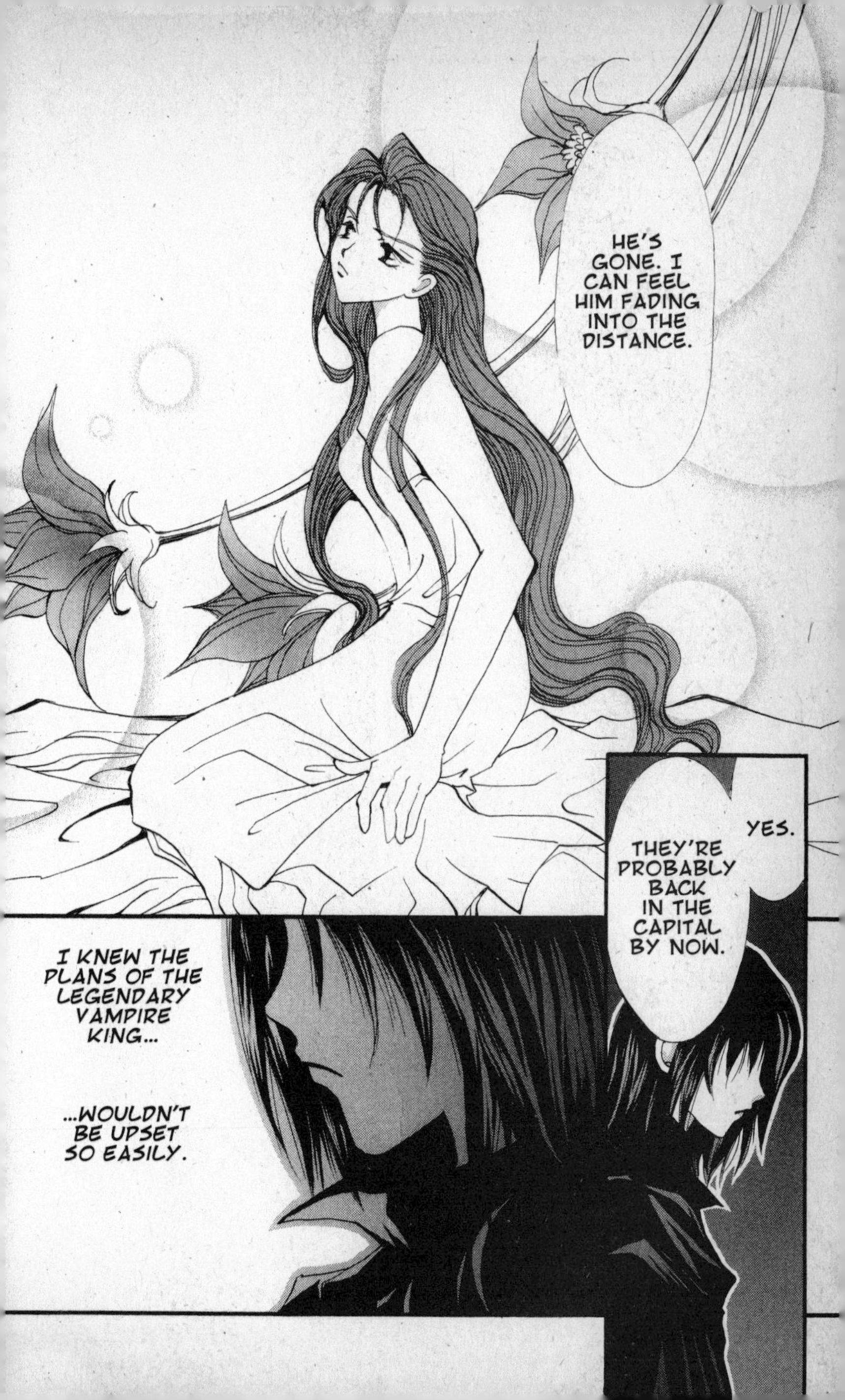
HE'S GONE. I CAN FEEL HIM FADING INTO THE DISTANCE.
YES.
THEY'RE PROBABLY BACK IN THE CAPITAL BY NOW.
I KNEW THE PLANS OF THE LEGENDARY VAMPIRE KING...
...WOULDN'T BE UPSET SO EASILY.

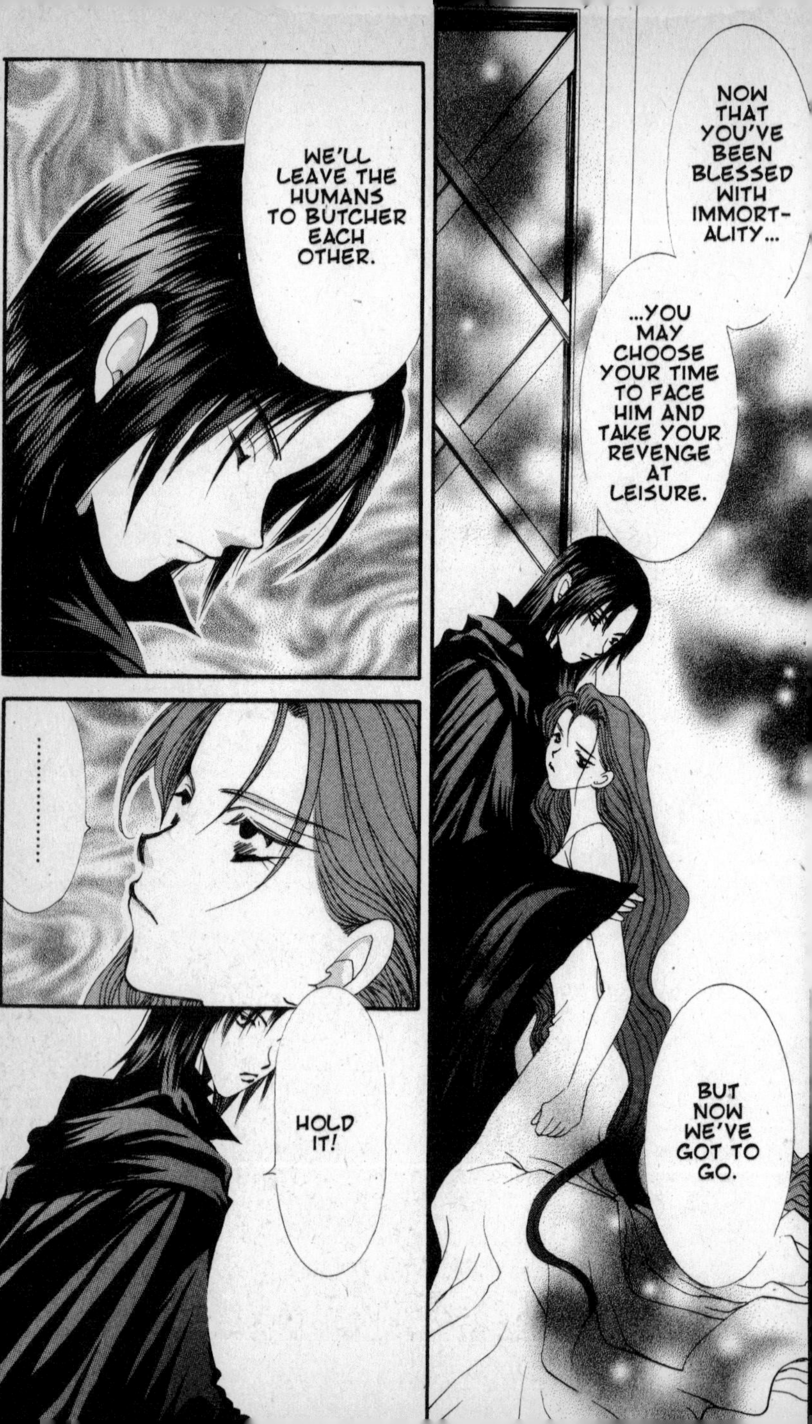
NOW THAT YOU'VE BEEN BLESSED WITH IMMORT-ALITY...
...YOU MAY CHOOSE YOUR TIME TO FACE HIM AND TAKE YOUR REVENGE AT LEISURE.
BUT NOW WE'VE GOT TO GO.
WE'LL LEAVE THE HUMANS TO BUTCHER EACH OTHER.
....
HOLD IT!

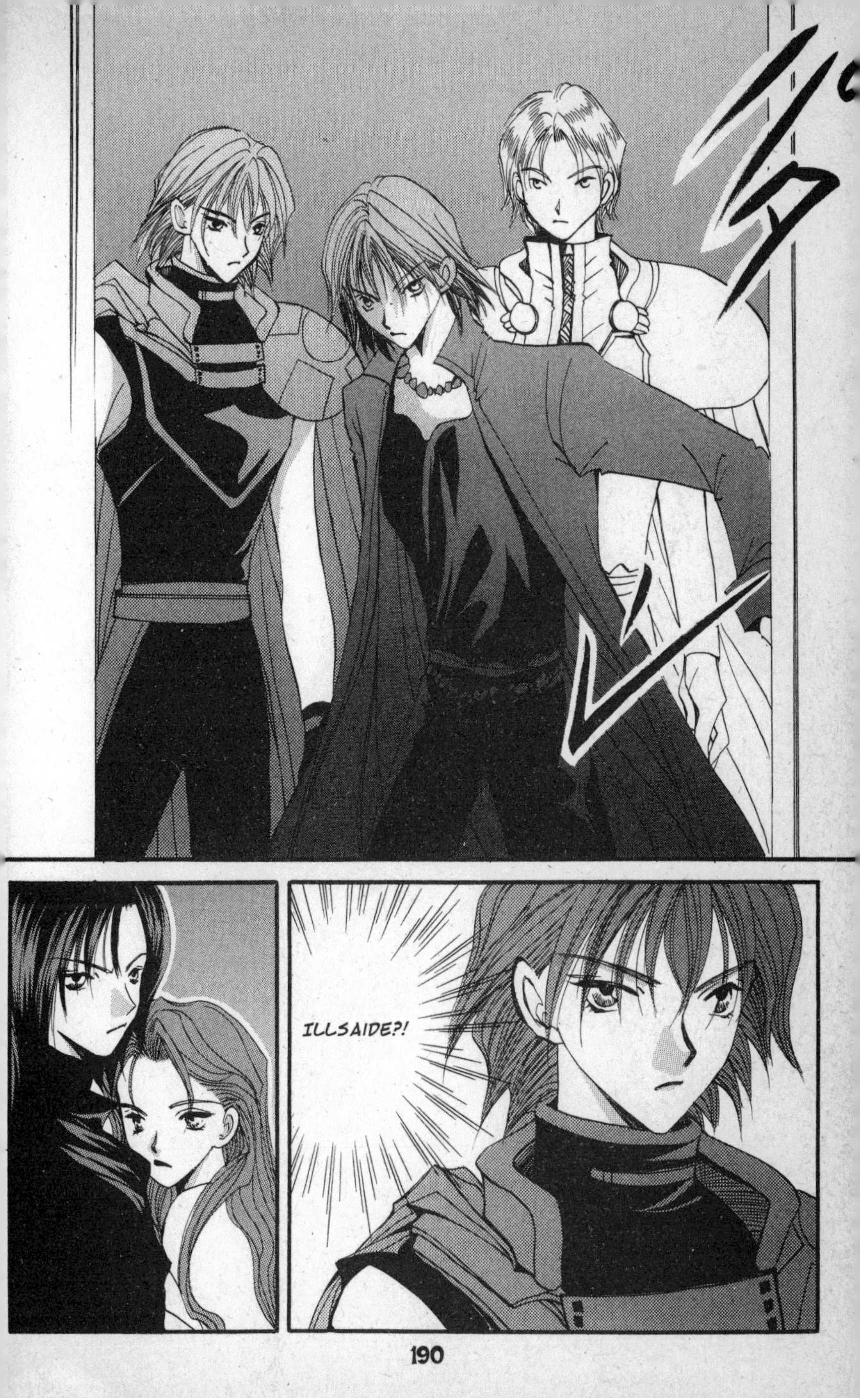
ILLSAIDE?!

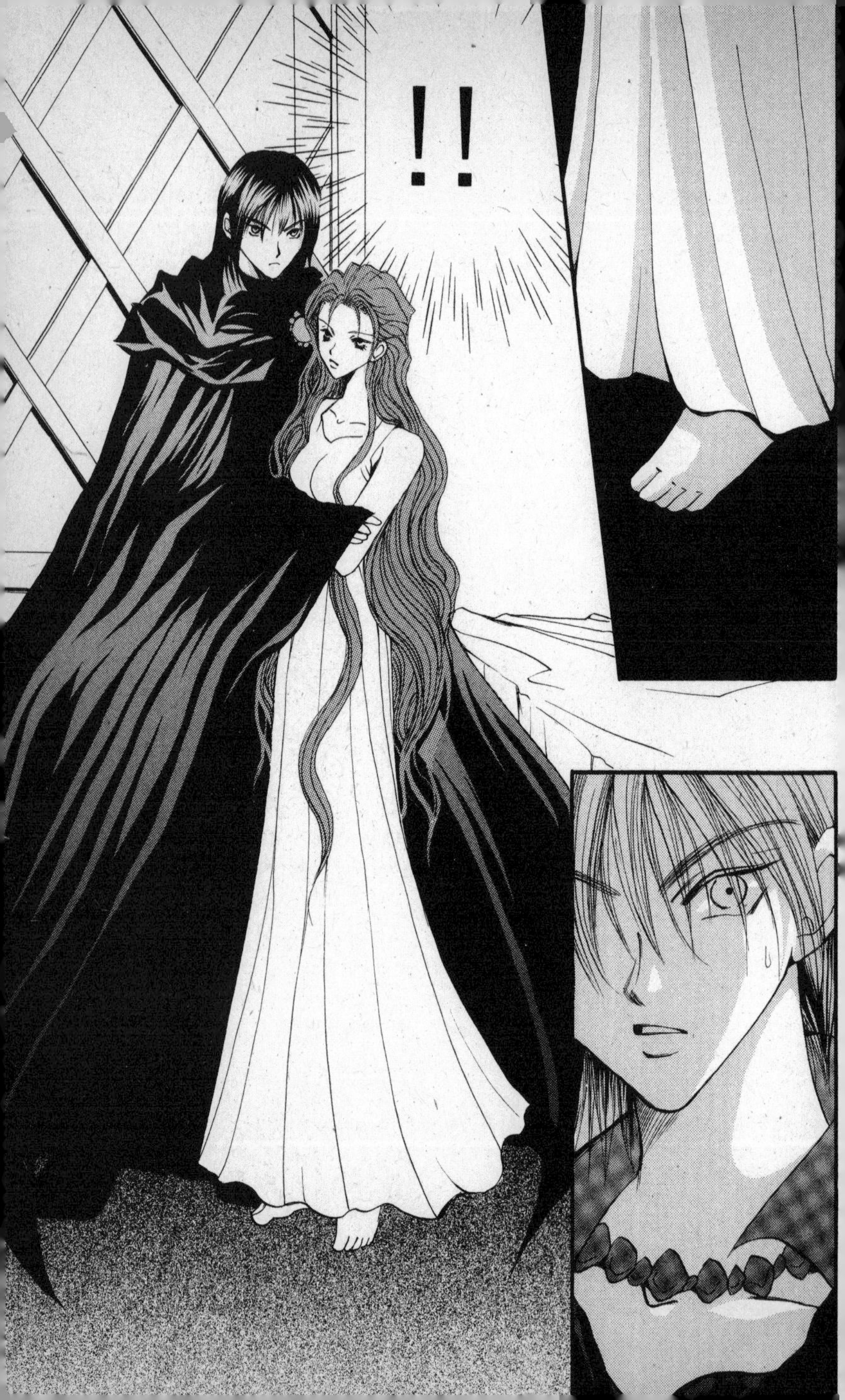
!!

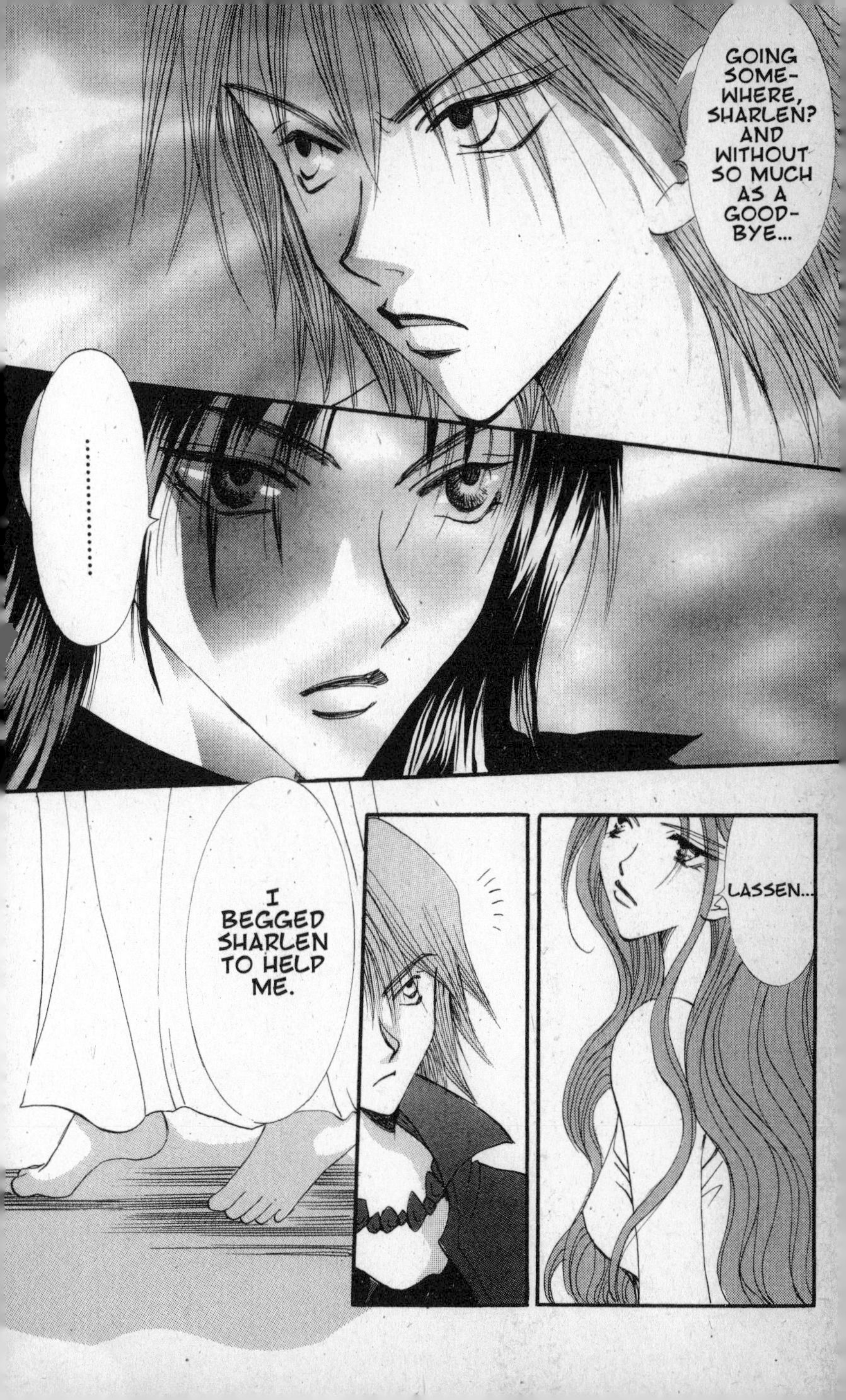
GOING SOME-WHERE, SHARLEN? AND WITHOUT SO MUCH AS A GOOD-BYE...
....
LASSEN...
I BEGGED SHARLEN TO HELP ME.

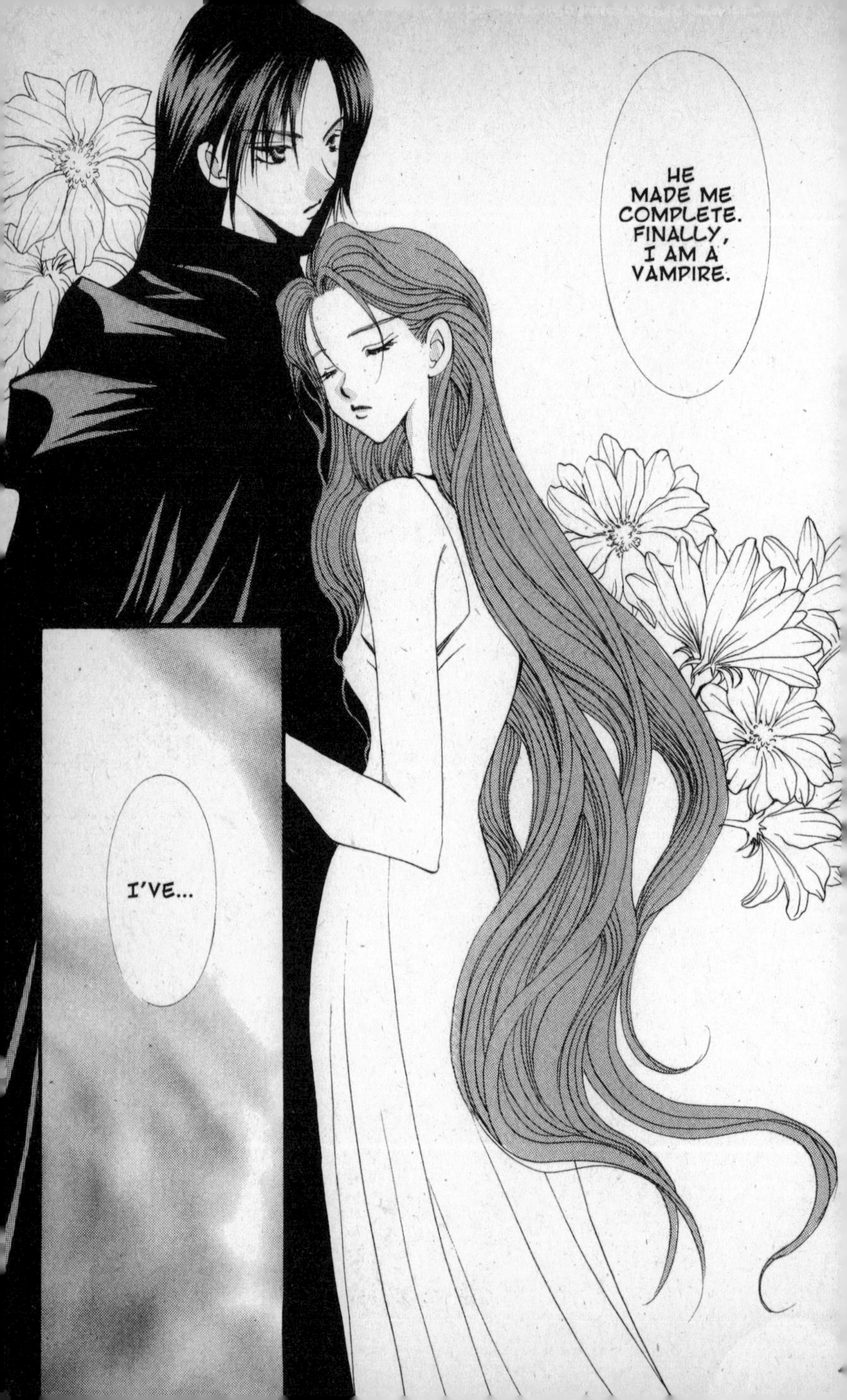
HE MADE ME COMPLETE. FINALLY, I AM A VAMPIRE.
I'VE...

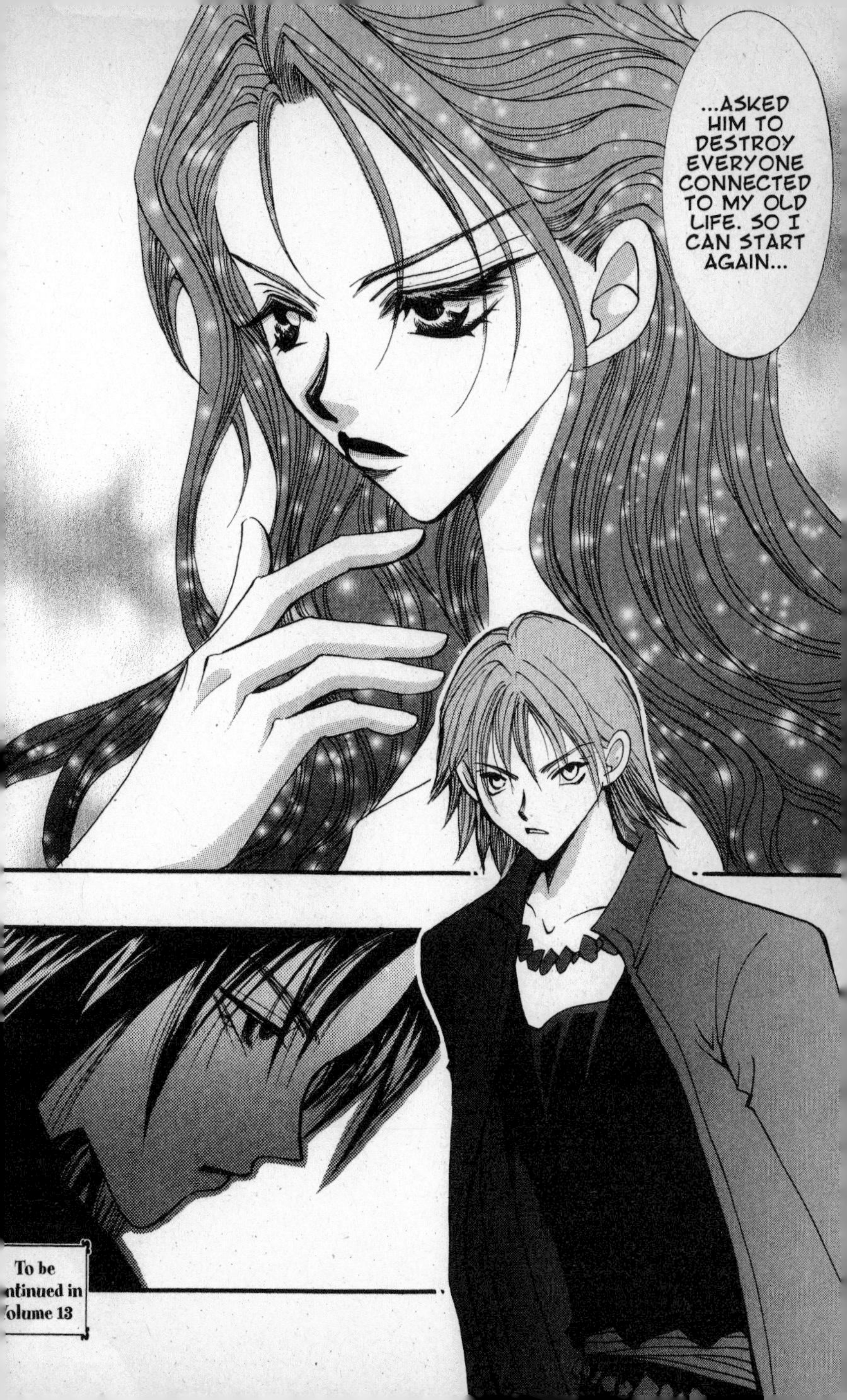
...ASKED HIM TO DESTROY EVERYONE CONNECTED TO MY OLD LIFE. SO I CAN START AGAIN...
To be ntinued in olume 13

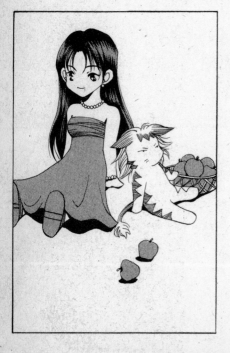

An Entertaining Epilogue

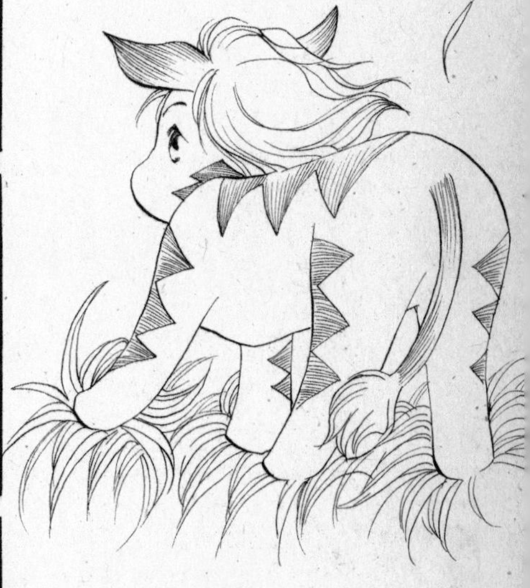

Hey there!

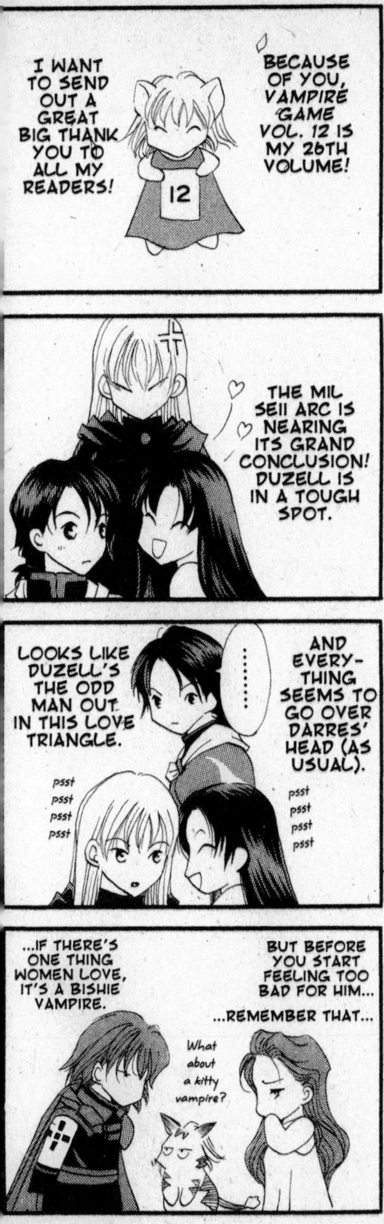

BECAUSE OF YOU, VAMPIRE GAME VOL. 12 IS MY 26TH VOLUME!
I WANT TO SEND OUT A GREAT BIG THANK YOU TO ALL MY READERS!
12
THE MIL SEII ARC IS NEARING ITS GRAND CONCLUSION! DUZELL IS IN A TOUGH SPOT.
AND EVERYTHING SEEMS TO GO OVER DARRES' HEAD (AS USUAL).
....
LOOKS LIKE DUZELL'S THE ODD MAN OUT IN THIS LOVE TRIANGLE.
psst psst psst psst
psst psst psst psst
BUT BEFORE YOU START FEELING TOO BAD FOR HIM...
...REMEMBER THAT...
...IF THERE'S ONE THING WOMEN LOVE, IT'S A BISHIE VAMPIRE.
What about a kitty vampire?

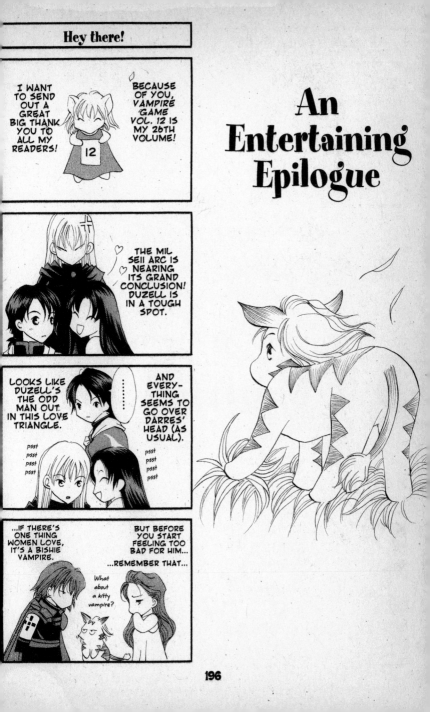

Alternate Universe Part 1

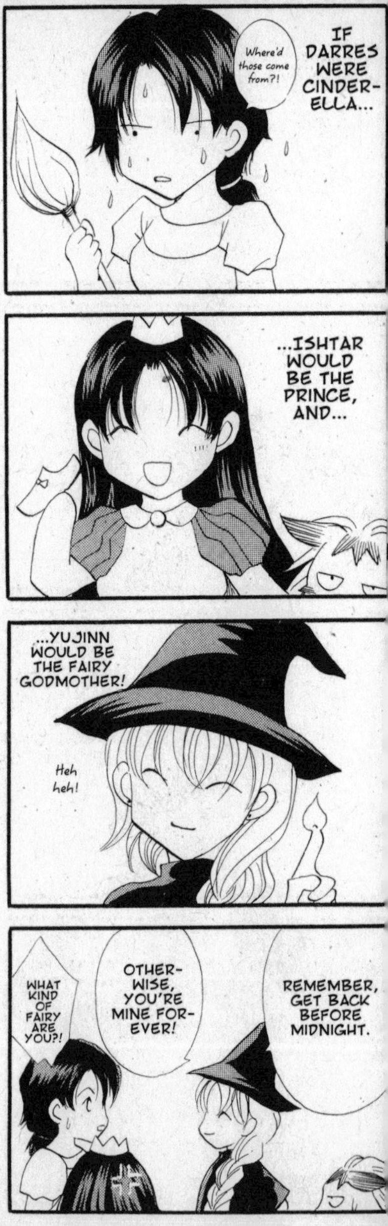
IF DARRES WERE CINDERELLA...
Where'd those come from?!
...ISHTAR WOULD BE THE PRINCE, AND...
...YUJINN WOULD BE THE FAIRY GODMOTHER!
Heh heh!
REMEMBER, GET BACK BEFORE MIDNIGHT.
OTHERWISE, YOU'RE MINE FOREVER!
WHAT KIND OF FAIRY ARE YOU?!

Alternate Universe Part 2

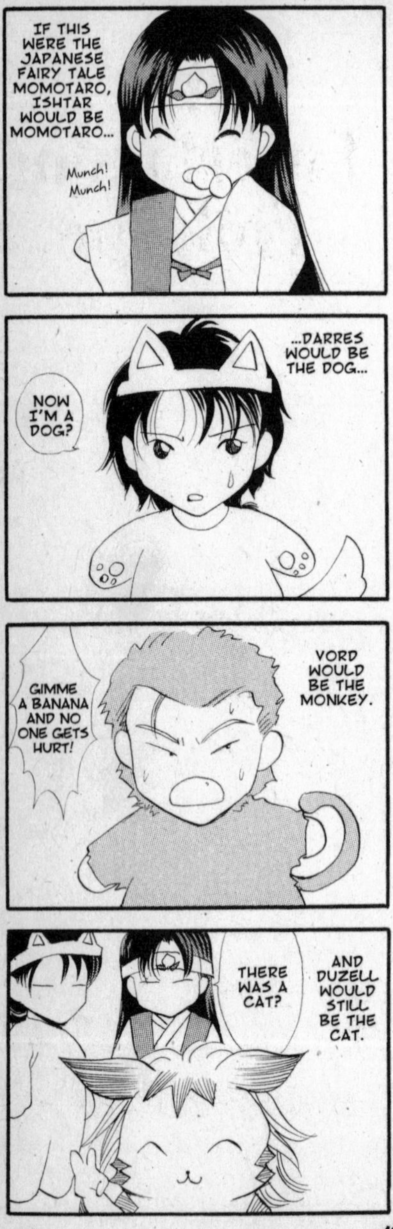
IF THIS WERE THE JAPANESE FAIRY TALE MOMOTARO, ISHTAR WOULD BE MOMOTARO...
Munch! Munch!
...DARRES WOULD BE THE DOG...
NOW I'M A DOG?
VORD WOULD BE THE MONKEY.
GIMME A BANANA AND NO ONE GETS HURT!
AND DUZELL WOULD STILL BE THE CAT.
THERE WAS A CAT?

Alternate Universe Part 3

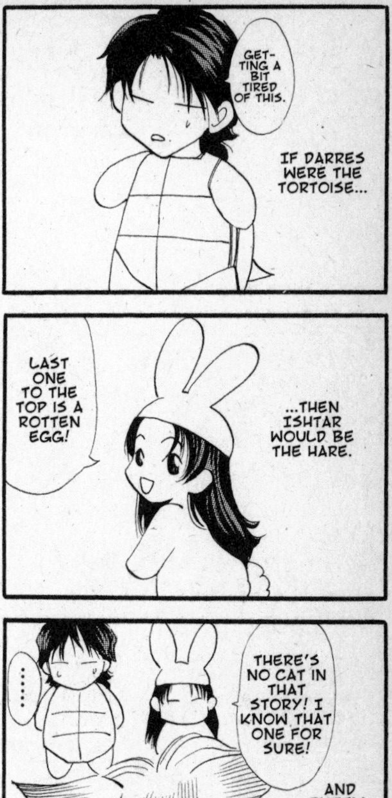
IF DARRES WERE THE TORTOISE...
GET-TING A BIT TIRED OF THIS.
...THEN ISHTAR WOULD BE THE HARE.
LAST ONE TO THE TOP IS A ROTTEN EGG!
AND DUZELL WOULD STILL BE THE CAT.
THERE'S NO CAT IN THAT STORY! I KNOW THAT ONE FOR SURE!
......
WELL, MAYBE YOU'RE RIGHT, BUT THE TURTLE STILL COMES OUT ON TOP!
Z Z
Z Z
DEPENDING ON HOW YOU LOOK AT IT, OF COURSE.

Alternate Universe Part 4

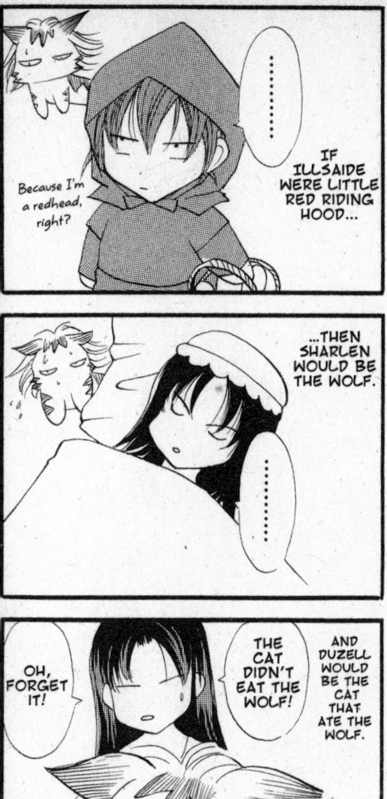
IF ILLSAIDE WERE LITTLE RED RIDING HOOD...
....
Because I'm a redhead, right?
...THEN SHARLEN WOULD BE THE WOLF.
....
AND DUZELL WOULD BE THE CAT THAT ATE THE WOLF.
THE CAT DIDN'T EAT THE WOLF!
OH, FORGET IT!
WHY IS GRANDMA'S TUMMY SO BIG?
AND THEY ALL LIVED HAPPILY EVER AFTER! (WELL, ALMOST...)
MEEEEOW!
(BECAUSE MY DINNER DOESN'T AGREE WITH ME.)

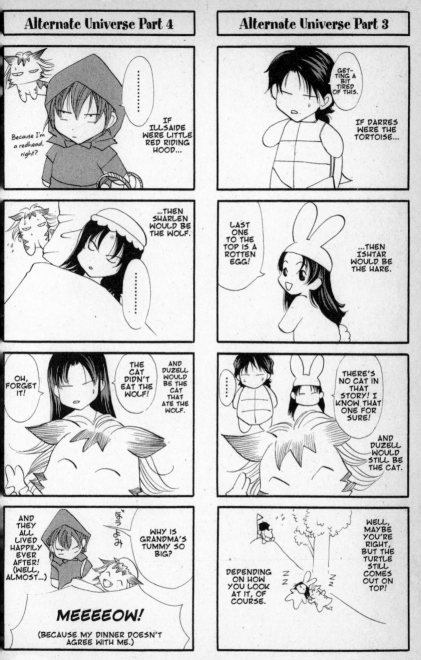

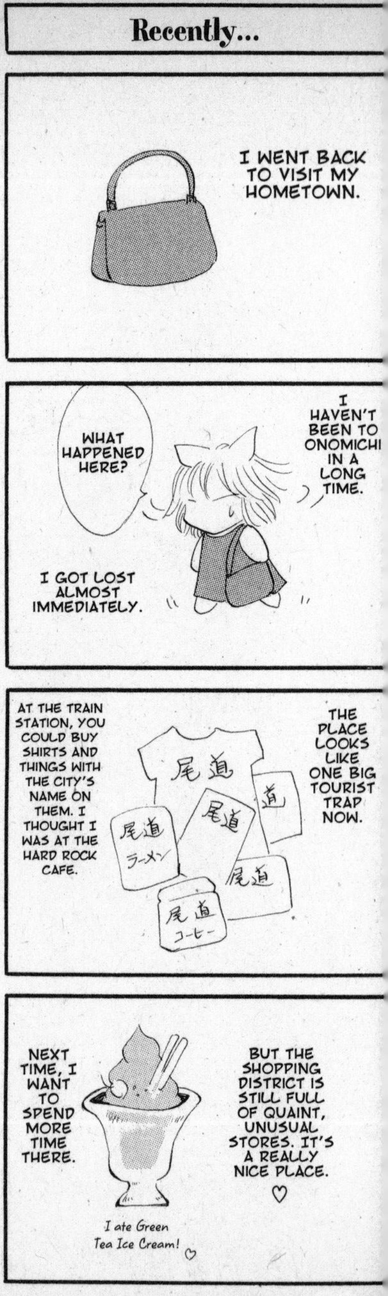
Recently...
I WENT BACK TO VISIT MY HOMETOWN.
I HAVEN'T BEEN TO ONOMICHI IN A LONG TIME.
WHAT HAPPENED HERE?
I GOT LOST ALMOST IMMEDIATELY.
THE PLACE LOOKS LIKE ONE BIG TOURIST TRAP NOW.
尾道
道
尾道
尾道
尾道 ラーメン
尾道 コーヒー
AT THE TRAIN STATION, YOU COULD BUY SHIRTS AND THINGS WITH THE CITY'S NAME ON THEM. I THOUGHT I WAS AT THE HARD ROCK CAFE.
BUT THE SHOPPING DISTRICT IS STILL FULL OF QUAINT, UNUSUAL STORES. IT'S A REALLY NICE PLACE. ♡
NEXT TIME, I WANT TO SPEND MORE TIME THERE.
I ate Green Tea Ice Cream! ♡

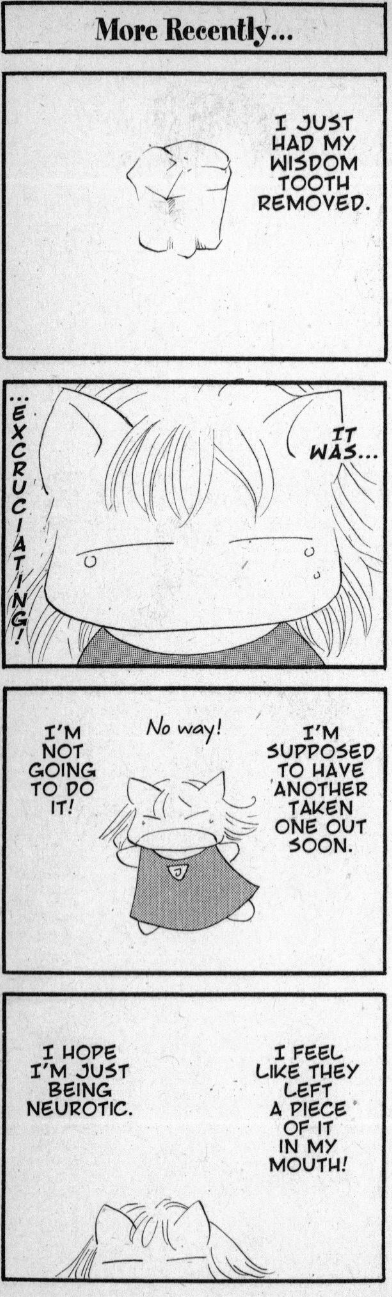
More Recently...
I JUST HAD MY WISDOM TOOTH REMOVED.
IT WAS...
...EXCRUCIATING!
I'M SUPPOSED TO HAVE ANOTHER TAKEN ONE OUT SOON.
No way!
I'M NOT GOING TO DO IT!
I FEEL LIKE THEY LEFT A PIECE OF IT IN MY MOUTH!
I HOPE I'M JUST BEING NEUROTIC.

Even More Recently...

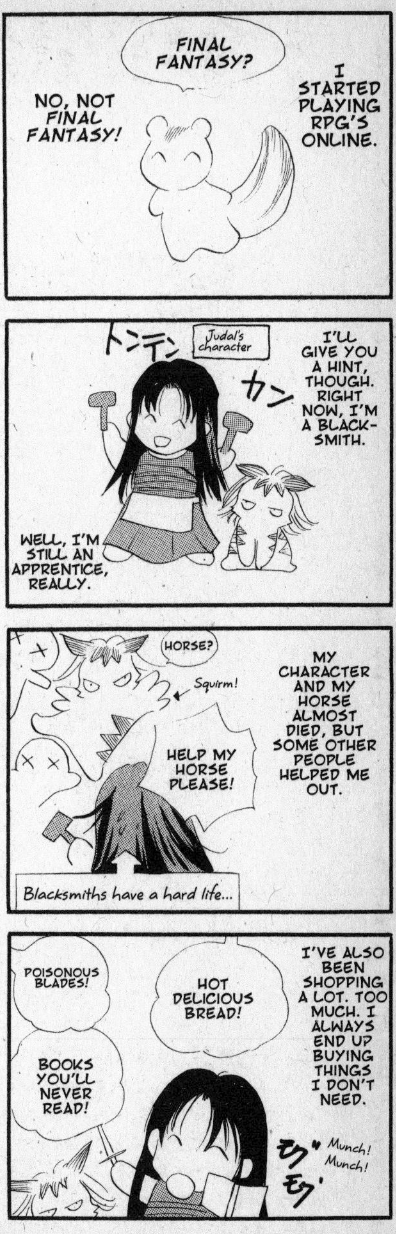

I STARTED PLAYING RPG'S ONLINE.
FINAL FANTASY?
NO, NOT FINAL FANTASY!
I'LL GIVE YOU A HINT, THOUGH. RIGHT NOW, I'M A BLACK-SMITH.
Judal's character
トンテン
カン
WELL, I'M STILL AN APPRENTICE, REALLY.
MY CHARACTER AND MY HORSE ALMOST DIED, BUT SOME OTHER PEOPLE HELPED ME OUT.
HORSE?
Squirm!
HELP MY HORSE PLEASE!
Blacksmiths have a hard life...
I'VE ALSO BEEN SHOPPING A LOT. TOO MUCH. I ALWAYS END UP BUYING THINGS I DON'T NEED.
HOT DELICIOUS BREAD!
POISONOUS BLADES!
BOOKS YOU'LL NEVER READ!
モグ モグ
Munch! Munch!

Finally...

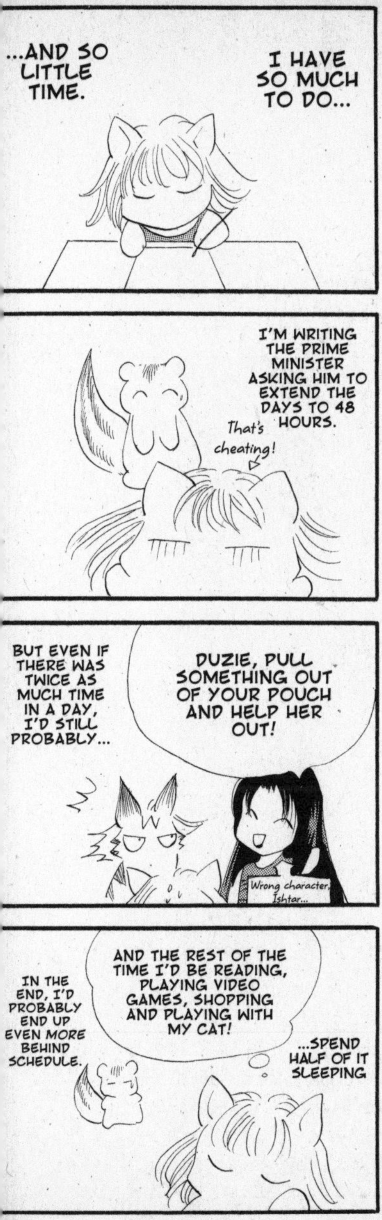

I HAVE SO MUCH TO DO...
...AND SO LITTLE TIME.
I'M WRITING THE PRIME MINISTER ASKING HIM TO EXTEND THE DAYS TO 48 HOURS.
That's cheating!
DUZIE, PULL SOMETHING OUT OF YOUR POUCH AND HELP HER OUT!
BUT EVEN IF THERE WAS TWICE AS MUCH TIME IN A DAY, I'D STILL PROBABLY...
Wrong character, Ishtar...
...SPEND HALF OF IT SLEEPING
AND THE REST OF THE TIME I'D BE READING, PLAYING VIDEO GAMES, SHOPPING AND PLAYING WITH MY CAT!
IN THE END, I'D PROBABLY END UP EVEN MORE BEHIND SCHEDULE.

VAMPIRE GAME

Next Volume...

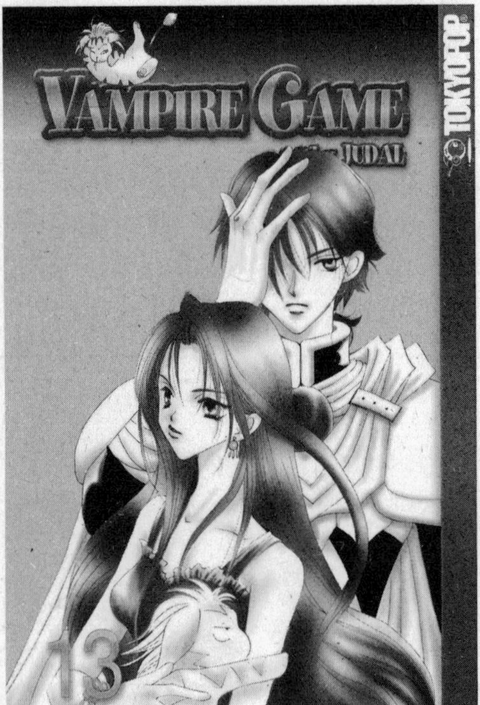
VAMPIRE GAME
JUDAL
TOKYOPOP
13

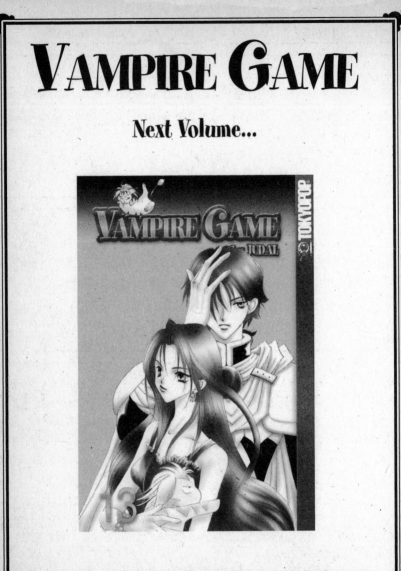

Danger! Drama!! Lots of dead guys!!! Pheliosta stands on the brink of civil war, and about all we can tell you is that considering who's running the smaller kingdoms, we're damned surprised it didn't happen sooner! Volume 13 also marks the start of the Pheliosta arc, Duzell and Ishtar's final adventure. Will Duzell carry out his vow to kill the reincarnation of Phelios? Does he still even want to, or have his growing feelings of affection for Ishtar quenched his thirst for revenge? It's the beginning of the end in the next can't-miss volume of *Vampire Game!*

TOKYOPOP SHOP

WWW.TOKYOPOP.COM/SHOP

HOT NEWS!
Check out the TOKYOPOP SHOP! The world's best collection of manga in English is now available online in one place!

SAIYUKI RELOAD

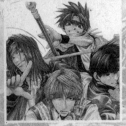

.HACK NOVEL

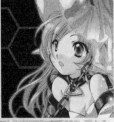

BIZENGHAST

Bizenghast and other hot titles are available at the store that never closes!

- **LOOK FOR SPECIAL OFFERS**
- **PRE-ORDER UPCOMING RELEASES**
- **COMPLETE YOUR COLLECTIONS**

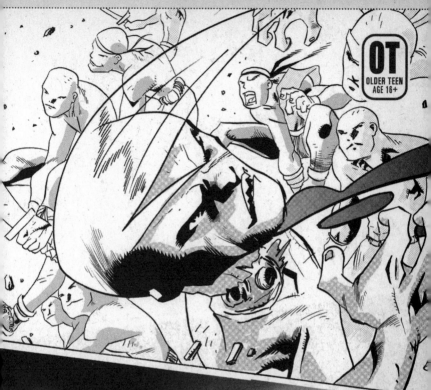

In the deep South, an ancient voodoo curse unleashes the War on Flesh—a hellish plague of voracious Ew Chott hornets that raises an army of the walking dead. This undead army spreads the plague by ripping the hearts out of living creatures to make room for a Black Heart hive, all in preparation for the most awesome incarnation of evil ever imagined… An unlikely group of five mismatched individuals have to put their differences aside to try to destroy the onslaught of evil before it's too late.

VOODOO MAKES A MAN NASTY!

WAR ON FLESH

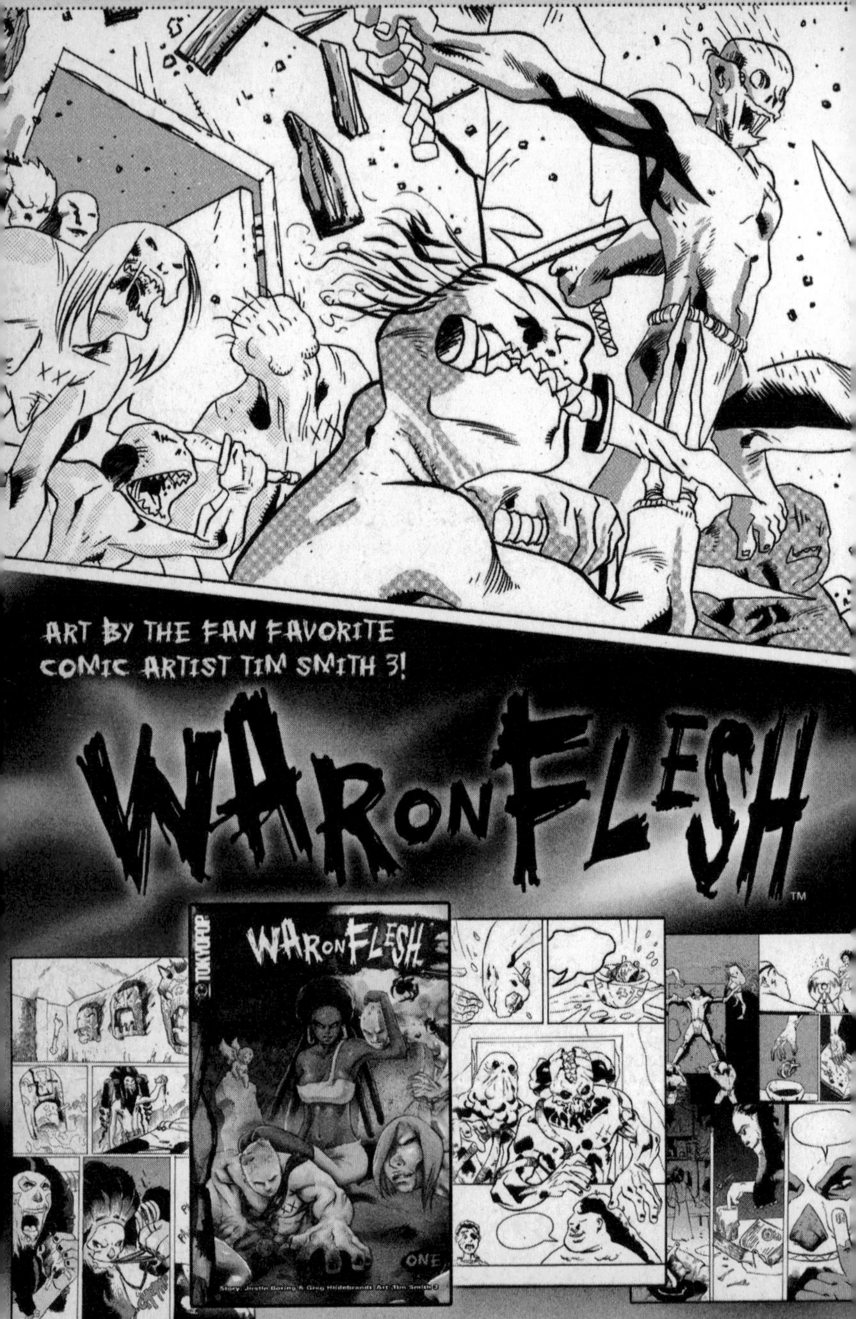

ART BY THE FAN FAVORITE
COMIC ARTIST TIM SMITH 3!
WAR ON FLESH™
WAR ON FLESH
TOKYOPOP
ONE
Story: Justin Boring & Greg Hildebrandt Art: Tim Smith 3

EDITORS' PICKS

TOKYOPOP MANGA SUPPLEMENT

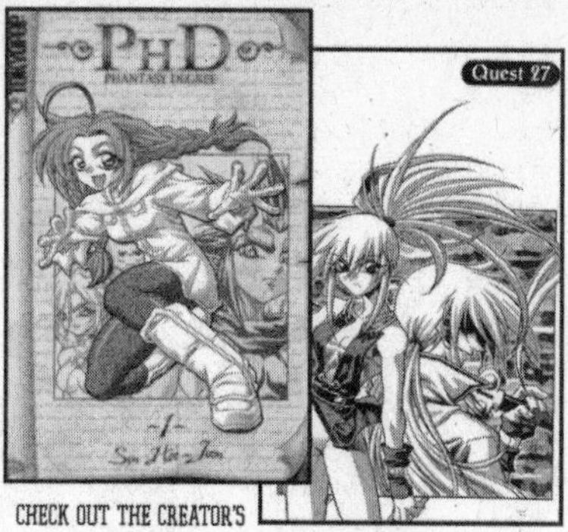
PhD
Quest 27

CHECK OUT THE CREATOR'S *iD_eNTITY*

BY SON HEE-JOON

PhD: PHANTASY DEGREE

So you think you've got it rough at *your* school? Try attending classes at Demon School Hades! When sassy, young Sang makes her monster matriculation to this arcane academy, all hell breaks loose—literally! But what would you expect when the graduating class consists of a werewolf, a mummy and demons by the score? Son Hee-Joon's underworld adventure is pure escapist fun. Always packed with action and often silly in the best sense, *PhD* never takes itself too seriously or lets the reader stop to catch his breath.

~Bryce P. Coleman, Editor

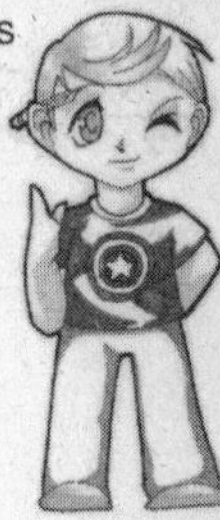

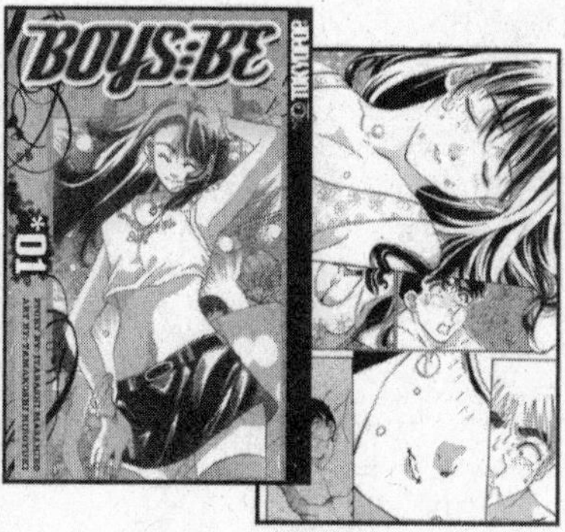
BOYS:BE
01

BY MASAHIRO ITABASHI & HIROYUKI TAMAKOSHI

BOYS BE...

Boys Be... is a series of short stories. But although the hero's name changes from tale to tale, he remains Everyboy—that dorky high school guy who'll do anything to score with the girl of his dreams. You know him. Perhaps you *are* him. He is a dirty mind with the soul of a poet, a stumblebum with a heart of sterling. We follow this guy on quest after quest to woo his lady loves. We savor his victory; we reel with his defeat...and the experience is touching, funny and above all human.

Still not convinced? I have two words for you: fan service.

~Carol Fox, Editor

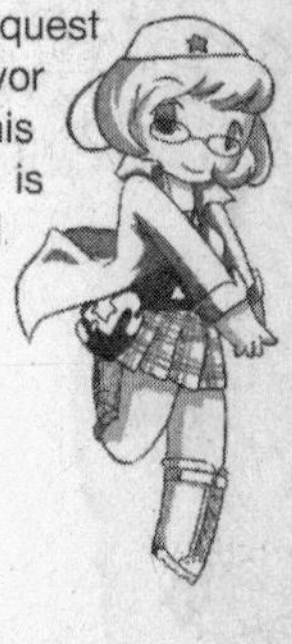

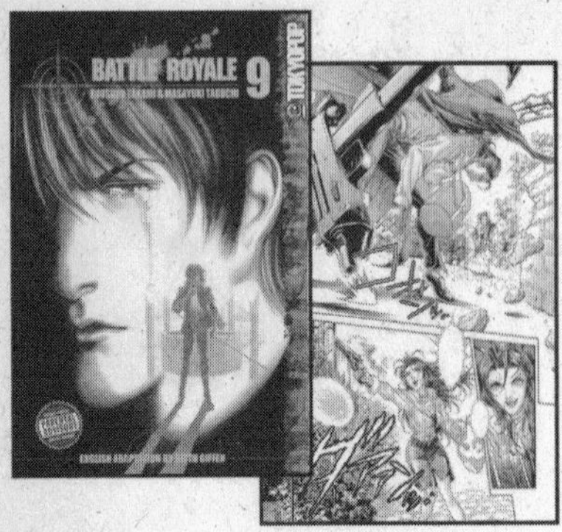
BATTLE ROYALE 9
TOKYOPOP

BY KOUSHUN TAKAMI & MASAYUKI TAGUCHI

BATTLE ROYALE

As far as cautionary tales go, you couldn't get any timelier than *Battle Royale*. Telling the bleak story of a class of middle school students who are forced to fight one another to the death on national television, Koushun Takami and Masayuki Taguchi have created a dark satire that's sickening, yet undeniably exciting as well. And if we have that reaction reading it, it becomes alarmingly clear how the students could be so easily swayed into *doing* it.

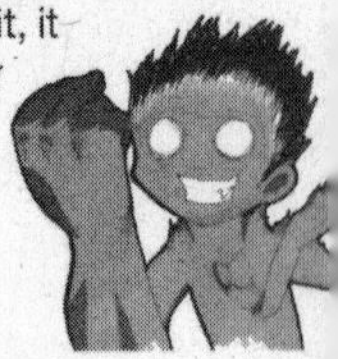

~Tim Beedle, Editor

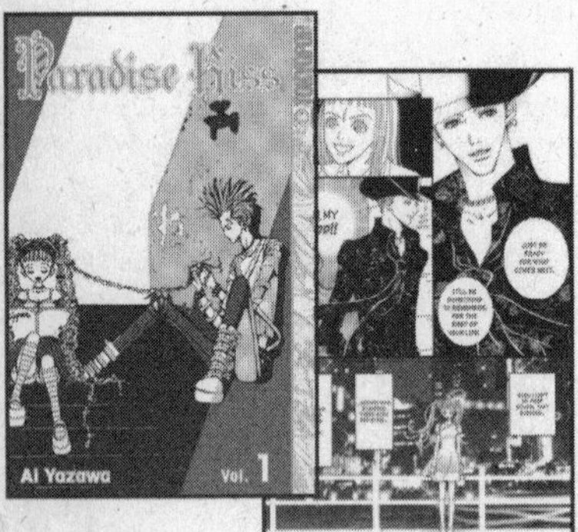
Paradise Kiss
Ai Yazawa
Vol. 1
TOKYOPOP

BY AI YAZAWA

PARADISE KISS

The clothes! The romance! The clothes! The intrigue! And did I mention the clothes?! *Paradise Kiss* is the best fashion manga ever written, from one of the hottest shojo artists in Japan. Ai Yazawa is the coolest. Not only did she create the character designs for *Princess Ai*, which were amazing, but she also produced five fab volumes of *Paradise Kiss*, a manga series bursting with fashion and passion. Read it and be inspired.

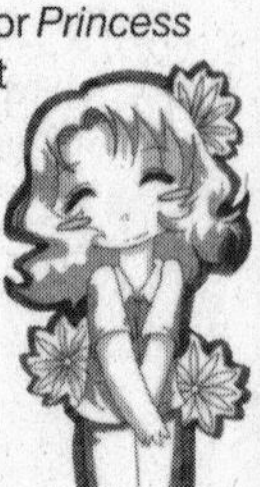

~Julie Taylor, Sr. Editor

STOP!

This is the back of the book.
You wouldn't want to spoil a great ending!

This book is printed "manga-style," in the authentic Japanese right-to-left format. Since none of the artwork has been flipped or altered, readers get to experience the story just as the creator intended. You've been asking for it, so TOKYOPOP® delivered: authentic, hot-off-the-press, and far more fun!

DIRECTIONS

If this is your first time reading manga-style, here's a quick guide to help you understand how it works.

It's easy... just start in the top right panel and follow the numbers. Have fun, and look for more 100% authentic manga from TOKYOPOP®!

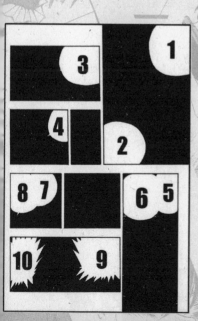

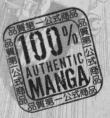